English Academic Writing and Language Styles

英语学术论文写作及语体风格

主 编 马 莉　副主编 宋秀平

北京大学出版社
PEKING UNIVERSITY PRESS

图书在版编目(CIP)数据

英语学术论文写作及语体风格/马莉主编. —北京:北京大学出版社,2011.10
ISBN 978-7-301-19620-5

Ⅰ. ①英… Ⅱ. ①马… Ⅲ. ①英语-论文-写作-教材 Ⅳ. ①H315

中国版本图书馆 CIP 数据核字(2011)第 203562 号

书　　　名：英语学术论文写作及语体风格
著作责任者：马　莉　主编
责 任 编 辑：刘秀芹　王业龙
标 准 书 号：ISBN 978-7-301-19620-5/H·2961
出 版 发 行：北京大学出版社
地　　　址：北京市海淀区成府路 205 号　100871
网　　　址：http://www.pup.cn　电子邮箱：law@pup.pku.edu.cn
电　　　话：邮购部 62752015　发行部 62750672　编辑部 62752027
　　　　　　出版部 62754962
印 刷 者：北京虎彩文化传播有限公司
经 销 者：新华书店
　　　　　　730 毫米×980 毫米　16 开本　21 印张　400 千字
　　　　　　2011 年 10 月第 1 版　2021 年 1 月第 5 次印刷
定　　　价：42.00 元

未经许可,不得以任何方式复制或抄袭本书之部分或全部内容。
版权所有,侵权必究
举报电话:010-62752024　电子邮箱:fd@pup.pku.edu.cn

前　言

　　随着近十几年来高等教育人才培养过程的规范化,英语学术论文写作成为《高等学校英语专业英语教学大纲》中规定的必修课,目的是使学生了解英语论文写作的一般过程和英语学术论文的写作格式,并掌握其写作规范。同时,随着我国与国外的交往越来越频繁,学术论文愈来愈成为介绍、交流科研学术成果的主要媒介,越来越多的学者和科技工作者希望自己的学术文章和科研成果能够在国际刊物上发表或是在国际会议上宣读。许多科研人员已有了使用英语撰写符合国际标准的学术论文的迫切需求。对科研水平不断提高的中国社会来说,这也成为一种日益增长的社会需要。本教程为实现切实培养和提高英语专业学生及其他写作者英语写作能力的目的而编写。

　　本教程有以下主要特点:

　　(1) 注重学习者科研素质和综合能力的培养。探讨如何利用信息资料进行科学研究,如何运用专业理论,实现理论与实践的结合,以达到培养创新能力与科学思维能力的目标。

　　(2) 密切联系时代需求和专业实际需要,便于学以致用。对现代信息源的运用和论文规范作了系统介绍;通过对文学理论、语言学理论、翻译理论和文化学理论方面的选题分析,培养英语专业学生独立解决实际问题等方面的能力;同时,通过对不同语言类型在文本中的不同语体效果的对比,根据选题切实实现语言运用的功能性。

　　(3) 文字浅显、通俗易懂,希望对初次撰写英语科研学术论文的读者有所裨益。

　　本教程分为"学术论文写作篇"和"语体风格篇"。"学术论文写作篇"共十二章,由华东政法大学马莉编写。内容包括学术论文的类型及写作的基本要求和原则,论文的选题,资料的查阅和利用,论文的格式和写作的程序,论文的答辩及成绩评定。在第十一章"专题毕业论文写作与评析"里,分别介绍了"英美文学"、"翻译理论与实践"、"英语语言学"、"英美文学及中西文化对比"四个专题的一些基本专业知识及相关论文题目,同时在第十二章各附一篇有代表性的论文范例。"语体风格篇"由三章组成:第一章由郑州大学张慧编写,第二章由郑州大学李鸣翠编写,第三章由上海师范大学宋秀平编写。本篇包含不同体裁文章的写作特征及策略,还包含不同语言类型在文本中创造的不同语体效果。本教程主要面对高校英语专业学生,但也适用于初次撰写科研、学术论文的各类人员,包括高校各专业学生及青年科研人员等。

  本书所引成篇论文或介绍性论文,有作者署名或出处的,均已注明;段落和单句的作者及出处则从略。编著者在此对这些作者表示感谢,没有他们的耕耘,就不可能有这本教材。

编著者

2011 年 1 月

目 录

学术论文写作篇

第一章　学术论文概述 ……………………………………………… (3)
  1.1　学术论文的特点 ……………………………………………… (3)
  1.2　学术论文的主要类型 ………………………………………… (3)
  1.3　英语专业毕业论文的类型 …………………………………… (4)
  1.4　毕业论文的性质 ……………………………………………… (4)
  1.5　学术论文的构成部分 ………………………………………… (6)
  1.6　学术论文的写作步骤 ………………………………………… (6)
  1.7　练习 …………………………………………………………… (7)

第二章　确定选题 ……………………………………………………… (9)
  2.1　选题的原则 …………………………………………………… (9)
  2.2　选题的方法 …………………………………………………… (10)
  2.3　选题的过程 …………………………………………………… (13)
  2.4　中心论题 ……………………………………………………… (14)
  2.5　练习 …………………………………………………………… (15)

第三章　撰写开题报告 ………………………………………………… (16)
  3.1　论文题目 ……………………………………………………… (16)
  3.2　研究现状 ……………………………………………………… (17)
  3.3　研究目的和意义 ……………………………………………… (18)
  3.4　研究方法 ……………………………………………………… (20)
  3.5　练习 …………………………………………………………… (22)

第四章　收集资料 ……………………………………………………… (23)
  4.1　资料来源 ……………………………………………………… (23)
  4.2　图书分类法 …………………………………………………… (24)
  4.3　文献检索 ……………………………………………………… (29)
  4.4　常用信息载体 ………………………………………………… (30)

第五章　组织及引用资料 (36)
　　5.1　临时参考资料目录的罗列 (36)
　　5.2　资料的分析及评估 (37)
　　5.3　阅读的方法及步骤 (38)
　　5.4　资料的收集及分类 (40)
　　5.5　资料的整理 (40)
　　5.6　记笔记 (41)
　　5.7　避免剽窃、抄袭 (42)
　　5.8　练习 (44)

第六章　撰写初稿 (46)
　　6.1　编写提纲 (46)
　　6.2　撰写引言 (48)
　　6.3　撰写文献综述 (50)
　　6.4　正文的写作 (54)
　　6.5　调研类论文的结构 (56)
　　6.6　结语 (59)
　　6.7　练习 (62)

第七章　修改与定稿 (63)

第八章　提供文献目录 (65)
　　8.1　芝加哥论文格式 (65)
　　8.2　现代语言学会论文格式 (68)
　　8.3　美国心理学会论文格式 (69)

第九章　论文格式及后期工作 (70)
　　9.1　论文各部分的要求 (70)
　　9.2　论文标题 (71)
　　9.3　论文提纲 (72)
　　9.4　正文 (73)
　　9.5　文中引述 (73)
　　9.6　摘要 (75)
　　9.7　致谢 (83)
　　9.8　练习 (85)

第十章　论文答辩 (86)
　　10.1　毕业论文答辩概述 (86)

10.2　答辩的目的和意义 ································ (87)
　10.3　毕业论文答辩的程序 ·························· (88)
　10.4　如何准备毕业论文答辩 ······················ (88)
　10.5　答辩方法与技巧 ································ (89)
　10.6　毕业论文评定标准 ···························· (91)

第十一章　专题毕业论文写作与评析 ················ (93)
　11.1　英美文学 ··· (93)
　11.2　翻译理论与实践 ······························ (101)
　11.3　英语语言学 ···································· (105)
　11.4　英美文化及中西文化对比 ················· (118)

第十二章　英语专业毕业论文实例 ··················· (121)
　12.1　英美文学类毕业论文实例 ················· (121)
　12.2　翻译类毕业论文实例 ························ (136)
　12.3　语言学类毕业论文实例 ···················· (147)
　12.4　中西文化对比类毕业论文实例 ··········· (160)

参考文献 ·· (172)

语体风格篇

Chapter 1　Types of Essays ························· (175)
　1.1　理论简介 ··· (175)
　1.2　Description ····································· (178)
　1.3　Narration ······································· (185)
　1.4　Exposition ······································ (190)
　1.5　Argumentation ································ (205)

Chapter 2　Rhetorical Devices in English ······ (213)
　2.1　理论简介 ··· (213)
　2.2　Rhetorical Devices in English ·········· (216)
　2.3　Phonological Rhetorical Devices ······ (216)
　2.4　Semantic Rhetorical Devices ··········· (225)
　2.5　Syntactical Rhetorical Devices ········· (273)

Chapter 3　Introduction of Stylistics ············· (307)
　3.1　理论简介 ··· (307)

3.2　The Noun Phrase …………………………………………（308）
3.3　The Verb Phrase …………………………………………（309）
3.4　The Function of the Pronoun ……………………………（310）
3.5　The Function of the Tense ………………………………（312）
3.6　Ellipsis ……………………………………………………（312）
3.7　The Discourse Markers …………………………………（313）

参考答案 ………………………………………………………（315）

参考文献 ………………………………………………………（328）

学术论文写作篇

第一章 学术论文概述

1.1 学术论文的特点

一般学术论文是指对教育领域的某个问题,通过某种方法进行科学的探索和思考而写成的以论述为主的文章,是科学研究成果的文字表述。

学术论文突出的是学术性,具体表现为以下三个方面。

1) 创新性

学术论文在自己所研究的范围内,理论上要有所发展,方法上要有所突破,能为某一领域提供新知识,或为新的研究提供新材料和新观点,对今后的研究有所启示。

2) 科学性

学术论文要以精确可靠的数据资料为论据,经过严密的逻辑推理进行论证。理论观点要清楚明白,有说服力,经得起推敲和验证。

3) 实践性

学术论文的学术性还表现为在社会实践中有现实意义,能在实践中操作运用,而不是空洞的理论堆砌。

1.2 学术论文的主要类型

学术论文按不同的标准划分,存在着各种不同的类型。按学术论文的性质功能,学术论文可分为:

1) 论说性论文,即用大量的事实、数据和材料,正面阐述,以证明自己的观点。考证性文章归入此类。

2) 综述性论文,即对某一时期某一学科领域的研究进展情况加以概括总结,分析现状,指出问题,并明确发展方向和趋势。

3) 评论性论文,即对某一学术成果、期刊论文或专著的内容进行估价、鉴定,指出其成就,分析其价值,挑明其中的问题与不足。

4) 驳论性论文,即反驳对方的观点,提出自己不同的见解。我们常见的商榷性文章就属此类。

大学四年级要写毕业论文。毕业论文要能反映运用大学几年中所学的知识分析解决学术问题的实际能力，要有一定的学术价值。硕士论文应该对本专业的基本问题和重要疑难问题有一定的独到见解。博士论文则必须在掌握某一学科深邃广博知识的基础上，获得较大突破，从而对学科的发展起到重要的作用。除此之外，还有投稿论文、命题论文等等。不同类型的学术论文各有其特色、风格和要求，只有有的放矢，才能写出质量较高的学术论文。

1.3　英语专业毕业论文的类型

英语专业毕业论文选题可分为以下几个学科方向：
1) 语言学(语言学一般理论的研究)
2) 英美文学(英美文学的文化研究、作品分析等)
3) 翻译(翻译理论与实践探讨、译本研究以及名家名著翻译作品对比研究等)
4) 英美文化与中西文化对比研究(英、美、加、澳、新等西方文化以及中西文化的对比研究)
5) 教学法(英语教学法、测试学等方面的研究)
6) 特殊用途英语(根据所属院校类别的专业类选题，如法律、金融、贸易等)

1.4　毕业论文的性质

毕业论文从文体上看，归属于议论文中学术论文的种类。所谓议论文，是指一种证明自己观点正确的文章。它包括政论、文论、杂论在内的一切证明事理的文章，或说理，或评论，或辩驳，或疏证，以达到明辨是非、解除疑惑、综陈大义、驳斥谬误等目的。毕业论文就其内容来讲，一种是解决学科中某一问题的，用自己的研究成果予以回答；一种是只提出学科中某一问题，综合别人已有的结论，指明进一步探讨的方向；再一种是对所提出的学科中某一问题，用自己的研究成果，给予部分的回答。毕业论文注重对客观事物作理性分析，指出其本质，提出个人的学术见解和解决某一问题的方法和意见。毕业论文就其形式来讲，具有议论文所共有的一般属性特征，即论点、论据、论证是文章构成的三大要素。文章主要以逻辑思维的方式为展开的依据，强调在事实的基础上，展示严谨的推理过程，得出令人信服的科学结论。

毕业论文是高等院校毕业生提交的一份有一定学术价值的文章。它是大学生完成学业的标志性作业，是对学习成果的综合性总结和检阅，是大学生从事科学研究的最初尝试,是在教师指导下所取得的科研成果的文字记录,也是检验学生掌握知识的程度、分析问题和解决问题基本能力的一份综合答卷。

毕业论文虽属学术论文的一种,但和学术论文相比,又有自己的特点:

一是指导性。毕业论文是在导师指导下独立完成的科学研究成果。毕业论文作为大学毕业前的最后一次作业,离不开教师的帮助和指导。对于如何进行科学研究,如何撰写论文等,教师都要给予学生具体的方法论指导。在学生写作毕业论文的过程中,教师要启发引导学生独立进行工作,注意发挥学生的主动创造精神,帮助学生最后确定题目,指定参考文献和调查线索,审定论文提纲,解答疑难问题,指导学生修改论文初稿,等等。学生为了写好毕业论文,必须主动地发挥自己的聪明才智,刻苦钻研,独立完成毕业论文的写作任务。

二是习作性。根据教学计划的规定,在大学阶段的前期,学生要集中精力学好本学科的基础理论、专门知识和基本技能;在大学的最后一个学期,学生要集中精力写好毕业论文。学好专业知识和写好毕业论文是统一的,专业基础知识的学习为写作毕业论文打下坚实的基础;毕业论文的写作是对所学专业基础知识的运用和深化。大学生撰写毕业论文就是运用已有的专业基础知识,独立进行科学研究活动,分析和解决一个理论问题或实际问题,把知识转化为能力的实际训练。写作的主要目的是培养学生具有综合运用所学知识解决实际问题的能力,为将来作为专业人员写学术论文作好准备,它实际上是一种习作性的学术论文。

三是层次性。毕业论文与学术论文相比要求比较低。专业人员的学术论文,是指专业人员进行科学研究和表述科研成果而撰写的论文,一般反映某专业领域的最新学术成果,具有较高的学术价值,对科学事业的发展起一定的推动作用。大学生的毕业论文由于受各种条件的限制,在文章的质量方面要求相对低一些。这是因为:第一,大学生缺乏写作经验,多数大学生是第一次撰写论文,对撰写论文的知识和技巧知之甚少。第二,多数大学生的科研能力还处在培养形成之中,大学期间主要是学习专业基础理论知识,缺乏运用知识独立进行科学研究的训练。第三,撰写毕业论文受时间限制,一般学校都把毕业论文安排在最后一个学期,而实际上停课写毕业论文的时间仅为十周左右。在如此短的时间内要写出高质量的学术论文是比较困难的。当然这并不排除少数大学生通过自己的平时积累和充分准备写出较高质量的学术论文。

撰写毕业论文的过程,同时也是学习专业知识的过程,而且是更生动、更切实、更深入地学习专业知识。首先,撰写毕业论文是结合科研课题,把学过的专业知识运用于实际,在理论和实际相结合过程中进一步消化、加深和巩固所学的专业知识,并把所学的专业知识转化为分析和解决问题的能力。其次,在搜集材料、调查研究、接触实际的过程中,既可以印证学过的书本知识,又可以学到许多课堂和书本里学不到的活生生的新知识。此外，学生在毕业论文写作过程中，对所学专业的某一侧面和专题作了较为深入的研究，会培养学习的志趣，这对于他们今后确定具体的专业方向，增强攀登某一领域科学高峰的信心大有裨益。

1.5　学术论文的构成部分

1）论文题目

要求准确、简练、醒目、新颖。

2）目录

目录是论文中主要段落的简表(短篇论文不必列目录)。

3）内容提要

内容提要是文章主要内容的摘录，要求短、精、完整。字数少可几十字，多以不超过300字为宜。

4）关键词

关键词(或主题词)是从论文的题名、提要和正文中选取出来的，是对表述论文的中心内容有实质意义的词汇。

5）论文正文

(1) 引言：引言又称"前言"、"序言"和"导言"，用在论文的开头。引言一般要概括地写出作者意图，说明选题的目的和意义，并指出论文写作的范围。引言要短小精悍、紧扣主题。

(2) 论文正文：正文是论文的主体，应包括论点、论据、论证过程和结论。主体部分包括以下内容：a. 提出问题——论点；b. 分析问题——论据和论证；c. 解决问题——论证方法与步骤；d. 结论。

6）参考文献

一篇论文的参考文献是将论文在研究和写作中参考或引证的主要文献资料，列于论文的末尾。参考文献应另起一页，标注方式按国家标准 GB7714-87《文后参考文献著录规则》进行。对所列参考文献的要求是：

(1) 所列参考文献应是正式出版物，以便读者考证。

(2) 所列参考文献要标明序号、著作或文章的标题、作者、出版物信息。

1.6　学术论文的写作步骤

1）选择题目

对学术论文题目应该尽可能地进行明确的界定，题目宜小不宜大。实际上并不存在太小的题目，一切话题中都可以发掘出能写论文的东西，重要的是明确地界定题目的范围。

2) 查找与搜集材料

所谓广泛搜集资料,就是尽可能多地了解前人对这一问题已经发表过的意见。这些意见可以给我们启发。掌握某一问题的全部资料,写出的论文就具有了坚实的基础,就能立于不败之地,也就有重要的学术价值。有时受条件的限制,百分之百地获取资料不易做到,但是,重要的、有代表性的资料是一定要阅读、考察的。

3) 整理笔记

记录对论文有用的观点并把重要的资料归类、整理、分段。收集了与题目有关的第一手资料之后,就可以列出初步的分段,在撰写论文的过程中可能会对其进行经常修改。论文的分段应该条理清楚、合乎逻辑。

4) 确定论据

在确定题目后,可结合进一步调研考虑缩小题目范围。在此基础上,要有文章的中心论题(thesis statement)。针对中心论题,要提出问题和假设检验现有论点,拟定提纲。

5) 撰写初稿

初稿包括引言(introduction)、文献综述(literary review)、主体(main body)和结论(conclusion)。

6) 修改与定稿

对论文的整体结构和逻辑性、连贯性、表达方式及引文的规范性等进行评价,同时检查语法及修辞的准确性。

1.7 练 习

1. 学术论文与散文的主要区别是什么?
2. 阅读一篇关于"文化差异"的论文的导言,根据学术论文的特点,从中找出该论文的几个论点。

Cultural Differences Between West and East

Everything is relative, cultural differences being no exception. Culture, as the total pattern of human behavior and its products, oversteps geographical limits and historical conditions in many ways, and it is characterized by its strong penetrativeness and fusibility. They affect people's ways of thinking and their views of the world, which are reflected in the areas of customs, etiquettes, beliefs, business management, legal systems, education, entertainment, relationship between people and nature, linguistic features (such as metaphorical usage, refusal strategies...), non-verbal communication styles (such as body language, sense of time and distance, symbols, etc). Therefore, the culture differences are everywhere.

In terms of communication, cultural differences between the West and the East are categorized into the following major patterns: high-context vs. low-context, individualism vs. collectivism, high uncertainty avoidance vs. low uncertainty avoidance, equality vs. hierarchy and assertiveness vs. interpersonal harmony.

第二章 确定选题

毕业论文是高校各专业教学计划的一个有机组成部分,是完成专业培养目标的一个重要教学环节,是对学生综合运用所学的基本知识、理论、技能和分析解决问题能力的基本训练。选择论题是毕业论文写作的第一步。"题好一半文",论题选得好,可以使毕业论文有较高的学术价值、实用价值。论题选得不好,不仅会为收集整理材料、提炼论点、安排文章的结构和动笔写作带来一系列的困难,而且可能造成半途而废,即使勉强完成写作,质量也堪忧。因此,选题是决定论文成败的重要前提和主要环节之一,也是本科学生在撰写毕业论文时最为困惑的问题。

2.1 选题的原则

1) 专业性原则

毕业论文写作要体现作者的专业特点,论点要根据专业内容而定,切忌写成工作总结或调研报告,也不能写成纯专业性的说明文,更不能写与专业无关的文章。学术论文是作者运用系统的专业知识,去论证或解决专业领域里某一个学术方面尚未解决的问题。学术论文是运用专业术语和专业性图表、符号表达内容的。它主要是写给同行看的,所以不在乎其他人是否看得懂,而是要把学术问题表达得简洁、准确、规范,专业术语也用得很多。因此,选题应注意其专业性要求。

2) 学术性原则

所谓学术是指较为专门而有系统的学问,以学术问题为论题,以学术研究成果为表述对象。毕业论文以学术见解、观点为立论目标。因此,学术性既是它的出发点,也是它的核心和依据,是评价和衡量选题质量的重要尺度。

3) 创新性原则

创新是选题的价值所在,要求论题必须有自己的独到见解,体现专业创新。在前人没有探索过的新领域中或没有做过的新题目上做出成果;或在前人成果的基础上作进一步研究,从理论的完备性、研究方法的科学性上进行高度的评判、分析。如果要选择同一论题,就一定要对自己已有的工作条件认真审视,从一个新角度把已有的材料或观点加以概括和表述,重新确定自己的新论点,新的着眼点,该论文才有意义。选题过于平淡,缺乏新意,人云亦云,乃论文之大忌。虽然对于本科毕业论文过于强调原创性不太现实,要想有很大的创新是不可能的,但论文中作者应有自己的独到见解,哪怕是一点点,否则选题将失去意义。

4) 可行性原则

所谓可行性,是指毕业论文的选题一定要切合实际,不能泛泛空想,不着边际。首先,论文选题往往受到主观和客观条件的限制。有些论文选题虽然非常好,价值非常大,但由于写作者自身条件的限制,或研究条件等客观原因的限制,即使选择了这一选题,最后也无法完成。其次,选题的现实性还表现在适宜性方面,即选题要从实际出发。针对不同学生,应选择与其能力相符的题目,或个人有浓厚兴趣的题目。遵循可行性原则需要考虑以下几点因素:

- 时间性。选题难度适当,工作量适中,在规定的时间内能够圆满完成写作。
- 选题范围适中。题目过小,在规定的时间内很难深入研究;题目过大,需要大量时间查阅文献资料,难以按期完成,或导致写作中难以驾驭,毕业论文达不到预期效果;选题过于保守,会妨碍自身水平的充分发挥,使论文缺乏学术水准。
- 资料可获取性。一旦确定论题,就要根据论题获取论据材料。如果缺乏足够的证据支撑论点,则选题无法展开。

2.2 选题的方法

17世纪法国著名的思想家笛卡尔曾经说过:"最有价值的知识是关于方法的知识。"要选好毕业论文的题目,只了解选题原则还不够,还需要了解和掌握选题的一些具体方法。下面介绍几种常见的选题方法。

1) 浏览捕捉法

所谓浏览捕捉法,就是学生先根据自己对所学专业知识或实践领域的熟悉和兴趣程度划定一个或若干毕业论文的选题范围,然后通过对占有的文献资料快速地、大量地阅读,浏览相关的报纸、杂志上面刊登的属于自己选题范围内的文章,边读边思,从中捕捉适合自己的毕业论文选题。用这种方法选题难免要花费很多工夫。但是,由于在浏览的过程中学生的思维始终处于目的性很强的活跃状态,外部信息很容易激发调动起学生平时积累的潜在知识和智能,从而灵感顿生,形成很好的毕业论文选题。

浏览捕捉法一般可按以下步骤进行:

第一步,广泛地浏览资料。记下资料中对自己影响最深刻的观点、论据、论证方法等,记下脑海中涌现的点滴体会。第二步,将阅读所得到的方方面面的内容进行分类、排列、组合,从中寻找问题、发现问题。材料可按纲目分类。第三步,将自己在研究中的体会与资料分别加以比较,找出不同的观点和不同的资料类型。把这种想法及时捕捉住,再作进一步的思考,选题的目标也就会渐渐明确起来。

2) 追溯验证法

学生经常会遇到一些前人已研究过但尚未解决、尚未形成共识的学术问题,一般来说也就是各学科的学术难题。他们往往对这些难题比较感兴趣,总想发表超越前人的见解,形成自己的学术创建,甚至也有了自己的"拟想",但是必须用追溯验证法来确定。所谓追溯验证法是指在学生准备把前人争论不休的问题选作自己的毕业论文题时,要在自己对此问题有一定理解的基础上,查阅前人对此问题研究争论的有关资料,弄清前人的主要观点和依据,明确自己对此问题是否确实有与众不同、超越前人的独到见解。

要善于捕捉一闪之念,抓住不放,深入研究。在阅读文献资料或调查研究中,有时会突然产生一些思想火花,尽管这种想法很简单、很朦胧,也未成形,但千万不可轻易放弃。因为这种思想火花往往是在对某一问题作了大量研究之后的理性升华,如果能及时捕捉,并顺势追溯下去,最终形成自己的观点,是很有价值的。追溯验证的选题方法,是以主观的"拟想"为出发点,沿着一定方向对已有研究成果步步紧跟,一追到底,从中获得"一己之见"的方法。但是,这种主观的"拟想"绝不是"凭空想象",必须以客观事实、客观需要等作为依据。这些"拟想",到了该写毕业论文时,就自然构成自己的选题范围。如果经过追溯研究,发现自己并未形成超越前人的新见,那就只能放弃。因此,用追溯验证法选择毕业论文题是有一定风险而且要花费很大力气的,它比较适合那些科研能力较强、常能独抒新见的学生。

追溯验证法的优点也是显而易见的:首先,它所涉及的论题一般都有较高的学术价值,只要能形成与众不同的一家之言,就容易写出较高水平的论文来;其次,它使选题、选材、构思融为一体,一旦论题选定,论文的基本模样也就形成了;最后,追溯验证的过程也正是学生从别人那里汲取营养、锻炼能力、超越他人和自我的过程,因而运用这种方法对提高学生的学术水平有很大的帮助。

3) 积累精选法

积累精选法是指学生在平时学习中就要注重对所学专业相关学术问题的积累,最终精选出一个最合适的作为毕业论文题。积累的途径主要有两种:一是在课堂教学中,老师往往会把本学科尚待深入研究的重点和疑难问题介绍给学生,学生应把自己认为重要和感兴趣的问题随手记下来;二是平时要阅读与本专业有关的报刊,随时了解学术动态,对阅览中遇到的自己感兴趣的学术问题也随手记下来。挑选论题时，既要考虑这一论题当前的学术和实用价值的高低，又要特别考虑论题的规模大小、收集资料和构思以及写作的难易程度等因素。应尽量选择适合小题大做、学术和实用价值较高、在限定时间内有把握高质量完成的论题。实践证明，积累精选法是一种最好的毕业论文选题方法。

4）实践调研法

现代教育观不仅看重毕业论文的学术价值，更看重其实用价值，即指导当前实践的价值。因此，从实践中发现急需研究和解决的问题作为毕业论文题，也应成为当代大学生毕业论文选题的基本方法之一。特别是长期处于特定实践领域的成人学生，用这种方法选定毕业论文题就更加方便。但是，从实践中寻找恰当的毕业论文题，即使对于身处其中的成人学生来说，也并非轻而易举的事。只有善于观察、思考的学生才能从司空见惯的现象中发现有普遍意义的、在当前实践中迫切需要解决的问题。然而，发现问题还仅仅是第一步，还必须综合运用所学的知识对问题各方面作出深入调查研究，才能找到解决问题的有效方法。只有对问题的现象、原因和解决办法都弄清了，才能最终确定能否以此作为毕业论文题。

5）筛选变造法

使用筛选变造法，首先要从学校提供的毕业论文题库中初选出两三个作为自己论文的备用题目。为了减少初选的盲目性，学生一定要牢记毕业论文选题的三个原则：(1) 选适合小题大做的题，(2) 选熟悉和感兴趣的题，(3) 选有一定学术和实用价值的题。熟悉和感兴趣的题是指学生以前就对其所涉及的理论和实践知识有所积累并愿意深入钻研的题，选这样的题是学生较顺利地完成毕业论文和获得较好成绩的基本保障。初选之后，学生可以与同学和老师交流，征求他们对自己备用论题的规模、难度、价值等方面的意见，再对照自身的实际情况选定其中的一个作为毕业论文题。在这一过程中，学生往往会发现学校所提供的论题并没有一个完全适合于自己，这时就需要对原论题进行变造。这种变造一般来说主要是对原论题规模和角度的变造。

6）移植发挥法

移植发挥法是指以另一学科、另一领域的科研成果和知识来开拓新学科领域。此类选题可体现交叉学科的优势。对于英语专业的选题来说，可从心理学角度探讨文学作品中的人物性格；可在翻译领域探讨法律文本、新闻语体或外贸函电的翻译技巧；也可在文化对比领域探讨中西政治或法律体系的异同，等等。

总而言之，任何一种选题方法都要凸显题目的创新性。这种创新性体现在该题目应是该领域内前人未曾解决或尚未完全解决的问题方面。这些方法都要求学生广泛查阅文献资料和深入地开展调查，对理论的完备性、研究方法的科学性进行评价和分析，在此基础上重新确定自己的新论点。

2.3 选题的过程

了解了选题的原则和方法后,下面通过实例看看选题的过程。

1) 缩小选题范围

如果选题范围过宽,论文篇幅必然过大,必然会涉及大量的事实和观点,使作者无论在时间上或能力上都难以驾驭。如"论语言与文化"、"双语教育在中国的现状"等课题对于篇幅有限的毕业论文来讲无疑过宽,难以叙述清楚、分析透彻,论据也不易充分。

虽然选题范围没有明确的规则来限定,但我们应该了解的是,选题范围的深度、广度取决于论文的长度、可获取的资料(数量、质量等)、读者对象,也取决于写作时间及写作者组织素材的能力等因素。

为缩小选题范围,人们常采用的策略有:① 利用期刊索引提供的分目类,可将选题由宽变窄;② 先选择一个范围较宽的题目,然后逐次缩小其范围。如:

第一次选题:On Jane Austin

第二次选题:On the Writing Styles of Jane Austin

第三次选题:On the Origins of Jane Austin's Feminism

上例说明,可通过三次选题,每次缩小原有范围。

只有在较充分地掌握资料后,才有可能较准确地判断所选课题是否适当,因而通常在收集数据资料阶段才有可能将选题的范围逐步缩小。人们常在资料收集过程中发现收集的资料过多、过杂。出现此类情况,一般采用两种办法:了解图书馆目录上涉及所选课题的专著数量;了解期刊索引所提供的参考书目或论文的数量。

2) 扩充选题范围

范围太窄的课题通常可供参考的资料较少,对作者的研究能力要求较高。刚刚从事科研工作或初写科研论文的人,应尽量避免选择参考资料较少的那类课题。

下例说明如何将范围较窄的课题加以扩充,使其成为合适的课题:

第一次选题:On the Transference of Different Thinking Models in Legal Language Translation

第二次选题:On the Non-linguistic Factors in Legal Language Translation

第三次选题:On the Cultural Features in Legal Language Translation

3) 选择感兴趣的课题

初次撰写学术论文,一般应选择撰写者个人确实感兴趣的课题,而不应选那些看似"热点"的课题。当然,理想的选题对撰写者个人和读者来说都应是饶有趣味的。选题时,若不能提出符合个人兴趣的课题,可去图书馆查阅目录有趣的课题;也可翻阅报刊、参考资料等。

2.4 中心论题

论文的中心论题(thesis statement)就是它的中心思想,有着重要的作用,是整篇论文的灵魂。所以,写好中心论题,就等于论文写了一半出来。

中心论题必须是一个完整的句子,用来陈述一篇论文的结论和为什么会得出这个结论。下面是两个 thesis statement 的例子:

a. Health is achieved through a combination of exercise, proper diet, relaxation, and strong social relationships.

b. Body language, like verbal language, is also a part of culture. Different cultures have different body languages except some world known ones. And in intercultural communication, the same body language may mean different things.

中心论题有以下几个作用:

1) 能点明论文的主要论点和主线。一般是用一到三句话将所有要点涵盖其中,而且排在起始段落的最后。如下面这个段落(一篇论文的首段),其中画线的句子就是整篇论文的中心论题。

As modern theories of human rights are gradually accepted, people have begun to severely criticize the extreme inhumanity of death penalty and doubt its justification, and it has gradually been a global trend that such penalty should be restricted and completely abolished. However, China imposes the death penalty for over many crimes, and its death penalty system runs counter to the global trend. <u>Comparing the current situation of the death penalty in China with that in the world, plus some other factors, China should impose strict restrictions on death penalty.</u>

2) 能预示整篇论文的结构层次。例如上面段落中画线的中心论题句就预示着论文将对比中西死刑现状的差异,阐述中国不能废除死刑的种种原因和论据。

3) 能使读者尽早抓住文章的核心内容。要达到这一目的,论文作者还应在了解论题特征的基础上,注意以下几点:

(1) 要有清晰的单一主线。下面举出的这个论题示例就不符合这一点:

The Roman theater was inspired by the Greek theater which it imitated, and was eventually the Romans produced great plays in their theaters, such as those by Plautus, who was the best Roman comic writer because of his inventiveness.

这一论题示例设想了互相矛盾的两条思路:一方面说罗马戏剧从希腊戏剧

那里受到启发,其作品往往是从希腊戏剧那里模仿出来的;另一方面又说,像 Plautus 这样的著名喜剧作家基于其创造精神创作出许多伟大的戏剧作品。为避免这种自相矛盾,可将其改为:

Because of his robust language and novel comic plots, Plautus can be considered the best Roman comic playwright, whose plays are successfully staged today.

(2) 不要使用比喻。如:"Henry James is the Frank Lyoid Wright of the American novel." 这句话需要改成:"The novels of Henry James have the internal consistency because of the way he unifies his themes, patterns his episodes and orders his images." 这一表述更为直截了当。

(3) 语言要清楚明白,不要含糊其辞。如:"Cigarette smoking wreaks havoc on the body." 更为具体明白的说法应是:"Cigarette smoking harms the body by constricting the blood vessels, accelerating the heartbeat, paralyzing the cilia in the bronchial tubes, and activating excessive gastric secretions in the stomach."

(4) 不要使用问句。问句表示不肯定,无助于点明思路和要点。

(5) 不要使用太长的句子,特别是句子成分的层次结构不清晰,读起来感到困难的句子。

2.5　练　习

1. 创建三个你所学专业领域的选题,并为每个选题写出中心论题。

2. 以小组为单位论证每个选题,最终每人确认一个题目及修订后的中心论题,并以演示方式提交论证报告。

第三章 撰写开题报告

若撰写课程论文,在课题初步确定后应取得课程教师的同意;若撰写毕业论文,在课题初步确定后应取得论文指导和评审委员会的认可,同意就此课题开展研究并撰写论文。为此,需向有关方面提交论文方案。对于学位论文来说,就是提交开题报告。

开题报告是本科生毕业论文工作的重要环节,是指为阐述、审核和确定毕业论文题目而作的专题书面报告。它是本科生实施毕业论文课题研究的前瞻性计划和依据,是监督和保证论文质量的重要措施,同时也是训练本科生科研能力与学术作品撰写能力的有效的实践活动。写好开题报告要了解它的基本结构与写法。但"汝果欲学诗,功夫在诗外",写好开题报告或论文方案还需要大量的前期调研工作。首先,我们要了解别人在这一领域研究的基本情况。研究工作最根本的特点就是要有创造性,熟悉了别人在这方面的研究情况,我们才不会在别人已经研究很多、很成熟的情况下,重复别人走过的路,而是站在别人研究的基础上,从事更高层次、更有价值的研究。其次,我们要掌握与我们课题相关的基础理论知识。理论基础扎实,研究工作才能有一个坚实的基础,否则,没有理论基础,研究很难深入,很难有真正的创造。因此,在撰写开题报告之前,需要收集大量的资料,确定中心论题,并且掌握支撑中心论题的大量论据。在此基础上所写的开题报告或论文方案,才能更科学、更完善。

开题报告的内容一般包括:题目、立论依据(毕业论文选题的目的与意义、国内外研究现状)、研究方案(研究目标、研究内容、研究方法、研究过程、拟解决的关键问题及创新点)、条件分析等。一个清晰的题目,往往已经隐含着论文的基本结论,对现有文献的缺点的评论,也基本暗含着改进的方向。开题报告就是要把这些暗含的结论、论证结论的逻辑推理清晰地展现出来。

3.1 论文题目

论文题目就是课题的名称。这看起来是个小问题,但实际上很多人拟定的论文题目往往不准确、不恰当,从而影响整篇论文的形象与质量。首先,论文题目要准确、规范。准确就是论文题目要把课题研究的问题是什么、研究的对象是什么交代清楚。论文题目一定要和研究的内容相一致,要准确地将研究的对象、问题概括出来。其次,论文题目要简洁,不能太长。不管是论文或者课题,名称(包括副标题)一般不要超过20个字。

3.2 研究现状

重点要进行已有文献综述,认真介绍有关题目国内外的研究历史和现状,然后进行评述,阐述其研究的广度、深度、已取得的成果;寻找有待进一步研究的问题,从而确定本课题研究的平台(起点)。论文要写什么是根据文献综述得出来的,而不是论文作者的随意选择。没有文献综述,很可能被认为你在"拾人牙慧"。撰写研究现状不宜一味罗列,要有作者本人的分析和归纳,并适当举出观点或理论的实例。

下例为课题"On the Different Body Language Between U.S.A. and China"的研究现状:

> 身势语这一沟通方式产生在大约200万年至50万年前,谈话这一交流方式则在身势语产生了相当长一段时间后才产生并成为了人们沟通方式的一部分。直到20世纪60年代,对身势语所进行的全方位的研究才开始步入轨道。身势语研究领军人物阿尔伯特·麦拉宾发现:"一条信息所产生的全部影响中7%来自于语言,38%来自于声音,剩下的55%则全部来自无声的肢体语言。"可见,学者们已经认识到身势语的重要性。20世纪以前关于探究身势语的最富有影响力的作品之一是查尔斯·达尔文于1872年出版的《人类和动物的情感表达》一书。但是,这部作品以理论讲述为主,并不适合大众阅读。而21世纪风靡全球的作品,由亚伦·皮斯和芭芭拉·皮斯所著的《身体语言密码》,虽然更生动明了地解析了生活中的肢体语言,将各种不同文化环境下的肢体语言作对比,然而,这些对比中却没有中国这个独特的文化环境。另外,现实生活中,大多数人仍然将注意力都集中在了谈话上,而忽略了不同文化背景下身势语的差异,也忽略了全球化大环境下各国身势语互相影响、趋同的现状。本文意在以中美身势语之异同为例,通过分析比较中美不同文化环境下所造就的不同意义的身势语,探讨其内在与外在的原因,提出"和而不同"的、独特的对待各国身势语差异的思想方法。

3.3 研究目的和意义

研究的目的、意义也就是为什么要研究、研究它有什么价值。这一般可以先从现实需要方面去论述,指出现实当中存在这个问题,需要去研究,去解决,然后再写课题的理论和学术价值。这些都要写得具体、有针对性,忌大而空。主要内容包括:研究的有关背景(课题的提出),即根据什么、受什么启发而搞这项研究;通过对现实社会或本领域实际情况的分析,指出为什么要研究该课题、研究的价值、要解决的问题。

下例为课题"On the Protection of the Criminal Suspects in the Process of Public Prosecution"的研究目的和意义:

> 媒体报道出的一起起冤假错案,尤其是前段时间佘祥林的案子,引起了全社会对司法程序的公正性的热烈讨论,与此同时,也将被告人在整个公诉过程中的人权保障问题提上议题。尤其当我们看到佘祥林在被错关了几年释放之后对于整个社会表现出的强烈不适应感,更是让我们对被告人的人权给予了强烈的关注。
>
> 我国司法体系上的审讯方式沿用了大陆法系的究问制方式。在一定程度上,这使得在刑事诉讼中,有国家支持的公诉人与被告人之间的诉讼地位不能绝对的平等。因此,在法治社会、司法公正、人性化语境下的司法实践中,注重被告人人权保障是一种必然选择。
>
> 本文将从上述法理的<u>理论角度</u>以及现实社会要求的<u>实践角度</u>来探讨,尤其是从公诉过程中被告人人权保障的必要性、从实践中适用的各项原则及制度等角度来分析公诉过程中的被告人人权保障制度的发展过程,以及通过现实中出现的问题提出被告人人权保障制度仍需要完善的地方。本文研究的意义在于,在公诉过程中,做好对被告人的人权保障,有利于我们更好地构建社会主义和谐社会。在民众的监督之下,对被告人的公平公正对待,能使民众对我国的司法充满信心。同时,通过本文将法律保护意识进一步普及,可以使得民众更有效地用法律的武器保护自己。另外,加强我国在司法体系中的人权保护也是反驳西方舆论质疑中国人权的有力论点。

另外,理论和实践意义可先概括,再说明,如下例《法律语言的文化制约》的研究目的和意义:

> **研究意义**
>
> 理论意义:在全球化国际气氛下,文学批评、哲学思考及人类学等社会科学研究的重心和视角都发生了转移,在素有语言关怀传统的翻译理论领

域则表现为"文化热"的兴起。国内译界是否真正实现了"文化转向"尚有争议,但有一点已基本达成共识,即翻译活动的定位不仅在语言转换或文本间的互动以及对"译技"的研究上,更应在于文化之间的互动与交流。对法律语言翻译而言,在语言层面进行简单的"解码—重组"操作远远不能诠释文本背后的社会话语与异质概念内涵。从跨文化语际的视角来研究法律语言翻译,才能拓宽和深化法律语言翻译研究的维度。

本课题拟以翻译认知语境理论为主要框架,以"文化、语境和认知"机制为基础运作语言,运用翻译认知加工模式对译入语重新建构,在这一过程中也同时融入了建构主义翻译观和语用学的适应选择机制,以实现译文法律修辞的文化补偿。以文化形态的重构为支点,在法律语言翻译中辩证综合运用几种翻译模式,在理论上显示了一定的科学价值与难度。

现实意义:根据社会语言学理论,语言是文化的一部分,司法领域的语言学研究就理当属于文化研究,在这个层面上探讨法律文化语言学是有相当的理论意义的;随着中国社会的日益法制化并加入WTO,从法律文化语用的视角探讨法律语言的翻译,对于中国法律语言学的未来研究具有巨大社会价值,因此具有深远的现实意义。具体概括如下:

一、传播、记载和传承目标语的法律文化

法律语言是法律文化的重要组成部分。用文化语言学的眼光看,法律语言与法律文化关系密切;许多流传至今的历代优秀法律语言作品,包括有关法律语言认知和运用技术的著述,都是对本民族优秀法律文化的记载与传承。它既是法律文化的产物,又是记录法律文化的工具和载体。如古代汉民族法律语言即是中华法系的独特法律文化的产物和一种独特的表现形式。一批独特的法律词汇和概念术语作为这种法律文化的记录、表述工具,从而使中华法系的法律文化精髓得以保存、流传,并得以在全世界范围内进行交流。

二、促进在不同法系、不同社会制度及不同文化传统之间法律概念的沟通和理解

在不同的法系中,相同的语言符号可能会表示不同的概念。一国法律制度系统有其深刻的政治、经济以及文化根源,很少和他国的法律制度雷同,即使是基于相同法系的国家之间的法律也是如此。国与国之间对同一国际法律现象的认识常常也不一致。

社会制度是一个社会政治、经济、文化等根本制度的总和,它构成了一个社会的基础,影响到社会的方方面面,自然也会涉及法律的制定和执行。

在不同的法律文化背景中,往往因为不同的现实问题,需要制定专门的法律,采用特定的法律术语,也会产生不同的法制功能、法律制度及程序。

语意不对等有许多是由于法律文化的传统不同造成的。从某种角度上讲，法律词语是一定经济基础和体制的产物，其概念的产生与各国经济现状相适应。法律的多元性也表明了对法律文化诠释的必要性。

3.4 研究方法

开题报告里应进一步说明选择这个题目之后如何解决这个问题。也就是有了问题后，以什么方式寻求答案。撰写研究方法可简述自己的大体思路，同时重点阐述要用什么方法去研究。具体的研究方法可从下面选定：观察法、调查法、实验法、经验总结法、个案法、问卷法、比较研究法、文献阐述法、访谈法、定量研究等。确定研究方法时，还要要叙述清楚"做些什么"和"怎样做"。如下例为课题《试论网络新词》的研究方法：

1. 规范阐释方法

文中会就网络新词给出一个新的规范定义，并在这个层面上进行具体讨论。

2. 个案说明方法

文中会就网络新词举出个例，并就该例进行发展沿革分析。

3. 比较研究方法

文中会就不同领域新词的产生及发展进行比较，并进一步找出网络新词的发展特点。

4. 经验总结方法

文中会适当总结此领域现有的研究成果，并适当予以修整。

5. 文献资料方法

文中会大量引用前人的文献参考资料，作为有力的论据，同时也弥补作者本身在词汇学研究领域的理论上的不足。

另例为课题《对比中美国际直接投资中的比较优势》更为详细的研究方法阐述：

1. 比较研究的方法

本文以中国和美国为研究对象，为了更好地阐述笔者的观点，比较研究法是采用较多的一种研究方法。它强调资料的可比性、真实性、准确性和可靠性，并且要求的是资料之间的全面的、本质的比较。

在比较研究的过程中，笔者通过对中美国际直接投资中比较优势的对比和细致分析，避免了孤立地考察发达国家或是发展中国家在国际直接投资中的比较优势。

2. 规范阐释法

本文会引用前人对于国际直接投资中比较优势所阐述的理论，对于这些理论，笔者将进行系统的概念解释。通过对斯蒂芬·海默的垄断优势论、巴克利及卡森的内部化理论、弗农的产品生命周期理论以及邓宁的国际生产折衷理论这些经典理论的阐释，同时分析其应用背景，揭示其应用的局限性，说明在产品技术含量低且大多属于劳动密集型产业的中国国情下，需要进一步进行创造性研究。

在以上框架下，可结合各个学科，列出更为具体的方法。如在比较文学的研究框架中，还可运用心理学、文化学、形式分析等多种范式方法。比较文学研究方法本身更具有四种类型：最早的是源于法国的"影响研究"，继而又有美国首倡的"平行研究"，苏联创造的"历史类型学研究"，中国提出的"阐发研究"。

撰写学术论文，提倡使用综合的研究方法。一个大的课题往往需要多种方法，小的课题可能主要使用一种方法，但也要利用其他方法。在应用各种方法时，一定要严格按照该方法的要求，不能凭对一些基本概念的了解草率行事。要用调查法，就要讲清调查的目的、任务、对象、范围、调查方法、问卷的设计或来源等，最好能把调查方案附上。比如，如何通过调查了解情况，如何制订调查表，如何进行分析等，要有调查结果和论证的设计，而不是随便发张表，得出一些百分数、平均数了事。

下例为课题"The Future of Language E-learning"的研究方法中对调查过程较为详细的描述：

> 本论题主要通过对比线上与线下语言教学模式的差异，寻找网络语言教学的优势与不足，由此进行深化，试图寻找到网络语言教学的发展之路。在研究中，拟搜集充足的案例进行数据统计。通过调查研究、数据分析，可以直观地挖掘网络语言教学的现状与动态方向。调查研究的客体一般是一些较为成功的网络语言教学平台和某些语言类高校，以及社会上较为成功的语言培训中心。数据分析包括其上线人数（报名人数）、数据库大小、盈利模式、研发投入、培训效果（一般指各项考试成绩）等等。还有一部分的理论支撑来自于相关的书刊、网页等。这一部分也是不可缺的，因为网络语言教学这个平台开始阶段还是来自于理论构想与实际构建。只有合理地搭建模式，才能造就这一特殊的教育平台。通过阅览书籍，还可以找到更多的理论依据和实际案例。最后，通过总结找到网络语言教学面临的问题，并提出解决方案，由此勾画出一幅属于未来网络语言教学的蓝图。

3.5 练　习

1. 根据选题撰写开题报告。
2. 小组模拟开题答辩,重点阐明以下几点:
    - 研究现状:现有研究的广度、深度
    - 研究目的和意义:研究的特色或突破点、理论意义及实践意义
    - 研究方法:按示例结合题目简述各个方法

第四章 收集资料

4.1 资料来源

美国国家基金会在化工部的调查统计表明,科研人员工作时间分配为:计划思考7.7%,信息收集50.9%,实验研究32.1%,数据处理9.3%。由此可见,科研中大量的工作是阅读与课题有关的已出版的或未出版的文献资料。资料是论文写作的基础,没有资料,则"巧妇难为无米之炊",研究无从入手,观点无法成立,论文不可能形成。所以,详尽地占有资料是论文写作之前的另一项极重要的工作。

参考资料是指科研中需查阅的各种类型的资料,包括书籍、期刊、报纸、杂志、百科全书、词典等,也包括录音、书信、艺术品等。写成一篇五千字左右的论文,可能要搜集到几万甚至几十万字的资料。论文写作之前,至少应当占有如下几个方面的材料:

1) 第一手资料。第一手资料是指最原始和最直接的资料。如选题为某文学作品评论,第一手资料就包括该作品作者的原作、信札、日记、手稿、自传、采访录音等。第一手资料包括与论题直接有关的文字材料、数字材料(包括图表),譬如统计材料、典型案例、经验总结等,还包括自己在实践中获得的感性材料。这是论文提出论点、主张的基本依据。尚未经别人阐释、讨论或引用的成果和统计数据也是第一手资料。没有这些资料,撰写的论文就只能成为毫无实际价值的空谈。对第一手资料要注意及早收集,同时要注意其真实性、典型性、新颖性和准确性。

2) 第二手资料。所谓"第二手资料",是指经他人研讨、引用的和阐释而有所转化的资料。它可能是某作者针对某作品所撰写的专著、论文和评说,也可以是沿用他人调研结果和统计数据(需附加注释说明)的分析性或阐释性论文。文中所引用的某人的原话(引语)本身为第一手资料,而关于该引语的评价和阐释则为第二手资料。经过科学的自行设计而自然得出的客观实验、调查或统计数据资料为第一手资料,而在调查中所作的访谈录则为第二手资料。一般来说,第一手资料最有说服力,第二手资料要符合科学性、逻辑性,在使用时要注意甄别,例如在使用引语时常常要核查一下原来的出处。

3) 他人的研究成果。这是指国内外对该课题学术研究的最新动态,反映该课题研究现状和各家论述(包括研究方法)的资料。资料应包括不同研究阶段的代表性论述、不同视角下具有代表性的专家之言。要研读名人的有关论述、有关政策文献等。名人的论述极具权威性,对准确有力地阐述论点大有益处。

撰写论文不是凭空进行的,而是在他人研究成果的基础上进行的。因此,对于他人已经解决了的问题就可以不必再花力气重复进行研究,而是以此作为出发点,从中得到有益的启发、借鉴和指导。对于他人未解决的或解决不圆满的问题,则可以在他人研究的基础上再继续研究和探索。

4) 与论题相关的理论背景。如果你要写的论文题目是《论〈呼啸山庄〉的叙事手法》,你就必须通过研读资料,对叙事手法的基本理论有一个全面的了解,同时还要对作品的整体风格以及作者的写作风格有所把握。如果你要写"习语的翻译",你就要做必要的英汉语语言学或语义学方面的理论准备,在该领域收集一定量的基本理论知识,以展开论题。

5) 与论题有关的一般背景知识。例如,要评论某作家某篇作品的主题,往往需要了解和收集该作家生平方面的资料,其中包括该作家所处时代的社会背景、所受的哲学思想和文艺思潮的影响、所处的家庭环境、周围的人际关系、有哪些主要作品、作品的社会反响等。

6) 相关的其他学科的资料。收集的资料不仅仅是与论题相应的本学科的资料,还应有与论题有关的其他学科的资料。如要写一篇关于"修辞格"的论文,除了收集本辞格的资料外,还要收集与分析本辞格有关的哲学、心理学、逻辑学、美学、文化学、文艺学等方面的资料。只有这样,才有可能把论文写得透彻、有深度。

7) 中文参考资料。语言比较研究、中英(中美)文化比较研究以及英汉互译方面的论文少不了中文资料。除此以外,其他选题也常常需要从中文出版物中收集有用的信息,只不过在使用时需将这些汉语变通为英语罢了。一篇论文最好不要使用清一色的中文资料,因为不看英文原版资料,你往往会对所谈问题中关键术语的英语表达感到困难。通常情况下,收集英语的原版资料是第一位的,只有在特殊情况下(如英文资料匮乏,或中文资料有不可替代的参考价值时)才会考虑收集中文资料。

4.2 图书分类法

为充分使用文献资料,首先应了解本单位图书馆、资料室有哪些藏书,藏书如何编目分类。各单位图书馆或资料中心的编目体系不尽相同,因此也应熟悉各图书资料库图书分类法。

我国古代图书按经典、历史、哲学、诗歌等几类编目。随着人类知识不断拓宽深化,现代图书馆的图书分类要繁复得多。图书馆或资料中心一般都有目录卡。通常每一目录卡上提供作品的有关资料,如出版年月数、出版地点、出版商名称等等。较大规模的图书馆都采用计算机或胶片储存目录或资料。此类图书馆所藏的每一份资料通常按作者名、书(或论文)名及内容三种类型分别编目,因而每一份资料也就可能有三种检索的途径。例如,若只知作者姓名,可在作者姓氏目录中检索,若有两名或多名合著的作者,一般可在第一作者名下查到该资料,有些图书馆将合著的资料分别列入每一作者名下;若仅知某书名,可在书名目类内检索;也可按内容检索,按内容编目的一般采用美国国会图书馆图书分类法。

下面介绍三种主要的图书分类法。

1) 杜威十进分类法

杜威十进分类法(简称"杜威分类法",英文简称 DDC)将图书分为十大类,每一大类又分为若干类,在其下又复分为若干类。杜威分类法所分的十大类为:

000　总论
100　哲学
200　宗教
300　社会科学
400　语言
500　自然科学和数学
600　技术(应用科学)
700　艺术、美术和装饰艺术
800　文学
900　地理、历史及辅助学科

杜威分类法由马尔维·杜威创建于1876年。发展至今,各大类下出现了很多新的学科,例如哲学大类包括心理学、逻辑学;社会科学大类包括经济、教育及法律;科学类包括天文、生物学、物理学。

为简要说明杜威分类法,我们以语言学类为例列举复分类:

400　语言
410　语言学
420　英语和昂格罗—撒克逊语言
430　日耳曼语言 德语
440　罗曼语言 法语
450　意大利语、罗马尼亚语、里托—罗曼语
460　西班牙和葡萄牙的诸语言

470　意大利的诸语言 拉丁语
480　希腊语系 古典希腊语
490　其他语言

杜威分类法在某些图书馆可能根据内容进一步分类,这一级分类以一小点后跟数字表示,如:
- 1　哲学与理论
- 2　杂记
- 3　词典、百科全书等
- 4　各专用性的内容
- 5　系列出版物(如学术刊物)
- 6　组织与管理
- 7　教与学
- 8　历史
- 9　史地讨论

2) 美国国会图书馆图书分类法

美国国会图书馆图书分类法(LC)是现时不少大学图书馆采用的图书分类法,原因是它用了26个英文字母做分类代码,相比0—9的数字代码可以完成更仔细的分类。但是,这个分类法其实亦已采用了超过150年,所以仍有不少不足之处。

美国国会图书馆图书分类法的具体分类如下:
A　一般内容
B　哲学、心理学及宗教(注:有不少心理学内容其实归入了社会科学,如青少年问题、性学等)
C　历史学及相关科学总论
D　古代史及世界各国史
E　美国历史
F　美洲历史
G　地理、人类学、休闲活动
H　社会科学
J　政治学
K　法律
L　教育
M　音乐
N　艺术
P　语言及文学

Q 科学
R 医学
S 农业
T 技术及工程
U 军事科学
V 航海科学
Z 图书馆学

26个英语字母中,I、O、W、X、Y 5个字母未编用,留待今后扩充门类时使用。美国国会图书馆图书分类法中的26大类,每一类下又复分若干类,仍以语言类为例:

P 一般语言学及文学
PA 希腊、拉丁语言学及文学
PB 现代语言学、凯尔特人语言学
PC 罗马语系语言学
PD 德国语言学
PE 英国语言学
PF 西德语言学
PG 斯拉夫语言学、波罗的海语言学、阿尔巴尼亚语言学
PH 乌拉尔、巴斯克语言学
PJ 东方语言学及文学
PK 伊朗语言学及文学
PL 东亚、非洲、大洋洲语言学及文学
PN 一般文学
PQ 法国文学、意大利文学、西班牙文学、葡萄牙文学
PR 英国文学
PS 美国文学
PT 德国文学
PZ 小说与青少年文学

各大类除主表外,大多编有专用复分表(包括形式、地区、年代、主题等),且分别附有字顺索引。

美国国会图书馆图书分类法采用拉丁字母和阿拉伯数字相结合的混合标记符号。一、二级类目用字母标记,三至六级类目用数字标记,按顺序制编号。为了便于扩充,六级之后加一小数点,或用小数制展开,或用字母或字母—数字展开。例如,LC第4版农业大类:

S 农业

SB　植物栽培
189　禾谷类作物总论
- 5　育种
- 53　品种
- 54　细胞与组织培养

* * *

191　各种禾类作物，A—Z
- A42　苋属

野燕麦，见 W53
- B2　大麦
- M2　玉米

参见 SB191. P64，爆裂玉米
　　SB351. C7，甜玉米

3）中国图书馆图书分类法

中国图书馆图书分类法简称"中图法"。"中图法"将知识门类分为"马列主义、毛泽东思想,哲学,社会科学,自然科学,综合性图书"五大部类,在此基础上组成22个基本大类。该分类法使用字母与数字相结合的混合号码,基本采用层累制编号法,一个字母标志一个大类：

A　马克思主义、列宁主义、毛泽东思想、邓小平理论
B　哲学
C　社会科学总论
D　政治、法律
E　军事
F　经济
G　文化、科学、教育、体育
H　语言、文字
I　文学
J　艺术
K　历史、地理
N　自然科学总论
O　数理科学和化学
P　天文学、地球科学
Q　生物科学
R　医药、卫生
S　农业科学

T　工业技术
U　交通运输
V　航空、航天
X　环境科学、劳动保护科学(安全科学)
Z　综合性图书

"中图法"的 22 大类中除 T(工业技术)类对其下一级栏目的复分也采用字母表示外，其余大类后用数字表示大类下类目的划分，以语言类为例：

H　　　语言、文字
H0　　语言学(语音学、文字学、语义学、写作、修辞、词典方言、应用语言学)
H1　　汉语(语音、文字学、语义、词汇、词义)
H3　　常用外国语(英语普及读物)
H194　汉语言文学写作

在二级分类下再分类，则再加一位数字；再细分时，加一小点后再用数字表示。

4.3　文献检索

文献检索的目的主要是查找某种文献的出处和了解该文献的概况。常见的文献检索是通过使用书目(bibliographies)、索引(indexes)和文摘(abstracts)来实现的。书目、索引和文摘作为对文献进行控制和检索的工具，属于检索型工具书。它们的共同功能是记录和通报文献，提供识别文献的信息和检索文献的手段。

1) 书目

书目是关于记录资料来源的资料汇编，其内容不仅包括图书，还包括报刊、声像资料、数据库等其他信息形式与载体。"书目"一词还可泛指书目、索引和文摘类工具书。它不仅可以向读者提供一定历史时期的文献出版情况和各学科的发展概况，而且还可以向读者提供某一个国家、一个地区甚至世界各国文献收藏和出版的情况。

读者可以从特定的角度(例如著者、题名、主题)去查找各种书目资料。如可用美国的《累积图书索引》(Cumulative Book Index, a world list of book in the english language, CBI)去查找世界各地出版的英语图书，还可以利用《英国国家书目》(British National Bibliography, BNB)去查找英国出版的图书和新版期刊等。

书目的种类不一，除了国家书目、联合书目等综合图书目录之外，还有各种专科图书目录和期刊目录。图书馆目录(library catalog)是图书目录中的一种。

它记述图书馆入藏文献,并依一定的体系与排检方式进行组织,从而提供检索途径,是通报和利用图书馆藏书的主要工具。

值得注意的是,在英文中"catalog"和"bibliography"的意思是有区别的。前者常指某特定场所(如图书馆)收藏文献的有序化记录,而后者的收录范围则不限于此。不过,在当前联机书目数据库广泛使用的情况下,这种区别已趋于模糊。

2) 索引

索引是一种常用的提供文献线索的检索工具,它一方面能够按照人名和主题帮助人们迅速查检所需书刊文献的线索,另一方面又能够使读者通过检索词的使用,了解某一文献的主题内容以及某课题的发展概况和最新观点。

索引种类繁多,可按分析对象的不同分为期刊索引、报纸索引、专书索引、文集索引等,也可按内容的不同分为综合性索引、专科索引、专题索引和专门著作索引等。现介绍几种代表性的索引:

- Reader's Guide to Periodical Literature《读者期刊文献指南》
- Poole's Index to Periodical Literature《普尔氏期刊文献索引》
- Art-Index《艺术索引》
- Essay and General Literature Index《散文和一般文献索引》
- Book Review Digest《书评摘要》
- A Comparative and Systematic Concordance to the Works of Shakespeare《莎士比亚语词索引大全》

3) 文摘

文摘是索引的延伸,同索引一样具有指明材料来源的基本功能,并进一步揭示文献的内容要点和实质。文摘和索引的主要区别在于:① 文摘不仅能指明文献的出处,而且提供简明的内容摘要,这种内容摘要通常是客观地概括介绍原文的要点、研究方法、所争论的问题以及研究成果和结论;索引只指明何处可以查到某种资料,很少介绍具体或者较详细的内容。② 与索引相比,文摘倾向于更专门的学科范围,旨在收录某个狭窄主题内相对完整的资料。③ 在编排方式上,索引一般按著者、主题和题名排列;文摘大都是按分类排列或按收录编号排列。

4.4 常用信息载体

为了更高效地查找到所需资料,有必要对常用信息载体(资料源)及其性质与功能作一些了解。

1) 百科全书(encyclopedias)

百科全书是对人类现有知识的编排、整理和概要记述。它主要回答有关定义、概念、问题、历史沿革、当前状况和关于人物、事件的综合性问题。因此，它是获得知识信息和背景理论信息的理想载体。另外，由于百科全书的规模大，又是由权威人士集体编纂的，因此所载信息全面、系统、可靠，有很高的参考价值，因而引用率特别高。

常用的百科全书有：
- *The New Encyclopedia Britannica*(1985)《新不列颠百科全书》
- *Encyclopedia Americana*(1983)《美国百科全书》

英语专业常用的专科性百科全书有：
- *International Encyclopedia of the Social Science*(1968)《国际社会学百科全书》
- *Encyclopedia of Education*(1970)《教育百科全书》(包括教育哲学、教育史、教学管理、教学法与重要教育法规)
- *Encyclopedia of World Literature in the 20th Century*(1967—1971)《20世纪世界文学百科全书》
- *Cassell's Encyclopedia of World Literature*(1965)《卡西尔世界文学百科全书》
- *Encyclopedia of World Arts*(1983)《世界艺术百科全书》
- *Princeton Encyclopedia of Poetry and Poetics*《普林斯顿诗歌与诗学百科全书》

2) 英语词典(dictionaries)

对于学术论文的作者来说，词典的首要功能是提供术语的定义。如：何为 Oedipus Complex？何为 Libido？除此以外，语文(语言)词典还有语言研究功能。可以利用历时性词典(diachronic dictionaries)所提供的信息研究词的历史演化(词义、词形等)，也可以利用教学词典(又称"学生词典")研究英语教学问题，也可以利用英汉和汉英词典进行英汉语的比较研究。

常用的英语通用语文词典有：
- *Oxford English Dictionary*, 2nd Edition, Oxford: Clarendon Press, 1989.《牛津英语大词典》

该词典素有"词典之王"之称，几乎收录了自12世纪中叶以来英文文献中出现的全部词语，其主要特征在于按历史原则进行编纂(词形、词义都有历史演变)，例证大都选自名家的著作，因此权威性很高。

- *Webster's Third New International Dictionary of the English Language*, Springfield, Mass.: Merriam, 1961.《韦氏第3版新国际英语词典》

该词典摒弃以往的规定主义编纂传统，采用描写主义编纂原则，并开创了现代词典编纂的新风。

- *Webster's New World Dictionary of the American Language*, 3rd College Edition, New York: Collins Publication, 1988.《韦氏新世界美国英语词典》

该词典特别注重美国英语用法,词源信息在中型词典中最佳。

- *The Concise Oxford Dictionary of Current English*, 9th Edition, Oxford: Clarendom Press, 1998.《牛津简明英语词典》

该词典的释义简明、严谨,习语和词源信息丰富,是英国使用最广也是世界最畅销的一本中型英语词典。

- *Chambers English Dictionary*, New Edition, Edinburgh: Chamber, 1988.《钱伯斯英语词典》

以国外英语学习者为主要对象的英语教学词典,也属于通用词典的范畴,如我们所熟悉的 *Oxford Advanced Learner's Dictionary of Current English*(《牛津高阶英语词典》)和 *Longman Dictionary of Contemporary English*(《朗文当代高级词典》)。这两种词典国内都有英汉双解本,是英语专业师生必备的英语词典。

除了上述通用词典外,各种版本的文学术语词典、语言和语言学词典也是重要的信息源。例如:J. A. Cuddon 的 *Dictionary of Literary Terms and Literary Theory*(《文学术语及理论词典》),R. R. K. Hartmann 与 F. C. Stork 的 *Dictionary of Language and Linguistics*(《语言与语言学词典》),David Cristal 的 *A Dictionary of Language and Phonetics*(《现代语言学词典》)。另有一本别开生面的成语词典特别值得一提——*Brewer's Dictionary of Phrase and Fable*(《布留沃成语词典》)。这是一本记录词语背景信息的成语词典。可以说,该词典对人类文化的各个领域,如神话传说、民间故事、宗教历史、风俗、考古、建筑、雕刻、艺术、科学等无所不包,因而它是一本不可多得的语言与文化研究方面的重要参考书。

3) 专著(monographs)

专著不同于一般知识性书籍,它是著者对未知知识领域的探索,系一家之言。专著相对来说具有一定的规模和较完整的体系。公开出版的专著,无论是纯理论性质的,还是实际应用型的,都有相当高的参考价值,因而是学术论文写作最重要的参考信息源之一。

4) 教科书(textbooks)

学校基础理论课和专业理论课所用的教科书一般来说都是编著者关于本学域的系统性概括,所涉及的理论具有前沿性,所使用的概念和术语具有广泛性,也有不少教科书实际上是一部学术专著。所有这些就使教科书具有相当高的参考价值。

5) 期刊(periodicals)

期刊,特别是学术性期刊,是当今学术通讯系统中最主要的知识与信息源。学术性期刊定期集中发表论文、调查报告、统计报告等学术研究成果。学术期刊的最大特点是它的及时性和创新性。因此，期刊通常是学术论文写作中获得研究资料的来源。论文作者在着手收集资料时往往总是先从期刊文献开始，并由此获得更多的书目信息。

期刊大致可以分为大众期刊（普通杂志）和学术性期刊两大类。高等学校机构所出的学报（journal），学会、协会所出的会志（journal or translation）和书评杂志（book reviews）都属于学术期刊的性质。

英语专业师生常用的国外英文期刊如下：
- *Language*《语言》（美国语言学会会刊）
- *Applied Linguistics*《应用语言学》（牛津大学出版）
- *English Teaching Forum*《英语教学论坛》
- *Studies in Second Language Acquisition*《第二语言习得研究》（剑桥大学出版）
- *American Speech*《美国语》
- *Times Literary Supplement*《泰晤士报文学增刊》
- *Linguistic Studies*《语言学研究》
- *Time*《时代》
- *Newsweek*《新闻周刊》
- *Reader's Digest*《读者文摘》
- *U. S. News & World Report*《美国新闻与世界报道》

国内出版的关于英语语言、英美文学、英美文化和翻译方面的学术期刊有：
- 《中国翻译》（中国翻译工作者协会主办）
- 《中国科技翻译》（中科院主办）
- 《上海科技翻译》（上海大学主办）
- 《中国外语》（高等教育出版社主办）
- 《中国英语教学》（中国英语教学研究会会刊）（英文）
- 《当代语言学》（中国社科院语言研究所主办）
- 《外语教学与研究》（北京外国语大学主办）
- 《外语界》（上海外国语大学主办）
- 《外国语》（上海外国语大学主办）
- 《现代外语》（广东外语外贸大学主办）
- 《外语教学》（西安外国语大学主办）
- 《解放军外国语大学学报》
- 《外语学刊》（黑龙江大学主办）
- 《山东外语教学》（山东师范大学主办）
- 《四川外国语学院学报》

- 《外语与外语教学》(大连外国语学院主办)
- 《外国语言文学》(福建师范大学主办)
- 《外国文学评论》(中国社科院文学研究所主办)
- 《外国文学研究》(中国人民大学主办)
- 《国外文学》(北京大学主办)
- 《外国文学》(北京外国语大学主办)
- 《当代外国文学》(南京大学主办)
- 《外国文学研究》(华中师大文学院主办)

除此以外,大专院校的学报有时也刊登英语语言、英美文学、英美文化和翻译方面的论文。关于汉语语言与语言学研究的期刊则有:《中国语文》和《语言教学与研究》(北京语言大学主办)。

6) 学术会议论文集(proceedings)

国际或国内学术会议上宣读过或未能宣读的论文常以论文集的形式印发或作为专著正式出版,也可以作为期刊的专号(special issue)或附刊(supplement)出版。

7) 报纸(newspapers)

报纸在英文里称为"newspapers",可见它的主要内容是登载来自四面八方的新闻消息。从报纸中可以学到政治、经济、外交以及文化等方面的知识,还可以从它的书评、影评、剧评专栏中学到文艺理论。报纸的语言生动、活泼,语言最新的变化也往往最早体现在报刊之中。因此,可以利用英语报纸上的实际语言素材进行英语语言研究,如英语语言的变化、英语新词新义研究、新闻英语的语言特征、广告语言的特征等。

英国和美国都是世界上报业非常发达的国家,因此英语报纸种类颇多。比较有影响力的英美报纸主要有以下几种:

- *The Times*《泰晤士报》

英国驰名国内外的三大全国性日报之一,政治上自称是独立的,但实际上常反映保守党观点及政府和外交部的观点。

- *The Guardian*《卫报》

英国三大全国性日报之一,政治观点倾向于工党,在知识界有较大影响。

- *The Daily Telegraph*《每日电讯》

英国三大全国性日报之一,名义上独立,但实际上倾向于保守党。

- *Daily Express*《每日快报》

英国颇负盛名的大众化报纸,销量在日报中位居前茅。

- *Observer*《观察家报》

英国著名星期日报(Sunday Papers)之一,它的书评、影评、剧评很有影响。

- *The New York Times*《纽约时报》

美国三大有影响的报纸之一,读者主要是上层社会成员,包括政府官员和高级知识分子,其社论常反映国务院的观点。

- *Washington Post*《华盛顿邮报》

美国三大有影响的报纸之一,政治上接近国会,支持民主党,以登载政府"内幕"的报道而著称。

- *Los Angeles Times*《洛杉矶时报》

美国三大有影响的报纸之一,政治观点倾向于共和党。

- *Wall Street Journal*《华尔街日报》

美国有影响的财政金融业和贸易专业性报纸,以这些专业的新闻为主要内容,同时也登载内外政治新闻和评论。政治观点倾向于共和党。

- *Christian Science Monitor*《基督教科学箴言报》

它不是一份宗教性报纸,而是一家名为 Christian Science Monitor 的出版社(在波士顿)出版的、内容注重国际新闻的报纸。

除了上述英美报纸外,国内出版的英文报纸 China Daily(《中国日报》)的影响也很大,同时也是外国人士了解中国的重要窗口之一。

8)数据库(databases)与声像资料(audio-visual materials)

所谓数据库,即存贮和组织在磁、光介质(磁带、磁盘、光盘等)上的数据文件的集合。它的最大特点是一次输入,反复使用,一家输入,多家使用;便于计算机处理和电讯传递。数据库可分为两大类:一类只提供文献线索(出处和内容概要);另一类则提供详细完整的信息内容。可以购买所需资料的数据库磁盘或光盘在计算机上使用,也可以通过在线系统进行传递、处理或查阅。平时说的网上查询就是指的第二种情况。

声像资料是指与视、听有关的声像出版物。大致可以分为三大类:一是视觉资料,如幻灯片(slide);二是听觉资料,如留声机(phonograph)、录音磁带(magnetic tape)、唱片(compact disc);三是视听资料,如电影片(motion picture)、录像磁带(video tape)、激光视盘(VCD)、数字激光视盘(DVD)。

声像资料的最大优点是直接而形象、生动且真实。研究文学艺术、人物生平、历史发展、语言等方面的课题时往往有必要索查和使用声像资料。

第五章 组织及引用资料

5.1 临时参考资料目录的罗列

　　临时用的参考资料目录是一份参考书目单,开列作者已参阅的各参考资料。参考资料目录应尽可能完整地将已参阅的各种文献资料都编入其中,以供查阅用。这份目录也称做"工作用参考资料目录",在科研过程中可不断对其变更、增删。

　　每项资料的全部信息应尽可能记录在同一卡片上或列在一张目录单上,便于以后的检索。临时用的参考资料目录应尽量多记录每项资料的情况。

　　1) 若参阅的是书籍,记录中应包括下列各项基本内容:
- 作者,有多位作者的标出第一作者,姓前名后,如 Einstein, Albert;
- (若是编译资料)编者名,译者名;
- 书的全名;
- 出版地点、出版商、出版日期。

　　如:Boud, David. Moving Towards Autonomy. Boud, David (ed.). Developing Student Autonomy in Learning. London: Kongan Page Limited, 1988.

　　为便于查阅,也可包括:
- 参阅的章节或部分;
- 版次;
- (若是系列书中某部分内容)系列书名;
- 卷号;
- 资料所在的页码。

上述各项内容大部分都在图书的书名页及版权页上。

　　2) 参考资料若是论文,记录中应包括下列各项内容:
- 作者姓名;
- 标题;
- 刊物名;
- 卷号;
- 期号。

如：McDevitt, Becky. Learner Autonomy and the Need for Learner Training. Language Learning Journal, 1997：(9).

为便于查阅,也可包括：
- 刊物出版日期；
- 资料所在的页码；
- 论文的首页页码及末页页码。

3) 参考资料若来自网络,记录中应包括下列各项内容：
- 作者；
- 文章或书名；
- 网站网址,需用下划线标明；
- 访问日期。

如：Bush, Rosaline & Hacker, Nina George. Kids Without a Conscience, http://www.cfwa.org/library/family/1997-02-fv-fids-conscience.shtm, 2008-12-4.

可在卡片上或列表内重点标明作者的姓名(姓前名后)或书的图书编号,或采用其他任何方法,目的是便于以后能较快检索到已参阅的资料。

每张工作用参考资料目录卡或收录列表上也应注明收藏并摘引资料的图书馆。目录卡上应简略注明该资料哪些内容有助于课题研究。

工作用参考资料目录应多于最后的文献资料目录,因为在编制工作用参考资料目录时尚难确定哪些资料更有价值。

5.2 资料的分析及评估

整理参考资料时应对资料的来源进行分析,并作出正确的判断。首先要确定材料是否有用,是部分有用还是全部有用,以及可以用在什么地方。对有用的材料也要有个简单的分析和评估。同时,随着资料的不断增加,应对原有的资料重新评估,因为很多资料常经修订、增删后再行出版、发表。可能条件下应参阅最新出版的信息资料。对不同来源的资料应作比较,研究各论点或论点的依据是否矛盾。各种资料若不一致,需谨慎分析,去伪存真。参阅资料时也应了解编著参考书文的作者的有关情况。学术刊物在不同程度上向读者提供论文作者的背景情况。读者可从作者介绍中了解作者在该领域的研究经历和地位。总之,参考资料要真实、可靠、可信,方能具备参考价值。关于在具体对资料评估的操作中如何筛选具有较高参考价值或学术价值的论著,可参照以下几点：

1) 由专家或著名学者撰写的专业书(学术专著或教科书)和学术论文都有较高参考价值。如心理分析学方面的权威资料当属弗洛伊德所著；西方语言学理论专著当属乔姆斯基、韩礼德等所著；西方翻译理论论述当属奈达的作品。

2) 对于内容相近的众多资料,由著名出版商(出版公司、出版社)出版的书通常要比普通出版商出版的书更有价值。例如,牛津大学出版社和剑桥大学出版社就是享有世界盛誉的国际出版社,同时也是集中出版学术性著作的知识型的出版社。在我国,商务印书馆和中国社会科学出版社就是两家国家级的著名出版社,而像上海辞书出版社、中国民间文学出版社和外语教学与研究出版社则属于专业性出版社。

3) 在国内外知名学术期刊(包括知名大学学报、国家级或国际学会会刊等)上发表的论文相对来说有较高的学术价值。这些期刊的大多数都会列入"核心期刊"。

4) 经过修订再版的书要比旧版书更有价值,特别是在新版与旧版之间相隔的时间较长时,更是如此。经过修订而再版的书一般都要对原书中的错误加以纠正,或对一些观点加以修正,或者是对部分内容予以更新。因此,在可能条件下应尽量参阅最新版的图书资料。在论文写作中是否坚持这一原则有时会显得特别重要,如果你引用或参考的资料是未经修正过的资料,或者你引用的观点已在新版中有所更新,那么你的写作就会犯"拾人牙慧"的错误。

该情况同样适用于学术论文。两篇内容雷同的学术论文,出版或发表日期较近的可能会比早期面世的更全面,有更新颖的观点。

5) 在特定条件下,早期出版或发表的文献资料也可能比后期出版或发表的资料更有学术价值。例如,在较早的《不列颠百科全书》中收有许多常见的希腊罗马神话人物的词条,但在后来的新版(如第 15 版)中却大都被删去了。因此,如果查阅希腊罗马神话人物的情况,旧版的《不列颠百科全书》就成了更有价值的材料。另外还有一种情况是,许多权威著作的经典观点被后人大量复制,并无创新内容,因此需要我们在梳理资料时花费一些时间来辨析。

5.3　阅读的方法及步骤

1) 阅读的方法

查阅与课题有关的著作时,不必急于逐页细读,阅读应有正确有效的方法。一般来说,根据材料的不同性质应采取不同的方法,即略读、通读和研读。

略读是指粗略阅读书中某一部分,吸取引你注意的思想或观点。采用这一方法可防止浪费大量的时间或精力,发现该书无参考价值可立即停阅。阅读专业书时可先采取三步略读法,即略读书中内容目录;略读书后的索引;略读有兴趣的章节或段落。

略读目录时应注意以下几个问题:一是根据目录所列标题判断该书是否有较大篇幅或较多章节与课题有关。如有关的章节少,可能无法满足课题的要求。

但这不等于说该书没有查阅价值,有时就可能在这类书中发现一些新颖的内容或信息。二是书中的材料组织是否得当,组织不当会对查找资料造成困难。三是书中若有图表等材料,所附的图表是否有助于说明问题。直观易懂,内容丰富的图表胜过若干页文字说明。

略读书后的索引时也应注意几个问题:索引长度怎样？索引是否详尽？索引中能否查到与课题有关的内容。略读完一本书的目录及索引后,可以说对全书有了概略的了解。实际上在略读目录及索引时就可阅读有关的段落或章节,快速浏览,若所述内容与课题密切相关再作细读。

通读是指对段落、篇章信息从头到尾地阅读,其主要目的是了解和熟悉文中说了些什么,凡是文中说到的要点都是通读时需要掌握的,不可轻易遗漏。

研读是指对重要的信息内容进行研究性的阅读,如对一个篇章认真地、反复地、有评论地阅读,其主要目的是挖掘信息符号在信息结构中的意义,包括所指意义、内涵意义、交际意义、篇章意义等。其重点是讲究"精通"。

上述三种阅读方法可以依据信息载体的性质类型综合运用。

阅读学术论文与阅读专业书在方法上虽无根本性的差别,同样是略读、通读和研读,但科研论文的篇幅小,因而通读和研读的比率较大。

2) 阅读的步骤

阅读学术论文从标题开始,若对标题感兴趣,可先读其摘要。阅读摘要后对论文仍感兴趣,即可阅读论文全文;若仍无法确定该文是否有用,可参阅论文后所列的参考书目,参考书目一般反映出论文作者对有关文献资料熟悉了解的程度,从而反映出论文作者的科研水平。

以一篇研讨某一作家某一文体特色的论文为例,此类论文应涉及相当数量有代表性的参考资料。读者应注意论文所引资料发表的时间。若多数资料发表时间早,说明论文作者没有引用足够的最新资料。编写书、出版书需要较长时间,因此引用的资料可能陈旧些,但可能可靠些,所述内容较少争议。新近的论文因其中的实验可能尚未被其他科研人员重复作过,结论尚未经其他科研人员验证过,因而可能有误导的信息。

在阅读论文摘要及参考书目后,若确定该论文值得认真细读,仍可采取上述的略读、通读和研读三种阅读法。略读时先阅读论文前言的第二段,再略读其余各段,及此后"结论"部分。通读是阅读论文全文,了解论文作者的结论或观点的依据。研读是研究论文的内容。这就需要再次认真阅读全文,分析作者的论断或结论,核实论文结论与参考资料在观点上是否相符。

总之,在阅读专业书籍和学术论文时,要遵循详略得当的原则,根据不同的需要和目标确定具体的阅读方法。三种阅读法各有各的功能和优点,要学会综合运用,以达到科学地收集资料和运用资料的目的。

5.4 资料的收集及分类

1）资料的收集

收集资料的方法很多，常用的主要有以下几种：

第一，做卡片。使用卡片收集资料，易于分类、易于保存、易于查找，并且可分可合，可随时另行组合。一个问题通常写在一张卡片上，内容太多时也可以写在几张卡片上。当然，在收集资料的过程中，要不要做卡片，可根据个人习惯，不必有死板规定。

第二，做笔记。做笔记对于任何一个论文撰写者来说都是必要的，"好记性不如烂笔头"。阅读书报杂志时，搞调查研究时，要随身带笔和纸，随时记下所需资料的内容，或有关的感想体会、理论观点等。在做笔记时，最好空出纸面面积的三分之一，以供写对有关摘录内容的理解、评价和体会。此种方法亦可用于电子媒介的阅读，笔记可在另建的文档中记录。

第三，剪贴报刊。将有用的资料从报纸、刊物上剪下来，或用复印机复印下来，再进行剪贴。把剪下的资料分类贴在笔记本、活页纸或卡片上。这种方法的优点是可以节省抄写的时间。无论是用卡片收集资料，还是摘录资料，或是剪贴资料，都必须注明出处。如果是著作，则要注明作者、书名、出版单位、出版年月；如果是报纸，则要注明作者、篇名、报纸名称、发行年月日、版次；如果是杂志，则要注明作者、篇名、杂志名称、卷（期）号、页码等，以便附录在论文的后面。

2）资料的分类

对收集来的资料要认真阅读，仔细加以分类。主要的分类方法有以下两种：

第一种，主题分类法。按照不同的观点把资料编成组。这些观点可以是综合而成的观点，也可以是自己拟定的观点。例如，翻译中异化观点的学说形成沿革、主要倡导者、异化例证、作者个人评述；反之，同化学说的形成、名家论述、例证及个人评述等。

第二种，项目分类法。即按照一定的属性，把收集的资料分项归类。如：① 经典作家、名人言论；② 概念理论类项目；③ 科学的定义、定理、公式、法规；④ 一般公理、常识、成语、谚语、名言；⑤ 资料作者本人的观点，如资料作者所引用的古今中外的事实、人物活动、言论、诗词等事实类项目，各种统计数字、图表，资料作者的片断论述等。

5.5 资料的整理

资料的整理过程实质上是资料的辨析过程，这里有几方面的工作是不可缺少的。

一是辨析资料的适用性。选择资料的依据,只能是作者所要阐明的中心论点。什么资料可用,什么资料不能用,都要根据这个中心论点决定。论文的中心论点一经确定之后,它就是统帅一切的东西,资料必须服从于中心论点的统帅。不能把一些不能充分说明问题的资料搬来作牵强附会的解释,也不能将所有资料统统塞进文章里,搞得文章臃肿庞杂,扩大了篇幅,中心反而不突出。

二是辨析资料的全面性。如果资料不全面,缺少了某一方面的资料,论文的论述也往往不圆满、不全面,会出现偏颇、漏洞,或由于证据不足难以自圆其说。

三是辨析资料的真实性。资料真实与否直接关系着论文的成败。只有从真实可靠的资料中,才能引出科学的结论。在这方面要注意:其一,要尊重客观实际,避免先入为主的思想,选择资料不能夹杂个人的好恶与偏见,不能歪曲资料本来的客观性;其二,选择资料要有根有据,采用的第一手资料要有来历,选取的第二手资料一定要与原始文献认真核对,以求得最大的准确性;其三,对资料来源要加以辨别,弄清原作者的理论观点、生活背景、写作意图,并加以客观的分析评价,社会科学方面的资料更应该注意这一点。

四是辨析资料是否新颖。所谓新颖的资料,包括两方面的含义:一方面是指前所未有,近期才出现的新事物、新思想、新发现、新方向;另一方面是指虽早已存在,但人们尚未发现其价值的事物。

5.6 记 笔 记

收集资料时应记笔记。阅读中应摘录事实、数据、论点等各方面的资料,摘录时应记录资料的出处及来源,这些记录是科研中原始素材的主要组成部分。科研笔记中所摘录的撰写论文时可能有用的资料既可包括读者可能熟悉的资料,更应包括鲜为人知的资料。在开始科研时,应尽可能多摘录一些资料,随着调研的深入,有时会发现原先的思路不切实际,此时可根据摘录的资料自行进行调整或另辟途径。这就要求对已有的资料去粗取精。资料的取舍这项工作本身即是科研的组成部分。

用卡片记录(摘录)资料是人们普遍采用的记笔记的方法。随着计算机的普遍使用,建立文档记录资料也成为一种替代方式。

按照所记录的内容划分,笔记可分成四种类型:概要型、阐释性、引语型和个人评述型。现将各类型的笔记方法具体描述如下:

概要型(summary or précis)是对参考资料中那些重要的观点和事实所作的归纳和总结,其关键是既要简明扼要,又要忠于原文。也就是说,将原文内容压缩,但要概括原文的重要观点。另一种概要特称为梗概(précis),它和一般性概要(summary)的共同点是都是用自己的话对原文的要点进行归纳和概括;不同点在于,前者较为笼统,后者更为具体,且注重忠于原文,即在思想、观点的叙述顺序、文字的语体风格和文章的基调等方面要与原文保持一致。

阐释型(paraphase)是以自己的词语重述原文的内容,阐释者对原文的审视角度稍有差异,但所改写的内容和基调必须与原文相同。与概要(梗概)相比,阐释并非着重于压缩,因其长度与原文是大致相同的。作好阐释的关键是对原文的正确理解和阐释词的选择,而且要注意的是,应在论文中就所阐释内容的出处予以说明。

引语型(quotation)是直接引用他人的话语。当感到用概要和阐释有损于原汁原味时,可采用这样的方式记录原材料。引用内容要加引号,以区别于阐释。引语确切地说是"直接引语",内容应绝对准确,不可以有任何改动或遗漏(包括词的拼写、大小写形式和标点符号)。引语既可以出自第一手资料(如文学作品中的具体内容),也可以来自第二手资料(如局外人对局中人或事物的看法)。

个人评述型(personal comment)是对参考资料内容所作的评价。在研究分析资料时常常会引发对某种具体内容的看法,需及时予以记录,以免转瞬即逝,因为这种看法有可能成为撰写论文初稿的素材或思路。

5.7 避免剽窃、抄袭

在撰写论文时,首先要避免剽窃或抄袭。剽窃是指在使用他人的观点或语句时没有作恰当的说明,或有意无意地使用他人的观点、数据或词句等,但未标明出处,似乎论文中所述的内容都源于作者本人。许多人认为,只有剽窃他人的观点(包括实验数据、结果)才算剽窃,而使用别人的语句不算剽窃。也有人认为,只有照抄他人论文的结果、讨论部分才算剽窃,而照抄他人论文的引言部分不算剽窃。事实上,引言部分在介绍前人的成果时,也不能直接照抄他人的语句。对剽窃的另一个误解是,只要注明了文献出处,就可以直接照抄他人的语句。在引用别人的观点时,同样不能照抄他人论文或综述中的表述,而必须用自己的语言进行复述。如与他人表述相同,则必须加引号并标明出处。下例为参考:

Technology has significantly transformed education at several major turning points in our history. In the broadest sense, the first technology was the primitive modes of communication used by prehistoric people before the development of spoken language. Mime, gestures, grunts, and drawing of figures in the sand with a stick were methods used to communicate—yes, even to educate. Even without speech, these prehistoric people were able to teach their young how to catch animals for food, what animals to avoid, which vegetation was good to eat and which was poisonous.

源自:Frick, T. (1991). *Restructuring Education Through Technology*. Bloomington, IN: Phi Delta Kappa Educational Foundation.

抄袭:In examining technology, we have to remember that computers are not the first technology people have had to deal with. The first technology was the primitive modes of communication used by prehistoric people before the development of spoken language.

该例为抄袭,作者将原文逐字照搬,没有提到原文作者,也没有在参考文献中列出来源。

正确引用:In examining technology, we have to remember that computers are not the first technology people have had to deal with. Frick (1991) believes that "... the first technology was the primitive modes of communication used by prehistoric people before the development of spoken language" (p.10).

References:Frick, T. (1991). *Restructuring Education Through Technology*. Bloomington, IN: Phi Delta Kappa Educational Foundation.

同样是逐字照搬,但后者使用了引号,在引言前提到了原作者和原著出版年份,在参考文献中也列出了原作。

避免抄袭除了正确引用之外还有另外一个方法,即释义(paraphrase),在写作中也称"改写"。但释义并不等于不用提及原作或按照原作的结构替换部分词语,它是将原作者的语言变成自己的语言,也可以说是对原作意图的提炼浓缩。这一方法也同样要依照上述的规则,以避免剽窃之嫌。下例为参考:

原文:Developing complex skills in the classroom involves the key ingredients identified in teaching pigeons to play ping-pong and to bowl. The key ingredients are: (1) inducing a response, (2) reinforcing subtle improvements or refinements in the behavior, (3) providing for the transfer of stimulus control by gradually withdrawing the prompts or cues, and (4) scheduling reinforcements so that the ratio of reinforcements in responses gradually increases and natural reinforcers can maintain their behavior.

源自:Gredler, M. E. (2001). *Learning and Instruction: Theory into Practice* (4th ed.). Upper Saddle River, NJ: Prentice-Hall.

抄袭:Inducing a response, providing for the transfer of stimulus control by gradually withdrawing prompts or cues, reinforcing subtle improvements in the behavior, and scheduling reinforcements so that natural reinforcers can maintain their behavior are the key ingredients identified both in teaching pigeons to play ping-pong and in developing complex skills in the classroom.

References: Gredler, M. E. (2001). *Learning and Instruction: Theory into Practice* (4th ed.). Upper Saddle River, NJ: Prentice-Hall.

这一例子有抄袭嫌疑，因为作者只是把原作的语言移位，另个别删加了几个词语；同时，对于与原作完全相同的词语也未加引号，且在文中没有标明出处。

合理释义：According to Gredler (2001), the same factors apply to developing complex skills in a classroom setting as to developing complex skills in any setting. A response must be induced, then reinforced as it gets closer to the desired behavior. Reinforcers have to be scheduled carefully, and cues have to be withdrawn gradually so that the new behaviors can be transferred and maintained.

References: Gredler, M. E. (2001). *Learning and Instruction: Theory into Practice* (4th ed.). Upper Saddle River, NJ: Prentice-Hall.

该例可被视为正确引用，因为原作者不仅在后面参考书目中被提到，在文中也同样被标出。因为是释义，所以不必用引号。

另外，在论文中引用他人已经正式发表的成果，无须获得原作者的同意。但是，如果要引用他人未正式发表的成果（例如，通过私人通信或学术会议的交流而获悉的成果），必须征得原作者的书面许可。

以下几种情形可被视为合理使用：

1) 使用他人作品的历史背景、客观事实、统计数字。但是，完全照搬他人描述客观事实、历史背景的文字，有可能被认定为抄袭。

2) 对于基本常识或学术界的常识，可以不注明出处。例如，在提及地心引力学说或相对论时，没有必要特地注明源于该理论的创立者或源于某部著作。必须对别人的观点注明出处的一般是指那些比较新颖、比较前沿的观点，如果不作说明就有可能被误会为是论文作者的原创。

3) 引用别人某些简短或非常格式化的表述。例如，对实验材料和方法的描述，不同的人书写的结果都差不多，那么就不存在剽窃的问题。

5.8 练 习

修改下面这段有剽窃嫌疑的引用并指出其不合理之处：

Original Source Material: Theories differ from philosophies and models of teaching. A philosophy is a value system, whereas a theory seeks to explain real-world events and can be certified through scientific investigation. Models of teaching are approaches to the management of some aspect of classroom instruction and they may not be independent of subject area, grade level, age of the student, or the setting for learning. A characteristic of learning theories is that they address the underlying psychological dynamics of events. Thus, they provide a mechanism for understanding the implications of events related to learning in both formal and informal settings.

Source: Gredler, M. E. (2001). *Learning and Instruction: Theory into Practice* (4th ed.). Upper Saddle River, NJ: Prentice-Hall.

Plagiarized Version: Theories and philosophies are different from each other because theories seek to explain real-world events and can be certified through scientific investigation. Learning theories address the underlying psychological dynamics of events, so they provide a mechanism for understanding the implications of events related to learning in both formal and informal settings.

第六章 撰写初稿

6.1 编写提纲

1) 提纲概述

从写作程序上讲,编写提纲是作者动笔行文前的必要准备;从提纲本身来讲,它是作者构思谋篇的具体体现。所谓构思谋篇,就是组织设计论文的篇章结构。学术论文的写作不像写抒情的文章或散文那样随感而发,信手拈来,用很少的素材就可以表达一种思想感情,而是要用大量的资料、较多的层次、严密的推理来展开论述,从各个方面阐述理由、论证自己的观点。因此,构思谋篇就显得非常重要。编制写作提纲,才能有条理地安排材料、展开论证。

提纲可使作者易于掌握论文结构的全局,提纲挈领,分清层次,明确重点,掌握全篇论文的基本骨架,使论文的结构完整统一;提纲能周密地谋篇布局,使总论点和分论点有机地统一起来,也就能够按照各部分的要求安排、组织、利用资料,决定取舍,最大限度地发挥资料的作用;提纲有利于及时调整,避免大返工。在学术论文的研究和写作过程中,作者常常会产生新的联想或新的观点,如果不认真编写提纲,动起笔来就会被这种现象干扰,不得不停下笔来重新思考,甚至推翻已写的从头来过。提纲犹如工程的蓝图,只要动笔前把提纲考虑得周到严谨,就能形成一个层次清楚、逻辑严密的论文框架,从而避免许多不必要的返工。

2) 简单提纲

从内容上,论文提纲可分为简单提纲和详细提纲两种。简单提纲是高度概括的,只提示论文的要点,如何展开则不涉及。这种提纲相当于内容提要,可以不包括引言和结语。一般学术专著或教学参考书都有反映全书内容的提要,以便读者一翻提要就知道书的大概内容。在动笔前把论文的题目和大标题、小标题列出来,再把选用的材料插进去,就形成了论文的简单提纲。虽然简单,但由于它是作者经过深思熟虑构成的,可使写作按照一定的框架顺利进行。没有这种准备,边想边写,则很难顺利地写下去。

以课题"On Cultural Differences Embodied in E-C Translation of Metaphor"为例,简单提纲可以写成下面这样:

Topic: On Cultural Differences Embodied in E-C Translation of Metaphor

1. Introduction of Culture and Translation
2. Definition and Characteristics of Metaphor
3. E-C Translation of Metaphor in View of Cultural Differences

3)详细提纲

详细提纲,是把论文的主要论点和展开部分较为详细地列出来。从形式类型上,详细提纲可以分为词组型、句子型和段落型。以词组型为例:

Topic: On Cultural Differences Embodied in E-C Translation of Metaphor

Chapter 1　Introduction
　1.1　Literature Review
　1.2　The Close Relationship Between Translation of Metaphor and Cultural Difference

Chapter 2　Culture and Translation
　2.1　Culture
　2.2　Language, Culture and Translation

Chapter 3　Metaphor
　3.1　Definition of Metaphor
　3.2　Characteristics of Metaphor

Chapter 4　E-C Translation of Metaphor in View of Cultural Differences
　4.1　Cultural Translation of Metaphor
　　4.1.1　Interpretation of Cultural Factors in Translating English Metaphors
　　4.1.2　Cultural Connotation of Metaphor
　4.2　Corresponding Relations and Approaches to the Translation of English Metaphors
　　4.2.1　Approaches to Full-corresponding Relation
　　4.2.2　Approaches to Semi-corresponding Relation
　　4.2.3　Approaches to Non-corresponding Relation

Chapter 5　Conclusion
　5.1　A General Review of the Thesis
　5.2　The Growing Importance of Cultural Awareness in E-C Translation of Metaphor

句子型和段落型是将主要论点和次要论点或具体实例说明都编入,多适用于篇幅较长的论文。

6.2 撰写引言

论文的前言也叫引言,是正文前面的一段短文。前言是论文的开场白,目的是向读者说明本研究的来龙去脉,吸引读者对本篇论文产生兴趣,对正文起到提纲挈领的作用。引言提出问题,本论分析问题,结论解决问题。引言是开篇之作,写引言于前,始能疾书于后。正所谓万事开头难,引言是全文最难写的一部分。这是因为,作者对有关学科领域的熟悉程度,作者的知识水平和科研潜力,研究的意义何在、价值如何等问题,都在引言的字里行间得以充分体现。引言的主要任务是向读者勾勒出全文的基本内容和轮廓。它可以包括以下五项内容中的全部或其中几项:

1)介绍某研究领域的背景、意义、发展状况、目前的水平等;

2)对相关领域的文献进行回顾和综述,包括前人的研究成果、已经解决的问题,并适当加以评价或比较;

3)指出前人尚未解决的问题、留下的技术空白,也可以提出新问题及解决这些新问题的新方法、新思路,从而引出自己研究课题的动机与意义;

4)说明自己研究课题的目的;

5)概括论文的主要内容,或勾勒其大体轮廓。

下例为论文《On Sino-US Cultural Differences in Relationship Marketing》的引言节选:

Chapter 1   Introduction

With the development of economy, people got better living quality and then the consuming behavior is also changed. Under this kind of change, traditional marketing strategy can no longer satisfy people's needs and how to maintain the relationship with customers has become a key issue giving the theory of relationship marketing a good stage to perform. This study tries to explore the Sino-US cultural differences from the perspective of relationship marketing. The research will be divided into five sections. Research background and literary review in the first chapter; Sino-US relationship culture in the second section; the introduction of relationship marketing in the third part; comparison and deep analysis of cultural differences in the fourth; the expectation in the last.

Review

Although it is nothing new for companies to build relationships with customers, it has generally been done on a one-to-one basis. In recent years, however, technological developments have made it possible to build up individual relationships with clients on a much larger scale, and this more sophisticated kind of operation is known as relationship marketing which initiates from the West gradually becoming one of the most popular models in domestic marketing field. Many Chinese companies take it as an efficient way to explore some potential customers and pursue a stable mutually beneficial relation. With the great success of relationship marketing in Chinese market, the word "guanxi" has been frequently mentioned in the mainstream media at home and abroad, because the Chinese translation of relationship is guanxi.

Ye Shenghong and Wang Chenghui, the professors at Jinan University, believe that some philosophic terms as "benevolent love", "peace is precious" and "people-oriented" in Confucianism reflect the relationship marketing theory such as "taking customer demand as the core value", "coordination and cooperation", "emphasis on social responsibility" and "the importance of human capital" concept. Although relationship culture and relationship marketing are closely related, in practice, the understanding of relationship marketing is different between China and the West, proven by strong manifestation of culture itself.

The paper of Zhang Jinlai and Meng Xianzhong from Shanghai Jiaotong University analyses Confucian culture impact of Chinese marketing practice and puts forward four tips to promote the relationship marketing localization: first is more open to localize the strategies; second is to have a comprehensive insight on both market and customer needs; third is to attach importance to business moral and social responsibilities; last is to take the advantages over disadvantages.

Wilfried R. Vanhonacker referred in *When Good Guanxi Turns Bad* that relationship marketing is not its original pattern in China's practice and he admitted that the influence of Chinese "guanxi" culture would be a good spur and advantage for future theoretical development. However, good guanxi turns bad when the malign competition happens by means of bribery or get-in by the back door.

Significance

Although relationship and guanxi are the same in Chinese characters, significant differences exist between the "relationship" in American academic context and what Chinese people are familiar with, the Chinese "guanxi".

The theory of relationship marketing is introduced into China in 90s. Chinese relationship marketing features stand out under the great impact of Chinese culture after almost 20 years' development. Culture as the external factor of marketing plays a dramatically intensive role in the multinational corporation activities nowadays. Confucius understanding of relationship has both similarity and differences with that of the West. It is a good topic to investigate why the original theory turns different and how the relationship marketing in Chinese context emerges. Therefore, it is essential and necessary to make further study in this field.

America as the biggest country and economy in the world is the typical icon of western relationship marketing, so the paper takes American illustration to explain theoretical evolution of relationship marketing, the differences and similarity between America and China, and finally relationship marketing in Chinese context, its problems and strategies for future reform.

Purpose

Based on domestic and foreign literature review, the paper uses comparative research methods through citing, analyzing and demonstrating by some examples. The purpose of the paper is to indicate the discrepancy in Chinese and Western cultural features and then help people get a thorough and positive understanding of relationship marketing and its proper application in the specific context of Chinese situation, by means of comparison in two kinds of interpersonal relationship on the basis of cultural differences.

6.3 撰写文献综述

文献综述(literary review)是利用已发表的文献资料为原始素材撰写的论文。由于不同的作者对所研究对象认识的深度是不同的,有待研究的主要内容相应采用的研究方法也不尽相同。撰写学术论文首先要熟悉前人相关研究成果,站在别人研究的基础上,从事更高层次、更有价值的研究。所以,应了解该学科或专业的发展历史,分析它现在处于什么样的发展阶段,然后根据各个阶段的不同特点选择研究课题,从而确定论文题目。因此,我们在确定论文题目时写文献综述就很有必要。综述包括"综"与"述"两个方面。所谓"综"就是指作者必须对占有的大量素材进行归纳整理、综合分析,使材料更加精炼、更加明确、更加层次分明、更有逻辑性。所谓"述"就是评述,是对所写专题的比较全面、深入、系统的论述。因而,综述是对某一专题、某一领域的历史背景、前人工作、争论焦点、研究现状与发展前景等方面,以作者自己的观点写成的严谨而系统的评论性、资料性科技论文。文献综述不仅是对学术观点和理论方法的整理,而且还是评论性的,要带着作者本人批判的眼光来归纳和评论文献,而不是对相关领域学术研究成果的"堆砌"。所以,在写文献综述时应该瞄准主流文献,随时整理文献(如对文献进行分类,记录文献信息和藏书地点),按照问题来组织文献综述。

综述与论文本身不同。论文注重研究方法的科学性和结果的可信性,特别强调结果。而综述要写出主题(某一专题、某一领域)的详细情报资料,不仅要指出发展背景和工作意义,而且还应有作者的评论性意见,指出研究成败的原因;不仅要指出目前研究的热点和争论焦点,而且还应指出有待于进一步探索和研究的新领域;不仅要介绍主题的研究动态与最新进展,而且还应在评述的基础上,预测发展趋势和应用前景。因此,综述的书写格式比较多样化,大体由以下几部分组成:

1) 前言:与一般科技论文一样,综述的前言又称"引言",是将读者导入论文主题的部分,主要叙述综述的目的和作用,概述主题的有关概念和定义,简述所选择主题的历史背景、发展过程、现状、争论焦点、应用价值和实践意义,同时还可限定综述的范围,使读者对综述的主题有一个初步印象。这部分约200—300字。

2) 主体部分:综述主体部分的篇幅范围特别大,短者几千字,长者可达几万字,其叙述方式灵活多样,没有必须遵循的固定模式,常由作者根据综述的内容自行设计创造。一般可根据主体部分的内容多寡分成几个大部分,每部分标上简短而醒目的小标题。各部分的区分标准也多种多样,有的按年代,有的按问题,有的按不同论点,有的按发展阶段。然而,不管采用何种方式,都应该包括历史发展、现状评述和发展前景预测三方面的内容。

(1) 历史发展:按时间顺序,简述该主题的来龙去脉、发展概况及各阶段的研究水平。

(2) 现状评述:重点是论述当前国内外的研究现状,着重评述哪些问题已经解决,哪些问题还没有解决,提出可能的解决途径;指出目前存在的争论焦点,比较各种观点的异同并作出理论解释,亮明作者的观点;详细介绍有创造性和发展前途的理论和假说,并引出论据,指出可能的发展趋势。

(3) 发展前景预测:通过纵横对比,肯定该主题的研究水平,指出存在的问题,提出可能的发展趋势,指明研究方向,提示研究的捷径。该部分也可以放在最后。

3) 总结部分:总结部分又称为"结论"、"小结"或"结语"。书写总结时,可以根据主体部分的论述,提出几条语言简明、含义确切的意见和建议;也可以对主体部分的主要内容作出扼要的概括,并提出作者自己的见解,表明作者赞成什么,反对什么;对于篇幅较小的综述,可以不单独列出总结,仅在主体各部分内容论述完后,用几句话对全文进行高度概括。

4) 参考文献:参考文献是综述的原始素材,也是综述的基础。因此,拥有并列出足够的参考文献显得格外重要。它除了表示尊重被引证作者的劳动及表明引用的资料有其科学依据以外,更重要的是为读者深入探讨该主题提供查找有关文献的线索。对学位论文来说,参考文献可只在最后列出,而不用与文献综述连为一体。

Language and Gender: A Brief Literature Review

With the general growth of feminist work in many academic fields, it is hardly surprising that the relationship between language and gender has attracted considerable attention in recent years. In an attempt to go beyond "folklinguistic" assumptions about how men and women use language (the assumption that women are "talkative", for example), studies have focused on anything from different syntactical, phonological or lexical uses of language to aspects of conversation analysis, such as topic nomination and control, interruptions and other interactional features. While some research has focused only on the description of differences, other work has sought to show how linguistic differences both reflect and reproduce social difference. Accordingly, Coates (1988) suggests that research on language and gender can be divided into studies that focus on dominance and those that focus on difference.

Much of the earlier work emphasized dominance. Lakoff's (1975) pioneering work suggested that women's speech typically displayed a range of features, such as tag questions, which marked it as inferior and weak. Thus, she argued that the type of subordinate speech learned by a young girl "will later be an excuse others use to keep her in a demeaning position, to refuse to treat her seriously as a human being" (1975, p.5). While there are clearly some problems with Lakoff's work—her analysis was not based on empirical research, for example, the automatic equation of subordinate with "weak" is problematic—the emphasis on dominance has understandably remained at the Centre of much of this work. Research has shown how men nominated topics more, interrupted more often, held the floor for longer, and so on (see, for example, Zimmerman and West, 1975). The chief focus of this approach, then, has been to show how patterns of interaction between men and women reflect the dominant position of men in society.

Some studies, however, have taken a different approach by looking not so much at power in mixed-sex interactions as at how same-sex groups produce certain types of interaction. In a typical study of this type, Maltz and Borker (1982) developed lists of what they described as men's and women's features of language. They argued that these norms of interaction were acquired in same-sex groups rather than mixed-sex groups and that the issue is therefore one of (sub-)cultural miscommunication rather than social inequality. Much of this research has focused on comparisons between, for example, the competitive conversational style of men and the cooperative conversational style of women.

While some of the more popular work of this type, such as Tannen (1987), lacks a critical dimension, the emphasis on difference has nevertheless been valuable in fostering research into gender subgroup interactions and in emphasizing the need to see women's language use not only as "subordinate" but also as a significant subcultural domain.

Although Coates' (1988) distinction is clearly a useful one, it also seems evident that these two approaches are by no means mutually exclusive. While it is important on the one hand, therefore, not to operate with a simplistic version of power and to consider language and gender only in mixed-group dynamics, it is also important not to treat women's linguistic behaviour as if it existed outside social relations of power. As Cameron, McAlinden and O'Leary (1988) ask, "Can it be coincidence that men are aggressive and hierarchically-organized conversationalists, whereas women are expected to provide conversational support?" (p. 80). Clearly, there is scope here for a great deal more research that

- is based on empirical data of men's and women's speech;
- operates with a complex understanding of power and gender relationships (so that women's silence, for example, can be seen both as a site of oppression and as a site of possible resistance);
- looks specifically at the contexts of language use, rather than assuming broad gendered differences;
- involves more work by men on language and gender, since attempts to understand male uses of language in terms of difference have been few (thus running the danger of constructing men's speech as the "norm" and women's speech as "different");
- aims not only to describe and explain but also to change language and social relationships.

References

Coates, J. and D. Cameron (Eds.) (1988). *Women in Their Speech Communities*. Harlow: Longman.

Cameron, D., F. McAlinden and K. O'Leary (1988). *Lakoff in Context: The Social and Linguistic Function of Tag Questions*. In J. Coates and D. Cameron (op. cit.). pp. 74—93.

Coates, J. (1988). Chapter 6: Introduction. In J. Coates and D. Cameron (op. cit.) pp. 63—73.

Lakoff, R. (1975). *Language and Woman's Place*. New York: Harper and Row.

Maltz, D. N. and R. A. Borker (1982). *A Cultural Approach to Male-female Miscommunication*. In J. Gumperz (Ed.), *Language and Social Identity*. Cambridge: Cambridge U. P.

Tannen, D. (1987). *That's not What I Meant*. London: Dent.

Zimmerman, D. & C. West (1975). *Sex Roles, Interruptions and Silences in Conversation*, In B. Thorne & N. Henley (Eds.), *Language and Sex: Difference and Dominance*. Rowley, Mass: Newbury House.

撰写文献综述的注意事项：

(1) 综述内容应是前人未曾写过的。如已有人发表过类似综述，一般不宜重复，更不能以他人综述之内容作为自己综述的素材。

(2) 对于某些新知识领域、新技术，写作时可以追溯该主题的发展过程，适当增加一些基础知识内容，以便读者理解。对于人所共知或知之甚多的主题，应只写其新进展、新动向、新发展，不重复别人已综述过的前一阶段的研究状况。

(3) 综述的素材若来自前人的研究报告，必须忠实于原文，不可断章取义，阉割或歪曲前人的观点。

(4) 撰写综述时，收集的文献资料应尽可能齐全，切忌随便收集一些文献就动手撰写，更忌讳阅读了几篇中文资料，便拼凑成一篇所谓的综述。

6.4　正文的写作

正文(main body)是论文的主体部分，也称"本论"，是对问题展开分析、对观点加以证明的部分，是全面、详尽、集中地表述研究成果的部分。

正文部分的篇幅长、容量大，一般不会只由一个层次或一个段落构成。不同的层次或段落之间有着密切的结构关系，按照层次或段落之间的结构关系的不同，可以把本论部分的结构形式分为并列式、总分式、对照式、递进式和混合式四种。

1) 并列式

并列式结构又称"横式结构"，是指各个小的论点相提并论，各个层次平行排列，分别从不同的角度、不同的侧面对问题加以论述，使文章内容呈现出一种齐头并进式的格局。例如，论文"On the Differences of Family Education Between China and America"，先从中美教育目标、内容、方法和结果几个方面同时对比，又从社会背景、经济模式、社会条件及传统文化几个部分分别探讨，就是采用并列的结构。

Chapter 1　A Brief Introduction to Family Education
  1.1　The Definition of Family Education
  1.2　The Importance of Family Education
Chapter 2　The Differences Between Chinese and American Family Education
  2.1　The Comparison of Family Education Objects
  2.2　The Comparison of Family Education Contents
  2.3　The Comparison of Family Education Methods
  2.4　The Comparison of Family Education Results
Chapter 3　The Reasons of the Differences Between Chinese and American Family Education
  3.1　Different Historical Backgrounds
  3.2　Different Economic Patterns
  3.3　Different Social Conditions
  3.4　Different Traditional Cultures
Chapter 4　Conclusion
  4.1　Suggestions About Chinese Family Education
  4.2　Conclusion of the Research

2）总分式

总分式结构是先总说后分说，总说提出中心论点，分说则横向开拓，分解论点，论证中心。这种关系还可以演变为"分—总"或"总—分—总"的结构方式。例如，"On Sino-US Cultural Differences in Relationship Marketing"一文采用的就是"总—分—总"的结构，提纲如下：

Chapter 1　Introduction
  1.1　Literary Review
  1.2　Research Significance and Methods
Chapter 2　Sino-US Relationship Culture
  2.1　Guanxi
  2.2　Relationship in Chinese Confucianism Culture
  2.3　Relationship in American Culture
Chapter 3　Relationship Marketing
  3.1　The Establishment of Relationship Marketing Theory
  3.2　Definition of Relationship Marketing Theory
  3.3　Three Levels in Relationship Marketing
Chapter 4　Cultural Differences in Relationship Marketing
  4.1　Comparison in Features of Relationship Culture

    4.2   Comparison in Sino-US Relationship Marketing
        4.2.1   Similarities
        4.2.2   Differences
    4.3   Relationship Marketing in Chinese Context
        4.3.1   Problems and Side Effects
        4.3.2   Strategies in Chinese Context
Chapter 5   Conclusion

该文先总说"relationship culture";然后对中美"relationship culture"分别阐述,再归纳两者的差异;最后着重分析"relationship culture"在中国社会环境下的问题和对策。

3) 对照式

对照式结构是指文中两部分内容或进行对比,或用这部分内容烘托另一部分内容。例如鲁迅先生的《中国人失掉自信力了吗》一文,前一部分反面批驳了敌论中的论据不能证明论点,即中国人失掉的是"他信力",发展的是"自欺力",而不是"自信力",直接批驳了敌论;后一部分从正面列举事实,提出正确的论点,我们中国人没有失掉自信力,间接地批驳了敌论。

4) 递进式

递进式结构又称"纵式结构"或"直线式结构",是指由浅入深,一层深于一层地表述内容的结构方式。各层次之间呈现出一种层层推进、步步深入的逻辑关系,后一个层次的内容是对前一个层次的内容的发展,后一个论点是对前一个论点的深化。

5) 混合式

所谓混合式结构,是把并列式同递进式混合在一起的结构形式。与其内容的复杂性相适应,学术论文的结构形式也极少是单一的。有的文章的各大层次之间具有并列关系,而各大层次内部的段落之间却具有递进关系,或者在彼此之间具有递进关系的大的层次的内部,包含着具有并列关系的段落,并列中有递进,递进中有并列;有的文章的各大层次之间所具有的结构关系就不是单一的,并列关系与递进关系分别存在于文章不同的层次之间。

从格式上说,为使本论部分更有条理性,人们常在这一部分的各个层次之前加上一些外在的标志,这些用以区分层次的外在标志主要有序码、小标题、序码和小标题相结合及空行等几种。

6.5   调研类论文的结构

一般来说,若正文包括许多调查研究,就要有对研究方法的详细描述和对研究结果的详细分析。实验类的科研论文更是如此。在明确了所要解决的问题和撰写完文献综述后,很自然地就要提出自己解决问题的思路和方案。这也是读者评估课题意义的重要手段。如果科研中程序有误,研究结果的可靠性就值得怀疑,因而应以充分的理由说明拟采用方法的可靠性和正确性。在写作方法上,一是要通过比较显示自己方案的价值,二是让读者了解方案的创新之处或有新意的思路、算法和关键技术。在与文献资料中的方案进行比较时,首先要阐述自己的设计方案,说明为什么要选择或设计这样的方案,前面评述的优点在此方案中如何体现,不足之处又是如何得到了克服,最后完成的工作能达到什么水平,有什么创新之处。如果自己的题目是总方案的一部分,要明确说明自己承担的部分及对整个任务的贡献。这一部分包括:调查与研究对象,实验和观测方法,仪器设备,材料原料,实验和观测结果,计算方法和编程原理,数据资料,经过加工整理的图表,形成的论点和导出的结论等。当然,其中的结论可以单独设一部分(或一节)展开叙述。

下例摘选自一篇有关阅读理解中图式理论的论文,题为"Toward Content and Linguistic Schemata":

* * *

The purpose of the study is to address to the following hypothesis:

(1) Content schemata has more influence on the second language learners' comprehension than linguistic proficiency

(2) Language proficiency compensate for the learners' content schema inadequacy

2.1 Method

(1) Participants

Participants in the study were 74 freshmen and 78 sophomore non-English major attending university. They are composed of two classes of freshmen (35 and 36 in number respectively) and two classes of sophomore (33 and 35 in number respectively). 68 of them are females and 84 of them are males. The sophomore group has taken CET4 and the freshmen have just been at the college for 3 months. Their level of English proficiency is supposed to be different.

(2) Reading Materials:

An experimental test was conducted in order to get the data for the impact of linguistic instruction and background knowledge for the two groups of participants. The two reading passages were selected from CET6 sample tests, one is about the reform of British legal system and the other is about the function of liver. These two readings are chosen on the ground that they may be challenging and relatively unfamiliar to most of the students. Although they are not lengthy and the passage lines are not very technical, both selections do presuppose content-specific information that most of the student's lack.

(3) Procedures

A final exam was taken two weeks after the passage test. It intends to provide the most up-dated reference of the participants' L2 proficiency level to compare their performance in the experimental situation. To reinforce the validity of the final exam and to further identify the significance of the preview in the experiment, we referred back to the student's previous performance in CET4 and the National Entrance Exam (NEE) respectively and took them as the frame of reference for the students' language proficiency in each group. CET4 was the most recent English test the sophomores had taken. And NEE was what the freshmen had done three month ago, a month later than the time of CET4 for the sophomores. The time of the exams suggests their English proficiency before the experiment. The data was obtained from the questionnaire we delivered before the experiment. The questionnaire includes the items relating to their age, sex, scores in major English tests (NEE for freshmen and CET4 for sophomore), their background knowledge about the prospective reading passage, their particular interests and their learning styles. This procedure is also served to gather data for their personality traits in the following chapter.

In the experimental test (reading passages), one of the freshmen classes and one of the sophomore classes were given some background information about the reading passages and each of the counterpart class was given the linguistic instruction prior to reading the target passage. Then the participants were tested in the context of their classroom groups and the test was administered during the regular class time.

(4) Score and Data Analysis

The analysis was made on the basis of experimental passage test scores and the scores in the final exam. The results of entrance English examination were taken as the covariates for the freshmen group and the results of CET4 for the sophomores.

20 questions were designed in the form of multiple choices, with ten questions for each passage. Statistical analysis were conducted by applying the SPSS 10.0 package of statistical programs, using independent T-test repeatedly for freshmen group and sophomore group separately first and then the compare means procedure which is comparable with the analysis of mean scores. Table 1 is the description of the independent T-test for the related tests.

Table 1 Report of T-test of Entrance English Examination, Passage and Final Exam for the Freshmen Group

		Levene's Test for Equality of Variances		T-test for Equality of Means		
		F	Sig.	t	df	Sig. (2-tailed)
NEE	Equal variances assumed	.278	.600	2.264	69	.027
	Equal variances not assumed			2.259	66.299	.027
Passage	Equal variances assumed	4.229	.044	15.595	69	.000
	Equal variances not assumed			15.519	60.627	.000
Final	Equal variances assumed	.004	.947	1.400	69	.166
	Equal variances not assumed			1.400	68.993	.166

* * *

2.2 Discussion and Further Analysis

Addressing to hypothesis 1, we can see that content schema does not significantly affects reading comprehension for the less proficient L2 learners' comprehension as much as the more advanced learners. Linguistic instruction plays a more important role at the lower level learning. Thus information gap may result from the linguistic inadequacy for the less advanced learners. But for the more advanced learners, the prior background knowledge of content specific information has more influence.

* * *

6.6 结　　语

论文的结语(conclusion)部分,应反映论文中通过实验、观察研究并经过理论分析后得到的学术见解。结语应是论文最终的、总体的结论。换句话说,结论应是整篇论文的结局,而不是某一局部问题或某一分支问题的结论,也不是正文中各段的小结的简单重复。结论应当准确、完整、明确、精练,体现作者更深层的认识,且是从全篇论文的全部材料出发,经过推理、判断、归纳等逻辑分析过程而得到的新的学术总观点、总见解。结语一般应包括以下几个方面:

1) 本文研究结果说明了什么问题;

2) 对前人有关的看法作了哪些修正、补充、发展、证实或否定；

3) 本文研究的不足之处或遗留未予解决的问题，以及解决这些问题的可能的关键点和方向。

结束语也可以用"后记"的形式写出，可以总结论文中得出的结论并进行批判性的反思。

上例"Toward Content and Linguistic Schemata"结语节选：

2.3 Conclusion

Some scholars contend that successful L2 learning depends on the possession of a "critical mass of knowledge," of which one part is strictly linguistic knowledge. But linguistic knowledge must interact with other parts of the "mass" as "background knowledge assumptions and relevant formal and content schemata (Devine, 1991, 267)." As Steffensen et al. (1979, 19) said, "the schemata embodying background knowledge about the content of a discourse exert a profound influence on how well the discourse will be comprehended, learned, and remembered." This suggests that as far as both language instruction and background information are to have a positive impact on L2 learners' comprehension, they are the components never to be isolated in the classroom instruction. What this investigation reminds us is:

First, beginning L2 readers are thought to focus on low-level process strategies (e.g., word identification), whereas more proficient readers shift attention to more abstract conceptual abilities and make better use of background knowledge; that is, they use textual information to confirm and predict the information in the text.

Second, since each of the two groups of participants showed significant effects of both linguistic instruction and background information, both of the factors appear to be important to address in second language comprehension pedagogy. Moreover, as the relative strength of linguistic instruction and background knowledge differ to each group, the relative attention and weight to be given to each of these factors in L2 teaching may need to vary for different groups of learners. The learners at lower L2 proficiency levels may need relatively greater help linguistically whereas the learners with better language processing skills may gain more by the contextual sources. The question the classroom teachers must answer should be how to make the best devotion of class time to the different levels of learners and how best to help learners to use various types of textual information.

Finally, the facilitating effect of some strategies cannot be neglected. Data suggests that some participants performed much better than the others regardless of different contexts. They are good at making associations between the clues within the text;

they tend to make inference within their limited vocabulary. Retrospective investigation reveals part of it is due to the participant's awareness of strategy employment. We hypothesize the sophomore owe their greater achievements in L2 processing to their language proficiency and partly to their knowledge in processing strategy. Strategy training poses its pedagogical significance in this sense. Learners should be aided in becoming a better analyzer not at a vocabulary level but also at a more content-based level.

* * *

Implications for teaching are drawn from the findings of the investigations about contextual factors influencing Chinese adult learners' L2 comprehension and the information reconstruction should be based on how to build the bridges between the L2 learners' existing schemata and the new knowledge, thus achieving the reconstruction of information. . . .

In regard to content and cultural teaching. Further studies are to be made from the perspectives of textbooks, teaching pedagogy as well as the language teacher. Our suggestions to cultural teaching are that a broader definition of the cultural content of texts is called for; explicit contrastive analysis is to be taken as an effective methodology by the L2 language teachers in order to raise the learners' awareness of intercultural issues; special efforts are to be made in developing the learners' pragmatic competence in L2 classroom teaching, and finally, the attention should be given to the enhancement of the L2 teachers' cultural competence.

* * *

Though being a tip of the huge iceberg in the field of linguistic research, the exploration of the contextual factors for the Chinese adult learners' L2 language comprehension in this study attempts to provide some insights into the L2 learning/teaching in China. Inevitably, there are more related factors that deserves attention but remains uncovered in this paper. Therefore, further in-depth research is needed in this area.

综上所述,论文的各个部分可简单地概括为对如下问题的回答：

Why am I doing it?	Introduction Significance
What is known? What is unknown?	Review of research Identifying gaps
What do I hope to discover?	Aims
How am I going to discover it?	Methodology

(续表)

What have I found?	Results
What does it mean?	Discussion
So what? What are the possible applications or recommendations? What contribution does it make to knowledge? What next?	Conclusions

6.7 练 习

写一篇关于你所拟定选题的文献综述,字数为五百个单词左右,内容须包括:研究现状、研究目的和意义、研究方法。

第七章　修改与定稿

　　修改是在初稿完成后对初稿进行再阅读、再思考和再撰写的一个创造性过程。修改工作需要严谨的态度和审视能力，因为它需要超越自我以便追求更高的境界和更好的效果。

　　常见的修改方法有四种：一是扩展，即增加新的内容；二是压缩，即删除不必要的内容；三是修正，即改正错误的东西；四是润饰，即改善语言效果。以下从评价论文的几点标准逐项检查修订：

　　1）观点

　　要重审文章中的观点是否抓住题目的主要问题。观点是论文的重要组成部分。如果观点不明晰，或论据说明的是另外的论点，那么就要对文章中的观点进行调整。对观点的修改一般只能是微调，如果全部否定观点的话，文章就要重写。观点的修改既包括对论点的增加或删减，也包括对观点的订正。但无论是那一种修改，都要使文章显得论点突出、明了。

　　2）论证材料

　　文章有了立论后就要证明自己的观点，可采用的论证方式通常有例证法、引证法、对比法、类比法、比喻法、因果分析等方法。在修订中要重审文章是否证明了立论假设并举出相应的例子。检查论文中的论证或材料是否清楚地说明了观点。材料是为观点服务的，如果材料不足以说明观点，就必须增加材料；如果材料过多，使文章显得烦琐、累赘，就必须删减材料。如果发现有更好的材料能说明观点，就必须更换或增加材料。有了恰当的论证材料后，还要检查的是该例证的来源是否可靠。

　　3）结论

　　文章的结论要能简要反映全文的内容。如果文章的结论不能准确反映文章的内容，或文章的结论不足以反映文章的内容，则结论要进行调整。

　　4）内容

　　论文的各个部分是否连接紧密（线索）？阐述时是否紧扣题目？论文的发展是否符合题目的逻辑性？论文的结构是否条理清楚、顺理成章、符合逻辑？是否遵守论文的分段？论文在表达方式上是否为读者所接受？语法及修辞是否有错误？修改的另一个重要方面是锤炼字句、润色文字。写作过程中不可避免地会出现一些病句,或重复啰唆语句,通过修改能避免这些错误的出现。

5) 文献和引文

所使用的文献应出现在参考书目中;转引的内容应在文中说明;所采用的引文或别人的观点有应有所表明。

第八章 提供文献目录

论文作者在正文之后必须提供论文中全部引文的详细出版情况，即文献目录页。提供文献目录是对论文中使用他人的信息资料（包括直接引语和间接引语，第一手资料和第二手资料）的内容和出处作出详细的说明。它既可以表示出论文作者对所引资料的承认与感谢，也可以增强资料来源的可信度，同时还能方便读者对资料来源的核对。提供参考文献目录不仅体现了学术论文的学术性、科学性和规范性，也反映了作者严谨的科学态度。

提供英语论文的文献目录须遵守一定的文体格式，常见的有以下三种：

8.1 芝加哥论文格式

芝加哥论文格式（Chicago Manual Style）是一种既有一定权威性又不局限于某一学科的研究论文格式，被社会科学及许多其他专业本科生和研究生广泛采用。语言和文学均属人文学科，因此许多英语语言文学专业本科生的毕业论文首选芝加哥论文格式。

芝加哥论文格式有两种基本的引注形式：① 注释和参考书目（人文类形式）（Notes and Bibliographies（Humanities Style））；② 作者—年份引注和参照表（Author-Date Citations and Reference List）。

这两种形式可以混用，只要维持全论文统一即可。在此以介绍第一种形式为主。

1）注释和参考书目（人文类形式）

批注以数字顺序安插在论文中，注释依序放在每一页的最下方（页尾注），或在文章结尾（结尾注）。在第一次引注时，批注包括完整的参考数据。参考书目一般只列出该论文中使用的数据来源，中、日文条目依作者姓氏笔画排列，西文依作者姓氏的字母排列，必须包括完整的参考数据之信息。

芝加哥论文格式要求对引述资料的第一次注释，必须包括所有可辨识与指认的资料来源：作者的全名、书籍的完整名称、编辑者的名字、出版地、出版社、出版日期、引注资料的页数。再次参考该数据时，只需注明作者的姓，再加上逗点，书籍名称的简写，逗点，页数。每一个注释编号后加上句点，空一格之后再写注释。每一个注释必须空五格(或和每一段论文本文起始空格相同)。如果文本是双行间距,则注释也必须采双行间距。

基本格式如下：

书籍——注释编号.(空一格)作者名,书籍名称(以斜体字或画底线处理),(出版地:出版社,出版年),页数。

文章——注释编号.(空一格)作者名,文章篇名(放在引号中),刊物名称(以斜体字或画底线处理),卷数,(发行期数),页数。

范例：

Book (first note) 书籍(第一次注释)
1. Hayden Herrera, *Frida*: *A Biography of Frida Kahlo* (New York: Harper and Row, 1983), 356.
Book (subsequent note) 书籍(再次引注)
2. Herrera, Frida, 32.
Periodical article (first note) 期刊(第一次注释)
3. Zbigniew Brzezinski, "Post-Communist Nationalism," *Foreign Affairs*, 68, no.4 (1989), 20.
Periodical article (subsequent note) 期刊(再次引注)
4. Brzezinski, "Post-Communist Nationalism," 22.

注意事项：

如何在论文中加批注	在论文中引述句子、词汇或总结的句子后加上上标。 • 例如:This is how one acknowledges a source in Chicago/Turabian documentation.[1]
批注的位置	将批注放在： • 每一页的最下方； • 和论文本文以一条1.5英寸的线相隔。 某些指导老师要求将页尾注改为结尾注,以批注(Notes)为标题,置于所有附录后,放在论文最末。

	(续表)
批注的格式	• 与论文中的数字相同; • 在注释编号后加句点,并空一格。 • 单行间距(如果论文文本双行间距则采双行间距); • 首行与左缘间距五格(或与论文文本段落起始空格同)。
在一段中对某一位作者参考数次	如果在一段文字之中参考某一作者数件作品,可以在最后一段引文、词汇或总结后用一个批注数字,以指明该段中所有引用数据的来源。
缩写	通常没有必要在页数之前加上 p. 或 pp. 这种缩写,只要列出适当的数字即可。

2) 作者—年份引注和参照表

这种形式近年使用的人数日渐增加。作者—年份引注(例如,(Smith 1996))置于论文之中或在一段引文之后,并在论文的最末列出完整的引注信息。如果作品有两位或三位作者,必须注明所有作者的名字(例如,(Jackson and Jones 1998))。如果作者超过三人以上,使用第一作者的姓,并加上缩写 et al. (例如,(Brown et al. 1982))。如果引注某一特定页数、图形、章节或其他元素,则应在日期之后加上逗点,再加上页码等(例如,(Smith 1996, 42))。

与注释和参考书目(人文类形式)相比,作者—年份引注和参照表形式的特点如下:

- 只写出作者的名字(不必写全名)。
- 年份紧接在作者名字之后。
- 只有标题和次标题的第一个字母大写。
- 引注资料不包括期刊文章、章节、短篇文献的标题。

范例: Stoller P. and C. Olkes. 1987. *Sorcery's Shadow*. Chicago: University of Chicago Press.

芝加哥论文格式建议对特定引述如书籍和期刊的标题以印刷体斜体字(Italics)处理,除非指导教授要求,或者打字机或文字排版软件没有斜体字,才使用画底线(Underlining)。

3) 电子引注

The Chicago Manual of Style 第 14 版提供了电子引注格式。脚注和尾注为(作者+文章题目+网络发布时间)。

范例：

（1）书籍：

Peter J. Bryant. "The Age of Mammals," in Biodiversity Conservation April 1999, < http：//darwin. bio. uci. edu/ ~ sustain/bio65/index. html > （11 May 1999）.

（2）报刊文章：

Christopher Wren. "A Body on Mt. Everest, a Mystery Half-Solved," The New York Times on the Web, 5 May 1999, < http：//search. nytimes. com/search/daily/bin/fastweb？ getdoc + site + site + 87604 + 0 + wAAA + % 22a% 7Ebody% 7Eon% 7Emt. % 7Everest% 22 > （13 May 1999）.

（3）出版文件：

George Bush. "Principles of Ethical Conduct for Government Officers and Employees," Executive Order 12674, 12 April 1989, pt. 1, < http：//www. usoge. gov/exorders/eo12674. html > （30 October 1997）.

（4）专业和个人网站：

Joseph Pellegrino. "Homepage," 12 May 1999, < http：//www. english. eku. edu/pellegrino/default. htm > （12 June 1999）.

Gail Mortimer. "The William Faulkner Society Home Page," 16 September 1999, < http：//www. utep. edu/mortimer/faulkner/mainfaulkner. htm > （19 November 1997）.

（5）电子期刊文章：

Teague, Jason Crawford. "Frames in Action," Kairos：A Journal for Teachers of Writing in Webbed Environments, 2, no. 1, 20 August 1998, < http：//english. ttu. edu/kairos/2.1 > （7 October 1999）.

（详见 *The Chicago Manual of Style* 或网络介绍文章 *A Reference Guide to Using Internet Resources*。）

8.2　现代语言学会论文格式

现代语言学会论文格式（Moden Language Association Style, MLA）多使用于社会科学和自然科学类学术论文中，现在也广泛使用于人文学科。该格式的基本体系为"文中夹注 + 文献目录"（parenthed note + works cited）。具体细节参见 *MLA Handbook for Writers of Research Papers*。

8.3 美国心理学会论文格式

美国心理学会论文格式(American Psychological Association Style, APA)的使用范围与现代语言学会论文格式基本相同,但自然科学类论文更倾向于使用美国心理学会论文格式。该格式的基本体系是"文中夹注+文献目录"(parenthetical note + references)。具体细节参见 Publication Manual of the American Psychological Association。

第九章　论文格式及后期工作

虽然语言和内容是评判一篇英语论文质量高低的重要依据,但是写作格式规范与否亦是一个不可忽略的衡量标准。因此,规范英语论文的格式,使之与国际学术惯例接轨,对我们开展英语学术论文写作,促进国际学术交流都具有重要意义。

由于英语论文写作规范随学科不同而各有所异,本书拟就人文类学科英语论文的主要组成部分,概述美国教育界、学术界通行的人文类英语论文写作规范,以供读者参考。

9.1　论文各部分的要求

1) 标题

标题应简短、明确、有概括性。标题字数要适当,不宜超过 20 个字。标题过长的,可以分成主标题和副标题。

2) 摘要

论文摘要包括中文摘要和英文摘要。论文摘要概括研究课题的主要内容,中文摘要 300 字左右,英文摘要 250 个实词左右。

3) 关键词

关键词是对表述论文的中心内容有实质意义的词汇。关键词一般以 3—5 个为宜。

4) 目录

目录按三级标题编写,第一层级为"一",第二层级为"(一)",第三层级为"1",要求层次清晰。目录标题应与正文标题一致。

5) 正文

正文包括文献综述、正文主体和结论。

文献综述是对论文所论述专题的相关情报资料经综合分析后形成的概要叙述。文献综述的字数一般在 800 字左右。

正文主体是对研究工作的详细表述。其内容包括问题的提出、研究工作的基本前提、假设和条件；基本概念和理论基础；理论论证，理论在课题中的应用，课题得出的结果以及对结果的讨论等。

6）参考文献与附录

参考文献是毕业论文不可缺少的组成部分，反映毕业论文的取材来源、材料的广博程度和可靠程度，也是作者对他人知识成果的承认和尊重。参考文献不宜过多，但应列出主要文献 10 篇(部)以上。

附录是不宜放在正文中但有参考价值的内容。如文章中引用的符号较多时，为便于读者查阅，可以编写一个符号说明，注明符号代表的意义。附录的篇幅不宜过大。

7）谢辞

即以简短的文字对在课题研究和论文撰写过程中曾直接给予自己帮助的人员(例如指导教师、答疑教师及其他人员)表示谢意。这不仅是一种礼貌，也是对他人劳动的尊重，是治学者应有的品格和修养。

9.2 论文标题

一篇较长的英语论文(如英语毕业论文)一般都需要标题页，其书写格式如下：第一行标题与打印纸顶端的距离约为打印纸全长的 1/3，与下行(通常为"by"一词，居中)的距离则为 5 cm，第三、第四行分别为作者姓名及日期(均居中)。如果该篇英语论文是学生针对某门课程而写，则在作者姓名与日期之间还需分别打上教师学衔及姓名(如：Dr./Prof. C. Prager)和本门课程的编号或名称(如：English 734 或 British Novel)。打印时，如无特殊要求，每一行均需 double space，即隔行打印，行距约为 0.6 cm(论文其他部分行距同此)。学位论文标题页可参照如下格式：

> **On the Differences of Family Education Between China and America**
>
> Presented in Partial Fulfillment of the Requirements for
> the Degree of Bachelor
>
> in the Foreign Languages School
> In ** University
> by
>
> **Li Lin**
>
> Under the Supervision of
>
> **Professor Wang Hua**
>
> ** University
> **Shanghai**
>
> April. 2011

就学生而言,如果英语论文篇幅较短,亦可不做标题页(及提纲页),而将标题页的内容打在正文第一页的左上方。第一行为作者姓名,与打印纸顶端距离约为 2.5 cm,以下各行依次为教师学衔和姓、课程编号(或名称)及日期;各行左边上下对齐,并留出 2.5 cm 左右的页边空白(下同)。接下来便是论文标题及正文(日期与标题之间及标题与正文第一行之间只需隔行打印,不必留出更多空白)。

9.3 论 文 提 纲

英语论文提纲页包括论题句及提纲本身,其规范格式如下:先在第一行(与打印纸顶端的距离仍为 2.5 cm 左右)的始端打上 Thesis 一词及冒号,空一格后再打论题句,回行时左边须与论题句的第一个字母上下对齐。主要纲目以大写罗马数字标出,次要纲目则依次用大写英文字母、阿拉伯数字和小写英文字母标出。各数字或字母后均为一句点,空出一格后再打该项内容的第一个字母;处于同一等级的纲目,其上下行左边必须对齐。需要注意的是,同等级的纲目必须是两个以上,即:有 Ⅰ 应有 Ⅱ,有 A 应有 B,以此类推。如果英文论文提纲较长,需两页纸,则第二页须在右上角用小写罗马数字标出页码,即 ii(第一页无需标页码)。

9.4 正　　文

　　有标题页和提纲页的英语论文,其正文第一页的规范格式为:论文标题居中,其位置距打印纸顶端约 5 cm,距正文第一行约 1.5 cm。段首字母须缩进五格,即从第六格打起。正文第一页不必标页码(但应计算其页数),自第二页起,必须在每页的右上角(即空出第一行,在其后部)打上论文作者的姓,空一格后再用阿拉伯数字标出页码;阿拉伯数字(或其最后一位)应为该行的最后一个空格。在打印正文时尚需注意标点符号的打印格式,即:句末号(句号、问号及感叹号)后应空两格,其他标点符号后则空一格。

9.5 文中引述

　　正确引用作品原文或专家、学者的论述是写好英语论文的重要环节;既要注意引述与论文的有机统一,即其逻辑性,又要注意引述格式(即英语论文参考文献)的规范性。引述别人的观点,可以直接引用,也可以间接引用。无论采用何种方式,论文作者必须注明所引文字的作者和出处。目前美国学术界通行的做法是在引文后以圆括弧形式注明引文作者及出处。现针对文中引述的不同情况,将部分规范格式分述如下:

　　1) 若引文不足三行,则可将引文有机地融合在论文中。如:

　　The divorce of Arnold's personal desire from his inheritance results in "the familiar picture of Victorian man alone in an alien universe" (Roper 9).

　　这里,圆括弧中的 Roper 为引文作者的姓(不必注出全名);阿拉伯数字为引文出处的页码(不要写成 p.9);作者姓与页码之间需空一格,但不需任何标点符号;句号应置于第二个圆括弧后。

　　2) 被引述的文字如果超过三行,则应将引文与论文文字分开。如下例所示:

　　Whitman has proved himself an eminent democratic representative and precursor, and his "Democratic Vistas" is an admirable and characteristic diatribe. And if one is sorry that in it Whitman is unable to conceive the extreme crises of society, one is certain that no society would be tolerable whose citizens could not find refreshment in its buoyant democratic idealism. (Chase 165)

　　这里的格式有两点要加以注意:一是引文各行距英语论文正文的左边第一个字母十个空格,即应从第十一格排起;二是引文不需加引号,末尾的句号应标在最后一个词后。

3) 如需在引文中插注,对某些词语加以解释,则要使用方括号(不可用圆括弧)。如:

Dr. Beaman points out that "he [Charles Darwin] has been an important factor in the debate between evolutionary theory and biblical creationism" (9).

值得注意的是,本例中引文作者的姓已出现在引导句中,故圆括弧中只需注明引文出处的页码即可。

4) 如果拟引用的文字中有与论文无关的词语需要删除,则需用省略号。如果省略号出现在引文中则用三个点,如出现在引文末,则用四个点,最后一点表示句号,置于第二个圆括弧后(一般说来,应避免在引文开头使用省略号);点与字母之间,或点与点之间都需空一格。如:

Mary Shelley hated tyranny and "looked upon the poor as pathetic victims of the social system and upon the rich and highborn. . . with undisguised scorn and contempt. . . " (Nitchie 43).

5) 若引文出自一部多卷书,除注明作者姓和页码外,还需注明卷号。如:

Professor Chen Jia's A History of English Literature aimed to give Chinese readers "a historical survey of English literature from its earliest beginnings down to the 20th century" (Chen, 1: i).

圆括弧里的 1 为卷号,小写罗马数字 i 为页码,说明引文出自第 1 卷序言(引言、序言、导言等多使用小写的罗马数字标明页码)。此外,书名 "A History of English Literature" 下画了线。规范的格式是:书名,包括以成书形式出版的作品名(如《失乐园》)均需划线,或用斜体字;其他作品,如诗歌、散文、短篇小说等的标题则以双引号标出,如 "To Autumn" 及前面出现的 "Democratic Vistas" 等。

6) 如果英语论文中引用了同一作者的两篇或两篇以上的作品,除注明引文作者及页码外,还要注明作品名。如:

Bacon condemned Platoas "an obstacle to science" (Farrington, Philosophy 35).

Farrington points out that Aristotle's father Nicomachus, a physician, probably trained his son in medicine (Aristotle 15).

这两个例子分别引用了 Farrington 的两部著作,故在各自的圆括弧中分别注出所引用的书名,以免混淆。此处两部作品名均为缩写形式(如书名太长,在圆括弧中加以注明时均需使用缩写形式),其全名分别为 Founder of Scientific Philosophy 及 The Philosophy of Francis Baconand Aristotle。

7) 评析诗歌常需引用原诗句,其引用格式如下例所示:

When Beowulf dives upwards through the water and reaches the surface, "The surging waves, great tracts of water,/were all cleansed..."(l. 1620-21).

这里,被引用的诗句以斜线号隔开,斜线号与前后字母及标点符号间均需空一格;圆括弧中小写的 l 是 line 的缩写;21 不必写成 1621。如果引用的诗句超过三行,仍需将引用的诗句与论文文字分开(参见第二项内容)。

9.6 摘　　要

1) 摘要的概念和作用

摘要又称"概要"、"内容提要",是以提供文献内容梗概为目的,不加评论和补充解释,简明、确切地记述文献主要内容的短文。其基本要素包括研究目的、方法、结果和结论。具体地讲就是研究工作的主要对象和范围,采用的手段和方法,得出的结果和重要的结论,有时也包括具有情报价值的其他重要的信息。摘要应具有独立性和自明性,并且拥有与文献同等量的主要信息,即不阅读全文,就能获得必要的信息。对于一篇完整的科技论文,都要求写随文摘要。摘要的主要功能有：

(1) 让读者尽快了解论文的主要内容,以补充题名的不足。现代科技文献信息浩如烟海,读者检索到论文题名后是否阅读全文,主要就是通过阅读摘要来判断；所以,摘要担负着吸引读者和将文章的主要内容介绍给读者的任务。

(2) 为科技情报文献检索数据库的建设和维护提供方便。论文发表后,文摘杂志或各种数据库对摘要可以不作修改或稍作修改而直接利用,从而避免他人编写摘要可能产生的误解、欠缺甚至错误。随着电子计算机技术和 Internet 的迅猛发展,网上查询、检索和下载专业数据已成为当前科技信息情报检索的重要手段,网上各类全文数据库、文摘数据库,越来越显示出现代社会信息交流的水平和发展趋势。同时,论文摘要的索引是读者检索文献的重要工具。所以,论文摘要的质量高低,直接影响着论文的被检索率和被引频次。

2) 摘要的分类

按摘要的不同功能划分,大致有如下三种类型：

(1) 报道性摘要 (informative abstract)

报道性摘要是指明文献的主题范围及内容梗概的简明摘要,相当于简介。报道性摘要一般用来反映科技论文的目的、方法及主要结果与结论,在有限的字数内向读者提供尽可能多的定性或定量的信息,充分反映该研究的创新之处。学术论文如果没有创新内容,如果没有经得起检验的与众不同的方法或结论,是不会引起读者的阅读兴趣的。报道性摘要的篇幅以 150—300 字左右为宜。

◆ 范例 1

Title: Shoppers in Cyberspace: Are They From Venus or Mars and Does It Matter?

Internet shopping (or e-shopping) is emerging as a shopping mode and with its requirement of computer access and use, it is interesting to find out whether consumers associate e-shoppers with any gender-specific stereotypes. Such stereotypes may be expected because shopping is considered a "female typed" activity whereas technology is considered to be in the male domain. In this article, we address this central question in an empirical study that varies the shopping context in terms of outlet type, product type, and purchase purpose. The respondents are college students with Internet access and familiarity with online shopping. The experimental results suggest that the global stereotype, held by both male and female respondents, is that of a shopper as a woman. This stereotype reverses when the product purchased is technical and expensive (DVD player). In terms of personality attributions, the female shopper is seen to be less technical, less spontaneous, and more reliable and attributions regarding personal characteristics are not influenced significantly by product type, outlet type, or purchase purpose. (*Journal of Consumer Psychology* 13, no. 1/2 (2003): 171—176)

◆ 范例 2

Title: Freedom Is a Constant Struggle—The Dynamics and Consequences of the Mississippi Civil Rights Movement

(What the dissertation does) This dissertation examines the impacts of social movements through a multi-layered study of the Mississippi Civil Rights Movement from its peak in the early 1960s through the early 1980s. By examining this historically important case, the paper clarifies the process by which movements transform social structures and the constraints' movements face when they try to do so. The time period studied in this dissertation includes the expansion of voting rights and gains in black political power, the desegregation of public schools and the emergence of white-flight academies, and the rise and fall of federal anti-poverty programs.

(methodologies) Two major research strategies are used: (1) a quantitative analysis of county-level data and (2) three case studies.

(What materials are used) Data have been collected from archives, interviews, newspapers, and published reports.

(Conclusion) This dissertation challenges the argument that movements are inconsequential. Indeed, some view federal agencies, courts, political parties, or economic elites as the agents driving institutional change. Typically these groups acted in response to movement demands and the leverage brought to bear by the civil rights movement. The Mississippi movement attempted to forge independent structures for sustaining challenges to local inequities and injustices. By propelling change in an array of local institutions, movement infrastructures had an enduring legacy in Mississippi.

(2) 指示性摘要(indicative abstract)

指示性摘要是指明学术论文的论题及取得的成果的性质和水平的摘要,其目的是使读者对该研究的主要内容(即作者做了什么工作)有一个轮廓性的了解。创新内容较少的论文,其摘要可写成指示性摘要。所以,指示性摘要一般适用于学术性期刊的简报、问题讨论等栏目以及技术性期刊等。篇幅以 100 字左右为宜。

◆ 范例

Title: Grammar Teaching and the Real World

It is not surprising that grammar teaching still dominates English teaching in China. When Chinese students finally obtain opportunities to study in English speaking countries, does the English they have acquired through grammar teaching facilitate their life and academic study in the target countries? An investigation was conducted among the Chinese oversea students in the UK to find out the answers. The results reveal that the answer to the question contains both positive and negative aspects.

(3) 报道—指示性摘要(informative/indicative abstract)

报道—指示性摘要是以报道性摘要的形式表述论文中价值最高的那部分内容,其余部分则以指示性摘要形式表达。篇幅以 100—200 字为宜。

◆ 范例

Title: On the Differences of Family Education Between China and America

Family education is closely related to a person's whole life. With the introduction of Western education thoughts into China, more and more problems about family education have been emerging. Because of the different historical backgrounds, economic patterns, social conditions and traditional cultures between China and America, the concepts of educating children by families are very different from each other, which further leads to the continuous comparative study in this area.

This thesis analyzes the differences of family education between China and America. Chapter I is a general introduction of definition and importance of family education. Chapter II deeply discusses the differences between Chinese and American family education in the aspects of education objects, contents, methods and its results. Chapter III explores the main reasons that lead to the differences of family education. And finally Chapter IV forms the conclusion, pointing out China and America should learn form each other's family education mode and putting forward several pieces of advice to improve the family education in China at present.

Key words: family education; differences; China; America

以上介绍了三种可供作者选用的摘要形式。一般地说,向学术性期刊投稿,应选用报道性摘要形式;只有创新内容较少的论文,其摘要可写成报道—指示性或指示性摘要。论文发表的最终目的是要被人利用。在当今信息激增的时代,如果摘要写得不好,论文进入文摘杂志、检索数据库后,被人阅读、引用的机会就会少得多,甚至丧失。一篇论文价值很高,创新内容很多,若写成指示性摘要,可能就会失去较多的潜在读者。

3) 撰写摘要的基本规范和原则

(1) 论文摘要分为中文摘要和外文(一般为英文)摘要。关于摘要在篇幅方面的限定,不同的学校和机构有不同的要求,通常中文摘要不超过300字,英文摘要不超过250个实词,中英文摘要应一致。毕业论文摘要可适当增加篇幅。

(2) 撰写摘要应多向指导教师请教,并根据其提供的意见及时修改,以期达到更高水平。

(3) 摘要是完整的短文,具有独立性,可以单独使用,所以应叙述完整,突出逻辑性,结构要合理。即使不看论文全文的内容,仍然可以理解论文的主要内容,作者的新观点和想法,课题所要实现的目的、采取的方法、研究的结果与结论。

(4) 要求文字简明扼要,不容赘言,提取重要内容,不含前言、背景等细节部分,去掉旧结论、原始数据,不加评论和注释。采用直接表述的方法,删除不必要的文学修饰。摘要中不应包括作者将来的计划以及与此课题无关的内容,做到用最少的文字提供最大的信息量。

(5) 摘要中不使用特殊字符,也不使用图表和化学结构式,以及由特殊字符组成的数学表达式,不列举例证。

4) 摘要的四要素

目的、方法、结果和结论称为摘要的四要素。

(1) 目的:指出研究的范围、目的、重要性、任务和前提条件,不是对主题的简单重复。

(2) 方法:简述课题的工作流程,研究了哪些主要内容,在这个过程中都做了哪些工作,包括对象、原理、条件、程序、手段等。

(3) 结果:陈述研究之后重要的新发现、新成果及价值,包括通过调研、实验、观察取得的数据和结果,并剖析其不理想的局限部分。

(4) 结论：通过对这个课题的研究所得出的重要结论，包括对从中取得证实的正确观点进行分析研究，预测其在实际生活中运用的意义，理论与实际相结合的价值。

下例为一篇英语专业毕业论文的中英文摘要，题目为《浅析中美关系营销中的文化差异性》：

关系营销理论产生于西方，对中国而言，它是舶来品。但是，中国是一个重视人际关系的国家，基于本国儒教思想的文化基础，中国关系营销理论本土化的特征日益明显，中美两国的文化差异性则是造成这一结果的根本原因。"关系"一词在西方主流媒体中被广泛提及。然而，在中国学术界却很少看到关于关系营销中文化差异性的研究文章，针对中美关系营销文化差异的学术论文更是没有先例。因此，对该问题进行深入研究是很有意义的。

本文以美国作为西方关系营销理论的代表，以比较研究法为主，解释关系营销理论的发展和儒家文化下的中国人际关系文化，剖析中美文化的差异及在这种差异性下的当代关系营销演变。通过实际商业环境下的比较，本文总结出儒家文化确实对中国的关系营销理论发展有着重要影响，正是出于儒家传统文化中的"仁者爱人"、"义利合一"等思想的渗透，才会产生所谓的中国式关系营销。当然，由于美国与中国对"关系"一词的定义和理解是不同的，很难从同一出发点比较双方的关系营销方式，但确实存在一个现象，即目前中国企业所实行的关系营销已偏离了美国企业所认为的关系营销，正发展成为一种独具特色的自有模式营销策略。然而，运用好这一独具特色的关系营销理论，让关系营销在未来的中国市场中站稳脚跟，有待于市场、企业和政府多方面的相互配合。

[关键词] 关系　关系营销　文化差异

On Sino-US Cultural Differences in Relationship Marketing

Abstract

For Chinese people, the theory of relationship marketing that originated from Western world is exotic. Since China is an interpersonal—relationship-valued country, the trend of "relationship marketing in Chinese context" gradually became localized under the influence of Confucianism. Sino-US cultural difference is the fundamental reason for that result. "Relationship" as found in the Western mainstream media has been widely mentioned, but in the Chinese academic circle, the research articles on cultural differences in relationship marketing are rarely seen, let alone an academic paper on Sino-US cultural differences in relationship marketing. Therefore, in-depth study of the issue is of great significance.

In this paper, the United States, as the representative of the Western relationship marketing theory, is compared with China to explain the development of the theory of relationship marketing and the interpersonal relationships in Chinese Confucian culture, and to analyze Sino-US cultural differences and differences in the contemporary relationship marketing evolution. Through the comparison of the actual business environment, the conclusion comes that Confucian culture has a great impact on the development of relationship marketing theory in China and so-called relationship marketing in Chinese context, because the philosophic Confucianism of "benevolent love", "peace is precious" and "people-oriented" concept. Of course, since "relationship" is defined and understood differently in these two countries, it is hard to compare the two sides of the relationship marketing approach, but there is a phenomenon that relationship marketing practiced by Chinese companies has strayed from U. S. pattern and has been developed as a unique model of Chinese own marketing strategies. However, coordination is needed in regard to market, business and government so as to make the best use of the unique characteristics of relationship marketing theory in China in order to ensure its firm foothold in future Chinese market.

Key words: guanxi; relationship marketing; cultural difference

5) 摘要的撰写步骤

摘要作为一种特殊的陈述性短文,其书写的步骤也与普通类型的文章有所不同。摘要的写作时间通常在论文完成之后,但也可以采用提早写的方式,然后再边写论文边修改摘要。首先,从摘要的四要素出发,通读论文全文,仔细将文中的重要内容一一列出,特别是每段的主题句和论文结尾的归纳总结,保留梗概与精华部分,提取用于编写摘要的关键信息。然后,看这些信息能否完整、准确地回答摘要的四要素所涉及的问题。若不足以回答这些问题,则重新阅读论文,摘录相应的内容进行补充。最后,将这些零散信息组成符合语法规则和逻辑规则的完整句子,再进一步组成通畅的短文,通读此短文,反复修改,达到摘要的要求。

6) 英文摘要

(1) 英文摘要的写作方法要依据公认的写作规范。

(2) 尽量使用简单句,避免句型单调,表达要求准确、完整。

(3) 正确使用冠词。

(4) 使用标准英语书写,避免使用口语,应使用易于理解的常用词,不用生僻词汇。

(5) 表述作者所做工作用过去时,结论用现在时。

(6) 多使用主动语态。

7）关键词

关键词是为了文献标引工作从报告、论文中选出来用以表示全文主题内容信息的单词术语。每篇报告、论文选取 3—8 个词作为关键词，以显著的字符另起一行，排在摘要的左下方。如有可能，尽量用《汉语主题词表》等词表提供的规范词。为了国际交流，应标注与中文对应的英文关键词。主题词是一种新型检索词汇，多用于计算机网络检索。关键词是主题词中的一类。

关键词分为中文关键词和与之对应的英文关键词，分别置于中文摘要和英文摘要之下。为便于他人检索，不能使用过于宽泛的词语。选择关键词既可以从论文的各级标题入手，也可以从论文本身的内容选取，将选出的关键词按照所涉及领域的范围从大到小的顺序列出。

8）常见句型

目前，摘要编写中的主要问题有：无独立性与自明性；要素不全，或缺目的，或缺方法；繁简失当，多数过于简单化；重复题名已有的信息；把引言中出现的内容写入摘要；习惯使用"本文介绍了……"作为摘要开头。

常见的摘要句型有：

(1) This paper deals with...

(2) This article focuses on the topics of (that, having, etc.)...

(3) This essay presents knowledge that...

(4) This thesis discusses...

(5) This thesis analyzes...

(6) This paper provides an overview of...

(7) This paper elaborates on...

(8) This article gives an overview of...

(9) This article compares...and summarizes key findings.

(10) This paper includes discussions concerning...

(11) This paper presents up-to-date information on...

(12) This article covers the role of chemicals in...

(13) This paper addresses important topics including...

(14) This paper touches upon...

(15) This paper strongly emphasizes...

(16) This essay represents the proceedings of...

(17) This article not only describes...but also suggests...

(18) This paper considers...

(19) This paper provides a method of...

(20) This paper introduces an applicable procedure to analyze...

(21) This paper offers the latest information regarding...

(22) This paper is devoted to examining the role of...

(23) This article explores...

(24) This paper expresses views on...

(25) This paper reflects the state of the art in...

(26) This paper explains the procedures for...

(27) This paper develops the theory of...

(28) This article reviews the techniques used in...

(29) This paper investigates the techniques and procedures to...

(30) This article is about...

(31) This essay is related to...

(32) This paper concerns...

(33) This paper gives an account of...

(34) This article tells of...

(35) This paper tries to describe...

(36) This paper provides an analysis of...

(37) This paper reports the latest information on...

(38) The author of this article reviews...

(39) The writer of this paper discusses...

(40) The writer of this essay tries to explore...

(41) The aim of this paper is to determine...

(42) The purpose of this article is to review...

(43) The objective of this paper is to explore...

破题用语，一般有：

(1) The author of this article reviews (or: discusses, describes, summarizes, examines) something...

(2) This article reviews (or: reports, tells of, is about, concerns) something...

(3) This article has been prepared (or: designed, written)...

(4) The purpose of this article is to determine something...

(5) The problem of something is discussed...

结论和建议，一般有以下几种写法：

(1) The author suggests (recommends, concludes) that...

(2) This article shows that...

(3) It is suggested that...

(4) The author's suggestion (or: conclusion) is that...
(5) The author finds it necessary to...

9.7 致 谢

1)致谢的概念及范例

致谢(Acknowledgements)是指作者在论文完成后对曾经给予支持或帮助的单位或个人表示感谢。致谢辞要写得诚恳、真切,可以用第一人称(如范例1、范例3),也可以用第三人称(如范例2)。

◆ 范例1

I would like to express my gratitude to all those who helped me during the writing of this thesis. A special acknowledgement should be shown to Professor X, from whose lectures I benefited greatly. I am particularly indebted to Mr. X, who gave me kind encouragement and useful instructions all through my writing. Finally I wish to extend my thanks to the library assistants who supplied me with reference materials of great value.

◆ 范例2

The author is indebted to Mr. X for his constructive suggestions, to Mr. Y who helped work out an outline of this paper, and kindly eliminated many of the errors in it. The author is also indebted to Miss X for permission to quote material from the past examination papers in the course of Advanced English.

◆ 范例3

First and foremost, I would like to show my deepest gratitude to my supervisor, Dr. Liu Hong, a respectable, responsible and resourceful scholar, who has provided me with valuable guidance in every stage of the writing of this thesis. Without his enlightening instruction, impressive kindness and patience, I could not have completed my thesis. His keen and vigorous academic observation enlightens me not only in this thesis but also in my future study.

I shall extend my thanks to Mrs. Liu for all her kindness and help. I would also like to thank all my teachers who have helped me to develop the fundamental and essential academic competence. My sincere appreciation also goes to the teachers and students from No. 16 Senior Middle School and Guangdong University of Foreign Studies, who participated this study with great cooperation.

Last but not least, I'd like to thank all my friends, especially my three lovely roommates, for their encouragement and support.

2）致谢中的一些惯用表达方式

（1） I would like to acknowledge my indebtedness to. . .

（2） I should like to acknowledge with deep gratitude the assistance and guidance given to me by. . .

（3） I gratefully acknowledge the help of. . .

（4） I want to acknowledge the invaluable help of Mr. X, who has been my constant consultant in my writing this essay. If there are any errors, they are not his, but all mine.

（5） I would like to thank Mr. X for his suggestions on my writing the first earlier draft.

（6） I would extend my sincere thanks to my tutor. . .

（7） I would like to take this opportunity to thank. . .

（8） I especially appreciate the guidance of. . .

（9） I wish to express my special appreciation of Mr. X's help. . .

（10） I am also indebted to the following for permission to reproduce copy-right material:. . .

（11） I have a real debt of gratitude to. . .

（12） Likewise I am grateful to. . .

（13） Most particularly, I must thank. . .

（14） I am in debt to. .

（15） My gratitude also goes to. . .

（16） My heartfelt thanks are also due to. . .

（17） My work also owes much to. . . for his encouragement and great help.

（18） A real debt is owed to Mrs. X for her valuable help in my writing.

（19） My grateful thanks to all of you, most of all to. . .

（20） The author is deeply indebted to. . .

（21） The author's special thanks should be given to. . .

（22） This thesis would not have been. . . without. . .

（23） I have eternal gratitude to. . . , my tutor, for his inestimable help and valuable instruction, and to Professor. . . , for his insightful lectures, which inspire me to compose this dissertation.

（24） I am greatly indebted to Professor. . . for his allowing me to have access to his books pertinent to this dissertation.

（25） I also thank those who help me in course of the writing and whose names I can't list here one by one.

(26) I want to take this golden opportunity to express my sincere gratitude to my mentor for her generous professional instruction and my friends for their support and help. Without her patience and profound knowledge, I could not expect this paper finish in time and with good quality.

9.8 练　　习

根据下列导言和提纲,撰写一篇三百个单词左右的报道性文摘,并于适当的位置在括弧内注明其 "*Problem*(*background*),*Methodology*,*Results and Conclusion Implications*" 等要素。

The concepts of educating children by families are very different from China and the West. This further leads to the differences between Chinese and American family education.

This thesis concluded that China and America should learn form each other's family education mode, and suggests the family education in China turn "talent" education into "human" education and "close" education into "open" education.

Contents

Chapter 1　A Brief Introduction to Family Education	1
1.1　The Definition of Family Education	2
1.2　The Importance of Family Education	3
Chapter 2　The Differences Between Chinese and American Family Education	4
2.1　The Comparison of Family Education Objects	4
2.2　The Comparison of Family Education Contents	5
2.3　The Comparison of Family Education Methods	6
2.4　The Comparison of Family Education Results	8
Chapter 3　The Reasons of the Differences Between Chinese and American Family Education	10
3.1　Different Historical Backgrounds	10
3.2　Different Economic Patterns	10
3.3　Different Social Conditions	11
3.4　Different Traditional Cultures	11
Chapter 4　Conclusion	13
4.1　Suggestions About Chinese Family Education	13
4.2　Conclusion	14

第十章 论文答辩

10.1 毕业论文答辩概述

毕业论文答辩是指答辩委员会成员(以下简称"答辩老师")和撰写毕业论文的学员面对面,由答辩老师就论文提出有关问题,让学生当面回答。它有"问"有"答",还可以有"辩"。

答辩是辩论的一种形式。辩论按进行形式不同,分为竞赛式辩论、对话式辩论和问答式辩论。答辩就是问答式辩论的简称。与竞赛式辩论相比,论文答辩有以下几个特点:

1) 答辩具有明显的不平等性

首先,人数不对等。毕业论文答辩组成双方的人数是不对等的,参加答辩会的一方是撰写论文的作者,只有一个人,另一方是由教师或有关专家组成的答辩小组或答辩委员会,一般有三人或三人以上。其次,地位不对等。一般地说,答辩小组或答辩委员会始终是处在主动的、审查的地位上,而论文作者则始终处在被动的、被审查的地位上,并且双方的知识、阅历、资历、经验方面都相差悬殊。

2) 答辩委员会具有双重身份

竞赛式辩论除了参加辩论的双方外,还设有专门的裁判,即有个"第三方"对辩论双方的高下是非作出评判。而论文答辩虽然也要作出评判,但它不是由特设的裁判员来评判,而是由参加答辩会的一方——答辩小组或答辩委员会对另一方即论文作者的论文和答辩情况作出评价。可见,在毕业论文答辩会上,答辩老师是具有双重身份的:既是辩论员,又是裁判员。

3) 毕业论文作者的答辩准备范围广泛

为了顺利通过答辩,毕业论文作者在答辩前先需要作好充分准备。毕业论文答辩会上的题目是由参加答辩会的一方——答辩老师根据另一方提供的论文拟就的,所要答辩的题目不是一个,而是多个,一般是三个或三个以上,并且答辩小组拟就的题目对论文的作者事先是保密的,到答辩会上才亮出来。答辩老师提出问题后,一般有两种情况:一种情况是让学员即论文作者独立准备一段时间(一般是半小时以内)后再当场回答;另一种情况是不给学员准备时间,答辩老师提出问题后,学员就要当即作出回答。因此,虽然在举行论文答辩会以前,学员也要为参加答辩会作准备,但难以针对答辩会上提出的问题(因为事先不知道)作准备,只能就自己所写的论文及有关的问题作广泛的思考和准备。

4)表达方式以问答为主,辩论为辅

论文答辩一般是以问答的形式进行,由答辩老师提出问题,论文作者作出回答。在一问一答的过程中,有时也会出现作者与答辩老师的观点相左的情况,这时也会而且也应该辩论。但从总体上说,论文答辩是以问答的形式为主,以不同观点的辩论为辅。

10.2 答辩的目的和意义

毕业论文答辩的目的,对于组织者——校方,和答辩者——毕业论文作者而言是不同的。

校方组织毕业论文答辩的目的简单说有以下三点:

第一,进一步考查和验证毕业论文作者对所著论文的认识程度和当场论证论题的能力。一般说来,从学员所提交的论文中,已能大致反映出各个学员对自己所写论文的认识程度和论证论题的能力。但由于种种原因,有些问题没有充分展开细说,有的可能是限于全局结构不便展开,有的可能是受篇幅所限不能展开,有的可能是作者认为这个问题不重要或者以为没有必要展开详细说明;有的很可能是作者深入不下去或者说不清楚而故意回避了的薄弱环节,有的还可能是作者自己根本就没有认识到的不足之处等等。通过对这些问题的提问和答辩,就可以进一步弄清作者是由于哪种情况而没有展开深入分析,从而了解学员对自己所写论文的认识程度、理解深度和当场论证论题的能力。

第二,进一步考查毕业论文作者对专业知识掌握的深度和广度。虽然通过论文也可以看出学员已掌握知识的深度和广度,但是撰写毕业论文的主要目的不是考查学员掌握知识的深广度,而是考查学员综合运用所学知识独立地分析问题和解决问题的能力,培养和锻炼其进行科学研究的能力。学员在写作论文中所运用的知识有的已确实掌握,能融会贯通地运用;有的可能是一知半解,并没有转化为自己的知识;还有的可能是从别人的文章中生搬硬套过来,连其基本含义都没搞清楚。在答辩会上,答辩小组成员把论文中阐述不清楚、不详细、不完备、不确切、不完善之处提出来,让作者当场作出回答,从而就可以检查出作者对所论述的问题是否有深广的知识基础、创造性见解和充分的理由。

第三,审查毕业论文是否学员独立完成,即检验毕业论文的真实性。撰写毕业论文,要求学生在教师的指导下独立完成。但它不像考试、考查那样,在老师严格监视下完成,而是在一个较长的时期(一般为一个学期)内完成,难免会有少数不自觉的学生投机取巧,采取各种手段作弊。尤其是像电大、函大等开放性大学,学员面广、人多、组织松散、素质参差不齐,很难杜绝捉刀代笔、抄袭剽窃等不正之风。指导教师固然要严格把关,可是在一个教师要指导多个学员的不同题目、不同范围论文的情况下,对防止作假舞弊很难做到没有疏漏。而答辩小组或答辩委员会由三名以上教师组成,鉴别论文真实性的能力就更强些,并且在答辩会上还可通过提问与答辩来暴露作弊者,从而保证毕业论文的质量。

对于答辩者(毕业论文作者)来说,答辩的目的是通过答辩,按时毕业,取得毕业证书。学员要顺利通过毕业论文答辩,就必须了解上述学校组织毕业论文答辩的目的,然后有针对性地作好准备,继续对论文中的有关问题作进一步的推敲和研究,把论文中提到的基本材料搞准确,把有关的基本理论和文章的基本观点彻底弄懂弄通。

通过答辩固然是大学毕业生参加毕业论文答辩所要追求的目的,但如果大学毕业生们对答辩的认识局限在这一点上,其态度就会是消极、应付性的。只有充分认识到毕业论文答辩具有多方面的意义,答辩者才会以积极的姿态,满腔热忱地投入到毕业论文答辩的准备工作中去,满怀信心地出现在答辩会上,以最佳的心境和状态参与答辩,充分发挥自己的才能和水平。

10.3　毕业论文答辩的程序

第一步,在毕业论文答辩时,答辩老师首先要求答辩者简要叙述其毕业论文的内容。叙述中要表述清楚答辩者写这篇论文的构思(提纲)、论点、论据、论述方式(方法)。陈述时间一般约五分钟。答辩老师可通过答辩者的叙述,了解其对所写论文的思考过程,考查其分析和综合归纳能力。

第二步,进行现场答辩。答辩老师向答辩者提出2—3个问题后,答辩者作即兴答辩。其中,第一个问题一般针对论文中涉及的基本概念、基本原理提出,考查学生对引用的基本概念、基本原理的理解是否准确。第二个问题一般针对论文中所涉及的某一方面的论点,要求答辩者结合工作实际或专业实务进行讲(论)述,考查其理论联系实际的能力。

10.4　如何准备毕业论文答辩

毕业论文答辩是一种有组织、有准备、有计划、有鉴定的比较正规的审查论文的重要形式。为了作好毕业论文答辩,在举行答辩会前,校方、答辩委员会、答辩者(撰写毕业论文的作者)三方都要作好充分的准备。

答辩前的准备,最重要的是答辩者的准备。要保证论文答辩的质量和效果,关键在答辩者一方。论文作者要顺利通过答辩,在提交了论文之后,就不要有松一口气的思想,而应抓紧时间积极准备论文答辩。

第一,要写好毕业论文的简介,主要内容应包括论文的题目,指导教师姓名,选择该题目的动机,论文的主要论点、论据和写作体会以及本课题的理论意义和实践意义。

第二,要熟悉自己所写论文的全文,尤其是要熟悉主体部分和结论部分的内容,明确论文的基本观点和主论的基本依据;弄懂弄通论文中所使用的主要概念的确切含义,所运用的基本原理的主要内容;同时还要仔细审查、反复推敲文章中有无自相矛盾、谬误、片面或模糊不清的地方,有无与党的政策方针相冲突之处等等。如发现有上述问题,就要作好充分准备——补充、修正、解说等。只要"认真设防,堵死一切漏洞",在答辩过程中就可以做到心中有数、临阵不慌、沉着应战。

第三,要了解和掌握与自己所写论文相关联的知识和材料。如对于自己所研究的这个论题学术界的研究已经达到了什么程度,目前存在着哪些争议,有几种代表性观点,各有哪些代表性著作和文章,自己倾向哪种观点及理由;重要引文的出处和版本;论证材料的来源渠道等等。对于这些方面的知识和材料都要在答辩前做到有比较全面的了解和掌握。

第四,要认识到论文还有哪些应该涉及或解决,但因力所不及而未能接触的问题。

第五,对于优秀论文的作者来说,还要搞清楚哪些观点是继承或借鉴了他人的研究成果。

10.5　答辩方法与技巧

1)熟悉内容

作为将要参加论文答辩的学生,首先而且必须对自己所著的毕业论文内容有比较深刻的理解和比较全面的熟悉。这是为回答答辩老师就有关毕业论文的深度及相关知识面而可能提出的论文答辩问题所作的准备。例如题为《创建名牌产品,发展民族产业》的论文,答辩老师可能会问"民族品牌"与"名牌"有何关系。尽管毕业论文中未涉及"民族品牌",但参加论文答辩的学生必须对自己的毕业论文有"比较全面的熟悉"和"比较深刻的理解",否则就会出现尴尬局面。

2)图表穿插

许多毕业论文,无论是文科还是理科,都或多或少地涉及用图表表达论文观点的可能,故应该有此准备。图表不仅是一种直观的表达观点的方法,更是一种调节论文答辩会气氛的手段,特别是对私人论文答辩委员会成员来讲,长时间地听述，听觉难免会有排斥性，不再对你论述的内容接纳吸收，这样必然对你的毕业论文答辩成绩有所影响。所以，应该在论文答辩过程中适当穿插图表或类似图表的其他媒介，以提高你的论文答辩成绩。

3）语速适中

进行毕业论文答辩的同学一般都是首次参加答辩。无数事实证明，他们进行论文答辩时，说话速度往往越来越快，以致答辩老师听不清楚，影响了答辩成绩。故毕业论文答辩学生一定要注意在论文答辩过程中的语流速度，要有急有缓，有轻有重，不能像连珠炮似的轰向听众。

4）目光移动

毕业生在论文答辩时，一般可脱稿，也可半脱稿或完全不脱稿。但不管哪种方式，都应注意自己的目光，使目光时常地瞟向答辩老师及会场内的同学们。这是你用目光与听众进行心灵的交流，使听众对你的论题产生兴趣的一种手段。在毕业论文答辩会上，由于听的时间过长，答辩老师们难免会有分神现象，这时，你用目光的投射很礼貌地将他们的注意力"拉"回来，使答辩老师们的思路跟着你的思路走。

5）体态语辅助

虽然毕业论文答辩同其他论文答辩一样以口语为主，但适当的体态语运用会辅助论文答辩，使论文答辩效果更好。特别是手势语言的恰当运用会使答辩者显得自信、有力、不容辩驳。相反，如果你在论文答辩过程中始终直挺挺地站着，或者始终如一地低头俯视，即使你的论文结构再合理、主题再新颖、结论再正确，论文答辩效果也会大受影响。所以，在毕业论文答辩时，一定要注意使用体态语。

6）时间控制

一般在比较正规的论文答辩会上，都对辩手有答辩时间要求。因此，毕业论文答辩学生在进行论文答辩时应重视论文答辩时间的掌握。对论文答辩时间的控制要有力度，到该截止的时间立即结束，这样显得是有备而来，对内容的掌握和控制也轻车熟路，容易给答辩老师一个良好的印象。故在毕业论文答辩前应该对将要答辩的内容有时间上的估计。当然，在毕业论文答辩过程中灵活地减少或增加内容也是对论文答辩时间控制的一种表现，应该予以重视。

7）紧扣主题

对于答辩老师来说，他们不可能对每一位答辩者的毕业论文内容有全面的了解，有的甚至连论文题目也不一定熟悉。因此，整个论文答辩过程能否围绕主题进行，能否最后扣题就显得非常重要了。另外，答辩老师们一般也容易就论文题目所涉及的问题进行提问，如果能自始至终地以论文题目为中心展开论述就会使答辩老师思维明朗，对你的毕业论文给予肯定。

8）人称使用

在毕业论文答辩过程中必然涉及人称使用问题，建议尽量多使用第一人称，如"我"、"我们"。即使论文中的材料是引用他人的，也要用"我们引用"了哪儿哪儿的数据或材料。特别是毕业论文作者大多称论文是自己独立完成的，所以要更多使用而且是果断地、大胆地使用第一人称"我"和"我们"。

10.6　毕业论文评定标准

优秀

1）论文选题好，内容充实，能综合运用所学的专业知识，以正确观点提出问题，能进行精辟透彻的分析，并能紧密地结合实际情况，有一定的应用价值和独特的见解及鲜明的创新。

2）材料典型真实，既有定量分析，又有定性分析。

3）论文结构严谨，文理通顺，层次清晰，语言精练，文笔流畅，书写工整，图表正确、清晰、规范。

4）答辩中回答问题正确、全面，比较深刻，并有所发挥，口语清晰、流利。

良好

1）论文选题较好，能运用所学的专业理论知识联系实际，并能提出问题，分析问题。所论述的问题有较强的代表性，有一定的个人见解和实用性，并有一定的理论深度。

2）材料真实具体，有较强的代表性。对材料的分析较充分，比较有说服力，但不够透彻。

3）论文结构严谨，层次清晰，行文规范，条理清楚，文字通顺，书写工整，图表正确、清楚，数字准确。

4）在答辩中回答问题基本正确、中肯，口语比较清晰。

中等

1）论文选题较好，内容较充实，具有一定的分析能力。

2）独立完成，论点正确，但论据不充足或说理不透彻，对问题的本质论述不够深刻。

3）材料较具体，文章结构合理，层次比较清晰，有逻辑性，表达能力也较好，图表基本正确，运算基本准确。

4）在答辩中回答问题基本清楚，无原则性错误。

及格

1）论文选题一般，基本上做到用专业知识去分析解决问题，观点基本正确，基本独立完成，但内容不充实，缺乏自己的见解。

2）材料较具体，初步掌握了调查研究的方法，能对原始资料进行初步加工。

3）文章有条理，但结构有缺陷；论据能基本说明问题，能对材料作出一般分析，但较单薄，对材料的挖掘缺乏应有的深度，论据不够充分，不够全面。

4）文字表达基本清楚，文字基本通顺，图表基本正确，无重大数据错误。

5）在答辩中回答问题尚清楚，经提示后能修正错误。

不及格

凡论文存在以下问题之一者，一律以不及格论：

1）文章的观点有严重错误。

2）有论点而无论据，或死搬硬套教材和参考书上的观点，未能消化吸收。

3）离题或大段抄袭别人的文章，并弄虚作假。

4）缺乏实际调查资料，内容空洞，逻辑混乱，表达不清，语句不通顺。

5）在答辩中回答问题有原则性错误，经提示不能及时纠正。

第十一章 专题毕业论文写作与评析

11.1 英美文学

11.1.1 文学种类

1)"二分法":即根据是否押韵而把所有的作品分为韵文和散文两大类的方法。

2)"三分法":依据文学作品塑造形象的不同方式,而把文学作品分为三大类:即抒情文学、叙事文学、戏剧文学。

3)"四分法":"四分法"是指根据综合文学作品在形象塑造、语言运用、结构体制和表现方法等方面的不同,而把文学作品分为诗歌、小说、散文、戏剧文学四大类别的分类方法。"四分法"的长处:其一,划分时既注意到形象塑造的不同方式,也注意到了体裁上的差别。其二,突出了小说、散文的地位。其三,"四分法"是我国"五四"以来传统的文学体裁的分类法,它既注意了塑造形象、反映社会生活的不同方式,又注意到作品体裁上的差别,符合文学实际。另外,"四分法"也有缺陷,例如分类标准不很统一。各种分类方法都有其相对性。

11.1.2 文学理论

文学理论是对古今中外一切文学活动实践的总结,它的出发点和基础只能是文学活动的实践。先有文学活动的实践,然后才会有文学理论的概括,关于文学活动的本质,文学创作,作品构成,文学接受,文学发展的基本原理、概念范畴以及相关的方法,无一不是从文学活动的实践中总结、提炼出来的。

文学理论的基本形态有如下几种:

1) 文学哲学

文学创作是对社会生活的反映,即作家作为主体反映作为客体的生活。作品论、接受论中也有不少哲学层面的问题。这样,反映论这个马克思主义的哲学视角,成为揭示文学活动的基本视角,因此以反映论为基础的文学哲学是文学理论的一个基本形态。马克思主义的认识论的文学哲学,以其科学性超越了以前的文学哲学,成为文学理论的基石。

2）文学心理学

创作——作品——接受的过程，是一个心理转换过程，无论是文学创作还是文学接受，都是特殊的心理行为。因此，采用心理学的视角，建立起文学心理学，才能切入这些特殊的心理行为进行研究。文学心理学是文学理论的又一重要形态。

3）文学符号学

创作——作品——接受的过程，又是一个符号化的过程，因为文学创作旨在向人们传递特殊的审美信息，创作必须运用语言符号，作品则是语言符号的结晶。文学接受则首先要破译语言符号，这样符号学的视角对文学理论来说就显得极为重要，而文学符号学也理所当然地成为文学理论的一种基本形态。

4）文学社会学

现在再从文学创造——艺术价值——文学消费这个流动的系统看，首先，从文学创造到文学消费是一个组织起来的社会文化过程，这一过程不得不受一定的社会关系的制约，而浸润着社会思潮，反映着社会风貌，直接或间接地回答社会问题，即或文学创造和消费的是一些空灵的、超脱的、虚玄的、恬淡的产品，也不可能达到完全的"纯净"而不带社会性。因此，社会学的视角无疑是一个重要的视角，文学社会学无疑是文学理论一种重要的形态，而且在所有的形态中具有特别重要的地位。

5）文学价值学

文学创造到文学消费的过程，又是文学的艺术价值产生、确立和确证的过程。所谓价值是指某事物对人所具有的意义。文学作品显然对人具有特殊的意义，因此它具有价值。这种价值一般不是指实用价值，而是一种特殊的艺术价值。这种艺术价值在文学创造中产生，在文学作品中得以确立，在文学消费中得以确证。

6）文学文化学

面对创作——作品——接受和文学创造——艺术价值——艺术消费这统一的文学活动系统，还有一种把各种视角和方法融合在一起的理论，这就是文学文化学。这种形态的文学理论以"泛文学"作为研究对象，可以说是最古老的文学理论。我国先秦到魏晋以前的文学理论基本上属于这一形态，西方从古希腊到 18 世纪以前也基本上属于这一形态。但是，随时代的变化和各门科学中综合倾向的发展，人们又在一个更高的层次上去实现对文学活动的多视角的协同和综合研究，如西方的文化批评理论在某种意义上是又回归到文学文化学的路子上去了。因此，文学文化学又可以说是一种最新的文学理论形态。

7）文学信息学

创作——作品——接受系统又是特殊的信息系统，从创作到作品发表，是特殊信息的传播，文学接受则是特殊信息的接收，从文学接受再到文学创作则是信息的反馈。这样一来,从信息学的视角研究文学活动必然要形成一个新的学科——文学信息学。

11.1.3 文学批评

文学批评是对以文学作品为中心兼及一切文学活动和文学现象的理性分析、评价和判断。文学批评是文学活动的一个重要组成部分。自有文学作品及其传播、消费和接受以来,文学批评就随之产生和发展,并且构成文学理论不可或缺的重要内容和文学活动整体中的一种动力性、引导性和建设性因素,既推动文学创造,影响文学思想和文学理论的发展,又推动文学的传播与接受。

1) 文学批评的意识形态评价效用

首先,从批评对象来说,作为主要对象的文学作品,不管诗歌、散文,还是小说、剧本,都是精神创造的产物,都是一种意识形态话语。其次,从文学批评的效能来说,文学批评也表现为一种意识形态评价。具体可概括为:第一,文学批评是一种与一定社会意识形态深刻联系的批评话语,它运用这种话语来判断文学作品的意识形态价值,从而决定其相应的态度。第二,文学批评通过对文学思潮、文学运动的评估,对文学批评自身的检讨,以及对其他文学现象的衡定,也表现出它作为意识形态评价的效能。第三,文学批评作为意识形态评价的效用,还表现在它通过这种评价所肯定的价值取向影响和造就文学新人,扶持有利于确立一定意识形态领导地位的创作和批评队伍,特别要使批评者成为具有一定权威的人,以尽可能发挥其在意识形态评价上的作用。

2) 文学批评的模式

文学批评史上,出现过各式各样的批评流派,也形成了种种不同的批评模式。伦理道德批评、社会历史批评、审美批评,这些都属于传统批评模式。现代批评模式主要为:心理学批评、语言学批评、文化批评。这些多样的文学批评模式,既反映出文学自身的复杂性和多样性,也反映出批评思维的活跃性。

(1) 传统批评模式

伦理道德批评

伦理道德批评是以一定的道德意识及由之而形成的伦理关系作为规范来评价作品,以善、恶为基本范畴来决定对批评对象的取舍。这种批评着重于对文学作品的道德意识性质和品位的评价,实现作品的伦理价值及道德教化作用。

社会历史批评

这种批评强调文学与社会生活的关系,认为文学是再现生活并为一定的社会历史环境所形成的,因而文学作品的主要价值在于它的社会认识功用和历史意义。其基本的原则是:分析、理解和评价作品,必须将作品产生的时代背景、历史条件以及作家的生活经历等与作品联系起来考察。

审美批评

第一，审美批评首先是一种情感性评价；第二，审美批评又是一种体验与超越矛盾统一的批评，这种批评往往具有"超功利"的性质；第三，审美批评还常常是一种形式或形象的直觉批评。

(2) 现代批评模式

心理学批评

心理学批评主要是指运用现代心理学的成果对作家的创作心理及作品人物心理进行分析，从而探求作品的真实意图，以获得其真实价值的批评。

语言学批评

语言学批评认为文学作品是一个独立自足的整体，是一种有组织的符号结构，作品的意图只需要从文本去寻求而无需借助于外部因素加以说明。语言的语境、语义、能指性、信息作用是构成形象、形成结构的极其重要的因素，因而，只有通过对文本的语言进行分析，才能探求到作品的意图。

文化批评

文化批评既不是囿于文学文本或单纯文学的批评，也不是所谓的从"外部"的批评，而是在解读甚至审读文本的前提下"联系"文学外部诸文化现象的批评，尤其是联系权力/文化关系的批评。它是一种泛文学的批评，又是一种泛学科的批评。

文学批评多种多样，常用的方法有形式批评（Formalist Criticism）、生平批评（Biographical Criticism）、历史观批评（Historical Criticism）、性别观批评（Gender Criticism）、心理分析批评（Psychoanalytic Criticism）、社会学批评（Sociological Criticism）、神话批评（Mythological Criticism）、读者反应批评（Reader-response Criticism）、解构批评（Deconstructive Criticism）等。形式虽然没有定规，但还是有原则可循，即"批评五要"：了解对象，选点切入，确定要旨，布局安排，力求创见等。文学批评具有强烈的实践性。文学批评实践，是实现文学批评效能的根本途径。

11.1.4 文学类论文写作要点

1) 认真研读文本

文本是文学研究的第一手资料，因此选择一个可靠的文本并认真加以研读非常重要。所谓可靠的文本，是指由权威出版商出版的，经过考证、整理和校勘的文本。如能选到附有"导言"和"注释"的文本那就更好，因为"导言"会对作品的历史渊源、作者的生平、该文本与作者其他作品的关系等情况有侧重点不同的介绍，这对于全面地理解文本以及论文写作都会有直接的帮助。"注释"则会帮助我们解决研读中的疑难问题。文本选定之后，就要认认真真地通读和研读文本了。阅读文学文本时既要注意要点、重点,也要注意不漏掉细节。所谓"要点"就是作品的内容结构和形式结构框架,例如小说的中心思想、主要故事情节、主要人物关系和主流叙述方法等。诗歌则首先要弄清它的中心思想、诗节结构、韵律形式以及语言形象的象征意义等。剧本则首先要弄清人物(角色)关系、场景的内涵、剧情等。所谓"重点"主要是指与所研究课题直接相关的东西。对重点要不止一遍地阅读,还要用卡片和笔记记下原文的内容和出处(第几页,第几行,第几场),以备后用。所谓"细节"是指文本中与课题研究有直接关系但却容易被忽略的"枝节"内容,如一草一木之类的背景,某个次要人物的一句话,诗歌中的某些个别意象等。

2) 运用好文学理论与文学批评方法

在决定运用某种文学理论(文学批评方法)之后,首先要对该理论有一个深入的研究。具体办法是先从文学术语词典或百科全书中找到有关词条,了解其梗概,然后再参考文学史和文论之类的专著,了解它的全貌。最好是根据自己的理解,用自己的话归纳出它的基础知识要点。有不懂的地方,要请教导师,直至弄明白为止。只有这样,才能从文本中选用适合自己的材料,将论文写得内容到位、言之有物、方法正确、运用贴切。

其次,在实际运用中,也可能不只运用一种批评方法。例如,在分析一首诗时,既可以用历史批评方法去分析它的题材和主题思想,同时又可以用形式批评去分析它的韵律格式及其作用。在研究作品与作者的关系时,既可以用生平分析法为主要切入点,同时又可以用心理分析法分析该作者的创作心理。

再次,要善于辩证地看待和处理所使用的文学理论或文学批评方法,不仅看到它的长处,也要看到它的缺点和局限性。例如,在运用神话—原型批评理论的时候,既要吸取它注重人类的文化形态分析和文化模式研究的一面,又要对它的不妥和偏执之处(如用人类学与神话学抹去文艺学的特性,或者说以集体无意识、原型、神话仪式这些文艺的部分属性取代文艺的全部属性)有一个清醒的认识。再如,在运用解构主义文学理论时,既要肯定它具有可行性的一面(如对审美现象作深层结构的模式化研究),又不能忽视它的缺点与错误(如它在注重语言学因素的同时,忽视了文学形象的特征与作用)。

最后一点,也是极为重要的一点,那就是无论使用何种文学理论与批评方法,都要有自己的思想和见解,绝不可机械地照搬书本上现成的条文或乱发没有文本基础的空洞议论。这类论文有没有创新性,关键就在于对理论的精华和内核能否活学活用。

3) 选题时应优先考虑文学史上公认的重要作家的作品

重要作家是指像莎士比亚、斯威夫特这样的"经典"作家,像雪莱、拜伦、勃朗特姐妹、狄更斯、杰克·伦敦、马克·吐温这样的重要文学流派代表人物,以及像叶芝、萧伯纳、刘易斯、高尔斯华绥(Galsworthy)、赛珍珠(P. Buck)、T. S. 艾略特、福克纳、海明威、斯坦伯克(Steinbeck)、贝娄(Bellow)这样的诺贝尔文学奖获得者。研究这类作家的作品一是不会遇到参考资料过少的问题；二是对他们的基本情况平时多有了解；三是不乏多角度研究样板，从中可以得到启发或直接借鉴。例如，我们可以用精神分析法去研究莎士比亚作品中的悲剧人物，用女权批评法去研究莎士比亚笔下的女性，用接受美学理论去研究莎剧的读者反应和社会影响，用生平分析法和社会历史分析法去研究赛珍珠，等等。

与上述这些重要作家相比，选择近期的、时髦当代作家则写起来有较大的难度。一方面是由于研究资料会相对匮乏（最新研究成果不容易看到），另一方面，这些时髦作家往往会因"现代主义"思想和手法盛行一时，但对这些"现代派"的文学理论，学生还缺乏准确的把握。例如，超现实主义（包括达达主义、荒诞派）、存在主义、后现代主义等都属于此类。

4）在选择比较文学研究时，要特别注意两部作品必须要有可比性

要重点分析两部作品的相同之处和不同之处及其原因（作者的思想、风格、历史及文化因素）。要点明作比较的意义，避免"为比较而比较"的盲目做法。

5）要紧扣题目，避免"节外生枝"

在撰写文学类毕业论文时，一个最常见的错误做法就是"节外生枝"，说一些远离题目或与题目无直接关系的话。有不少同学虽然题目选得不错，但写起来却往往会无视题目所提示出来的重点，而习惯于千篇一律地从作家的生平和创作经历写起。其主要动机据说是不这样写就达不到篇幅要求。正确的做法是"开门见山"，并使所写内容紧扣题目。以下就是"开门见山"和"紧扣题目"的两个例子：

例1 （开门见山）

Growing Pains: On *The Catcher in the Rye*

The Catcher in the Rye is a landmark book for the post-World War II period. There have been pros and cons in the criticism of the novel, from downright approval to questions about Salinger's attitudes, the free use of profanity and whether the book is fit for young readers. But one thing is for sure, that the character of Holden Caulfield has become an icon, a figure that is the most frequently talked about by people in relation to growing pains, adolescent development, teenager rebellion and so on.

Holden's growing seems strange and twisted, but in fact, it is very much the same as many young people's. Stuck in between the adults' world and the children's world, Holden has many pains and disbeliefs. Through struggling and seeking, he will find the truth and the right way.

例2 （紧扣题目）

以大纲形式体现：

Title: The American Dream Reflected by *The Great Gatsby*

Chapter 1　Introduction
　　1.1　The Content of the American Dream
　　1.2　About *The Great Gatsby*
Chapter 2　The Real American Dream in the Book
　　2.1　The Elements of the American Dream
　　2.2　The Symbols of the American Dream
Chapter 3　The Americans' American Dream
　　3.1　The Development of the American Dream
　　3.2　Influences on the Development of Society
Chapter 4　Conclusion
　　4.1　The Restriction of the American Dream
　　4.2　The Proper Attitudes Should Be Taken

11.1.5　英语专业毕业论文文学类参考选题(范围)

1. A Comparative Study of Tao Yuanming and William Wordsworth
2. Jane Eyre's Search for Christianity
3. *Jane Eyre*, a Symbol of Feminism
4. The Colonialist Discourse in *Jane Eyre* and *Wide Sargasso Sea*
5. *Jane Eyre*: A Great Masterpiece with Prejudice—We Should Analyze a Work Dialogically
6. Analysis of the Characters in *Jane Eyre*
7. On the Techniques of Emily Bronte's Dual Personalities in *Wuthering Heights*
8. The Realism of the *Adventure of Huckleberry Finn*
9. Love Stories in William Cather's *O Pioneers*
10. An Analysis of the Source of Tess' Tragedy
11. A Picturesque Novel, *Tess of the D'Urbervilles*
12. The Light of the Dark: the Greatest Works of Conan and Agatha
13. The Ambiguity in *The Scarlet Letter*
14. The Symbolism in *The Scarlet Letter*
15. Hawthorne's Theory of Romance and *The Scarlet Letter*
16. Does Hester Get Rebirth? Reexamination of the Heroine in *The Scarlet Letter*

17. Amazing Return—An Analysis of the Character of Hester Prynne in *The Scarlet Letter*
18. The Literature Characteristics in *A Tale of Two Cities*
19. On Wordsworth's View of Nature
20. On the Symbolism of D. H. Lawrence's *The Rainbow*
21. Three Structures in *Pride and Prejudice*
22. Revelation of Four Couples in *Pride and Prejudice*
23. Love and Lust—*Pride and Prejudice*
24. The Character Analysis of *Pride and Prejudice*
25. The Brief Analysis of Shakespeare's Tragedy Tradition
26. The Versification of English Poetry and Metrical
27. Contrast Between Chinese Poetry and Sonnets
28. Social Reality Reflected in *Ode to the West Wind*
29. Comment the Themes of *The Merchant of Venice*
30. To Love or To Be Loved? Analysis of Major Characters in *Wuthering Heights*
31. Gothic Features in *Wuthering Heights*
32. The Appearance of New Women：On Carrie's New Image
33. The Comparison of the Character of Carrie Meeber and Jennie Gerhardt
34. The Philosophy of Life in Ernest Hemingway's *The Old Man and the Sea*
35. The Cuban Culture Contest of *The Old Man and the Sea*
36. Reexamination of Santiago—Hero of *The Old Man and the Sea*
37. Mark Twain—The Pessimist Who Brought Laughter to The World
38. Humor and Realism of Mark Twain's *The Celebrated Jumping Frog of California County*
39. *Robinson Crusoe* and the Colonial Empire
40. A Probe into the Ambiguity and Symbolization of Eliot's Poetry
41. *A Farewell to Arms*—A Clear Mirror
42. *Gone with the Wind* and the Awakening of Women
43. Comparison of *Gone with the Wind* and *The Collector*—An Analysis of Women's Problem
44. The Sound of Heart-Reverie and Melancholy in Emily Dickinson's Poems
45. The Negative Influence of Society on the *Oliver Twist*
46. Comment on the Biblical Images in *Paradise Lost*, *Paradise Regained*, *Samson Agonistes*
47. The Typical Characteristic of O. Henry's Short Story—Comment on *The Gift*

of the Maggie

48. Destruction of Tess in *Tess of the D'Urbervilles*
49. Morals Affect on the Fate of Tess
50. *Jude the Obscure* as the Masterpiece by Hardy

11.1.6 Tasks

1. Try to find some new perspectives on the books of *Jane Eyre*, *Tess of the D'Urbervilles*, *Pride and Prejudice*, *The Old Man and the Sea*, *The Scarlet Letter*, etc.

2. Try to develop a topic on one of them for yourself on the basis of the methods introduced.

11.2 翻译理论与实践

11.2.1 翻译的性质和分类

翻译是指把一种语言文字的意义转换成另一种语言文字。简言之,翻译是一种用不同的语言文字将原文作者的意思准确地再现出来的艺术。翻译是跨语言(cross-linguistic)、跨文化(cross-cultural)、跨社会(cross-social)的交际活动。对翻译的性质,有过许多描述,其中奈达(Eugene A. Nida)的论述是:"翻译是指从语义到文体在译语中用最切近而又最自然的对等语再现原文的信息。"翻译是科学,因为它涉及思维和语言,反映了存在与认识、主体与客体的关系,这种关系可用受一定规律支配的语言加以描述,即翻译有科学规律可循;翻译是艺术,因为翻译是译者对原文再创造的过程,译者不可避免地带有自己的主观色彩,有自己的独创性;翻译是技能,因为译者需采用增词、减词、切分、转换等方法。

翻译的类型可从如下几个角度划分:
1) 从译出语和译入语的角度
2) 从涉及的语言符号的角度:语内翻译(intra-lingual translation)、语际翻译(inter-lingual translation)和符际翻译(inter-semiotic translation)
3) 从翻译手段的角度:口译、笔译和机器翻译
4) 从翻译题材的角度:专业性翻译、文学翻译、一般性翻译
5) 从翻译方式上的角度:全译、摘译和编译

11.2.2 翻译类论文的形式

英语专业的翻译类毕业论文有以下几种常见形式:

1) 纯理论研究型

此类论文主要是指翻译学(translatology)研究,其研究课题包括翻译学的定义、性质、功能、任务、体系框架和翻译方法论等理论问题。

翻译学是一门独立的学科,其研究的范围与对象主要包括:翻译活动的全过程及其所涉及的原作者、原作、原作读者、译者、译作、译作读者及与之相关的历时和共时的客观世界。它的研究目的是揭示翻译过程中的规律和特点,从而指导翻译实践。

翻译学所研究的内容可分为三大部分:(1)翻译史和翻译理论发展史;(2)翻译理论;(3)翻译实践论。其中,翻译理论主要论述翻译理论的科学基础和翻译理论的本体系统。前者是从横向角度论述哲学、语言学和符号学、逻辑学、心理学、文化学、美学、信息论等不同学科与翻译理论的关系以及对翻译理论的贡献,以揭示其跨学科特征。翻译理论的本体系统是翻译理论的核心部分,具体涉及翻译原理、翻译过程、翻译方法论、翻译风格、翻译美学和翻译批评等。其中,翻译原理旨在明确翻译的本质和标准等。对翻译过程的研究旨在揭示理解和表达等翻译活动的内在规律。翻译方法论旨在总结各种翻译技巧及其运用场合。翻译风格着重于研究译者个性在翻译中的体现。翻译美学旨在追求翻译作品在内容、形式和风格上的高度统一。翻译批评的目的是促进翻译达到理想的美学境界。翻译实践研究主要包括口译、笔译等翻译实践的研究和翻译人才的素质与培养研究。

翻译学有两个大的分支:一是普通翻译学,研究不同语言翻译的共同规律,并以此从宏观上对翻译现象进行解释和指导;二是本位翻译学,研究不同语言国家各自(本国)的翻译活动及其规律,其立足点是本国国情下的翻译对策,其目的是指导本国的翻译实践和为普通翻译学提供依据。我国的本位翻译学就是中国翻译学。

2) 翻译实践总结型

此类论文主要是通过对译者翻译实践的分析,揭示并归纳出一些规律性的东西,以此进一步指导翻译实践。这种方法是典型的"从实践中来,到实践中去"的翻译研究方法,也是初学者培养和提高自己翻译研究能力的常用方法。此种论文成功的关键有两条:一是论文作者必须有较深厚的翻译理论素质以及由表及里或者是从具体到一般的概括、归纳和升华能力;二是所选用的实例必须具有一定的典型性和代表性,只有这样,所总结出的规律才有说服力和实践指导意义。在选择翻译实践案例时,既可选择论文作者本人的译作,又可以选择别人的;既可以选择集中于某一译作的翻译案例,又可以选择不同译作中的"零散"案例。经过分析所得出的结论,既可以是关于翻译理论的,又可以是关于翻译技巧的;既可以是体系性的,又可以是对某一主题的"一得之愚"。

3）翻译批评型

所谓翻译批评,是指运用翻译理论对译品和译者(翻译思想)进行具体的分析。它包含两方面的内容:翻译欣赏和翻译批评。翻译欣赏是直接的,体现欣赏者的主观感受。翻译批评是客观的,着眼于科学的分析、研究和判断。翻译批评的功能主要是为了规范翻译实践,提高翻译质量,繁荣翻译事业。批评能否做到客观与批评者的素质和出发点有密切关系。批评者应该以公正的态度并以现代翻译理论为指导,坚持科学性和客观性,运用适当的批评方法进行翻译批评。可以从批评者的角度,也可以从欣赏者的角度,还可以从一般读者的角度,对译作进行评价。常见的批评方法有:

(1) 逻辑分析法

主要是用逻辑推断的方法分析译文内容是否忠实地再现了原作的内容。如译者对原文的理解是否准确,上下文关系是否顺理成章,译文是否从整体上把握了原文的实质内容等,都可以通过逻辑分析加以验证。

(2) 定量定性分析法

可以先通过对全篇译文、译文的重点部分和译文的难点部分进行定量分析,然后作出定性的判断。

(3) 语义分析法

通过观察对词的外延意义的理解及多义词词项的选择是否正确,以及是否注意到了词义的内涵意义等,判断译文是否忠实地传达了原文的意思。

(4) 抽样分析法

被评译文的篇幅过大,不宜作全面评价时,可采用抽样方法,只对抽样部分进行分析,然后作出判断。这种分析虽不能概括全貌,但只要样品选择得当(有代表性),还是能够在较大程度上客观反映译作的质量水平的。

4）典型案例分析型

此种论文一般是从翻译实践中选择具有代表性的典型案例进行详细和深入的分析和研究,然后得出具有认识价值、实用价值或学术价值的结论。它既不同于翻译实践的分析与总结,也不同于抽样分析式的翻译批评。一般的翻译实践与总结着重于实践的积累、整理和升华,而典型案例分析则侧重于"以点代面",突出"榜样"的启迪作用和示范作用。抽样分析属于翻译批评的一个组成部分,典型案例分析则属于一项完整的应用研究或理论研究。

5）不同译本比较型

此种论文的撰写适用于同一本原著有两种以上译本(version)的情况。如《红楼梦》两种译本的对比、《中华人民共和国合同法》两种译本的对比、杜甫诗歌的几种译法等都属于此类。

6) 佳作欣赏型

此种论文属翻译批评中的翻译欣赏类，其欣赏对象一般是翻译名家的佳作。这种论文的写作不仅可以寓学习于研究之中，即通过研究活动使学生学到不少知识和本领，而且还可以起到提高翻译品位和弘扬优良译风的作用。

11.2.3 英语专业毕业论文翻译类参考选题（范围）

1. The Translation of Trade Marks and Culture
2. Interpreting and Interpreting Skills
3. On the Origins of Legal Terms and Their Translation
4. The Appropriateness and Comparison of Poem Translation
5. Analysis of Transliterated Brand Names from English to Chinese
6. The Social and Cultural Factors in Translation Practice
7. On the Domestication in the Translation of Advertisements from E-C
8. English Pun Translation—From a Sociosemiotic Perspective
9. On Literal Translation and Free Translation
10. Translation for EST
11. On Translation Methods of Numerals in Chinese and English
12. On the Translation of Du Fu's Poems
13. The Comparison and Translation of Chinese and English Idioms
14. Review on the Translation of Movie Titles
15. Equivalence and Its Application in Translation
16. Cultural Equivalence in Translation
17. Onomatopoeia and Its Translation
18. On the Cross-Culture Pragmatic Failure in English Translation
19. Remarks on the Translation of Chinese Set Phrase
20. What Is an Ideal Translation?
21. A Brief Comparison Between Two Basic Translation Methods—Literal Translation and Free Translation
22. A New Understanding of TE Based on Pragmatic Adaptation Theory
23. Learning a Foreign Language Through Translation
24. Arts in Verse Translation
25. On Translating the Passive Voice in Scientific and Technology English into Chinese
26. A Probe into Translation Theory and English Versions of Some Tang Poems
27. The Translation of English Idioms and Culture

28. Features and Translation of Idioms
29. The Translation of Long Sentences
30. English News Headline and Its Translation
31. A Contrastive Study of the Cohesive Devices Between English and Chinese and the Translation of Them

11.2.4　Tasks

Give some analysis to the above topics and categorize them on the basis of topic types in translation study introduced.

11.3　英语语言学

11.3.1　语言学的内容及主要学派

1）语言学概述

语言学是以人类语言为研究对象的学科,探索范围包括语言的结构、语言的运用、语言的社会功能和历史发展,以及其他与语言有关的问题。传统的语言学称为**语文学**,以研究古代文献和书面语为主。语文学是为其他学科服务的。现代语言学则以研究当代语言和口语为主,而且研究的范围大大拓宽。现代语言学是一门独立的学科。广义的语言学包括语文学。研究语言在某一时期的情况,叫做**共时语言学**;研究语言在不同时期所经历的变化,叫做**历时语言学**或**历史语言学**。对多种语言作综合研究,试图找出其中的共同规律,叫做**普通语言学**。把语言学知识运用于实际工作,叫**应用语言学**。通过语音和词形的比较追溯某些语言的亲属关系,叫**历史比较语言学**。用比较方法发现人类各种语言的某些共同现象,叫**类型语言学**。为了解决教学或翻译问题而对比两种语言的异同,叫**对比语言学**。

语音、语法、词汇及文字这些学科都注目于语言的结构本身,是语言学的中心,有人叫**微观语言学**。研究语音的物理属性、人类的发音方法、语音感知的生理过程等的是**语音学**;研究一种语言有多少个不同的音,彼此之间有何区别和关系的是**音系学**或**音位学**。研究词的构成方式和屈折方式的是**形态学**,也叫**词法**;研究如何把词组成短语或句子的是**造句学**,也叫**句法**。按传统语法,形态学和造句学合起来就是**语法学**。研究词汇项目、词汇意义、词语演变的是**词汇学**;追溯词的来源和历史的是**词源学**;搜集许多词项,把它们分类、比较、注释的是**词典学**。研究词项与概念及指称对象的关系,揣摩各种词义的异同、正反、上下、交叉等关系,剖析整个句子或其中某些成分的意义,这是**语义学**。研究文字的形状、体系、起源、演变和发展的学科是**文字学**。

语言教学是语言研究的动力,又是语言理论发挥作用的场所。语言教学分为第一语言教学、第二语言教学和外语教学。第一语言教学所教的是母语。第二语言教学在双语社团中进行,既教母语,又教另一种语言。在外语教学中,学生所学的是外国语。翻译要求把原以某种语言写成的作品的内容用另一种语言表达出来。即使同一民族语言,语音、词汇、语法格式也因地区而异,因使用者的社会地位而异,还因交际场合和使用目的而异。研究这些问题的是**社会语言学**。与社会语言学关系密切的是**方言学**。研究区域方言的学科称为**方言地理学**。**语体学**近似社会语言学,研究在不同条件下语言使用的语体差异。**文体学**研究如何造成不同的文章风格。与此近似的传统学科是**修辞学**,包括雄辩术和作文法。文体学可以说是现代的修辞学。**心理语言学**从语言出发研究心理,摸索语言与感知、注意、记忆、学习等心理作用的关系。**神经语言学**探索人们学习语言、运用语言的神经学基础,试图作出人脑控制言语和听觉的模拟。研究伴随着语言交际而发生的种种现象的学科,叫**副语言学**,也叫**伴随语言学**。**人类语言学**研究社会制度、宗教信仰、职业、亲属关系等对语言习惯的影响以及语言对这些东西的或多或少的影响。**民族语言学**只研究民族类型、民族行为程式与人们的语言之间的关系。**数理语言学**是研究语言中的数学性质的学科。使用数学方法研究语言,最初是统计音素、语素、词汇等项目,后来人们运用数量计算学并使用各种模式来处理语言材料。数理语言学目前包括代数语言学、统计语言学和应用数理语言学。**计算语言学**阐明如何利用电子计算机进行语言研究,其项目有统计资料,检索情报,研究词法、句法,识别文字,合成语音,编制机助教学程序,进行机助翻译等等。

2) 语言学的主要学派

语言学的主要学派如下:

- 自然主义学派(Naturalistic Linguistics)
- 新语法学派(Neogrammarians)
- 社会学学派(Social Linguistics)
- 唯美主义学派(Aestheticism)
- 结构主义学派(Structuralism)
- 语符学派(Glossematics)
- 美国描写语言学派(Descriptive Linguistics)
- 格位语法学派(Case Grammar)
- 关系语法学派(Relation Grammar)
- 形式主义学派(Formalism)
- 衍生语法学派(Generative Grammar)

- 衍生语意学派(Generative Semantics)
- 词汇功能语法学派(Lexical-Functional Grammar)
- 核心词组语法学派(Head-Driven Phrase Structure Grammar)
- 认知—功能主义学派(Cognitive-Functionalism)
- 功能语法学派(Functional Grammar)
- 系统功能语法学派(Systematic Functional Grammar)
- 角色指涉语法学派(Role and Reference Grammar)
- 认知语法学派(Cognitive Grammar)

概括来讲,语言学可分为传统语言学、现代语言学和当代语言学。

传统语言学：传统语言学一般指19世纪以前的语文学和19世纪以来的历史比较语言学。早在公元前2—3世纪,我国战国时代哲学家荀子在《正名篇》中就提出名称同其所代表的事物没有必然联系的观点。荀子说:"名无固宜,约之以命,约定俗成谓之宜,异于约则谓之不宜。"此后,《尔雅》——我国第一部语义词典,《方言》——我国第一部方言词典,《说文解字》——我国第一部按部首编排的字典,汉代刘熙的《释名》,隋朝陆法言的《广韵》,宋朝陈彭年的《切韵》,以及清代大家的语言研究著作,谱写了中国语言研究色彩纷呈的篇章。这些著作是中国传统语言学的重要成果,是语言研究中宝贵的遗产。

古印度的学者对语言的研究也比较有价值。著名学者巴尼尼对《吠陀》的语法进行了研究,其作品《梵语语法》提出了近四千条规则。该书讨论问题的深入程度、自身的系统性以及表述的简练性是其他语法书无法比拟的。

古希腊的学者对于语言喜欢作哲学上的辩论。大约在公元前5世纪,古希腊人就对语言问题进行过两场有名的大论战。其中一场论战是在"自然发生派"和"约定俗成派"之间展开的,论战的焦点集中在语言的形式和意义之间的关系上。早期的希腊学者对语言的研究主要侧重于词源学、语音学和语法学等方面。比较著名的是亚里士多德的语法理论。此外,斯多葛派、亚历山大里亚学派等在语言研究中也作出了很大贡献,特别是亚历山大里亚学派的狄奥尼修斯。

文艺复兴以后,16世纪末就开始有了语言的比较研究。18世纪末—19世纪初,逐步形成了历史比较语言学,其奠基人是丹麦语言学家拉斯克,德国语言学家葆朴、格林,俄国语言学家沃斯托科夫。历史比较语言学使语言研究摆脱了其他学科的附庸,走上了独立发展的道路。历史比较语言学的一些研究方法如谱系分类,至今影响着对亲属语言的研究。

随后,在历史比较语言学的基础上,普通语言学概括了众多语言的特点而逐步形成,开始对人类语言进行系统的理论研究,形成了一些学派,如以德国语言学家缪勒为代表的自然主义学派,以德国语言学家洪堡特为代表的浪漫主义学派,以美国人类学家萨丕尔为代表的观念主义学派等。洪堡特被认为是普通语言学的奠基人,他的理论对索绪尔有一定的影响。

进入20世纪后,现代语言学的理论与方法兴起,但它没有完全代替传统语言学。从古到今,传统语言学依然源远流长,发挥着它应有的作用,其中一部分已与现代语言学合流。

现代语言学:现代语言学是20世纪初以来建立在索绪尔语言理论基础上的各语言学流派和分支学科的总称。瑞士语言学家索绪尔提出了一系列理论和方法,于1906年—1911年在日内瓦大学讲授普通语言学,被称为"日内瓦学派"(Geneva School)。他成功地区分了语言和言语、共时和历时、内部语言和外部语言等。他的语言理论是语言发展的一个转折点,标志着现代语言学的形成。他的代表著作《普通语言学教程》成为现代结构主义语言学的理论基础。以索绪尔的语言理论为基础的语言学派还有:① 布拉格学派(Prague School)。其研究重点是把语言作为一种功能体系进行研究和分析。该派在音位学方面的研究成果尤为突出。② 20世纪30年代在丹麦形成的以叶尔姆斯列夫为代表的哥本哈根学派(Copenhagen School)。他们完全赞同索绪尔的观点,认为语言是形式而不是实体,并试图建立一门新兴的语言学——语符学。

英国共时语言学研究始于语音学和音位学研究。斯威特是19世纪下半叶用共时描写方法研究语音学的杰出代表。琼斯继承和发展了斯威特的理论和学说,并用"宽式音标"和"严式音标"来代替斯威特的区别意义和不能区别意义的两类音素。在20世纪初的英国语言学界,弗斯对普通语言学理论的建立与发展所作出的贡献最为突出。在他的学术生涯中,对他影响最大的要属他的同事、人类学教授马林诺夫斯基。马林诺夫斯基在《原始语言中的语义问题》一文中强调语言对社会的依赖性。

在共时语言学方面,影响最为深远的当属20世纪初发展起来的美国结构主义语言学派。这一学派在语言描写上取得的成就最大,所以被称为"美国描写语言学派"。鲍阿斯和他的学生萨丕尔是美国描写语言学派的"开路先锋"。鲍阿斯首先提出:语言的结构分析应该在语音、词汇和句法三个层次上进行。萨丕尔对鲍阿斯体系作了进一步的发展。美国描写语言学派最重要的人物是布龙菲尔德,他在1933年出版的《语言论》被称为美国描写语言学派的"圣经",是一段时期内每位从事语言研究人员的必读书。弗里斯、特雷格、史密斯、弗朗西斯、黑斯、希尔、哈里斯等人都对美国描写语言学派的发展作出过重要贡献。结构主义语言学的主要特点是:重视共时研究,重视"活"的口语研究,严格区分语言和言语,依靠归纳方法对收集的语言事实进行分类,客观地描写和研究语言事实。

当代语言学:1957年,美国语言学家乔姆斯基的《句法结构》一书出版,标志着转换生成语言学的诞生。乔姆斯基改用转换的方法,把抽象的深层结构转换为具体的表层结构。他的成就在于:证明了能够用形式和逻辑的方法描述一种自然语言,研究了人类普遍具有的生成话语的语言能力。这是前人没有做到的。

转换生成语言学从20世纪50年代到80年代经历了五个发展阶段:古典理论、标准理论、扩充式标准理论、修正的扩充式标准理论、支配和约束理论。

转换生成语言学的兴起打破了结构主义语言学一统天下的格局,使当代语言学出现了百花齐放的局面。除了格语法、生成语义学等对转换生成语言学有一定的修正以外,在转换生成语言学的直接挑战下,原有的语言学派不断完善自己并产生出一些新的学派,如序位语法派就是在结构主义的基础上通过改进而产生的一个语言学派别,代表人物是派克。层次语法学派则是在美国描写语言学派和哥本哈根语符学的基础上发展起来的一个语言学派别,代表人物是美国语言学家兰姆。系统功能语言学是在英国语言学家弗斯的理论的基础上发展起来的,代表人物是英国语言学家韩礼德。

当代语言学克服过去语言学的种种局限,向深度和广度发展。其发展趋势是:重视语义研究,语言学对象扩大为语言体系、言语活动和言语机制,语言学边缘学科涌现,语言学理论广泛应用,语言学研究重点从结构转向建构(建构—指利用语言体系中的材料构成话语;一指利用话语中的创新,在其约定俗成后充实语言结构体系;一指个体在习得和学习一种语言后,逐步建构个体的语言体系,使之接近于全民语言体系)等。建构语言学要求在继续研究语言结构体系、描写语言现象的同时,更多地研究建构规律,以便更好地建构话语,并建构语言本身。

3) 交叉学科

语言学与社会学、心理学、数学、逻辑学、信息论、神经生理学、计算机科学、通讯工程等学科互相渗透,形成了许多边缘学科:

- 社会语言学
- 心理语言学
- 应用语言学
- 数理语言学
- 神经语言学
- 语言病理学
- 实验语音学
- 宇宙语言学

11.3.2 语言学的研究方法

对语言的研究可以分为共时和历时两种。共时是指对某一历史时期的语言进行研究,例如对现代汉语的研究;历时是指对语言从一个时代到另一个时代的历史进行研究。这里主要介绍社会语言学和应用语言学两个领域的研究方法。

1) 社会语言学(sociolinguistics)

社会语言学是一门语言学的分支学科,研究社会的各层面对语言运用的影响,包括文化准则、社会规范或情境。社会语言学也研究社会本质和差别对语言的影响,如族群、宗教、地位、性别、教育程度、年龄等,和语言的差别如何能用来区分一个人在社会阶层中的地位。

有人亦把后设语言学(metalinguistics,亦作"元语言学")归类为社会语言学的一部分。

(1) 研究范围

社会语言学研究的是语言的社会本质和差别,以及影响它们的社会因素。在传统的语言地理学中也有相同的研究,但是自社会语言学出现以后,这些内容都归入社会语言学的范畴了。

对社会本质的研究包括:
- 语言的社会本质的特点及其规律
- 语言、意识、社会在起源上的相互关系
- 民族语言和民族形成的关系
- 民族共同语的形成与社会发展的关系
- 语言演变与社会演变的关系

对语言差异的研究包括:标准语与方言、行话的差异,如发音差异、用词差异和地位差异;同一语言在不同国家、地区以及社会所产生的差异,如英语在不同国家或地区的传播中产生了变异,出现了美式英语、港式英语、新加坡式英语等;同一国家或社会中通行几种语言所造成的差异,如有两种或两种以上官方语言的国家或地区,如加拿大(英语、法语)、新加坡(英语、中文、马来语);不同的语言使用者在语言运用上的差异,如性别差异导致男女使用有差异的语言;不同社会场所所使用语言的差异,如一般中国人在家庭环境中使用家乡方言,在工作学习时用普通话。

(2) 研究方法

使用调查研究法对各地区、各行业、各阶层等的人的语言运用进行考察。使用数学分析法对口语材料和文献资料进行数学统计和数理分析。使用对比研究法分析社会因素,研究语言差异。使用实验分析法用语音或心理实验仪器对语言差异进行实验分析,并作出定量和定性的描述。

2) 应用语言学(applied linguistics)

应用语言学是研究语言在各个领域中实际应用的语言学分支。它着重解决现实当中的问题,一般不涉及语言的历史状态,也不大介入一般理论上的争辩。可以说,它是鉴定各种理论的实验场。

19世纪初,语言理论方面的研究和应用方面的研究开始分化。19世纪末,

J. N. 博杜恩·德·库尔德内提出了应用语言学这个概念，但没有引起广泛关注。20 世纪以后，语言科学得到了进一步的发展，应用范围空前扩大，语言应用方面的研究和理论方面的研究明确地区分开来，"应用语言学"这个名词开始被广泛运用，并促成了应用语言学和理论语言学的分化。

（1）研究范围

应用语言学的研究范围由实践的需要决定，通常分为一般应用语言学和机器应用语言学。

一般应用语言学按其应用领域，分为以下几个方面：a) 语言教学。这是传统意义上的应用语言学。编辑高质量的教材和参考书，研究切合实际的教学方法，一直是语言教学研究中的重大课题。除一般的语言教学外，还有为不同目的和不同对象服务的第二语言教学、科技外语教学、双语制教学、聋哑盲教学。b) 标准语的建立和规范化，文字的创制和改革。建立通用于各方言区的标准语是很重要的。应用语言学要解决的问题是如何选好这种标准语的基础方言和标准音。为无文字的语言创制文字时，基础方言和标准音更是重要的依据。文字改革包括文字系统（字母表、正词法和标点符号）的部分改进和彻底更换。标准语的建立只是语言规范化的开始。为了确定语音、语法、词汇规范，需要编出相应的正音词典、规范语法和各种类型的词典。c) 辞书编纂。词汇是语言中变化最快部分，新词新义不断涌现。及时、准确地把这些新词新义固定在词典中，指导人们如何运用，这是辞书对语言规范化最有效的影响。d) 翻译。这是在两种语言之间进行的综合性创造活动。如何处理好意义的传达和形式的转换，有很多问题要探讨。

除上面这些课题外，一般应用语言学还涉及言语矫正、舞台语言研究、建立国际辅助语、制定速记系统等。

机器应用语言学研究如何利用电子计算机等先进工具处理自然语言。

（2）研究方法

A. 选择课题

选择研究课题可以从两方面着手：第一，从亲身感受中去考虑有哪些言语现象值得研究；第二，从前人的研究成果中吸取养料，寻求合适的课题。

B. 建立假设

研究人员对要探讨的社会因素与语言变异之间的联系作出初步的判断，这一步骤就叫做建立假设。建立假设须特别注意以下问题：第一，对假设应力求具体可测。注重对假设的研究，其结论要归结到检验假设上。因此，假设中的变量必须具体可测。第二，对自变量应加以限定。在现实生活中，影响语言变异的因素是多方面的。我们如果不从一开始就注意限定自变量的范围，就会导致对观察的结果难以作出准确的评估和推断。例如我们根据经验作出如下假设：男子说话比女子说话要干脆,表现在句法上,男子较多地使用陈述句,女子则较多地使用疑问句。

C. 确定调查对象

对有关言语共同体中的每个成员都一一进行一番调查是不可能的,可采用抽样调查和非随机抽样。

D. 搜集资料

搜集资料的方法包括访谈法、观察法和问卷法。访谈法就是由调查人员与被调查者进行面对面谈话。访谈法的关键在于如何诱导受访人说出调查人员所需了解的话语,提供有关语言变体的原始材料。观察法即研究人员通过直接观察研究对象的言语行为以获取资料。问卷法是用书面形式进行社会调查的一种方法。问卷的内容主要是根据调查项目编写而成的一系列问题,此外还应当包括有关填表人背景的项目。所列问题按其回答的方式可分为封闭式和开放式两种。封闭式问题就是把问题的若干种可能的答案用简明的语言陈述清楚,供填表人选择;开放式问题就是对回答不限范围,让填表人自由表达意见。

上述研究方法各有利弊,要根据选题和现实条件进行合理调整和组合。

3) 英语教学

语言教学研究属于应用语言学,它涉及语言学、心理语言学、社会语言学、跨文化交际理论、教育学和教学法等研究领域,因此也是一门交叉学科。关于语言教学研究,主要是研究语言学的研究成果在教学领域的运用,特别注重语言习得(language acquisition);现代教学流派、心理语言学、社会语言学、跨文化交际学对语言教学理论的影响和对语言教学实践的指导意义。

英语在我国属于外语(foreign language),在有些国家,如新加坡,则属于第二语言(second language)。将英语作为"外语"的教学(TEFL)和将英语作为"第二语言"的教学(TESL)均具有第二语言习得的特点,它们与第一语言习得,即母语习得,有着至关重要的区别。首先,与第一语言习得相比,信息的输入与交流、社区文化和正规教育起着至关重要的作用;其次,学习材料的输入要符合循序渐进的规律;最后,学习者的年龄、主导学习动机和学习策略等个人因素对第二语言习得的效果也有非常重要的影响。可见,语言习得理论对英语教学有直接的指导作用。

除了语言习得理论以外,传统语法、结构主义语言学、TG 语法、交际功能理论、系统功能语法等理论也都对英语教学产生过重大影响。

在撰写英语教学研究类论文时,首先必须对有关的重要语言学理论有一个深入的了解和把握,才能选好题目,写出高质量的论文。

11.3.3 选题思路和选题范围

英语专业毕业生可结合自己的学习经历,认真回顾教师的英语教学情况,重点从下列几个方面选择论文题目。

第一,英语教学理论研究,包括这些语言学理论对英语教学实践的指导意义。例如,语言习得理论、结构主义、跨文化交际理论、心理语言学、社会语言学、系统功能语法和交际语法等。

第二,英语教学法(methodology)研究,可主要侧重于教学流派的研究和各教学法之间的比较研究。这些教学方法包括:

- 传统语法教学法(traditional grammar approach):又称"语法—翻译法"(grammar-translation approach),其特点有:偏爱"纯洁"英语,即以拉丁语模式和优雅的文学语言为教学内容;重视对语言细节的分析,而不重视对整个篇章的分析;强调阅读与理解,忽视口语与交流;教学活动以语法练习和翻译为主;以教师为中心。

- 结构教学法(structural approach):以语法项目和句式结构为主线安排教学内容,强调共同语法范畴内的词项的替换。结构教学法因一味强调语法形式和孤立的机械性句式练习,却忽视它们在实际情景中的应用而受到批评。

- 情景教学法(situational approach):又称"听说法"(aural-oral approach)。该教学法接受语言的交际性,主张把对象语的语言材料编织在精心设计的情景中来教授。该教学法因强调情景对话和角色表演而被认为优于语法—翻译法和结构法,但它的实质仍是语法的(情景是按语法设计的),以教师为中心的。

- 认知法(cognitive approach):它追求学习者对语言体系和规则的内化,强调语言能力和交际能力的培养,重视语法规则以及"四会"(会听、会说、会读、会写)能力的平衡发展。

- 意念—功能教学法(notional-functional approach):所谓"意念"是指说话人要表达的意思;而"功能"则是指用语言来做什么。例如,"Would you please tell me how to get to the library?"这句话所要表达的"意念"就是"询问",其"功能"则是"问路"。"意念"属语义—语法范畴,"功能"属交际功能范畴。该教学法的最大优点是把抽象的语言形式与实际生活情景和特定文化联系起来。它的另一大优点是能最大程度激活学习者的学习动力。其不足之处有三:一是语言中往往并不存在一对一的"意念—功能";二是不可能把语言现象都归在"意念—功能"之下;三是仍将语言看成孤立的结构单位,因而并不十分有利于交际能力的培养。

- 交际教学法(communicative approach):其目的在于培养学习者的交际能力,并强调交际的过程。所谓交际能力(communicative competence),包括语用能力(如话语功能,适当的文体、文化规则等)和语言能力(如语音、词汇、句法等知识)。教学目标是教授那些能够表达不同"功能"的语言形式,即学生在交际中最可能使用的语言。该教学法的基石是"意念—功能法"和"功能法"。目前,在我国的英语教学中,该教学法已得到广泛的应用。

- 十足的交际法(fully communicative approach):该教学法是传统语法教学的一个极端。它强调语言能力不过是交际能力的一部分,声称"我们要教的是用语言来进行的交际,而不是服务于交际的语言"。它认为教师只要能把学生置于交际活动中,就可以使他们自然而然地学到语言。因此,它显然忽视了必要的语言知识的作用。
- 交际—语法教学法(communicative-grammatical approach):这是近年来部分国内外学者提出的一个新的教学法理论。其主要思想是:应该用新的眼光来看待语法教学。它认为,语法对语言技能和交际能力的培养也有重要作用;语法教学与交际法之间并没有根本的冲突。因此,有必要在交际法中加入直接的语法教学。

第三,针对学生的实际的英语教学对策研究。例如:不同学习法、兴趣和动机对学习的影响及其教学对策研究,不同个性(内向型、外向型)对学习的影响以及教学对策研究,正迁移(positive transfer)和负迁移(negative transfer)①下的教学研究等。

第四,新的教学理念的研究,如"英语教学与素质教育"、"启发式教学"、"因材施教"、"以学生为中心"、"面向21世纪"等教学理念的研究。

第五,教学设备与教育技术的研究,如多媒体辅助教学、计算机辅助教学。

第六,课堂教学研究,如教学组织、教师的语言艺术等。

第七,教材的分析与评价研究。

第八,听、说、读、写等教学环节的研究。

11.3.4　英语专业毕业论文语言学类参考选题(范围)

社会语言学及应用语言学类

1. Latin's Influence on the English Vocabulary in the History Perspective
2. The Recognition of Componential Analysis and Its Application
3. On English Language Historical Changes
4. On English Vocabulary Acquisition
5. Study on Compliments

---

① 所谓学习迁移,是指原已学过的知识、技能和方法对后继学习产生的作用和影响。学习迁移有正迁移和负迁移之分,对后继学习产生积极作用和影响的叫正迁移,反之叫负迁移。

6. The Functional Analysis of Advertising Headlines
7. Sexual Differentiation and Sexism in English Language
8. An Exploration of Body Language
9. The Linguistic Characteristics of Advertising English
10. On the Merit and Application of Computer-Assisted Instruction
11. Multiple Intelligence Theory and Language Teaching—Considering Student-Countered
12. Body Language on Nonverbal Communication
13. Analysis of Language Characteristics in Advertising English
14. A Dialectical Analysis of Fussy Expressions in Legal Language
15. Pragmatic Failures in Cross-Cultural Communication
16. The Pragmatic Function of Ambiguity
17. The Functional Analysis of Ambiguity in Advertising English
18. Pragmatic Functions of Address Forms in English
19. Pragmatic Functions of Irony
20. Gender Differences in Conversation
21. The Analysis of Rhetorical Features in Advertising English
22. A Comparative Study of Formation of Words in English and Chinese Advertising
23. A Comparative Study of Words in English and Chinese Advertising
24. A Comparative Study of Figures of Speech in English and Chinese Advertising
25. An Analysis of Factors Affecting College Students' English Autonomous Learning
26. A Pragmatic Analysis of Verbal Humor
27. A Contrastive Study of Courtesy Language in English and Chinese
28. A Semantic Approach to Verbal Humor Analysis
29. The Context Analysis of Humor
30. The Rhetoric Analysis of English News Headline
31. Lexical Features of English News Headline
32. Grammatical Features of News English
33. An Analysis of Ambiguity in English Newspaper Headlines
34. A Comparative Study of English and Chinese Newspaper Headlines
35. A Contrastive Study on Puns Between English and Chinese
36. Cognition and Culture of Metaphor in English and Chinese Language

37. On English Vocabulary Acquisition
38. Translating the Titles of Chinese Classic Poetry
39. Common Errors in Translation: An Analysis
40. English Idioms and the Translation
41. Reflection on the English Taboo Words
42. The Importance of Comprehension in Translating
43. The Importance of Knowledge in Translating
44. Stylistic Comparison Between Broadcast News and Newspaper News
45. News Headlines: Their Features and Style
46. Tendency of the Modern Linguistics
47. The Obstacle of Intercultural Communication
48. The Influence of Cultural Origin of East and West on Intercultural Communication
49. Emotive Factors and English Language Learning
50. The Function of the Cooperative Principle in Improving Harmonious Relationship among People
51. The Study on Relevance Theory in Reading Instruction
52. On the Use of Euphemism—The Purpose and Principles of Euphemism
53. An Exploration of Body Language
54. The Criterion of Poetic Translation
55. The Translation of the English Film Titles
56. A Comparison of English and Chinese Euphemisms
57. The Role of Sentence Production in Vocabulary Learning
58. Cultural Differences Between Chinese and English Idioms
59. Cultural Connotations of Color Words and Their Reflections in English Idioms
60. The Analysis of Chinglish Being Popular in China
61. News Headlines: Their Structures and Features
62. Lexical Cohesion of English
63. Studies in English Implied Conditional Sentences
64. On the English Negative Sentences
65. The Polite Language in English
66. The Features of Black English
67. Lexical Cultural Connotation Comparison Between Chinese and English

教学法类

1. The Application of Schema Theory in Reading Comprehension
2. Body Language in English Teaching
3. The Diversification of English Language Teaching
4. The Present Situation of Bilingual Education
5. Some Designs on English Learning
6. Creating Learning Environments
7. Collaborative Learning: Group Work
8. The Activities Used to Improve the English Teaching Class
9. Practice of Task-Based Teaching Approach Based on Construction
10. Teach Reading in Senior Middle School
11. Cooperative Learning in the Secondary School
12. A Balanced Activities Approach in Communicative Foreign Language Teaching
13. On Communicative Way in Grammar Teaching
14. Culture Education in English Teaching
15. Consideration on Bilingual Teaching
16. Cross-Culture Communication and English Teaching in Middle School
17. The English Teaching Based on Multimedia
18. The Contrast of Middle School Education Between China & West
19. Culture Lead-In in English Teaching
20. Psychological Factors in English Teaching in Middle School
21. Making Use of Resources on the Internet to Assist English Teaching
22. Communicative Language Teaching and the Teaching in English Class
23. Grammar Teaching Within a Communicative Framework
24. Cultural Awareness in English Teaching
25. The Impact of Different Interpersonal Relationship
26. The Social Psychological Factors of Foreign Language Learning
27. On Pair Work and Group Work and Their Use in English Language Teaching
28. Initiation and Situation in English Learning Motivation
29. Cognitive Approach in Oral English Teaching
30. Self-Access Learning's Effects on the Application of the Balanced Activities Approach
31. International Communicative Activities into College English Language Teaching

32. The Application of Communication Approach to English Teaching
33. A Comparative Study of Compliments: Cross-Culture Perspectives
34. Cross-Cultural Communication and English Teaching
35. Increasing Cultural Awareness of English for Middle School Students

11.4　英美文化及中西文化对比

文化是人的思想观念及其物化存在,体现为人的生存方式和生活方式。

1871年英国著名人类学家爱德华·泰勒的《原始文化》可被看做文化学的创始之作。他提出一个经典定义:"所谓文化或文明,乃是包括知识、信仰、艺术、道德、法律、习俗以及包括作为社会成员的个人而获得的其他任何能力、习惯在内的一种综合体。"

《现代汉语词典》(2002)的定义是:"人类在社会历史发展过程中所创造的物质财富和精神财富的总和,特指精神财富,如文学、艺术、教育、科学等。"

《辞海》(1980)的定义是:"从广义来说,指社会历史实践过程中所创造的物质财富和精神财富的总和。从狭义来说,指社会的意识形态,以及与之相适应的制度和组织机构。"

从以上定义可以看出,人们对"文化"有广义的理解和狭义的理解。广义的文化指人类作用于自然界和社会的成果的总和,包括一切物质财富和精神财富。狭义的文化指意识形态所创造的精神财富,包括宗教、信仰、风俗习惯、道德情操、学术思想、文学艺术、科学技术、各种制度等。作为意识形态的文化,是一定社会的政治和经济的反映,又作用于一定社会的政治和经济。每一种社会形态都有与其相适应的文化,每一种文化都随着社会物质生产的发展而发展。社会物质生产发展的连续性,决定文化的发展也具有连续性和历史继承性。随着民族的产生和发展,文化具有了民族性。

英语专业学生撰写文化类毕业(学术)论文,应侧重于对英语国家(特别是英美)民族文化的研究、汉文化与英语国家文化的比较研究以及文化语言、文化与交际之间的关系研究。

11.4.1　文化研究的意义

语言是文化的载体,并对文化起着至关重要的作用。语言和文化相互影响、相互作用,语言不能脱离文化而存在。研究英美文化与英语语言的学习有着密不可分的关系。主要体现在以下几点:

1)探讨与总结英美文化的共性,可研究它们对语言的影响与在语言中的表现。

2) 英语语言与地理、政治、经济、社会及工业变革息息相关,每一次重大的社会变动(如英国历史上 1066 年的诺曼征服,文艺复兴,英国工业革命,美国历史上的西进运动等等),都会有一批相应的词汇特别是习语出现。

3) 可将体现在语言中的英美文化现象与中国文化现象进行比较,找出其中的差异之处,从而最终实现为英语教学服务,使英语学习者全面、准确地掌握英语,以期减少在交际过程中因文化差异而造成的误会。

4) "他山之石,可以攻玉"。英美文化是人类先进文化的重要组成部分,在英美两国分别于 19 世纪与 20 世纪中期成为世界第一强国的过程中,英美文化传统所起的作用不容小觑。我国目前正处于向现代化发展的进程当中,一方面要探索适合我国国情的具有中国特色的现代化道路,另一方面也要吸收人类先进的文化遗产,使得我们在现代化建设过程中少走弯路,少犯错误。在现代化的发展过程中,如何处理好现代化与传统文化的关系,是任何一个国家与民族必须尽最大努力解决好的问题。

11.4.2 英语专业毕业论文英美文化及中西文化对比类参考选题(范围)

1. A Brief Discussion on Cultural Difference Between Chinese and English
2. The Euphemism in English
3. Characteristic and Cultural Differences of the English and Chinese Idioms
4. Culture Differences in English Learning
5. Animal Expressions in Chinese and Western Culture
6. On the Chinese and Western Cultures in Terms of Symbolic Colors
7. Chinese and Western Culture Values in Advertising Language
8. Globalization in Intercultural Communication
9. A Comparison of Color Words Between Chinese and English
10. The Similarities and Differences Between Chinese and English Culture
11. Deep-Structure Transfer in Cross-Cultural Communication
12. Cultural Differences in Nonverbal Communication
13. English and Chinese Idioms
14. Proverbs and Culture
15. Body Language Functions in Different Cultures
16. Difference and Similarities of the Word: Black
17. The Differences Between China and America in Food Culture
18. Euphemism——Their Construction and Application
19. Cultural Differences Seen from the Chinese and Western Customs
20. Exotic Cultures Influence on English Vocabulary

21. The Future Emergence of Chinese English
22. Euphemism in English
23. The Differences Between Chinese and Western Education
24. Differences Between American and English on Lexis
25. Similarities and Differences in the Connotation of Animal Words in English
26. Analysis on the Difference of Dietetic Culture Between China and Western Countries
27. Differences Between American and British English
28. Cultural Differences in Idioms
29. Religious Cultural Factors Affecting the Differences of Meanings of Words
30. A Brief Comparison of Spring Festival & Christmas Day
31. On the Cultural Connotation Between Chinese and English Vocabulary
32. The Differences of Family Values Between China and America
33. Comparative Study of Chinese and American Young Generations' Values
34. The Comparison of Chinese and Western Interpersonal Relationships
35. Cultural Differences in English-Chinese Communication

第十二章　英语专业毕业论文实例

12.1　英美文学类毕业论文实例

On Attitudes Toward Marriage in *Pride and Prejudice* with the Theory of Hierarchy of Needs by Maslow

Ⅰ. Introduction

A. Situation of Study

Pride and Prejudice has been studied thoroughly after its publication. As one of the most widely chosen topics of the novel, the attitudes towards love and marriage have been extensively concentrated on. For years, scholars have studied this topic from various aspects, and a large number of critics in China have associated the topic with sociology, such as Hu Qing's *On Attitudes Toward Marriage in Pride and Prejudice*. Recently, some scholars also choose to adopt psychological theory in their analyses. For instance, in *A Preliminary Discussion of Maslow's Theory of Hierarchy of Needs Reflected in Pride and Prejudice*, Huang Rui and Jia Peng have used this theory to analyze the different couples' orientations of marriage in the novel. Maslow's Hierarchy of Needs Theory, a theory that has long been regarded as important in the realm of humanistic psychology, has often been used to interpret the characteristic and pursuit of a certain figure in a literary work in recent years.

B. Thesis Statement

According to Maslow's Hierarchy of Needs Theory, the differences of the four couples' attitudes toward marriage in *Pride and Prejudice* are mainly due to different human motivations, which vary from the physiological needs, the safety needs, the love needs and the esteem needs to the need for self-actualization respectively. That is to say, it is these human needs that make the couples choose different marriages.

C. Purpose and Significance of the Study

Love and marriage are the eternal themes of countless literature works. Jane Austen's *Pride and Prejudice* has also focused on these topics and offered readers a chance to get closer to the real life of the British Middle Class in the 19th century. Instead of following the former critics' way to analyze the marriages in the story with the ideas in sociology, emphasizing how economic and social conditions would affect marriage, this thesis will use Maslow's Hierarchy of Needs Theory and try to interpret the characters' different choices of marriage by exploring their inner motivations. Such an analysis, which does not confine itself merely within a certain period of time and society but extends the theme by connecting it with the inner needs of the human race, will help readers in modern times understand the attitudes toward marriage in the book much better.

II. Maslow's Hierarchy of Needs Theory

A. Background: Humanistic Psychology and Abraham Maslow

Humanistic psychology is a school of psychology that emerged in the 1950s and has its root in existentialist thought. Many psychologists, like Abraham Maslow and Carl Rogers, believe that psychoanalysis has paid too much attention to mentally ill or neurotic people and has overlooked research on the meaning of behaviors and on the positive development of people. Therefore, the most distinctive feature of humanistic psychology is that instead of focusing on the problematic sides of the human race, humanistic psychology pays more attention to the positive aspects and values of mankind and put more emphasis on an individual's development, which can be called "self-actualization". That is to say, humanistic psychology values positive psychological development and personal improvement.

Many psychologists have made significant impacts on people's understanding of the world. Abraham Maslow is one of them. Abraham Maslow (1908—1970), was an American psychologist. He is noted for his conceptualization of a "hierarchy of human needs" and is considered as the founder of humanistic psychology because of his unique and inspiring thought.

B. A Brief Introduction to the Theory

1. Basic Contents of the Theory

As a humanistic psychologist, Abraham Maslow holds that every individual has a strong desire to realize his or her full potential, and to reach a level of self-actualization. To prove that humans are not simply blindly reacting to situations, but trying to accomplish something greater, Maslow studied mentally healthy individuals instead of people with serious psychological problems.

A visual aid Maslow created to explain his theory, which he called the Hierarchy of Needs, is a pyramid depicting the levels of human needs, psychological and physical. It was proposed in his 1943 paper *A Theory of Human Motivation*. At the bottom of the pyramid are the basic needs of a human being, which are called "physiological needs". The next level is "safety needs". These two steps are important to the physical survival of a person. Once these needs are fulfilled, people are likely to attempt to accomplish more. The third level of need is "love and belonging". The fourth level is "esteem needs", and this is a level of success and status to some degree. The top of the pyramid is the "self-actualization", which only occurs when individuals' four levels of lower needs are gratified and reach a state of harmony. [①]

2. Characteristics of the Basic Needs

In the first place, these basic needs are related to each other, the appearance of one need usually resting on the prior satisfaction of another, more pre-potent need. However, the sequence of these five levels of needs is not fixed or rigid all the time. Sometimes, the hierarchy can be reversed to some extent.

In the second place, when the human organism is dominated by a certain need, the whole philosophy of the future tends also to change.

What's more, sometimes certain people stick to some lower needs for such a long time that their higher needs might be permanently lowered and deadened.

C. Function and Significance of the Theory

Maslow's thinking was surprisingly original—most psychologists before him had been concerned with the abnormal and the ill only. His theory has reflected the general rule of human behavior and psychological activity. His theory—studying people by exploring and analyzing human needs and their relationship with human behavior—has given rise to several different therapies, all guided by the idea that people possess the inner resources for growth and healing. Its influence has even extended beyond psychology and the theory has been frequently used in courses of marketing. His theory has offered us a new way to analyze a person's choices and behavior in his or her life and thus has helped us to get a clearer understanding of human nature and human needs.

III. Analysis on Attitudes Toward Marriage in *Pride and Prejudice*

A. Plot Summary

Published in 1813, *Pride and Prejudice* is Jane Austen's second novel. The story was set in the aristocratic society of early 19th century England. The novel mainly

---

① Abraham H. Maslow, *Motivation and Personality* (Beijing: Huaxia Publishing House, 1987), 53.

portrays marriages of four couples—Elizabeth and Darcy, Jane and Bingley, Lydia and Wickham, and Charlotte and Collins.

　　Living in the country near a small town named Meryton, the Bennets has five daughters, and Jane, Elizabeth and Lydia are the three of them. Charlotte is a close friend of Elizabeth. Mr. Bingley, a young gentleman with a large fortune, has moved to the countryside, and Jane soon falls in love with him. Darcy is a friend of Bingley. Though Bingley soon establishes a good relationship with the country people, Darcy is regarded as a proud and disagreeable man at the beginning. He has gone through a lot of troubles and misunderstanding until he has won Elizabeth's love and respect at last. Collins is Mr. Bennet's cousin and, as Mr. Bennet has no son, heir to his estate. After being rejected by Elizabeth, he immediately turns to Charlotte and finally gets married with her. Wickham is an old acquaintance of Darcy from childhood. Acting as a charming gentleman, he is in fact a greedy and wicked person. He finally persuades Lydia to elope with him and does not marry her until Darcy forces him to.

B. Marriages Mainly Based on Physiological Needs and Safety Needs

1. Introduction of Physiological Needs and Safety Needs

　　Physiological needs are the lowest level of needs in Maslow's theory. They consist of needs for oxygen, food, water, sex or something like that. They are basic biological needs which are essential to an individual's survival.① And they are also the strongest needs, because if a person were deprived of all these needs, there is no way for him or her to live in this world. In this case, these physiological needs always come first in a person's search for satisfaction.

　　Safety needs are the most important needs which will become top priorities and begin to dominate a person's choice and behavior when an individual's physical needs have been satisfied relatively.② These needs, including needs for personal security, financial security, health and well-being, are significant elements for an individual's life and happiness as well. Therefore, they tend to influence a person's behavior and choice greatly.

2. Lydia Bennet and George Wickham: A Marriage Totally Driven by Physiological Needs

　　In *Pride and Prejudice*, Lydia Bennet and George Wickham elope at first and are forced to get married when they have been located by Darcy. What they have done be-

---

① Maslow, 42.
② Maslow, 44.

comes a scandal and the reputation of the Bennet has nearly been ruined because of their inappropriate deeds. According to the couples' words and actions in the novel, it is obvious that their marriage is driven by nothing but their basic physiological needs.

Lydia's choices are limited to the physiological level all the time, so she takes her sexual need as the most important thing when she wants to choose a spouse. This is fully confirmed by her deeds in the novel.

From the very beginning of the story, Lydia is always flirting with almost every man she meets, especially those soldiers who have moved to Meryton. She falls into extreme misery when she knows that the regiment is going to leave Meryton for Brighton and she goes into rapture when she is invited to go to Brighton with Mrs. Foster, the wife of the Colonel of the regiment. Her most imperative need has been described clearly by her imagination about her life in Brighton. In her imagination, Brighton will be full of officers and she is "the objection of attention to tens and to scores of them at present unknown"[①]. What's more, she sees herself "tenderly flirting with at least six officers at once"[②]. Apparently, Lydia indulges in her need for sex and asks for nothing else. In her eyes those officers in red uniforms are absolutely the most attractive men in the world so that she is always lost in them. It is also her strong need for sex that makes her elope with Wickham without any further consideration. Just like her sister Elizabeth says, she is "wholly unable to ward off any portion of that universal contempt which her rage for admiration will excite"[③]. According to Maslow's Hierarchy of Needs Theory, when a human being is dominated by a certain need, "the whole philosophy of the future tends also to change"[④]. Under the direction of such a certain single need, both of what an individual thinks and what an individual does are only to satisfy this single need. He or she lives for this need solely. As a result, Lydia's values and her perspectives of life are confined to the satisfaction of the lowest level of human needs—the physiological needs. Thus, she chooses Wickham, a man who has nothing but a handsome appearance, as her husband, for her attitude toward marriage is completely based on her need for sex.

George Wickham is a kind of men called "playboy". He chases women to meet his needs for money and sex rather than love.

First, as for Wickham, marriage is an easy way to gain a large sum of money.

[①] Jane Austen, *Pride and Prejudice* (Kuitun: Yili People Press, 2003), 266.
[②] Austen, 266.
[③] Austen, 264.
[④] Abraham H. Maslow, "A Theory of Human Motivation", *Psychological Review*, no. 50 (1943), 374.

Thus, as soon as he notices that Mary King is much richer than Elizabeth, he turns to chase that rich girl without any hesitation. Second, as for Wickham, going after a woman is simply to meet his sexual need. And this is exactly why he chooses Lydia. Obviously, there is no sign to prove that Wickham actually loves Lydia. The reason he selects Lydia is simply that he would like to have a woman to accompany him during his trip and Lydia happens to be the girl who can be seduced easily, because "neither her virtue nor her understanding would preserve her from falling an easy prey"[1]. Even though he marries Lydia at last, it is not because he has eventually fallen in love with her. It is because his debts will be paid and he will get a position in the army with the help of Darcy. Maslow's Hierarchy of Needs Theory believes that people's different choices are mainly due to their different needs. When it comes to Wickham, his choice only comes from his demand for money and sex.

In brief, physiological needs are "the most pre-potent of all needs"[2] and if a human being lacks everything in life, it is most likely that his or her major motivation would be the physiological needs rather than any others. In this way, it is reasonable that Lydia and Wickham choose to marry each other because their choices are totally motivated by their basic physiological needs. After they have got married, Wickham's affection for Lydia "soon sunk into indifference"[3]. Consequently, the couple's marriage can only satisfy their physiological needs.

3. Charlotte Lucas and William Collins: A Marriage Based on Physiological Needs and Safety Needs

The marriage between Charlotte Lucas and William Collins is decided soon after Collins has been refused by Elizabeth. The reason why Charlotte and Collins can come to an agreement at such a high speed is that both of them are eager to marry someone. In the Hierarchy of Needs Theory, all kinds of desires in our daily life are only the "means"[4] which assist us in achieving our goals but not actual goals themselves. Maslow holds that any motivated behavior, or any desire, should be seen as "a channel through which many basic needs may be simultaneously expressed or satisfied"[5]. As a matter of fact, Charlotte and Collins both use "marriage" as a tool to satisfy their own basic needs. Marriage is only a means, not the ultimate aim.

---

[1] Austen, 316.
[2] Maslow, "A Theory of Human Motivation", 373.
[3] Austen, 432.
[4] Maslow, 25.
[5] Maslow, 27.

Charlotte's choice of marriage is determined by her physiological needs and safety needs. First of all, Charlotte, like all the young women of small fortune at that time in England, always considers marriage as her "only honorable provision"①. The marriage with Collins will give her a permanent home and protect her from lacking various basic physiological needs such as need for a shelter, need for food, or something like that.

Apart from that, man is a "perpetually wanting animal"②, so new needs would appear as long as the more pre-potent ones have been satisfied. Therefore, when her physiological needs can be guaranteed, Charlotte's safety needs become high on her priority list. The ideal marriage that Charlotte longs for is one which is able to offer her a comfortable home and a stable relationship with the surroundings. Being a wife of a clergyman like Collins, Charlotte will get all these things with no doubt. Her life will consist of all sorts of housework and necessary communications with people in her neighborhood. All things seem fine and steady, nothing can do harm to her personal security and nothing unpredictable will ever happen in her future. As a result, just like Charlotte says in the novel, "considering Mr. Collins's character, connections, and situation in life, I am convinced that my chance of happiness with him is as fair as most people can boast on entering the marriage state"③. Of course, when Charlotte mentions "happiness", she means the fulfillment of her physiological needs and safety needs.

Perhaps, one may wonder if Charlotte would have some higher needs, such as need for love. Unfortunately, she does not have any of these higher needs. Her attitudes and behaviors before and after getting married do not give readers any trace of her affection for Collins. While she accepts Collins's proposal, Charlotte thinks that Collins is "neither sensible nor agreeable"④, and she also knows that Collins's attachment to her can be unreal. However, Charlotte has predicted that all her physiological needs and safety needs can be met through this marriage, so she focuses on the fulfillment of these basic needs and things like love are neither important nor necessary to her. Even after getting married, Charlotte still keeps Collins out of her life and tries her best to forget his existence. It seems that she have got used to the life without love. The explanation of this situation can be touched in Maslow's theory as

---

① Austen, 141.
② Maslow, "A Theory of Human Motivation", 395.
③ Austen, 144.
④ Austen, 141.

well. He believes that sometimes, in certain people the level of aspiration may be permanently deadened or lowered, "the less pre-potent goals may simply be lost, and may disappear forever"①. Living in an environment which lacks love for a long time, a rational woman like Charlotte has learned to concentrate on her lower needs and has got used to life without love.

Compared with Charlotte, Collins's choice of marriage is largely controlled by his safety needs.

At the beginning of the novel, it is known that Collins had become a clergyman and is going to inherit Mr. Bennet's estates after Mr. Bennet's death. Clearly, Collins's social status and the fortune that he is going to possess can sufficiently meet most of his physiological needs. In fact, it is almost impossible for people to have all their basic needs completely satisfied all the time. Thus, it is common that most normal people in society always have their basic needs partially satisfied. Collins has been content with most of his physiological needs, so he will have an increasing need for safety. His own words have also made this point quite clear when he proposes to Elizabeth. He thinks that getting married is a good way for him to "set the example of matrimony in his parish"②. Moreover, he declares that this marriage will please his patroness. Because Collins owes his present position to Lady Catherine, a wealthy woman who helps him to get the position as a clergyman of the district, he will do whatever he can to cater to the lady in order to protect his job and his personal security. In this way, since Lady Catherine has suggested that he should get married soon, Collins will absolutely strive to spot a bride as quickly as possible. When it comes to Collins, marriage is not a combination of two persons who love each other, but a practice which can protect his wealth and offer him a stable position in the society. He would like to marry any woman who will be the possible person to help him to achieve his goal. In this case, when he has been refused by Elizabeth, he is not really frustrated and soon turns to Charlotte. He does need a wife, a wife who will support him so that he can gain Lady. Catherine's favor and maintain his social position.

In a word, Charlotte actually marries Collins's status and fortune since these will meet her physiological needs and safety needs. Collins marries Charlotte because he is in need of this legal relationship to please his patroness and protect his safety needs. It is their physiological needs and safety needs that make them choose each other.

---

① Maslow, "A Theory of Human Motivation", 386.
② Austen, 121.

C. Marriages Mainly Based on Love Needs and Esteem Needs

1. Introduction of Love Needs and Esteem Needs

After physiological and safety needs are fulfilled, love needs will appear. Human beings need to feel a sense of belonging and acceptance.① As the third layer of human needs in Maslow's hierarchy of needs, the love needs involve needs for emotionally based relationship in general, such as friendship, intimacy, family and so on.

Esteem needs are the needs for respect and esteem.② They demonstrate the normal human desire to be accepted and valued by others. All people in our society have a need or desire for a stable, firmly based high evaluation of themselves, for self-respect, or self-esteem, and for the esteem of others.

2. Jane Bennet and Charles Bingley: A Marriage Mainly Based on Love Needs

Physiological and safety needs might have something to do with Jane's choice of marriage, but it is love needs that contribute to her final choice. Generally speaking, Jane's situation in the novel is quite analogous to Charlotte's situation. She is also well-educated but has no fortune because she is not allowed to inherit her father's estates. If she cannot have a rich husband as soon as possible, she might live the rest of her life in poverty and misery. As a result, we cannot deny that when Jane hears about Bingley for the first time, it is possible that his wealth and social status are very attractive to her.

Nevertheless, it is not her physiological and safety needs but her love needs that make her elect Bingley as her favorite. Although the hierarchy of human needs has a certain sequence, such a sequence is not completely rigid all the time.③ In Jane's case, it is evident that her expectation for love is much stronger than her other lower needs. There is a possibility that Jane is especially in need of a sense of belonging and acceptance, since she does so much to make her dream come true. This can be sensed in her sister's words. Elizabeth says that Jane is "a great deal too apt"④ and Jane is likely to "like people in general"⑤. If she does not have such a strong demand for love and belonging, Jane will not behaved like her sister described. And her love needs become even stronger when Bingley catches her eyes. She sees Bing-

---

① Maslow, 49.
② Maslow, 51.
③ Maslow, "A Theory of Human Motivation", 386.
④ Austen, 16.
⑤ Id.

ley as a man who deserves her love, so she strives to get intimate with him. Even after Bingley goes back to London, she still hopes that she will have the chance to see Bingley again and that they will have a closer relationship. If she pays more attention to other basic needs such as a good house to live in or a large sum of money that can ensure her daily expense, she will give up her love for Bingley and goes to search for another man who is capable of providing her with a comfortable and stable life. The difference between Jane and Charlotte is that Jane's attitude toward marriage is not limited to the basic physiological and safety needs. Just like she has said, "Do anything rather than marry without affection."① Her physiological and safety needs might take effect at first, but it is definitely her love needs that persuade her to make her choice at last.

Compared with Jane, Charles Bingley's choice is only based on his love needs, for his lower physical needs have already been satisfied. Bingley is a man from upper class and has inherited the property to an amount of nearly an hundred thousand pounds from his father. His status and fortune make him free from any lack of basic physical needs. In this way, "if both the physiological and the safety needs are fairly well gratified, then there will emerge the love and affection and belonging needs"②. Now, Bingley's pre-potent needs are his love needs and he will assume that he needs to be loved and to love someone else. And just at that moment, he meets Jane and almost falls in love with her at first sight. Although his love has been hindered by his sisters and by his friend Darcy because Jane's status and her humble relatives might have negative influence on Bingley's reputation, eventually he still chooses Jane to be his wife. At that time, all his actions, including his choice of wife, are meant to meet his strong desire for love. So he ultimately marries Jane because they love each other and this makes Bingley's love needs gratified.

In brief, the most essential needs that stimulate Jane and Bingley to choose their spouse are their love needs and in turn their marriage has fulfilled their needs.

3. Elizabeth Bennet and Fitzwilliam Darcy: A Marriage Determined by Love Needs and Esteem Needs

Being the protagonists of the novel, Elizabeth and Darcy's marriage is definitely the most dramatic and ideal one in the whole story. Their marriage is "a successful

---

① Austen, 417.
② Maslow, "A Theory of Human Motivation", 380.

combination between love and respect"①. Their marriage eventually perfects their love and esteem, and chances are that their marriage will lead them to self-actualization.

Elizabeth's choice is encouraged by her love needs and esteem needs and perhaps esteem needs play a more important role in her decision.

Like Jane and Charlotte, Elizabeth is an excellent woman without enough fortune, so her physiological needs and safety needs should be as strong as Charlotte's. And in fact she does not consider these needs nonexistent, for sometimes she does think about them. For instance, when she is going on a trip and pays a visit to Darcy's beautiful house in Pemberley, she feels that "to be the mistress of Pemberley might be something"②. Evidently, for one time, she is really attracted by his wealth and she does hope that her basic needs can be satisfied. Yet she does not merely regard marriage as a way to get her enough food and a warm shelter. She does not tend to marry a rich husband without any other consideration because she has put more emphasis on "the desire of being well married"③. Jane Austen describes Elizabeth as a woman "with more quickness of observation and less pliancy of temper than her sister, and with a judgment, too, unassailed by any attention to herself"④. As a consequence, in Elizabeth's opinion, her hierarchy of needs is different from that of ordinary people, for she thinks highly of the higher needs, or spiritual needs. Maslow has explained such a situation as an important exception—the ones that involve ideals, high social standards, high values and the like might become martyrs, for they are likely to give up everything for the sake of particular ideal, or value.⑤ When she refuses Darcy's proposal for the first time, her esteem needs have greatly exceeded other needs. She can not accept Darcy's love because Darcy does not regard her as an equal individual and hurts her self-esteem greatly. She longs for respect from her lover, but Darcy can not give her enough respect as she has expected. Her esteem needs do not allow her to accept a marriage like this.

If Darcy does not continue to try to understand and respect Elizabeth, the story of this couple may just end up here. It is not an accident that Elizabeth accepts his proposal at the end of the novel, for this time, her dreams of love and esteem are both realized. Darcy treats her relatives friendly and respectfully when Elizabeth is

---

① 季念:"婚姻的追求与层次的需要",载《衡阳师范学院学报》第 25 卷(2004),第 94 页。
② Austen, 279.
③ Austen, 28.
④ Austen, 16.
⑤ Maslow, "A Theory of Human Motivation", 387.

going traveling with them. What's more, Darcy does not look down upon her when he hears of Lydia's elopement, and he even makes great effort to help her family get out of the trouble. All these things make Elizabeth has a feeling that she is understood and respected by Darcy, and she has realized Darcy's merits at the same time. This makes her come to the conclusion that Darcy is "exactly the man who, in disposition and talents, would most suit her"①. She is sure that her marriage with Darcy will definitely gratify her love and esteem needs. The real love, according to Erich Fromm, should contain respect as one of the essential elements.② With no doubt, the love that she receives from Darcy, has got respect involved.

Darcy's attitude toward marriage is largely controlled by his love needs. His physiological and safety needs have already been gratified. His fortune and social status have ensured that he will live a rich and steady life. In this way, it is natural that his actions are driven by some higher needs. For him, the most important thing in his life at the moment is to fulfill his needs for love and belonging, and he thinks of Elizabeth as the ideal woman who can do him a favor. Although at first he has made it clear to his friends that Elizabeth's manners are not those of the fashionable world, he is soon attracted by their "easy playfulness"③. From then on, he grasps nearly every opportunity to communicate with Elizabeth and to have a better understanding of her. What he has done is encouraged by his needs for love. Just like Maslow has mentioned in his book, when an individual is in need of love, he or she will hunger for affectionate relations with people in general, namely, for a place in his group, and he will strive with great intensity to achieve this goal.④

Yet, at first, he keeps reminding himself of the inappropriate social status of her family and avoids showing his true feeling for her, because his high self-esteem gives him no reason to admit that he loves Elizabeth, a woman from a family much lower than his own. Therefore, Darcy's first proposal may sound somewhat ridiculous. He does express his love for Elizabeth, but at the same time, he also emphasizes her "inferiority"⑤, and makes his proposal like a "degradation"⑥. In his opinion, his love and proposal have taken his pride as a sacrifice. Such an idea implies that his

---

① Austen, 350.
② Erich Fromm, *The Art of Love* (Hefei: Anhui Literature and Art Publishing House, 1986), 22.
③ Austen, 26.
④ Maslow, 49.
⑤ Austen, 217.
⑥ Id.

love is still too superficial. Clearly, this immature idea of love has already offended, or even hurt Elizabeth, so he has been turned down completely. From Maslow's point of view, the love needs involve both giving and receiving love.① Consequently, Darcy's immature love receives no reply at first. But Darcy does not give up easily, his strong need for love makes him improve himself. This need urges him to try to accept Elizabeth's relatives, her social status and all other things in her life and urges him to respect her feelings. It is his love needs that make him do whatever he can to give Elizabeth a hand when he hears that Lydia has eloped with Wickham. He has also told the truth in the last part of the novel that all his actions are based on "the wish of giving happiness"② to Elizabeth. This time, his deeds have absolutely won Elizabeth's love and respect and his proposal is accepted. At last, his love has been accepted by Elizabeth and his love needs have been gratified. Apart from that, even though he does not show any strong need for esteem because his esteem needs have been met by his high social status, he has won the respect of Elizabeth at the same time when he has won her love.

When Elizabeth and Darcy have been content with their love and esteem needs, the need of a higher level—need for self-actualization will emerge naturally. Will their marriage eventually fulfill this kind of need? As far as this author is concerned, it is quite possible that they will finally get to self-actualization with the help of their happy marriage life. According to Maslow's theory, the need for self-actualization is a desire to become more and more what one is, to become everything that one is capable of becoming.③ A person who tries to meet the need for self-actualization will explore his or her potentialities and make full use of them to achieve his or her goal. Maslow also mentions that the specific form of self-actualization will of course vary greatly from person to person.④ Just like what Elizabeth has wished, their marriage is a union that must be advantageous to both of them, for Darcy's mind may be "softened"⑤ and his manners can be "improved"⑥ by Elizabeth's "ease and liveliness"⑦, and she will benefit from Darcy's "judgment, information, and knowledge of

---

① Maslow, 51.
② Austen, 409.
③ Maslow, 53.
④ Maslow, "A Theory of Human Motivation", 383.
⑤ Austen, 351.
⑥ Id.
⑦ Id.

the world"①. In this way, the couple both have benefited from the marriage and can improve themselves to some degree.

IV. Conclusion

A. Different Human Needs as the Inner Motivations of Different Marriages

Some readers may see the first two marriages mentioned in this thesis as unhappy and even complete failures. On the other hand, most readers might believe that Jane and Elizabeth's marriages are successful and the typical happy ones. Nevertheless, the aim of this thesis is not to evaluate whether these four marriages are successful or not, but to understand their choices of spouse and marriage by looking into the inner needs which motivate these characters to make these choices. This study clearly reveals that Lydia and Wickham's marriage is controlled by their basic physiological needs, Charlotte and Collins's marriage is determined by their physiological and safety needs, Jane and Bingley's marriage is mainly decided by their love needs, and Elizabeth and Darcy's marriage, the so-called most successful one, is mainly guided by their love and esteem needs. In one word, these people, smart or foolish, educated or vulgar, all take their inner human needs as the base of their choice of marriage. Generally speaking, different attitudes toward love and marriage result from different human needs.

B. Significance of the Result of this Analysis in Modern Society

Furthermore, having a clear idea of these characters' choices of marriage will have something to do with our attitudes toward marriage at present as well. Living in modern times when society is developing at a breath-taking speed, although we think that we are now much more civilized than those characters in the 19th century, our basic needs are still the same ones which they had two hundred years ago. It is the common experience of anthropologists that people, even in different societies or different times, are much more alike than we would think.② In a modern society, we still have all sorts of human needs and it is these needs that inspire us to make choices in our daily life. In the case of marriage, it is true that the elements which can satisfy our physiological and safety needs such as money and high social status are necessary for a better life, but if people are longing for a really happy marriage, they must take the higher spiritual needs into consideration. In order to be really contented and happy, one should choose a marriage which is able to fulfill both physical

---

① Austen, 351.
② Maslow, "A Theory of Human Motivation", 389.

and spiritual needs on the basis of love and respect.

Bibliography

Austen, Jane. *Pride and Prejudice*. Kuitun: Yili People Press, 2003.

Austen-Leigh, James Edward. *Memoir of Jane Austen*. Oxford: Oxford University Press, 1991.

Fromm, Erich. *The Art of Love*. Hefei: Anhui Literature and Art Publishing House, 1986.

Maslow, Abraham H. *Motivation and Personality*. Beijing: Huaxia Publishing House, 1987.

Maslow, Abraham H. "A Theory of Human Motivation", *Psychological Review*, no. 50 (1943): 370—396.

Stone, Lawrence. *The Family, Sex and Marriage in England 1500-1800*. New York: Harper & Row, 1977.

Teachman, Debra. *Understanding Pride and Prejudice: A Student Casebook to Issues, Sources and Historical Documents*. Westport, CT: Greenwood Press, 1997.

管先恒:"《傲慢与偏见》中的婚姻面面观",载《安徽工业大学学报》第20卷(2003),第78—79页。

胡晴:"论《傲慢与偏见》中的婚恋观",载《读与写杂志》第2卷(2008),第165页。

黄睿、贾鹏:"《傲慢与偏见》中体现的马斯洛需要层次理论",载《攀枝花学院学报》第26卷(2009),第94—96页。

季念:"婚恋的追求与需要的层次",载《衡阳师范学院学报》第25卷(2004),第92—95页。

梁亚敏:"《傲慢与偏见》中男主人公达西的性格分析",载《时代文学》第19卷(2008),第49—51页。

吴伟仁:《英国文学史及选读》,外语教学与研究出版社2001年版。

张世富:"人本主义心理学与马斯洛的需要层次论",载《学术探索》第9卷(2003),第66—68页。

(论文作者:郑州大学外语学院2006级学生　赵芳晔)

12.2 翻译类毕业论文实例

On Transliteration

Chapter 1 Introduction

1.1 What Is Transliteration?

As is known to all, translation of high quality will help a reader understand the original reading materials better. Since globalization in politics, economy, culture and many other aspects has gradually spread every corner of the world, translation, as an important means of communication among people across the globe, has played a more and more crucial role in our daily life. And as one of the main methods of translation, transliteration is supposed to be greatly valued. How to get an accurate and sound translation has become a heated topic.

What is transliteration? Transliteration is defined as "to represent or spell in the character of another alphabet" by the Merriam-Webster online dictionary. That is to say, to transliterate is to write words or letters of a different alphabet of language.

Transliteration is widely used in a variety of different fields, such as newspapers, advertisement, the Internet and so on, especially in news English, because news English involves large numbers of different states or communities. The vocabulary of news English is really large and various and new words are appearing daily with the development of news English itself, which has become an obstacle for understanding the reading materials and E-C translation. Therefore, it is very crucial for translators to make sure that appropriate and sound transliteration is made so as to help readers have comprehensive understanding of the original reading materials.

On the other hand, it is also necessary to study and improve the C-E transliteration because an outstanding transliteration does great help to propagate our Chinese civilization and facilitate understanding and friendship between Chinese people and people from different countries across the earth. Since quite a lot of people from English speaking countries learn little about our country and our traditional civilization for various kinds of reasons in the past years and even some of them hold the opinion that all Chinese men are still wearing long hair. It is common that our great treasure, Chinese traditional herbal medicine, is considered as witchcraft in many countries, which is the consequence of a lack of communication. In order to eliminate this kind of misunderstanding, we should have our traditional culture studied and understood by people from other countries and it certainly will entail translators to express our civilization to them. And we all know transliteration could play an important part in translating many Chinese specialized terms to English. Therefore, it is essential for translators to propagate our Chinese traditional culture and leave the world a better and more positive image of China through profound transliteration.

1.2 History of Transliteration in E-C and C-E Translation

Transliteration has undergone several stages of development in China. After the May 4th Movement of 1919, transliterated words of Indo-European language gradually appear in the sight of Chinese people. Many Chinese young people began to learn Western science and languages. It is known to all that language is the product of historic development. The close cultural and commercial communication between Chinese and Western people gradually broadened the range of transliterated words. However, from the establishment of PRC in 1949 to the late 1970s, transliteration was almost replaced by liberal translation. In 1980s, transliterated words came into our sight again as large numbers of joint ventures were founded in China. And in 1990s, transliterated words were more popular as a result of the reform and opening-up policy. And after entry into the 21st century, more and more transliterated words have sprung up with deeper communication of politics, economy and culture among countries around the world. Therefore, it is necessary to understand and study features and theories of transliteration.

Transliteration and liberal translation have their own advantages, which make them preferred in different aspects by different people. Generally speaking, scientists tend to adopt transliteration so as to have the original information expressed to readers accurately and completely while literary men prefer liberal translation in order to make the translation more graceful and beautiful. And young generation, especially those in large cities, might prefer to use transliterated words while the elder are more accustomed to accept liberally-translated words.[1] Whether we should choose transliteration or liberal translation reflects the orientation of cultural value. Even for a group of people who live in the same city, their various occupations, ages, education or mental conditions will have influence on their orientation of external words,[2] and

---

[1] 李玄玉:《略谈汉语音译词的地域文化差异》,载《语言与翻译》2002 年第 3 期。
[2] 李玄玉:《新时期的增义音译词》,载张新武、高莉琴主编:《新疆大学语言文化国际学术研讨会论文集》,新疆大学出版社 2002 年版,第 32 页。

drive them to choose one of the two different ways of translation.

1.3 Transliteration Can Not Be Neglected

It is impossible to judge which one is better. Both transliteration and liberal translation are essential for a translator to make a good translation work. But it seems that some people hold the mistaken opinion that transliteration is always considered as an impropriate means when translating English to Chinese or Chinese to English and only on occasions that liberal translation can not be used will translators adopt transliteration. However, the above idea is actually incorrect. We can see that transliteration has quite a long history in E-C translation. Take the word "logic" for example: our great translator Yan Fu used to translate "logic" into "名学" by the means of liberal translation, which was not widely accepted. Later he changed the translation to "伦理学" and this translation seemed to be adopted. During a certain time the transliterated word "逻辑" and the liberally-translated word "伦理学" were both used by people. But the transliterated word "逻辑" is more popular and is widely used in our text books, newspapers and daily life, which strongly embodies that good transliteration also plays an important role in E-C translation.

The quality of the transliteration is one of the factors that determine the translation quality, so how to get the transliteration appropriate and easily accepted is a key component of translation theories. And this essay aims at discussing the importance of the transliteration and some techniques of transliteration.

Chapter 2 Classification of Transliterated Words

It is beyond doubt that there are a lot of good transliterated words that are broadly used in our daily life. For example, many people like watching talk show on TV, and "talk show" is transliterated into "脱口秀" which is so vivid and alive that it is instantly accepted by us. Additionally, it is very common that many words have both transliteration and liberal translation and both are very popular. "武术" is quite familiar to Westerners and both the transliterated term "Chinese Kongfu" and the liberally-translated term "martial arts" are widely used in the Western countries. In E-C translation, it is a universal phenomenon, too. A typical example is the word "shopping". The liberal translation is "购物" and the transliterated word is "血拼". The former one expresses the meaning of buying commodities while the latter one gives us a more vivid image by the Chinese word "血". So the transliterated word "血拼" is quite popular among young generation. From the above two examples, we can know that good transliterated words which are both appropriate and vivid can be also easily accepted by people. Many transliterated words, such as 逻辑(logic), 拷贝(copy), 幽默(humor), etc., have been added into the "Modern Chinese Dictionary".

2.1 Names of People and Places

There have been some E-C translation principles and translators can even refer to the "English Personal Name Dictionary".① Many English peoples' names, especially names of historical people and celebrities, have common transliterated Chinese names. But translators can make some modifications in light of the specific conditions. For instance, "Vivien" is transliterated into "薇薇安", but the name of the British famous actress Vivien Leigh (1913-1967) is transliterated into "费雯丽" which sounds very beautiful.② So on some occasions translators can make some changes or modifications in accordance with the specific conditions.

The tone of Chinese has some correspondence to the pronunciation of English. If the vowel syllable on which the stress falls is open syllable [a, e], it could be transliterated into the 1st or 2nd tone of Chinese; if the vowel syllable on which the stress falls is closed syllable [i, u], it could be transliterated into the 4th tone of Chinese.③ If the weak syllable falls on the former part of the word, it could be transliterated into the 3rd tone of Chinese; if the weak syllable falls on the latter part of the word, it could be transliterated into the 4th tone of Chinese.

A consonant syllable needs to be first transferred to a complete weak syllable. The consonant syllable of the former part of the word could be translated into the 3rd tone of Chinese after transformation. The consonant syllable of the latter part of the word could be transliterated into the 4th tone of Chinese.

In accordance with the above principles, translators then could choose appropriate Chinese words from those words having the same pronunciation. The selected Chinese words must be familiar to readers and have no link to something bad, and they must embody both the original pronunciation and the gender of the person. For instance, the Chinese pronunciation of the name "Garnet", according to the above principles, should be Gā ni te. The Chinese name could be "加尼特" or "嘉妮特", and of course the former one is a man's name and the latter one is a female's name. Take "Scarlett" for another example. It could be transliterated into "司加利" or "斯嘉丽", and it is no doubt that the latter one is more suitable and appropriate

---

① 李忠华编:《英语人名词典》,上海外语教育出版社2002年版。
② 朱红梅:《英语人名翻译初探》,载《郑州轻工业学院学报(社会科学版)》2002年第1期。
③ 李玄玉:《增义音译法的原则》,载《山西大学学报(哲学社会科学版)》2003年第1期。

for a girl's name.

　　Except some right and proper transliteration of English names of celebrities, such as 耶稣基督—Jesus Christ, 亚力山大大帝—Alexander the Great, etc., many English names of ordinary people can be transliterated into Chinese names freely as long as the translator does it according to the pronunciation and the above principles. For instance, "Johansson" could be transliterated into both "约翰逊" and "约翰森".

　　But there is one key point in transliteration of people's names to be mentioned here in the essay: the selected Chinese words need to be the words that are frequently used in names of people. That is to say, when readers are reading the names they will not link the names of people to other kind of things. As a result, the translator has to choose the Chinese words that are most frequently adopted in translation of people's names. Besides that, the translator must pay attention to the following principle: do not transliterate the English name into a Chinese transliteration which sounds too similar to a Chinese local name because it may make readers feel confused about the nationality of the person. Take "John" for instance. Its conventional Chinese transliteration is "约翰". If the translator transliterates it into "江" or "张" merely according to its pronunciation, readers are likely to consider John as a Chinese man instead of a foreigner.

　　The transliteration of ordinary people's names will make it sense as long as it is transliterated following the principles of pronunciation and word selection, and it does not interfere readers with reading the passages. The transliteration that enables readers easily recognize it as a person's name is a qualified transliteration.

　　The transliteration of places is very similar to that of names. The transliteration that expresses the feeling or meaning of a place is to be a successful translation. But the translator has to notice that, the transliteration of places should not contain those words indicating any information linked to gender. Take the capital city of France for example. As the name of the capital city, Paris is transliterated into "巴黎" which involves no information about gender. But when it refers to the name of the American celebrity Paris Hilton, who is one of the two successors of the Hilton Group, Paris is transliterated into "帕丽斯", the Chinese words which are apparently and easily linked to female. To conclude, the selection of words of target language is badly important when translators are conducting transliteration work, as incorrect words may not express the correct image to readers and even may mislead them.

2.2　Names of Professional and Technical Terms in Varied Fields

Transliteration is quite often used in the translation of international units of measurement. Most of them are translated into Chinese by transliteration instead of liberal translation, such as ohm—欧姆(unit of resistance), volt—伏特(unit of voltage), ampere—安培(unit of electric current), etc. Transliteration of international units of measurement shares similar translating principles with transliteration of places.

Apart from that, transliteration is widely used in specialized fields, including science, medicine and other aspects. In these fields, translators tend to prefer transliteration rather than liberal translation. Many specialized terms are named after some celebrities who have made tremendous contributions to the study of his or her researching area, which makes transliteration more suitable than liberal translation.① When talking to these aspects, it is somewhat hard to transliterate English into Chinese but it is much more difficult to complete C-E transliteration. It is mainly because most English specialized words or phrases are new ones which can be understood by Chinese people while English speaking people may have trouble in understanding many Chinese things that are inherited from earlier generation. From Confucianism to Peking Opera, traditional herbal medicine to the 24 solar terms, all these Chinese traditional things have a fairly long history. Therefore, in order to have the original words more easily understood by readers, translators are supposed to write some explanation or detailed information after those specialized terms involving much expertise.② Let's start this topic from the English word "El Nino". If there was no explanation following the transliteration of technical terms "El Nino"—"厄尔尼诺", it would be a distinct possibility that Chinese readers were at a loss for "厄尔尼诺". Readers will easily get what is "厄尔尼诺" generally talking about if the translator write some Chinese explanation such as "一种严重影响全球气候的太平洋热带海域的大风及海水的大规模移动". On the other hand, the above method should also be applied into C-E transliteration when needed. As mentioned above, how to complete an excellent transliteration is a very important issue as a good C-E transliteration does great help to make people from other countries understand our civilization better.③ Since English speaking readers have little knowledge of our traditional culture, the translator needs to put some explanation behind the transliteration so as to help readers to

---

①　方小兵:《专有名词音译探讨》,载《皖西学院学报》2002年第2期。
②　李玄玉:《增义音译法的原则》,载《山西大学学报(哲学社会科学版)》2003年第1期。
③　史有为:《汉语外来词》,商务印书馆2000年版。

understand the translation. For example, our traditional holiday "清明" is usually transliterated into "Qing Ming", and in order to help foreign readers have a clear knowledge about the Chinese traditional holiday, the translator should put some explanation behind "Qing Ming", such as "a traditional Chinese festival to commemorate the dead observed in late spring". After reading the explanation, readers could easily get the general information of the transliteration. Take "阴阳" for another example. If the translator merely transliterates it into "Yin Yang" according to the pronunciation, perhaps no foreign readers can understand it.[①] They are likely to be completely confused. On occasions like this, explanation should be put forward. Readers will soon understand what "Yin Yang" is mainly talking about if the translator writes the following sentence "Yin and Yang represent the two opposite but nonantagonistic and mutually transformable sides in human nature and society". So one key principle of transliteration of Chinese traditional things is the translator must write some introduction or explanation behind his transliterated words to help readers get a general image of the words.

2.3 Words That Do Not Have Counterparts in Chinese

There are more and more borrowed words in modern Chinese language and there exist many different translation methods of external words, including pure transliteration (卡司—cast, 比基尼—bikini), combination of transliteration and liberal translation (奶昔—milkshake, 迷你裙—miniskirt), transliteration plus similar words (果酱—jam), whole liberal translation (电脑—computer, 冰箱—refrigerator), corresponding liberal translation (黑马—dark horse, 迷城—lost city), and so on. From the above several methods, it is true that transliteration is also an important means of the translation of those borrowed words, and thus the function of good transliteration is so crucial that should not be neglected. As a result, by reading and studying a lot of relevant books written by some great translators, some techniques and ways of transliteration will be discussed and studied in this essay for the sake of its important role in E-C translation.

As is known to all, it is so difficult for translators to acquire remarkable translation that the great translator Yan Fu had made such comments on translation, "it takes long time to translate merely a name." Take "laser" for instance. Actually there are two kinds of translation of laser: one is "镭射" and the other is "激光".

---

① 蒋建勇:《中医英译中的音译现象与翻译的等值理论》,载《贵州省翻译工作者协会 2005 年会暨学术交流会论文集》,2005 年。

"镭射" is the transliterated word widely accepted in Taiwan while "激光" is the liberally-translated word used in China mainland.① Someone may argue that "激光" is better than "镭射" while others may hold the opposite view. As far as I am concerned, "镭射" expresses "the action of the emission of radiation" while "激光" pays more attention to "light amplification". Both words have advantages. It is hard to say which one is better.

It is a common phenomenon that translators choose to translate some English words into Chinese by the transliteration means. The popular transliterated words are words that can stand the test of time. Those incoherent transliterated words that made it difficult for readers to understand finally were eliminated and replaced by other words. Take the English word "telephone" for instance, the liberally-translated word "电话" has got overwhelming support than the transliterated word "德律风". Some incoherent transliteration such as "德律风" will no doubt be abandoned at last.

Chapter 3   Means of Transliteration

However, there is still a long way to go before the transliteration can be widely accepted. Many translators tend to choose liberal translation mainly because they are afraid of being criticized not to translate the meaning of the words. This opinion is the result of the wrong conception that transliteration is equal to non-translation. Therefore, to change this conception, it is very essential and important to make the transliteration not only go with the original pronunciation but also easily accepted by Chinese people, which entails rich translation theories and gorgeous translation techniques. In order to make transliterated words become one component of the Chinese language system and absorbed by the Chinese language, we have to make some changes or modifications in pronunciation, intonation, syllable, the selection of Chinese words and other aspects, roughly including the following parts:

3.1   Modification of the Pronunciation

Although the external words come from other countries, they need to melt into Chinese language system. In order to be easily accepted by Chinese readers, the transliterated pronunciation of borrowed words will certainly somewhat different from the original English pronunciation. Take "laser" for example again. The original pronunciation has two syllables. But there are not counterparts of the single vowel of the

---

① Hsu J. L. Language Contact and Convergence: Englishization of Mandarin Chinese in Taiwan, 1994.

1st syllable [æ] and the consonance of the 2nd syllable [z] in Chinese pronunciation. So it needs to make some modification on syllables. Thus translators in Hong Kong and Taiwan changed the syllable [æ] to [ei] and the syllable [z] to [s] and then changed to [§]① so as to make the pronunciation more suitable to Chinese language. As a result, the widely used transliteration in Hong Kong and Taiwan "镭射" appeared and were accepted. If a syllable in English does not have a corresponding one in Chinese, the translator could find a similar syllable in Chinese to replace that original syllable.

3.1.1 Modification of Syllables

The core of the E-C transliteration is the modification of syllables. The main feature of Chinese language is that any Chinese word exists in the form of syllable unit. Therefore, in order to form the transliteration, external words should first be modified in syllables. For instance, "guitar" is transliterated into "吉他", and "tank" into "坦克". There is one point of Chinese language's custom to be put forward: Chinese words feature double syllables, so many transliterated words are composed of two syllables and one of the two syllables usually is transliteration while another one indicates the liberal translation of the original words.② For example, "beer" is translated into "啤酒". It is clear that "啤" is the transliteration of the pronunciation of "beer" and "酒" is the liberal translation of the word that expresses the meaning of "beer" to readers.

3.1.2 Modification of Intonation

The next point is about the modification of "Shengdiao" (which means the four different intonations in the pronunciation of a Chinese word, and in the following text I would call Shengdiao intonation for the sake of reading convenience). It is a unique phenomenon that Chinese words have four different intonations, which makes Chinese distinctive from any other language in the world.③ Only by sinicizing can external words be popular among Chinese people. That is to say, the translator needs to make the structure and intonation of the transliteration comply with the Chinese language system. It is also one of the factors determining the quality of the transliteration whether the intonation of the transliteration comforts to Chinese custom.

---

① 章恒珍:《浅谈汉语音译外来词的译音规范》,载《广东教育学院学报》2003 年第 3 期。

② 张张钰:《论英汉互译中文化特色与文化障碍的异化处理》,载《福建省外国语文学会 2004 年会论文集》,2004 年,第 8 页。

③ 汪榕培:《比较与翻译》,上海外语教育出版社 1997 年版,第 23 页。

3.2 Selection of Chinese Words

Selection of Chinese words is very important in transliteration, especially in the E-C advertising transliteration. The selected words in the transliteration are always related to some associations or imagination, which is part of Chinese people's national character, because we have learned large numbers of great Chinese poems full of beautiful words by discreet selection of millions of Chinese words, and this has helped to form the national character that Chinese people tend to be fastidious about the selection of words. An appropriate and excellently-selected Chinese word can make the transliteration shining, and vice versa. It plays an extremely important role in advertising transliteration.

The importance of choosing appropriate Chinese words in transliteration is extremely apparent in advertising translation as most branches' Chinese names are transliteration instead of liberal translation. A splendid transliteration not only expresses its content, but leaves a good image to customers so as to boost its sales. To achieve the goal, the translator must spare no efforts to select appropriate Chinese words, not just transliterating according to the pronunciation principles.① Different Chinese words should be selected in the transliteration of branches in different fields. The selected words should embody the feature and function of products of the branch, and if necessary, the chosen words have to clearly tell the information of the branch about its customer community's gender. The giant German automobile maker Benz enjoys high reputation across the globe. Its Chinese transliteration is "奔驰", which perfectly shows the image of high speed of the car. If the translator transliterated it into "笨死", it would certainly be rejected by all Chinese customers. There are several additional examples about the transliteration of names of cosmetics: Chanel—香奈尔, Guerlain—娇兰, Estee Lauder—雅诗兰黛, Lancome—兰蔻, etc. These Chinese names are terrific because they all clearly introduce the information of the branches to customers. Customers are able to immediately understand products of these branches are about cosmetics at the first sight of their Chinese names, as these names contain several Chinese words connected with females—"香", "娇", "兰", "蔻". The Chinese name "雅诗兰黛" is especially splendid as each one of the four selected Chinese words carries softness, smoothness, and beauty that symbolize females, which leaves customers a beautiful image. It is a successful case in transliteration of

---

① 柯金算:《商标译名初探》,载《福建省外国语文学会2001年年会论文集》,2001年。

branches. Let's take another branch in different fields for instance. Parker is a famous branch of pens. Its English pronunciation sounds smooth. And its Chinese name "派克" is also a terrific name. The Chinese word "派" is linked to meanings of elegant and gorgeous, which is very suitable for the name of pens and could easily give customers a positive image. There are many other examples of good advertising transliteration. And the common point of those examples is appropriate and discreet selection of Chinese words. An excellent selection of Chinese words will no doubt leave customers a splendid and shining image of the branch and will stimulate the sales of the products as well.

Chapter 4　Conclusion

The study of transliteration may still be at the initial stage. What has been explored in the paper is the academic value of transliteration as it plays a crucial role in the quality of translation work in many aspects. And it is beyond doubt that borrowed words really have broadened the horizon of Chinese and improved cultural communication. The study of transliteration is especially conducive to the economic, social and cultural communication between Chinese people and Westerners. Therefore, people from other English speaking countries across the world will understand Chinese civilization better and have a more positive image of China rather than being misled by the stereotypes of our country. So it is a thought-provoking topic playing a decisive role in facilitating globalization.

References

［1］Hsu, J. L. Language Contact and Convergence：Englishization of Mandarin Chinese in Taiwan, 1994.

［2］方小兵:《专有名词音译探讨》,载《皖西学院学报》2002年第2期。

［3］蒋建勇:《中医英译中的音译现象与翻译的等值理论》,载《贵州省翻译工作者协会2005年会暨学术交流会论文集》,2005年。

［4］柯金算:《商标译名初探》,载《福建省外国语文学会2001年年会论文集》,2001年。

［5］朱红梅:《英语人名翻译初探》,载《郑州轻工业学院学报(社会科学版)》2002年第1期。

［6］李忠华:《英语人名词典》,上海外语教育出版社2002年版。

［7］李玄玉:《略谈汉语音译词的地域文化差异》,载《语言与翻译》2002年第3期。

［8］李玄玉:《增义音译法的原则》,载《山西大学学报(哲学社会科学版)》

2003 年第 1 期。

［9］李玄玉:《新时期的增义音译词》,载张新武、高莉琴主编:《新疆大学语言文化国际学术研讨会论文集》,新疆大学出版社 2002 年版。

［10］史有为:《汉语外来词》,商务印书馆 2000 年版。

［11］汪榕培:《比较与翻译》,上海外语教育出版社 1997 年版。

［12］章恒珍:《浅谈汉语音译外来词的译音规范》,载《广东教育学院学报》2003 年第 3 期。

［13］张张钰:《论英汉互译中文化特色与文化障碍的异化处理》,载《福建省外国语文学会 2004 年会论文集》,2004 年。

（论文作者：华东政法大学外语学院 2004 级学生　徐敏洁）

12.3　语言学类毕业论文实例

A Comparative Study of Face-Enhancing Strategies in *A Dream of Red Mansions* and *Pride and Prejudice*

Ⅰ. Introduction

Face exists in all human communications so that it might seem obvious that face is simply a well-understood concept that pervades human interaction. In daily life, it is quite easy to give all kinds of examples of behavior related to saving, enhancing, threatening or losing face. Since face is so vulnerable that most people will protect it if it is threatened, it is very important to attend to each other's face in communication. Research on face and face theory is well done in a variety of settings and cultures recently. Scholars from the fields of anthropology, psychology, philosophy, and communication have done numerous studies to explore this universal construct in human interaction. Brown and Levinson claim that the Face Theory is valid for all cultures. In Brown and Levinson's framework, their rational person is endowed with "face"—an individual's self-esteem, a term adopted from Goffman.[①]

However, in different cultural contexts, people hold different ideas of the concept of "face". Therefore, the principles and tactics applied vary a lot according to different cultural backgrounds. The present thesis analyzes different strategies of face-enhancing in *A Dream of Red Mansions* against Chinese culture background and *Pride*

---

① Brown, P. & Levinson, S. *Politeness*: *Some Universals in Language Usage* (Cambridge: Cambridge Universities Press, 1987), 60.

and Prejudice in the individual-oriented western culture in order to help people from these two cultures communicate more easily.

On the one hand, *A Dream of Red Mansions* is a masterpiece in Chinese cultures, which mainly describes the love story between Pao-Yu and Tai-Yu, recreating the complex contradictions of the feudal family and revealing the decadence and degeneration of the feudal marriage, morality, culture and education. Moreover, hundreds of images are created with different educational backgrounds and social status to demonstrate an extremely vivid living environment of the typical feudal society which is bound to collapse. Their varied speech and behavior manners well display how Chinese enhance their hearers' faces. On the other hand, *Pride and Prejudice* written by the British novelist Jane Austen also shows how people in the other hemisphere do. There was also a very rigid hierarchy in 18th and 19th century in Britain when this story happened. Austen's witty, warm and ironic portraits of the privileged classes become a bountiful resource to study face and politeness. Through the description of their daily talks and doings of young men and women, this novel is also a good example for discussion.

To sum up, in order to develop an adequate pragmatic competence so as to function more effectively in English-Chinese cross-cultural communication, it is highly necessary to make a thorough study of face-enhancing strategies and accordingly an investigation into the cultural differences between English-speaking world and China.

II. The Conception of Face

Culture consists of not only language, behavioral norms, which can be observed, but also values and beliefs underlying them. Therefore, the conceptions of "face", which are closely connected with culture, differ from one another.

A. The Definition of Face

Goffman characterizes face as "the positive social value a person effectively claims for himself by the line others assume he has taken during a particular contact"[①]. He sees face not as a private or an internalized property lodged in or on the individual's body, but as an image located in the flow of events, supported by other people's judgments, and endorsed by impersonal agencies in the situation. Seen in this light, face is a public image that is on loan to individuals from society, and that will be withdrawn from them if they prove unworthy of it. To secure this public im-

---

① Goffman, E. *Interaction Ritual: Essays in Face-to-Face Behavior* (New York: Pantheon Books, 1967), 49.

age, people engage in what Goffman calls face-work, performing action to make whatever they are doing consistent with face while trying to save their own face. Goffman specifies two kinds of face-work: the avoidance process (avoiding potentially face-threatening acts) and the corrective process (performing a variety of redressive acts). Brown and Levinson clearly consider Goffman's conception of face-work as a set of maintenance strategies and partially incorporate his characterization of face into their concept of face. They define face as "the public self-image that every member wants to claim for himself"[①]. It consists of two related aspects:

(i) Positive face: the want of every member that his wants be desirable to at least some others;

(ii) Negative face: the want of every "competent adult member" that his actions be unimpeded by others.

In accordance with the differentiation of face wants, Brown and Levinson divide politeness into two types: (i) positive politeness, and (ii) negative politeness.

Positive politeness refers to any effort to meet a person's positive face wants, minimizing face-threatening acts (FTAs for short). Positive politeness is redress directed to the addressee's positive face, his perennial desire that his wants (or the actions/acquisitions/values resulting from them) should be thought of as desirable. Redress consists in partially satisfying that desire by communicating that one's own wants (some of them) are in some aspects similar to the addressee's wants. Positive-politeness utterances are used as a kind of metaphorical extension of intimacy, to imply common ground or sharing of wants to a limited extent even between strangers who perceive themselves, for the purposes of the interaction, as somehow similar[②].

Negative politeness is redressive action addressed to the addressee's negative face: his want to have his freedom of action unhindered and his attentions unimpeded[③].

B. Face in Chinese and Western Cultures

Face in Chinese is "脸" or "面子", which echoes the Confucian tradition, one that means subordinating the individual to the group or the community, and regards self-cultivation as an act of communicating with, and sharing in, an ever-expanding circle of human relatedness. Chinese attach much importance to the given community

---

① Brown, P. & Levinson, S. *Politeness: Some Universals in Language Usage* (Cambridge: Cambridge Universities Press, 1987), 60.
② Ibid., 66.
③ Ibid., 78.

where they interact with others. An individual takes seriously how the community judges and perceives his/her character and behavior. If a person is not welcome or respected by others, he/she will not stand. Thus, Chinese face emphasizes the harmony of individual conduct with the views and judgment of the community rather than the accommodation of individual "wants" or "desires". In this sense, to enhance face in China is more likely to mean to enhance their positive face.

In contrast, people pay more attention to individuality in western cultures. Individualism is probably the most basic of all their values, a notion including freedom, rights, and independence of action of man. It places the individual first. Personal achievement, exceptional performance, assertiveness, and material success all represent individual independence. By freedom, they mean an individual needs to be free of external impositions—a desire to be left alone to enjoy a sense of one's own privacy. He Zhaoxiong claims that regardless of its historicity, individualism is deeply rooted in English culture[①]. Due to an individual's liberty, rights, and independence will be considered polite while lack of it will appear to an English-speaker to be improper, and even rude. Thus, negative face is much more treasured in western cultures than in Chinese.

III. A Comparison of Positive-Politeness Strategies in *A Dream of Red Mansions* and *Pride and Prejudice*

Due to different conceptions of face in Chinese and western cultures which have been discussed in the last part, positive politeness is more valued in China than in the west. The strategies of enhancing hearers' positive face can be divided into four aspects: address form, praising hearers, self-denigrating and cursing, and showing warmth and attention. Dialogues in *A Dream of Red Mansions* and *Pride and Prejudice* can prove this point.

A. Address Form

The address form differs in different cultural backgrounds. What can be used in one culture is probably not applicable to another one. It would cause great problems not to understand the distinctive cultural customs underlying its address forms because how to address others is the first thing to consider in talks. If it is appropriately used, the distance of the interlocutors could be shortened so as to communicate smoothly; if

---

① He, Zhaoxiong. *Study of Politeness in Chinese and English Cultures* (Journal of Foreign Languages, 1995), 3.

not, the interlocutors would feel uncomfortable and awkward and their communication would be seriously impeded.

China used to be a feudal country where feudalism existed for at least two thousand years. The basic integrant of its society is the extensive family with several generations living together. Therefore, face and politeness are important in their community in order to defend feudal ethics. "Respect the old and cherish the young" is one of the traditional virtues passed down from ancestors. Seen in this light, the address form is the key token of personal social position and social recognition in China. The address form can be divided into two categories:

1. Others-Elevating Address Form

雨村忙起身亦让道:"老先生请便。晚生乃常造之客,稍候何妨。"(第一回)

雨村一面打恭,谢不释口,一面又问:"不知令亲大人现居何职?"(第三回)

这熙凤听了,忙转悲为喜道:"正是呢……竟忘了老祖宗,该打该打。"(第三回)

这门子忙上来请安,笑问:"老爷一向加官进禄,八九年来就忘了我了?"(第四回)

宝玉道:"你今日回家就禀明令尊……"(第七回)

水溶见他言语清楚,谈吐有致,一面又向贾政笑道:"令郎真乃龙驹凤雏,非小王在世翁前唐突,将来'雏凤清于老凤生',未可量也。"贾政忙赔笑道:"犬子岂敢谬承金奖。"(第十五回)

众清客在旁笑答道:"老世翁所见极是。如今我们有个愚见:……"(第十七回)

In Chinese, "老" is often used to address those who are distinguished, such as "老先生""老祖宗""老爷""老世翁". These words all show speakers' deference and respect for hearers so that hearers' social standing in the community is recognized or even raised.

2. Self-Despising Address Form

雨村忙起身亦让道:"老先生请便。晚生乃常造之客,稍候何妨。"(第一回)

如海道:"天缘凑巧,因贱荆去世……"(第三回)

那先生道:"依小弟的意思,竟先看过脉再说的为是……"(第十回)

水溶见他言语清楚,谈吐有致,一面又向贾政笑道:"令郎真乃龙驹凤雏,非小王在世翁前唐突,将来'雏凤清于老凤生',未可量也。"贾政忙赔笑道:"犬子岂敢谬承金奖。"(第十五回)

众清客在旁笑答道:"老世翁所见极是。如今我们有个愚见:……"(第十七回)

那张道士又向贾珍道:"……若论这个小姐模样儿,聪明智慧,根基家当,倒也配的过。但不知老太太怎么样,小道也不敢造次……"(第二十九回)

Contrary to "老", "小" is often used to despise oneself, such as "小弟" "小王" "小道". The speaker disparages himself with humble words in order to promote the addressee's positive self-image or personality. In Chinese vocabulary, there are many opposite words which can be used in different contexts. For example, "令郎" and "犬子" are relative—the former is used to praise the hearer's son while the latter is used to express one's own son is not so outstanding.

By contrast, there are not so many kinds of address forms in English. The reason for it is closely related to English cultures. English-speaking countries are mainly composed of nuclear families including only two generations. Due to individualism, children leave their parents and live an independent life when they grow up. Thus westerners pay much less attention to ties of blood. They think they are equal. It is common that the son call his father name in the west, but it is considered quite impolite and ungrateful in China. While "Mr." "Mrs." "Miss" "Ms" are used with high frequency in the west, few other words can express the speaker's positive politeness to the hearers. Take *Pride and Prejudice* for an example:

"My dear Mr. Bennet," said his lady to him one day, "have you heard that Netherfield Park is let at last?" (Volume Ⅰ, Chapter 1)

"Pardon me for interrupting you, Madam," cried Mr. Collins... (Volume Ⅰ, Chapter 20)

"Good Lord! Sir William..." (Volume Ⅰ, Chapter 23)

"My love, should not you like to see a place of which you have heard so much?" (Volume Ⅱ, Chapter 19)

There are few address forms to despise the speaker self in English, which are used widely in China. Moreover, "old" is an offensive word if it is used to address the old, because they still want to live independently without others' compassion and attention. So they are more likely to be called "Senior Citizens".

B. Praising Hearers

Chinese cultures as a whole advocate collectivism and object to independence and individual aggressive behavior. It originated in Confucius ethics. Chinese economy was mainly based on agriculture for thousands of years so that people were tied to the land and seldom moved away. As a result, it was not uncommon that all the inhabitants of a village were a clan or a family group. In society, people faced the outside world and problems in the form of group, not individually. Collectivism thus becomes the core of Chinese culture. And naturally, Chinese politeness manifests a collectivistic feature.

In order to satisfy the hearer's needs for his/her positive face, the speaker must raise the hearer's social dignity in the community. So giving direct praises is a good way. For example:

这熙凤携着黛玉的手,上下细细打量了一回,便仍送至贾母身边坐下,因笑道:"天下真有这样标致的人物,我今儿才算见了。何况这通身的气派,竟不像老祖宗的外孙女,竟是个嫡亲的孙女。"(第三回)

Xi Feng praises Tai-Yu, who is the grandchild of Madam Jia, in an exaggerated way in order to please Madam Jia and also make her feel contented.

秦氏道:"婶婶,你是个脂粉队里的英雄,连那些束带顶冠的男子也不能过你……(第十三回)

水溶笑道:"名不虚传,果然如'宝'似'玉'。"……"令郎真乃龙驹凤雏,非小王在世翁前唐突,将来'雏凤清于老凤声',未可量也。"(第十五回)

Although Shui Rong says Jia Zheng will be surpassed by his son Pao-Yu in the future, Jia Zheng is still satisfied because parents in China always hope their children could be more excellent. So on surface, the word threatens Jia Zheng's positive face; in fact, it is rightly the opposite in Chinese cultures.

老尼道:"这点子事,别人的跟前就忙的不知怎么样了,若是奶奶的跟前,再添上些也不够奶奶一发挥的。"(第十五回)

赵嬷嬷道:"那时谁不知道的?如今还有个口号呢,说东海少了白玉床,龙王来请江南王,这说的就是奶奶府上了。"(第十六回)

众人听了,都赞道:"极是!二世兄天分高,才情远,不似我们读腐了书的。"(第十七回)

那张道士先哈哈笑道:"无量佛寿!老祖宗一向福寿安康?众位奶奶小姐纳福?一向没到府里请安,老太太气色越发好了……托老太太万寿万福,小道也还康健……"(第二十九回)

In the west, such a device is also widely used. For example, in *Pride and Prejudice*:

"How good it was in you, my dear Mr. Bennet!"

"What an excellent father you have, girls." (Volume I, Chapter 2)

"My dear Madam," he replied, "this invitation is particularly gratifying, because it is what I have been hoping to receive; and you may be very certain that I shall avail myself of it as soon as possible." (Volume I, Chapter 22)

"He is the best landlord, and the best master that ever lived." (Volume III,

Chapter 1)

Moreover, some talks between westerners just show agreement rather than praise. For example:

—"Impossible, Mr. Bennet, impossible, when I am not acquaintance with him myself; how can you be so teasing?"

—"I honour your circumspection." (Volume Ⅰ, Chapter 2)

"That is very true," said Elizabeth... (Volume Ⅰ, Chapter 5)

"You are quite right..." (Volume Ⅱ, Chapter 17)

Therefore, there is much more kinds of words to praise others in China than in the west. In this sense, a conclusion can be drawn that Chinese more attend to enhancing the hearer's positive face than the westerners.

C. Self-Denigrating and Cursing

This method is similar to the self-despising address form. Speakers denigrate or curse themselves to be positively polite to hearers. This is culturally specific in China. Being humble in front of others has always been a traditional virtue since the ancient China. But in the west, people believe in individualism so that they think they are born equally.

张先生道:"晚生粗鄙下士,本知见浅陋,昨因冯大爷示知,大人家地谦恭下士,又承呼唤,敢不奉命。但毫无实学,倍增颜汗。"(第十回)

Zhang says himself has little knowledge to imply Jia Zheng is knowledgeable.

贾瑞道:"我在嫂子跟前,若有一点谎话,天打雷劈!"(第十二回)

宝玉急了,忙向前拦住道:"好妹妹,千万饶我这一遭儿罢,原是我说错了。若是有心欺负你,明日我掉在池子里,叫个癞头龟吞了去,变了大忘八,等你明日做了一品夫人,病老归西的时候,我往你坟上替你驮一辈子的碑去。"(第二十三回)

Pao-Yu curses himself in order to excite Tai-Yu and protect her positive face.

黛玉耳内听了这话,眼内见了这形景,心内不觉灰了大半,也不觉滴下泪来,低头不语。宝玉见他这般形景,遂又说道"……谁知你总不理我,叫我摸不着头脑,少魂失魄,不知怎样才好。就便死了,也是个屈死鬼,任凭高僧高道忏悔也不能超生,还得你申明了缘故,我才得托身呢!"(第二十八回)

张道士呵呵大笑道:"你瞧,我眼花了,也没看见奶奶在这里,也没道多谢……"(第二十九回)

D. Showing Warmth and Attention

This is also a Chinese-specific way. Warmth can make people feel they are welcomed and respected to maintain their positive self-image in the community. But in the west people would be offensive and feel that their privacy is infringed if others show too much warmth to them so that their negative face is threatened. For example:

又忙携黛玉的手问:"妹妹几岁了？可也上过学？现吃什么药？在这里不要想家。要什么吃的，什么顽的，只管告诉我。丫头老婆们不好，也只管告诉我。"一面又问婆子们:"林姑娘的行李东西可搬进来了？带了几个人来？你们赶早儿打扫二间下房，让他们去歇歇。"(第三回)

Xi Feng asks Tai-Yu three questions at first to show her great warmth so as to enhance Tai-Yu's positive face. If she does not ask these questions, Tai-Yu would think she is not welcome. But such a way is considered to encroach on the hearer's privacy and the hearer will be angry in the west.

From the above discussion, it is evident that Chinese mainly attend to their positive face. They pay much more attention to others' recognition of themselves and their public self-image. They want to be respected in their social community.

IV. A Comparison of Negative-Politeness Strategies in *Pride and Prejudice* and *A Dream of Red Mansions*

Because of individualism in western cultures, negative politeness is more important among westerners than among Chinese. Evidence for this point can also be found in *Pride and Prejudice* and *A Dream of Red Mansions*. Negative-politeness strategies can be divided into five parts:

A. Indirect Speech

Because direct request restricts hearers' freedom and privacy so as to threaten their negative face, indirect speech is widely used in the west. It can help avoid many troubles in communication. If the speaker reduces the degree of directness as much as necessary when making a request, the hearer is more likely to accept it. For example:

"If you are not so compassionate as to dine to-day with Louisa and me, we shall be in danger of hating each other for the rest of our lives, for a whole day's tête-à-tête between two women can never end without a quarrel." (Volume I, Chapter 7)

In the west, invitation is regarded as a means of infringing on others' freedom and privacy. Thus indirect invitation is required so as to be negatively polite. This example is an indirect invitation which is in the perspective of the hearer, avoiding threatening her negative face.

Moreover, it is common in China too. For example:

贾珍忙笑道:"婶子自然知道，如今孙子媳妇没了，侄儿媳妇偏又病倒，我看

里头着实不成个体统。怎么屈尊大妹妹一个月,在这里料理料理,我就放心了。"(第十三回)

Jia Zhen does not make a direct request at first. He just gives several reasons that his household work is in great disorder and then asks Xi Feng to come to help. In this way, Jia Zhen averts direct requirement.

However, in China, excessively indirect speech has effects contrary to what is intended. For example, if the above mentioned indirect invitation in *Pride and Prejudice* is used in China, the hearer may think the speaker does not really want to invite him or her.

B. Not Presuming

Western cultures support individuality and value independence. An individual has freedom to master his speech and behavior and to avoid imposition from others. Therefore, in communication, it is not polite to rashly assume what others think, want, believe or expect. It is also considered as a restriction of others' freedom and privacy. For example:

"Let me mend your pen, if you want me to." (Volume Ⅰ, Chapter 7)

The speaker presumes that the hearer's pen needs repairing, which threatens the hearer's negative face, but the if-clause evades the threat so as to relieve the chance of threatening the hearer's negative face.

This strategy is culturally specific in the west. In China, if the speaker can assume what others care or think correctly, the hearer's positive face can be raised. For example:

又忙携黛玉的手问:"妹妹几岁了?可也上过学?现吃什么药?<u>在这里不要想家</u>。要什么吃的,什么顽的,只管告诉我。丫头老婆们不好,也只管告诉<u>我</u>。"一面又问婆子们:"林姑娘的行李东西可搬进来了?带了几个人来?你们赶早儿打扫二间下房,让他们去歇歇。"(第三回)

Xi Feng presumes what Tai-Yu thinks and wants, which does not offend Tai-Yu but makes her feel she is cared by others. In this way, the hearer's positive face is enhanced.

C. Not Coercing the Hearer

The purpose of this strategy is also to leave freedom and privacy for the hearer; three ways can be used: being pessimistic, minimizing the imposition and giving deference.

1. Being Pessimistic

"Will you allow me, <u>or do I ask too much</u>, to introduce my sister to your acquaintance during your stay at Lambton."(Volume Ⅲ, Chapter 1)

The speaker wants to introduce his sister to the hearer's acquaintance. This is a request. So the speaker says "do I ask too much" to be pessimistic in order to protect the hearer's negative face.

2. Minimizing the Imposition

"May I ask whether these pleasing attentions proceed from the impulse of the moment, or are the result of previous study?"(Volume Ⅰ, Chapter 14)

"Will you give me leave to defer your raptures till I write again?"(Volume Ⅰ, Chapter 10)

"And pray may I ask?"(Volume Ⅱ, Chapter 18)

"May I take the liberty of asking your ladyship whether you left Mr. and Mrs. Collins well?"(Volume Ⅲ, Chapter 24)

These auxiliary words relieve the mood of command or request and minimize the imposition so as to enhance hearers' negative face.

3. Giving Deference

"Will you do me the honour of reading that letter?"(Volume Ⅱ, Chapter 12)

There are so many auxiliary words in English that they can express kinds of mood to ease the mood of imposition. However, in Chinese, there are no auxiliary words. Thus this strategy is less used in China than in the west.

D. Expressing Speakers' Wish of Not Impinging on Hearers

If the speaker says he or she does not want to impinge on the hearer, the hearer's negative face can be largely raised. This strategy can be classified into two ways: apology and impersonalization.

1. Apology

This method is common in China as well as in the west.

"Pardon me for interrupting you, Madam," cried Mr. Collins; "but..."(Volume Ⅰ, Chapter 20)

"I beg your pardon, madam, for interrupting you, but I was in hopes you might have got some good news from town, so I took the library of coming to ask."(Volume Ⅲ, Chapter 7)

"Forgive me for having taken up so much of your time, and accept my best wishes for your health and happiness."(Volume Ⅱ, Chapter 11)

"I have no wish of denying that I did every thing in my power to separate my friend from your sister, or that I rejoice in my success."(Volume Ⅱ, Chapter 11)

宝玉急了,忙向前拦住道:"好妹妹,千万饶我这一遭儿罢,原是我说错了。若是有心欺负你,明日我掉在池子里,叫个癞头龟吞了去,变了大忘八,等你明日做了一品夫人,病老归西的时候,我住你坟上替你驮一辈子的碑去。"(第二十三回)

The speaker apologies to the hearer for what he wants to say or do so that the latent conflict between them can be avoided in order to be negatively polite.

2. Impersonalization

This way either avoids mentioning oneself or the interlocutor, or to appeals to a public rule or institutional regulation. For example:

"It does not appear to me that my hand is unworthy your acceptance." (Volume I, Chapter 19)

"It seems likely to have been a desirable match for Jane." (Volume II, Chapter 2)

The English-specific sentence patterns "It appears that..." "It seems like..." avoid the use of "I" or "you" to show that some behavior has nothing to do with the speaker and the hearer. Therefore, the hearer can feel little imposition.

E. Redressing Other Wants of Hearer's

The speaker can provide compensation in some aspects in order to protect the hearer's negative face. For example:

"It pains me to offend you." (Volume II, Chapter 12)

The speaker has said something to offend the hearer, but he says it also pains himself. In this way, the loss of the hearer's negative face is deduced. However, this strategy is seldom used in China, because Chinese always avoid threatening the hearer's negative face.

From the above discussion, it is not difficult to find that the westerners mainly value their negative face. Due to individualism, they want to enjoy their freedom and have their own private space.

V. Conclusion: The Differences of Face-Enhancing Strategies in Chinese and English Cultures

People with different social-cultural backgrounds tend to have very different beliefs and values and such differences can be traced in the practice of saving face. Through the concrete examples of face-enhancing strategies from *A Dream of Red Mansions* and *Pride and Prejudice*, which are all representatives of its culture, it is evident that lack of knowledge about the diversities of face-enhancing ways or simply taking these differences for granted can easily lead to cross-cultural miscommunication, resulting in mutual misunderstanding or interpersonal conflicts.

Chinese culture differs from English culture in historical backgrounds and some basic values, and to acknowledge these differences is the first step to achieve mutual understanding and respect. A failure to do this will definitely lead to ethnocentric behavior. Because culture is highly influential in determining how people think, feel, and act, they use it as the means for judging the world around them. The culture one lives in becomes the center of everything, and its traits are seen as natural, correct, and superior to those of other cultures. The ways people in other cultures think, feel, and act are perceived as odd, amusing, inferior, or immoral. In English-Chinese cross-cultural communication, ethnocentric behavior can prevent people from understanding each other's culture. Only by overcoming one's ethnocentric view of the world can one begin to respect the other culture and thus function more effectively in it.

Despite its universality, face is, after all, culture-specific to some extent. In order to explain the cultural specificity of face, one needs to explore the specific values of the cultures in question. The information concerning face-enhancing strategies derived from the study can benefit cross-cultural communication.

To sum up, this paper provides an overview of how people in English-speaking world and in China have attempted to enhance the hearer's face, makes a comparison of some cultural differences between English and Chinese cultures, and gains an insight into certain cultural values such as collectivism and individualism. It claims that talking about face without taking the social norms and cultural values of a certain culture into consideration is just like a tree being cut off all its roots. Therefore, people who learn a foreign language are required to learn not only the grammatical rules of the target language, but also the knowledge of the target culture. Only by doing so can people achieve successful cross-cultural communication.

Bibliography

Brown, P. & Levinson, S. Universals in Language Usage: Politeness Phenomena. In E. N. Goody (ed.) *Questions and Politeness: Strategies in Social Interaction*. Cambridge: Cambridge Universities Press. 1978.

Brown, P. & Levinson, S. *Politeness: Some Universals in Language Usage*. Cambridge: Cambridge Universities Press. 1987.

Goffman, E. *Interaction Ritual: Essays in Face-to-face Behavior*. New York: Pantheon Books. 1967.

Gray, Donald. *Pride and Prejudice*. New York: W. W. Norton & Company, Inc. 2001.

He, Zhaoxiong. Study of Politeness in Chinese and English Cultures. *Journal of Foreign Languages*. 1995.

Klohf, D. W. *Intercultural Encounters*: *The Fundamentals of Intercultural Communication*. Englewood, Colorado: Morton Publishing Company. 1995.

曹雪芹、高鹗:《红楼梦》,人民文学出版社 2006 年版。

陈治安、刘家荣、文旭:《英汉对比语用学与英语教学》,外语教学与研究出版社 2002 年版。

何自然、陈新仁:《当代语用学》,外语教学与研究出版社 2002 年版。

(论文作者:郑州大学外语学院 2006 级学生　徐炜)

12.4　中西文化对比类毕业论文实例

A Comparison of Numeral Cultures in China and Western Countries

I. Introduction

1.1　Introduction to Numbers

When it comes to the concept—numbers, it is familiar to everyone. Numbers, in the field of science, which are combinations of different kinds of ideas and signs, are also a summary of people's exploration of the world. Naturally, we may see that numbers are often used to calculate, indicating the quantity and the order of things. Furthermore, in the world of human's inner-mind, numbers means a notion, a stream of awareness. Usually, numbers are endowed with kinds of mysterious and symbolic meanings, which show people's different cultural characters, whose meanings form a unique cultural concept, and influence people everyday. Thus, to some extent, those numbers have different cultural connotations under various backgrounds of languages and different cultures and are influenced by different traditions, religions, mythologies, historical stories, etc.

1.2　Introduction to Numeral Cultures

Numbers not only are frequently used to calculate or count, but also mean a notion, a stream of numeral cultural awareness. Culture information of numerals reflects various kinds of nation's connotations and characteristics to the culture, which are influenced by traditions, religions, mythologies, historical stories, etc. All nations have their own numeral culture. Now, the trend of globalization is inevitable, studying and comparing the Chinese and Western number symbolism with a cultural approach helps to learn cultural differences, eliminate cultural conflict and improve people's inter-culture of communication, for among which number culture plays a vital part.

According to the concept "number" and "numeral culture" mentioned above, to some extent, numbers are not signs for calculating, but in the language world of human's inner-mind, numbers mean notions, showing different cultural characters. Numbers gradually have different numeral cultures under various background of languages and different cultures. Some of them are influenced by different traditions, religions, historical stories, etc., which make some numbers have a lot of cultural information, profound local history and special cultural meanings.

As a result, it's more important to pay attention to the cognition of the numbers and numeral cultures. The author selects some representative numbers from Chinese and English languages to give a research. The aim is to show that the number as a culture, has different characteristics and implications, which enhance readers to have a special recognition of numbers.

II. The Relationship Between Numbers and Cultures

2.1 Different Definitions of Culture

2.1.1 Edward Burnett Tylor's definitions of culture

As we all know, culture has been named "the way of life for an entire society". As such, it contains different codes of manners, dress, language, religion, rituals, morality and systems of belief. Various definitions of culture reflect differing theories for understanding—or criteria for evaluating—human activity. Edward B. Tylor, described his definitions of culture from the perspective of social anthropology in 1871, "Culture or civilization, taken in its wide ethnographic sense, is that complex whole which includes knowledge, belief, art, morals, law, custom, and any other capabilities and habits acquired by man as a member of society." (2010: 36).

2.1.2 UNESCO's definitions of culture

Furthermore, the United Nations Educational, Scientific and Cultural Organization—UNESCO described "culture" like this: "... culture should be regarded as the set of distinctive spiritual, material, intellectual and emotional features of society or a social group, and that it encompasses, in addition to art and literature, lifestyles, ways of living together, value systems, traditions and beliefs."

2.1.3 Alfred Kroeber and Clyde Kluckhohn's definitions of culture

From the former two definitions, they cover a range of meaning, and don't exhaust the many uses of the term "culture". In 1952, Kroeber, A. L. and Kluckhohn as well made a list of more than 100 definitions of "culture" in *Culture: A Critical*

Review of Concepts and Definitions, "All kinds of different definitions in fact provide a catalog of the elements of culture. The items catalogued (e. g., a law, a stone tool, a marriage) each have an existence and life-line of their own. They come into space-time at one set of coordinates and go out of it another. While here, they change, so that one may speak of the evolution of the law or the tool." (1952: 47).

2.2 Culture and Numeral Culture

A number is at least, an integrated pattern of human knowledge, belief, and behavior that is both a result of and integral to the human capacity for learning and transmitting knowledge to succeeding generations.

Culture thus consists of language, ideas, beliefs, customs, taboos, codes, institutions, tools, techniques, works of art, rituals, ceremonies, and symbols. It has played a vital role in human's whole life and development, allowing human beings to adapt the environment to their own purposes rather than depend on natural selection to achieve adaptive success. Every nation has its owned culture. An individual's attitudes, values, ideals, and beliefs are greatly influenced by the culture in which he or she lives. As a result of ecological, socioeconomic, political, religious, or other fundamental factors affecting a society, culture change takes place. Number is an abstract entity that represents a count or measurement originally.

As a matter of fact, the main contents of the numeral culture are worship and taboo of the numbers. In ancient times, people endowed numeral mysterious powers because of some fear and ignorance of the natural phenomenon, which became the root of superstition and deeply affected people. With the running rife of the superstition and religious, people formed different ideas towards numbers. They still like some of them, and dislike others.

III. Cultural Differences Regarding Numbers

3.1 Numbers and Traditions

Tradition is anything transmitted or handed down from the past to the present. Material objects (the Iliad, the Parthenon), beliefs, images, practices, institutions, can all be traditions, which means things handed down. "It does demand a certain persistence or recurrence through transmission, because tradition has to be distinguished from mere fashion." (Edward Shils 2006: 85).

Ancestors believe that numbers not only are common signs, but also have some magic power to bless or curse people, so people should not use the unlucky numbers in daily life in order to avoid disasters. It is believed that numbers are in control of people's destiny. As a result, it makes people prefer the numbers with lucky symbols.

3.1.1 Numbers in China

Chinese have the tradition of pursuing peaceful, lucky and harmony awareness. Thus, the even numbers (except "4") have some lucky cultural connotations and are favored by Chinese people.

The number "6", pronounced "Liu", sounds like the word "流" which can mean "everything goes smoothly" is a lucky number pursued by Chinese people. For instance, people usually use "六六大顺" to wish and expect all the things will be well-developed and perfect. Meanwhile, from the point of view of an artist, "六法"、"六彩"、"六要" are the basic skills for an outstanding painters. According to ancient Pythagorean thinking, "6" is the most perfect number for it's both the sum and the product of its parts ($1 + 2 + 3 = 6$ and $1 \times 2 \times 3 = 6$). When selecting the phone numbers or the driving license, "666" is also considered one of the luckiest numbers. It can be seen prominently in many shop windows across China, and people there often pay extra money to get a cell-phone number including this string of digits in Shanghai and Shenzhen.

"10" and "2" are also favored by Chinese people. Chinese believe that "10" means all is perfect. When Chinese say something is perfect, they will say "十全十美". And when they are very confident about something, they will use the idiom "十拿九稳". In Cantonese, "2" is pronounced much like the word "易", hence it is considered good luck there, as well. It has widely been seen as a number of duality, contradiction and polarity. When Chinese people visit their friends, they will take some gifts in double to represent good luck. It is thought that good things come in pairs, which is a phrase that even appears in Western culture.

Furthermore, the combinations of some numbers are favored by Chinese too. Such as "168" (it implies that I prosper all the way and have a wish to get fortunes), "518" (it implies I will prosper), "5189" (it implies I will prosper for a long time) and "5918" (it implies I'm indeed to desire to win and prosper), etc.

On the other hand, "4" is considered the unluckiest number in Chinese culture, because it sounds like the word "死" (it means death). Due to that, many numbered product lines skip "4". Some buildings skip the 4th floor, particularly in heavily-populated Asian areas. In Hong Kong, some high-rise residential buildings skip all numbers with "4", for example, "4", "14", "24", "34" and all 40-49th floors to avoid the taboo.

Another taboo in China is number "7". In Chinese culture, "7" is another unlucky number to be avoided in people's daily life. If you want to send your friend presents, you mustn't send "7" presents to others. When people choose a lucky day to attend a wedding or to play outside, they won't choose day "7", "17" or "27". Maybe, it will attributes to the fact that Chinese people are in favor of even numbers but odd numbers.

3.1.2 Numbers in the Western countries

Compared with Chinese, Westerners much more like the odd number (except "13"). An example is "3" and "4". "3" is respected the lucky number in most Western countries, for it's a symbol of holiness, respect and luckiness. Westerners believe that the world is a combination of three parts: land, sea and sky. Nature contains three parts: animals, plants and minerals. Human have three qualities: body, soul and spirit. Christian believes that the trinity—the union of three divine persons, the Father, Son, and Holy Spirit, in one God. People's favor to "3" can be seen in the following proverbs, "Number three is always fortunate." (三号一定运气好), "The third time's the charm." (第三次一定灵). In the great playwright Shakespeare's drama appears, there is such a saying, "All good things go by threes." (一切好事以三为标准). From above, it is easy to know that the Westerners have a preference towards "3". Although "3" symbols luckiness in Western culture, Westerners do not want to be the third one when one lights a cigarette for them. It is because that in the Boer War (1899-1902), the third one who smoked has always been shot by the enemy. When it comes to the number "4", Western people regard it a magic symbol of justice and power.

3.2 Numbers and Mythology

Mythology is about narratives about divine or heroic beings, arranged in a coherent system, passed down traditionally, and linked to the spiritual or religious life of a community, endorsed by rulers or priests. Once this link to the spiritual leadership of society is broken, they lose their mythological qualities and become folktales or fairy tales. (Mircea Eliade 1991).

As is known to all, mythology is one of the most important soils in the culture, which influences every aspect of a nation.

The example is "13", which is regarded as the unluckiest number in the West. According to one of the stories in Norse mythology, Loki (the god of destruction and spirit of evil) crashed into a banquet and sat at the table together with Balder (the god of light) and the other gods. There were 13 gods sitting around the table, including Loki. In fact, Loki's intrusion was part of his artful scheme that caused Balder's death. From then on, all the gods cannot recover after a setback. The myth makes people regard "13" as an unlucky number, and believe that 13 persons sitting at a table to have a dinner was unlucky.

Meanwhile, the well-known story "the sleeping beauty" strengthens people's bias against "13". In the story, the king and the queen didn't have any child for many years. Finally, they had a daughter who was so pretty that the king could not contain his joy, and ordered a great feast. He invited twelve wise women to attend the party. When the party came to the end, the twelve wise women came to bestow magical gifts upon the baby. When the eleventh had made her promises, suddenly the thirteenth came in. she wanted to avenge for not having been invited, and cursed the baby to die. Everyone was shocked. Then, the twelfth woman gave the baby her good wish: the baby would sleep for a hundred years instead of being dead. After a hundred years, a prince came in and married her, they finally led a happy life.

3.3 Numbers and Religions

Religion and mythology have close relationship, just like the fish to the water. Religion is a system of social coherence based on a common group of beliefs or attitudes concerning an object, person, unseen being, or system of thought considered to be supernatural, sacred, divine or highest truth, and the moral codes with such belief or system of thought. It is sometimes used with "faith" or "belief system", but is more socially defined than that of personal convictions.

Furthermore, religion is the core of civilization history. Some western countries' history were dominated by the religion and lasted for thousands of years. One representative is Christianity, which is respected by the Westerners. That is why some numbers appear in the *Bible*.

"666" is an interesting number of combination. In Western culture and many Asian cultures, it goes to the extreme. As everyone knows, according to the *Bible*, "666" is of the beast and is synonymous with Satan. "666" might actually be the most frequently avoided number in Western culture, followed closely by "13". It was said that the former American president Ronald Wilson Reagan had bought a villa before his demission. When he knew the doorplate numbered "666", he was so shocked and changed it by using his power.

"13" has long been considered extremely unlucky because it has some bad associations with the tales from the *Bible*. According to the *Bible*, God created the first man, Adam. Then he took a rib from Adam's body and out of it created the first woman, Eve. Adam and Eve were assigned to look after the Garden of Eden, Paradise. There God made every tree grow. There was a tree pleasant to the sight and good for food, the tree of life, and the tree of knowledge of good and evil. The Lord God commanded them not to eat the fruit on the tree of knowledge of good and evil or they would die. Adam and Eve listened and promised that they would obey. But when Adam fell asleep, Eve met a serpent. The serpent handed her the fruit of the tree of knowledge and cheated her to eat. When Adam woke up, he ate some, too. The Lord God was very angry when he learnt this, and drove both Adam and Eve from Paradise. In due course of time they had two children, and then had many more. After they bent down with endless years of toil and misfortune, they died. It was said that Adam was created on a Friday the 13th and it was on Friday the 13th that Adam and Eve ate the forbidden fruit, and on a Friday the 13th they died.

The *Bible* tells that Christ sat down with his 12 disciples, which made up 13, at the last supper when Judas, one of the 12 disciples, sold his master for thirty pieces of silver. Christ was killed by nailing on the cross the following day—on a Friday. The story was painted into a homonymous painting by Leonardo Da Vinci, the great artist, and has made a far-reaching influence.

Due to the fear of "13", some tall buildings have resorted to avoiding "the 13th floor", either by numbering it "14" (though it's really still the 13th floor) or by designation the floor as "12A" or something similar. Likewise, some streets do not have a house numbered 13. It was said that when the former American president Franklin D. Roosevelt holding dinner party, in order to avoid "13", he would ask his secretary to be the fourteenth guest. What's more, he also made his special set out at 11:50 on the 12th designedly to avoid "13".

Another unlucky number in western culture is "40". It is also related to the *Bible*. In the *Bible*, many disasters have associations with "40". The most famous one is Noah's Ark. God saw that the whole world was corrupt and full of violence, and intend to destroy them. He told Noah to make an Ark. In the Ark, there should be himself, his wife, his sons and their wives, and living creatures, two of each kind, a male and a female. Noah did what God had commanded him. Towards the end of seven days the waters of the flood came upon the earth. In the year when Noah was 600 years old, on the 17th day of the second month, on that very day, all the springs of the great abyss broke through, the windows of the sky were opened, and rain fell on the earth for 40 days and 40 nights.... The flood continued upon the earth for 40 days. The waters increased and the mountains were covered to a depth of 15 cubits. Everything died. God wiped out every living thing that existed on earth, man and beast, reptile and bird; they were all wiped out over the whole earth, and only Noah and his company in the ark survived.

Different from "13", "7" is the luckiest number in western culture. In the story of Genesis, God created everything on earth in six days and ceased from all his work on the seventh day. God blessed the seventh day and made it holy, because on that day he ceased from all the work he had set himself to do. The Christian believe "the seventh heaven is the place where God and angels live, it's a Pure Land everyone wants."

In Chinese culture, "7" is related to Buddhism. It is said the initiator of Buddhism, Sakyamuni, had be faced to a wall for seven days without eating and drinking, and then he became immortal. Besides, Buddhism has seven treasures. In their books, sentence like "救人一命,胜造七级浮屠"(it means that if a man save one's life, the merits and virtues he get is more than he did) can be seen everywhere.

"3" is also closely related to the Taoism. In the book *Tao Te Ching*, Laozi said, "The way produced the One; the One produced Two; Two produced Three; and Three produced all things." All things are started by one, and then divided into two, and then three, then all. In their temple, they have a special San-qing Hall to worship the three gods of Taoism.

Mainly in some books, it's not difficult for us to find out the numbers are closely related to the religion. They are endowed with magic powers and become symbols of good or bad luck. Laozi once pointed out that everything has two sides. It is good or bad, right or wrong, active and quiet, above which suit for the Chinese's traditional customs and aesthetic psychology and tell the reason for numeral culture. Besides, Western number symbolism owes much to the philosophy of the Pythagoreans while Chinese number symbolism is also deeply engrained in ancient Chinese philosophy.

3.4 Numbers and Historical Stories

As a matter of fact, some other numbers have special associations with history. Most of these numbers originate from a special event.

An example is "Four Hundred". In the late nineteenth century, Caroline Webster Schermerhorn Astor, the wife of William Astor, who used her position as the heir, is the arbiter of New York high society. Her annual January ball was the social event of the year. In 1892, Mrs. Astor, finding that her list of guests exceeded her ball-room's capacity, asked Ward McAllister, a well-known socialite, to reduce it to four hundred. McAllister afterward boasted that "There were about four hundred people in New York society". The number had no significance because new millionaires soon received the social recognition to which, by American standards of conspicuous spending, they were entitled. Rather, "The Four Hundred" became a phrase denoting social exclusivity.

Another one is "The Fifth Column". It is a secret group that works against a country or an organization from the inside. This term was invented by General Emilio Mola during the Spanish Civil War on October 16, 1936, in which he said that he had "una quinta columna" (a fifth column) of sympathizers for General Franco among the Republicans holding the city of Madrid, and would join his four columns of troops when they attacked. The term was popularized by Ernest Hemingway. (1999: 3-32).

In the West, "Five it" is a common usage for people to express rejection. "Five it" originates from the Fifth Amendment of the Constitution of the USA. In the text, it says "No person shall be held to answer for a capital, or otherwise infamous crime, unless on a presentment or indictment of a Grand Jury, except in cases arising in the land or naval forces, or in the Militia, when in actual service in time of War or public danger; nor shall any person be subject for the same offense to be twice put in jeopardy of life or limb; nor shall be compelled in any criminal case to be a witness against himself, nor be deprived of life, liberty, or property, without due process of law; nor shall private property be taken for public use, without just compensation". So, people usually use "Five" to indicate the Fifth Amendment of the Constitution of the USA, and use "Five it" to refuse improper actions.

There are some other similar expressions, such as "Behind the eight ball", which means a difficult position from which it is unlikely that one can escape. It originates from the Eight Ball version of the game of billiards, which is played on a pool table. The balls are numbered and must be potted in order. A "behind the eight ball" position leaves a player in imminent danger of losing.

The idiom "Three sheets in the wind", also "Three sheets to the wind", usually indicates drunk, inebriated, as in "After six beers he has three sheets to the wind". This term is regarded to refer to the sheet—that is, a rope or chain—that holds one or both lower corners of a sail. If the sheet is allowed to go slack in the wind, the sail flaps about and the boat is tossed about as much as a drunk staggers. Having three sheets loose would be supposed to make the situation all the worse. Another explanation holds that with two or four sheets to the wind the boat is balanced, whereas with three it is not.

"The seventh son of a seventh son" is a concept from folklore regarding special powers given to, or held by, such a son. In this case, it refers to the man who is the seventh son of a man who is himself a seventh son. "7" has a long history of mystical and religious associations: seven sleepers, seven-league boots, seven ages of man, seven hills of Rome, seven lucky Gods of mythology, the Seven Sages, seven sisters, seven stars, seven wonders of the world, and so on.

In Chinese culture, there are some similar expressions, too. In ancient China, it indicated two kinds of martial formations, "五花阵" and "八门阵".

"三教九流" means all sorts of people, various religious sects and academicians. It's a general designation of three main religions (Confucianism, Taoism, and Buddhism) and nine schools. Generally, it refers to people in different professions.

"六亲" generally refers to all the relatives one have. People use "六亲不认" to say someone who is ruthless.

"三顾茅庐" is a story happened in the Three Kingdoms Period ("魏国", "蜀国" and "吴国"). The ruler of "荆州" (a place)—Liu Bei came to a famous wise man—Zhuge liang and asked him to assist him in conquering his enemies. Later, people use it to describe people who invite someone in all sincerity and eagerness.

Ⅳ. Cultural Similarities Regarding Numbers

4.1 Numbers in China

As what has been mentioned, Chinese people like the even numbers (except "4"), since they have some lucky cultural connotations.

In China, number "8" is regarded the lucky number and valued by all the people. In Mandarin, "8" is pronounced "Ba" and sounds similar to the word in Chinese "发", which means "fortune", "prosper" and "wealth". It's no wonder that the number "8" is considered the most fortuitous number in China and is made much coveted for addresses, phone numbers and bank accounts. Maybe no culture in the world is more fascinated with lucky numbers than the Chinese. At present, many youngsters are keen on collecting the phone number or credit number ended with the number "8", in spite of its high expenses and popularity in China.

On the other hand, like western people, the Chinese are favor of "9" and "7", too. When in period of Spring and Autumn and Warring States, the kings paid great attention to the number "9". He desired an everlasting dominion, and built a lot of constructions related to "9", like the Nine-Dragon Screen in the Beihai Park, which was made in 1756. Its screen wall is five meters high, 1.2 meters thick and 27 meters long. The whole thing is built with glazed bricks. On either side of it are nine dragons, also made of glazed bricks, each playing with a pearl amidst waves of clouds. Also, the Forbidden City has 9,999 rooms. The three main palaces are all

9.9 chi high, and the Gate of Supreme Harmony is as wide as 9 rooms, for each middle and upper stairways have 9 steps.

In China, folks have the tradition to hold the wedding on the day with double nine, because it sounds like "久久" (it means ever-lasting). In some places of China, on the ceremony, the Mother-in-law should give the bride RMB 2,999, which means that the new couple will have a happy life forever. Especially, in 1987, the English queen visited China on the Double Ninth Festival in particular, in order to express the best wish that two countries will be friends forever.

Although number "7" is a taboo in China, but in some districts in Sichuan, on the contrary, "7" become the lucky number for the pronunciation of "7" is equal to "起", which in the Sichuan dialect means "to rise up and make glory". Thus, "7" as well as "8", is pursued by people. It is obviously to find that the worship or dislikes to numbers are changing with the social development.

4.2 Numbers in the Western Countries

The westerners like "8", too. Because "8" is formed by two "0"s. People believe that it symbols endless eternity and harmony. In Germany, August 8th is the day that the largest number of new couples holds their ceremonies in the year. In order to make them hold their ceremonies at 8:08, the officials will start their work earlier. What's more, people will throw DEM88 on the new couple, and wish them have a good fortune.

Compared with Chinese, westerners much more like the odd numbers (except "13"). In western culture, "3" is closely related to mythology. In Greek and Roman mythology, the world was supposed to be under the control of three gods, i.e., Jupiter (Zeus), the ruler of Heaven; Neptune (Poseidon), the ruler of the sea; Pluto (Hades), the king of the Underworld. Jupiter's weapon was three-forked lightning, Neptune's, a trident, and Pluto's, a three-headed dog. So, "3" means power to some extent.

In Chinese mythology, there is a myth related to "3", too. Nezha, a superman in Chinese legend, has three heads and six arms; he is the god of justice. He can change into three, and has extraordinary power.

V. Conclusion

On a rough analysis of numbers from different aspects, which contains the introduction to numbers and numeral cultures, the relationship between numbers and cultures and cultural differences regarding the numbers, it is a proposal for a study between Chinese and western number symbolism with a cultural approach. Based on the accepted theories and typical facts and examples, the readers may get the sources of number symbolism and numeral cultures in China and western countries, revealing how extensively and profoundly numbers are ingrained in a nation's culture.

Numbers are closely related to daily life. Various associated meanings are bestowed on various figures by different nations. To some extent, some numbers are influenced by different traditions, religions, historical stories, etc., which make some numbers have a lot of cultural information, profound local history and special cultural meanings. As a result, numbers reflect different cultures of different nations. Therefore, a comparison and an analysis of the numbers will help people to understand the different cultures of China and western countries, as well as the way to promote the cultural communications and make people avoid misunderstandings or conflicts caused by cultural differences in communication.

Bibliography

Edward B. Tylor, *Primitive Culture*, England: Cambridge University Press, 2010.

Edward Shils, *Tradition*, Chicago: University of Chicago Press, 2006.

Ernest Hemingway, *The Fifth Column*, America: Harper San Francisco, 1999.

Kroeber, A. L. and Kluckhohn, *Culture*: *A Critical Review of Concepts and Definitions*, America: Harvard University Press, 1952.

Mircea Eliade, *World Religions*, America: Harper San Francisco, 1991.

毕继万、胡文仲:《跨文化非语言交际》,上海外语教育出版社1999年版。

邓炎昌、刘润清:《语言与文化》,外语教学与研究出版社1989年版。

黄兵:《英汉数字的文化内涵》,载《贵州民族学院学报》2002(3)。

刘利民:《语言与社会文化》,四川人民出版社2001年版。

王红:《中英文词汇的文化意蕴对比》,载《四川理工学院学报(社会科学版)》2005(2)。

殷莉、韩晓玲:《民族文化心理与英汉数字习语》,载《外语与外语教学》2004(9)。

(论文作者:上海大学外语学院2007级学生 沈玮)

参考文献

1. 邓秋香:《毕业论文答辩应注意的几个问题》,载《青年科学》2003 年第 8 期。
2. 高原:《谈谈毕业论文的选题方法》,载《阅读与写作》2005 年第 11 期。
3. 刘新民:《英语论文写作规范》,载《外语与外语教学》1999 年第 8 期。
4. 杨勤、吕冬生、李亚敬:《本科毕业论文选题探究》,载《九江学院学报》2009 年第 3 期。
5. 张霖欣:《英语专业毕业(学术)论文写作教程》,河南人民出版社 2006 年版。
6. 方舟子:《如何避免学术不端行为》,http://master.nwnu.edu.cn/ygb/Article.asp?ArticleID=17700,2010 年 8 月 19 日访问。
7. 《毕业论文的性质和写作意义》,http://www.diyifanwen.com/fanwen/lunwengeshi/119602393270635.htm,2011 年 2 月 8 日访问。
8. 《毕业论文答辩的目的和意义》,http://www.studa.net/zhidao/050526/122814.html,2010 年 12 月 8 日访问。
9. 《大学毕业论文答辩程序》,http://www.so100.cn/html/lwgs/2009-3/5/20090305152201.html,2011 年 3 月 12 日访问。
10. 《如何写好毕业论文中的"致谢辞"》,http://writingyu.blogcn.com/diary,15938222.shtml,2011 年 1 月 27 日访问。
11. 《学术论文的表现类型与写作格式》,http://kjzfxdzz.blog.163.com/blog/static/132847249201001410510888/,2011 年 1 月 27 日访问。
12. 《如何编写论文摘要》,http://jxdl.paperopen.com/news/default/2.aspx,2011 年 3 月 10 日访问。
13. 维基互动百科:语言学,http://www.hudong.com/wiki/%E8%AF%AD%E8%A8%80%E5%AD%A6,2011 年 4 月 7 日访问。
14. 《应用语言学的研究方法》,http://www.tde.net.cn/,2011 年 5 月 25 日访问。
15. 《芝加哥论文格式》,http://wenku.baidu.com/view/4e659b8a6529647d2728526b.html,2011 年 1 月 4 日访问。
16. 华东政法大学外语学院 04、05 届部分毕业论文
17. How to Recognize Plagiarism, https://www.indiana.edu/~istd/, visited at 2011-02-08.

语体风格篇

崔南善全集

Chapter 1　Types of Essays

1.1　理论简介

1.1.1　记叙文(Narration)

记叙文,又称"记事文"或"叙述文",是按照时间顺序叙述人物的经历和事情的产生、发展和变化过程的文章,通常包括日记、新闻报道、回忆录、游记、历史传记、寓言故事等。记叙既可写实,也可虚构。

1.1.1.1　记叙文的主要叙事方式

顺叙、倒叙、插叙和夹叙夹议是记叙文的主要叙事方式。顺叙(in sequence of time)通常是按事情发生的先后顺序进行叙述。倒叙(flashback)则把事件的结局提到前面叙述,然后再按事件的进展顺序进行叙述。插叙(narration interspersed with flashbacks)是在叙述过程中,由于某种需要,暂时把叙述的过程中断,插入与之相关的另外一件事。夹叙夹议(narration interspersed with comments)是一面叙述事情,一面对这件事情加以分析或评论。

1.1.1.2　记叙文的三个要素

情节(plot)、背景(background)和角色(character)构成记叙文的三个要素。

"情节"是整个记叙文的支柱和框架,由一系列精心安排的事件组成。在较长和复杂的记叙文中可能有两个或更多的重要情节,它们相互配合和穿插,次要情节服务于主要情节,以形成故事的主线。叙述中要围绕主题思想精心设计情节、选择细节,要选用与内容有关或能表现主要观点的细节,明确叙述的目的和读者。

"背景"指故事发生的时间和地点,以及有关的周围情况。例如,讲述一个人的历险故事时,可能讲到他的家庭出身、所处环境等。背景有助于烘托故事情节,使人物刻画更为真实可信。

"角色"包括人和物。大多数故事都有多个角色,分为主要角色和次要角色。角色必须有自己的个性和特征,角色塑造的效果直接影响着叙述的成功与否。背景和情节都是为塑造角色服务的。在塑造角色时要抓住三个关键:一是形象描写,二是语言特色,三是人物心理活动和行为。这三个方面都需要与情节有机地结合起来。

1.1.1.3 叙述角度

记叙文常用第一人称或第三人称进行叙述。第一人称叙述使读者感到所描绘的都是作者亲眼所见或亲自经历，因此读起来更真实生动。但是，这种叙述难以反映在同一时间内不同地点发生的事情。第三人称叙述没有这种局限性，作者能较自由地从不同角度和侧面展现事物的经过或表现不同人物的心理活动，使叙述更加灵活丰富、全面客观。好的叙述会灵活运用和变换叙述的角度。

1.1.1.4 展开记叙的两条线索

时间次序(temporal order)和空间次序(space order)是记叙文的两条基本线索。常用的表示时间概念的词语如：when, once, at the same time, now, while, then, before, after, next, all the time, during, on such occasions, simultaneously, soon, suddenly, 等。表示空间概念的词语有：next to, across, on the opposite side, to the left, to the right, below, nearby, 等。这些表达也是使语篇连贯的主要手段，以形成一个完整的记叙。

1.1.2 描写文(Description)

描写文就是用生动形象的语言把人物、事件、地点和环境进行具体的描绘和刻画。描写可分为人物(包括人物心理和动作)描写、景物描写和场面描写等。

1.1.2.1 描写文的特征

描写的目的是通过语言给读者或听者以生动、鲜明的形象，它强调人的感受。描写中多通过人的视觉、听觉、味觉和嗅觉所获得的感受来传达形象，这些形象虽然是以文字描写出来，但有时比用真实色彩绘成的形象更有感染力，因为它们不但有人或物的形状，还会让读者或听者感受到声响、思维变化以及颜料无法表达的一些韵味，从而给读者以真实感和美感。

1.1.2.2 描写文的写作技巧

1) 好的描写要抓住两个关键：突出的印象和丰实的细节。细节的选择至关重要。这就要求作者在语言的运用上要具体、生动，善于捕捉个性特征；不要写成千篇一律，不要过多使用概括性的语言。

2) 结构上，要精心设计描写的角度和次序。可用第一人称或第三人称来写；遵循一定的空间次序，如由上到下、由远到近等；也可按作者视线转移的顺序组织材料；有时还要兼顾静态与动态描写的结合。

3) 选词上，多使用形象、生动的实词来增强句子的活力。注意句式的多样化，避免使用过多的简单句。

4) 灵活运用各种修辞手法，如明喻、暗喻、拟人、扩张等，可使描述更生动、形象。如：

（1）Records fell like ripe apples on a windy day. （比喻）

（2）Death feeds on his mute voice, and laughs at our despair. （拟人）

（3）He ran down the avenue, making a noise like ten horses at a gallop. （夸张）

1.1.3　说明文（Exposition）

说明文是用来解释、阐述事物的文章。说明的对象可以是某一客观事物的特点、性质、操作程序、工作原理等，也可以是某种抽象概念或科学原理、自然现象或社会现象，有时也可以是对某一词语或概念的说明。

1.1.3.1　说明文的语言特点

由于说明文的目的是使读者对所解释的事物有一个清楚、完整的了解和认识，因此说明文的语言表述应尽可能客观、可信。说明文中通常不多个人的评论，写作多用一般现在时、被动语态，或引用权威的信息来源。

1.1.3.2　说明文的写作要点

1）限定说明的事物和范围，不要一篇文章介绍太多的事物。

2）要有足够多的、确切的例子阐述例证，用正确恰当的顺序摆出事实和观点。

3）遣词造句要准确明晰，避免使用华而不实的辞藻和含混不清的语言。

4）尽可能使说明的内容生动有趣，选用典型、新颖的素材吸引读者。在实际写作中，有意识地综合使用各种不同的写作方法。

1.1.4　议论文（Argumentation）

议论文是一种议论说理的文章，以抽象的思维方式，通过运用概念、判断、推理等逻辑形式论证和阐述作者的观点。议论文强调准确性和逻辑性，注意篇章结构，讲究修辞模式。此外，议论文多使用规范的书面语，以增强文章的说服力和读者对文章的信任感。

1.1.4.1　议论文的分类

按议论性质的不同，议论文可分为立论文和驳论文。立论文是从正面阐述论证自己的观点和主张，要求论点鲜明，论据充分，论证严密，以理和事实服人。驳论文则通过批驳别人的论点来树立自己的论点和主张。此外，议论文还可分为因果分析（建议）类议论文、比较分析类议论文和各抒己见类议论文等。

1.1.4.2　议论文的基本结构与写作要点

虽然不同的议论文有不同的写法，但议论文通常包括以下几个核心部分：

1）议论文的标题

议论文的标题要反映出议论的主题或作者的论点。常见的标题有：(1) 疑问句:如"Can Money Buy Happiness?","Which Is More Important, Heath or Wealth?","Could Smoking Be Banned?"。这类标题本身就体现了争论的焦点。(2) 陈述句:如"Life Can Be Happy and Meaningful","Rock Music Is Rotting Our Kids' Mind"。这类标题本身就是议论文的论点。(3) 名词短语:如"My Views on Space Research","Positive and Negative Aspects of Network"。这类标题没体现出论点,只是提供了议论的主题。(4) 介词短语:如"On Reading","Toward a Good Parents-Child Relationship"等。

2) 可争辩的论点

任何一篇议论文必须有论点。也就是说,提出的观点要能够从多方面探讨,从而引起争论。议论文对论点的要求是:正确、鲜明、新颖。提出论点也有多种方式,如:设问作答,引用名言,列举事实,假设情景,开门见山等。好的切题方式能把读者的注意力很快吸引到文章的中心议题上来。

3) 充分的证据

证据包括一般常识、具体事例、统计数字以及权威意见等。证据要与论题相关,充分而确凿。

4) 结论

在对论点进行了充分论证后,作者还要对论证进行总结,归纳或重申自己的观点,与主题相照应。

5) 清楚的逻辑推理

与其他文体相比,议论文的逻辑尤其重要,所提供的事实、例子、证据之间以及它们与全文的结论之间都要有合理的逻辑关系。通常使用的逻辑推理方法有:(1) 归纳法:即从个别到一般,从微观到宏观的论证方法。(2) 演绎法:从一般规律入手,推理到个别事物,从宏观到微观。(3) 类比法:这种论证方法根据两个对象在某种属性上的相同或相似推出结论。灵活使用这些方法可使论证更有力。

1.2 Description

1.2.1 An Overview

Description is intended to supply a word picture of persons, objects, scenes, etc. A good description creates a sensory experience with the use of words. Generally, description can be objective or subjective. The objective description faithfully records what the writer sees while the subjective description records what the writer sees with emotions or impressions. In a descriptive essay, the introduction, body, and conclusion all work together to bring a subject to life.

1.2.2 Strategies for Writing a Descriptive Essay

(1) The use of dominant impression

A descriptive essay usually has one, clear, dominant impression, a mood or atmosphere that reinforces the writing purpose. The dominant impression guides the author's selection of details and is thereby made clear to the reader in the topic sentence. Read the following description on "four skinny trees", and note how the writer's personal mood is expressed in the writing.

Sample paragraph:

They are the only ones who understand me. I am the only one who understands them. Four skinny trees with skinny necks and point elbows like mine. Four who do not belong here but are here. Four ragged excuses planted by the city. From our room we can hear them.

Their strength is secret. They send ferocious roots beneath the ground. They grow up and they grow down and grab the earth between their hairy toes and bite the sky with violent teeth and never quit their anger. This is how they keep. Let one forget his reason for being, they'd all droop like tulips in a glass, each with their arms around the other. Keep, keep, trees say when I sleep. They teach.

When I am too sad and too skinny to keep keeping, when I am a tiny thing against so many bricks, then it is I look at trees. Four who reach and do not forget to reach. Four whose only reason is to be and be.

(From *The House on Mango Street*, by Sandra Cisneros)

(2) The use of specific and descriptive details

To describe means to "picture verbally". First, the author pictures an experience in his mind, then he selects specific details to communicate that impression. The best details are those that appeal to people's five senses: hearing, seeing, smelling, tasting and touching. It is through the senses that the most vivid picture is created and through the vividness and sharpness provided by the sensory details enable the reader to share the writer's experience.

Sample paragraph:

The Middle Eastern bazaar takes you back hundreds—even thousands—of years. The one I am thinking of particularly is entered by a Gothic-arched gateway of aged brick and stone. You pass from the heat and glare of a big, open square into a cool, dark cavern which extends as far as the eye can see, losing itself in the shadowy distance. Little donkeys with harmoniously tinkling bells thread their way among the throngs of people entering and leaving the bazaar. The roadway is about twelve feet wide, but it is narrowed every few yards by little stalls where goods of every conceivable kind are sold. The din of the stall-holders crying their wares, of donkey-boys and porter clearing a way for themselves by shouting vigorously, and of would-be purchasers arguing and bargaining is continuous and makes you dizzy.

One of the most picturesque and impressive parts of the bazaar is the coppersmiths' market. As you approach it, a tinkling and banging and clashing begins to impinge on your ear. It grows louder and more distinct, until you round a corner and see a fairyland of dancing flashes, as the burnished copper catches the light of innumerable lamps and braziers. In each shop sit the apprentices—boys and youths, some of them incredibly young—hammering away at copper vessels of all shapes and size, while the shop-owner instructs, and sometimes takes a hand with a hammer himself. In the backyard, a tiny apprentice blows a big charcoal fire with a huge leather bellows worked by a string attached to his big toe—the red of the live coal glowing bright and then dimming rhythmically to the strokes of the bellows.

Elsewhere there is the carpet-market, with its profusion of rich colors, varied textures and regional designs—some bold and simple, others unbelievably detailed and yet harmonious. Then there is the spice-market, with its pungent and exotic smells.

(*The Middle Eastern Bazaar* from *Advanced English*, Book 1, 张汉熙编)

Sensory details are rich in the description. Pick out from the passage the words used to describe the light and heat; sound and movement; smell and colour.

(3) The different language styles of objective and subjective description

The language of a descriptive essay depends, to a great extent, on whether your purpose is primarily objective or subjective. If the description is objective, the language is usually straightforward, precise, and factual. If the description is subjective, the language used would be connotative and emotionally charged so that readers would share your feelings.

Read the following two passages and note the different language styles.

Sample 1:

Escaping from a Volcano

Three feet of pumice stone covered the ground. Ash floated in the air, poisonous gas came drifting from the crater, though people could still breathe. Roofs were collasping everywhere. The cries of the injured and dying filled in the air.

Rushing throngs, blinded by the darkness and the smoked, rushed up one street and down the next, trampling the fallen in a crazy fruitless dash toward safety. Dozens of people plunged into dead-end streets and found themselves trapped by crashing buildings. They waited there, too frightened to run farther, expecting the end.

Sample 2:

So with the lamps all put out, the moon sunk, and a thin rain drumming on the roof a downpouring of immense darkness began. Nothing, it seemed, could survive the flood, the profusion of darkness, which, creeping in at keyholes and crevices, stole round window blinds, came into bedrooms, swallowed up here a jug and basin, there a bowl of red and yellow dahlias, there the sharp edges and firm bulk of a chest of drawers.

Those sliding lights, those fumbling airs that breathe and bend over the bed, wearily, ghostlily, as if they had feather-light fingers widely used here, give examples and the light persistency of feathers, they would look, once, on the shut eyes, and the loosely clasping fingers, and fold their garments wearily and disappear. And so, nosing, rubbing, they wet to the window on the staircase, to the servants' bedroom, to the boxes in the attics; descending, blanched the apples on the dining-room table, fumbled the petals of roses, tried the picture on the easel, brushed the mat and blew a little sand along the floor. At length, all ceased together, gathered together, all sighed together; all together gave off an aimless gust of lamentation to which some door in the kitchen replied; swung wide; admitted nothing; and slammed to.

(From *To the Lighthouse*, by Virginia Woolf)

Here, "the darkness", "the night wind" in the quiet house are beautifully described with poetic language. Note the rhetorical devices used in the passage and talk about the artistic effects.

1.2.3 Three Types of Descriptive Essay

(1) Description of character

There are different ways of approaching the description of character, and many kinds of characters for the writer to create, each serving different purposes. In the broad, we can divide all characters into either types or individuals. In describing types, or flat characters, the writer chooses only those details that bear directly upon the one characteristic of nationality, occupation, social role, or personality. While in describing individuals, or round characters, the writer should not only present details of one's appearance, but reveal the person's personality, qualities, behaviour and manners. It's important to grasp the person's distinct features and habits from others.

Sample paragraph:

Elizabeth, or Beth—as everyone called her—was a rosy, smooth-haired, bright-eyed girl of thirteen, with a shy manner, a timid voice, and a peaceful expression, which was seldom disturbed. Her father called her "little Miss Tranquility"; and the name suited her excellently, for she seemed to live in a happy world of her own, only venturing out to meet the few whom she trusted and loved... And she was a house-wifely little creature, and helped Hannah keep home neat and comfortable for the workers, never thinking of any reward but to be loved. Long quiet days she spend, not only nor idle, for her little world was peopled with imaginary friends, and she was by nature a busy bee. There were six dolls to be taken up and dressed every morning, for Beth was a child still and love her pets as well as ever. Not one whole or handsome one among them, all were outcasts till Beth took them in; for, when her sisters outgrew these idols, they passed to her because Amy would have nothing old or ugly. Beth cherished them all the more tenderly for that very reason, and set up a hospital for infirm dolls.

(From *Little Women*, by Louisa May Alcott)

(2) Description of a place

Usually, when describing a place, the writer often takes a bird's eye view, and organizes his writing in terms of space or physical order.

Sample essay:

Piccadilly Circus

It is difficult to say what is the real center of London, but many people would choose Piccadilly Circus(皮卡迪利广场). This is because it is not only central but also the heart of London's entertainment world. Within a few hundred yards of it we find most of London's best-known theatres and cinemas, the most famous restaurants and the most luxurious night-clubs.

In the middle of Piccadilly Circus there is a statue said to be of Eros, the God of love. Few people know that it really represents the Angel of Christian Charity. This status is the first that was ever cast in aluminium. On Cup Final night and New Year's Eve it is boarded up to prevent over-enthusiastic revellers from climbing onto it.

The buildings around the Circus are rather nondescript, though some of them are large and quite imposing. Many of them are decorated with bright neon signs and advertising goods and entertainments; Piccadilly Circus at night is a colourful sight.

Underneath Piccadilly Circus there is an important tube station with escalators leading down to two different lines. The ticket-hall, which is just below street-level, is a vast circular hall with show cases, hired by various stores, let into the walls. There are entrances from all the main streets that meet at the Circus.

(From *Background to British*, by M. D. Munro Nackenzie and L. J. Westwood)

When describing a comparatively small place, the writer often takes a visitor's view, and writes to reveal a dominant impression or mood.

Sample essay:

It was a big, dull, brick house, exactly like all the others in its row, but that on the front door there shone a brass plate on which was engraved in black letters:

MISS MINCHIN

Selected Seminary for Young Ladies

Sara often thought afterwards that the house was somehow exactly like Miss Minchin. It was respectable and well-furnished, but everything in it was ugly; and the very armchairs seemed to have hard bones in them. In the hall everthing was hard and polished—even the red cheeks of the moon face of the tall clock in the corner had a severe varnished look. The drawing-room into which they were ushered was covered by a carpet with a square pattern upon it, the chairs were square, and a heavy marble timepiece stood upon the heavy marble mantel.

(From *A Little*, *Princess*, by Frances Hodgson Burnett)

(3) Description of a scene

A scene can be a natural one or a social one. In describing a scene, the writer needs to control the degree of detail of the description based on the purpose of describing.

Sample paragraph:

It grew dark before seven o'clock. Wind and rain whipped the house. John sent his oldest son and daughter upstairs to bring down mattesses and pillows for the younger children. He wanted to keep the group together on one floor. "Stay away from the windows," he warned, concerned about glass flying from storm-shattered panes. As the wind mounted to a roar, the house began leaking—the rain seemingly driven right through the walls. With mops, towels, pots and buckets the Koshaks began a struggle against the rapidly spreading water. At 8:30, power failed, and Pop Koshak turned on the generator.

The roar of the hurricane now was overwhelming. The house shook, and the ceiling in the living room was falling piece. The French doors in an upstairs room blew in with an explosive sound, and the group heard gunlike reports as other upstairs windows disintegrated. Water rose above their ankles.

Then the front door started to break away from its frame. John and Charlie put their shoulders against it, but a blast of water hit the house, flinging open the door and shoving them down the hall. The generator was doused, and the lights went out. Charlie licked his lips and shouted to John. "I think we're in real trouble. That water tasted salty. The sea had reached the house, and the water was rising by the minute!"

"Everybody out the back door to the cars!" John yelled. "We'll pass the children along between us. Count them! Nine!"

The children went from adult to adult like buckets in a fire brigade. But the cars wouldn't start; the electrical systems had been killed by water. The wind was too strong and the water too deep to flee on foot. "Back to the house!" John yelled. "Count the children! Count nine!"

As they scramble back, John ordered, "Everybody on the stairs!" Frightened, breathless and wet, the group settled on the stairs, which were protected by two interior walls. The children put the cat, Spooky, and a box with her four kittens on the landing. She peered nervously at her litter. The neighbour's dog curled up and went to sleep.

The wind sounded like the roar of a train passing a few yards away. The house shuddered and shifted on its foundations. Water inched its way up the steps as first floor outside walls collapsed. No one spoke. Everyone knew there was no escape; they would live or die in the house.

(From *Face to Face with Hurricane Camille*, by Joseph P. Blank)

In the description of fighting against hurricane, the writer makes effective use of verbs. List some verbs you consider used most effectively and give your reasons.

Writing assignment:

Write an essay about a particular place, or a person, a scene that you can observe carefully or that you know well. You might choose one of the following or something else that you think of:

- The waiting room at a train station, bus terminal or an airport
- An antique shop or some other small shop
- A rebellious child
- A close friend
- A friends gathering
- A school graduation ceremony

1.3 Narration

Narration is extensively used in present-day writing to relate imaginary events, record the happenings of personal and collective histories, and illustrate or explain ideas. Narration can be divided into two basic types: fiction and non-fiction. Some of the many forms it may take are popular fiction, diaries, anecdote, biography and journalism. Non-fiction recounts events that actually happened.

In writing a narrative composition, the writer should clearly tell readers the setting, times, places, participants, the process and outcome. He even needs to analyze the cause or make brief comments. However, mostly, the meaning of a narrative, like the point of a joke, is best left to the reader.

There are some strategies for writing a narrative essay:

(1) Be consistent in terms of the point of view of the narrative

When writing the body of the narrative essay, there are some elements to keep in mind. One of them is, the writer needs to keep a consistent point of view in terms of the person who is telling the story and in terms of time. The author can choose to tell in story from the point of view of any character in the story or as an observer. The story can be told in first person, second person, or third person. This point of view, however, should be maintained throughout the writing, or it will be very confusing to the reader.

(2) Write a good thesis

The story you tell must have a clear purpose: it must have a point. The specific point you want to make about it, is the essay's thesis. Certainly, it can be either implicitly or explicitly expressed. This thesis should serve to focus your narration. When recounting your narration, be sure readers are clear about your narrative point, or thesis.

(3) Select the right details

Select details carefully, giving just enough of the right kind to make your point. Selection must be aimed to help the reader identify with the characters and action, to evoke reader's interest, and carry massages at the same time, perhaps even to create the same kind of suspense as the fiction writer does. Even the briefest anecdote or narrative illustration should be lively and vivid.

(4) Arrange events in clear order

Arrange events in clear order, giving sufficient links to guide the reader through the action. One kind of link, or transition, is the use of time markers such as: first, second, then, next, later, finally, before, after, or the use of the calendar or concrete time to indicate sequence. As often as not, the sequence of verbs can also help to keep the events in order, whether the action is set in the past, the present, or the future.

(5) Use dialogues to make the narrative vigorous and immediate

As we know, our sense of other people comes, in part, from what they say, the way they sound. Conversational exchanges allow the reader to experience characters directly. The dialogue should fit the mood you want to create and reveal the character.

Sample essay 1:

A Test of True love

Six minutes to six, said the digital clock over the information desk in Grand Central Station. John Blandford, a tall young army officer, focused his eyesight to the clock to note the exact time. In six minutes he would see the woman who had filled a special place in his life for the past thirteen months, a woman he had never seen, yet whose written words had been with him and had given him strength without fail.

Soon after he volunteered for military service, he had received a book from this woman. A letter, which wished him courage and safety, came with the book. He discovered that many of his friends, also in the army, had received the identical book from the woman, Hollis Meynell. And while they all got strength from it, and appreciate her support of their cause, John Blandford was the only person to write Ms. Meynell back. On the day of his departure, to a destination overseas where he would fight in the war, he received her reply. Aboard the cargo ship that was taking him into enemy territory, he stood on the deck and read the letter again and again.

For thirteen months, she had faithfully written to him. When his letters did not arrive, she wrote anyway, without decrease. During the difficult days of wars, her letters nourished him and gave him courage. As long as he received letters from her, he felt as though he could survive. After a short time, he believed he loved her, and she loved him. It was as if fate had brought them together.

But when he asked her for a photo, she declined his request. She explained her objection:"If your feelings for me have any reality, and honest basis, what I look like won't matter. Suppose I'm beautiful. I'd always be bothered by the feeling that you loved me for my beauty, and that kind of love would disgust me. Suppose I'm plain. Then I'd always fear you were writing to me only because you were lonely and had no one else. Either way, I would forbid myself from loving you. When you come to New York and you see me, then you can make your decision. Remember, both of us are free to stop or to go on after that—if that's what we choose..."

One minute to six... Blandford's heart leaped.

A young woman was coming toward him, and he felt a connection with her right away. Her figure was long and thin, her spectacular golden hair lay back in curls from her small ears. Her eyes were blue flowers; her lips had a gentle firmness. In her fancy green suit she was like springtime come alive.

He started toward her, entirely forgetting to notice that she wasn't wearing a rose, and as he moved, a small, warm smile formed on her lips.

"Going my way, soldier?" she asked.

Uncontrollably, he made one step closer to her. Then he saw Hollis Meynell.

She was standing almost directly behind the girl, a woman well past forty, and a fossil to his young eyes, her hair sporting patches of grey. She was more than fat; her thick legs shook as they moved. But she wore a red rose on her brown coat.

The girl in the green suit was walking quickly away and soon vanished into the fog. Blandford felt as though his heart was being compressed into a small cement ball, so strong was his desire to follow the girl, yet so deep was his longing for the woman whose spirit had truly companioned and brought warmth to his own; and there she stood. Her pale, fat face was gentle and intelligent; he could see that now. Her gray eyes had a warm, kindly look.

Bladford resisted the urge to follow the young woman, though it was not easy to do so. His fingers held the book she had sent to him before he went off to the war, which was to identify him to Hollis Meynell. This would not be love. However, it would be something precious, something perhaps even less common than love—a friendship for which he had been, and would always be, thankful.

He held the book out toward the woman.

"I'm John Blandford, and you—you are Ms. Meynell. I'm so glad you could meet me. May I take you to dinner?" The woman smiled. "I don't know what this is all about, son," she answered, "That young lady in the green suit—the one who just went by—begged me to wear this rose on my coat. And she said that if you asked me to go out with you, I should tell you that she's waiting for you in that big restaurant near the highway. She said it was some kind of a test."

Questions and ideas for discussion:

1. The material in this narrative is neatly organized. How do you like its begin-

ning, middle and ending?

2. Every narrative makes some kind of point, either directly or indirectly. How do you think about this story?

Sample essay 2:

The Yellow Ribbon
by Pete Hamill

They were going to Fort Lauderdate, the girl remember later. There were six of them, three boys and three girls, and they picked up the bus at the old terminal on 34th street, carrying sandwiches and wine in paper bags, dreaming of golden beaches and the tides of the sea as the gray cold spring of New York vanished behind them. Vingo was on board from the beginning.

As the bus passed through Jersey and into Philly, they began to notice that Vingo never moved. He sat in front of the young people, his dusty face masking his age, dressed in a plain brown ill-fitting suit. His fingers were stained from cigarettes and he chewed the inside of his lip a lot, frozen into some personal cocoon of silence.

Somewhere outside of Washington, deep into the night, the bus pulled into a Howard Johnson's and everybody got off except Vingo. He sat rooted in his seat, and the young people began to wonder about him, trying to imagine his life: perhaps he was a sea captain, maybe he had run away from his wife, he could be an old soldier going home. When they went back to the bus, the girl sat beside him and introduced herself.

"We're going to Florida," the girl said brightly. "You going that far?"

"I don't know." Vingo said.

"I've never been there," she said. "I hear it's beautiful."

"It is," he said quietly, as if remember something he had tried to forget.

"You live there?"

"I did some time there in the Navy. Jacksonville."

"Want some wine?" she said. He smiled and took the bottle of Chianti and took a swig. He thanked her and retreated again into silence. After a while, she went back to the others, as Vingo nodded into sleep.

In the morning they awoke outside another Howard Johnson's, and this time Vingo went in. The girl insisted that he join them. He seemed very shy and ordered black coffee and smoked nervously, as the young people chattered about sleeping on the beaches. When they went back on the bus, the girl sat with Vingo again, and after a while, slowly and painfully and with great hesitation, he began to tell his story.

He had been in jail in New York for the last four years, and now he was going home.

"Four years!" the girl said. "What did you do?"

"It doesn't matter," he said with quiet bluntness. "I did it and I went to jail. If you can't do the time, don't do the crime. That's what they say and they are right."

"Are you married?"

"I don't know."

"You don't know?" She said.

"Well, when I was in the can I wrote to my wife," he said. "I told her that. I said I was gonna be away a long time, and that if she couldn't stand it, if the kids kept asking questions, if it hurt her too much, well she could just forget me. Get a new guy—she's a wonderful woman, really something—and forget about me. I told her she didn't have to write me or nothing. And she didn't. Not for three and a half years."

"And you're going home now, not knowing?"

"Yeah," he said shyly. "Well, last week, when I was sure the parole was coming through I wrote her. I told her that if she had a new guy, I understood. But if she didn't, if she would take me back she should let me know. We used to live in this town, Brunswick, just before Jacksonville, and there's a great big oak tree just as you come into town, a very famous tree, huge, I tole her if she would take me back, she should put a yellow handkerchief on the tree, and I would get off and come home. If she didn't want me, forget it, no handkerchief, and I'd keep going on through."

"Wow," the girl said. "Wow."

She told the others, and soon all of them were in it, caught up in the approach of Brunswick, looking at the pictures Vingo showed them of his wife and three children, the woman handsome in a plain way, the children still unformed in a cracked, much-handled snapshot. Now they were twenty miles from Brunswick and the young people took over window seats on the right side, waiting for the approach of the great oak tree. Vingo stopped looking, tightening his face into the ex-con's mask, as if fortifying himself against still another disappointment. Then it was ten miles, and then five and the bus acquired a dark hushed mood, full of silence, of absence, of lost years, of the woman's plain face, of the sudden letter on the breakfast table, of the wonder of children, of the iron bars of solitude.

Then suddenly all of the young people were up out of their seats, screaming and shouting and crying, doing small dances, shaking clenched fists in triumph and exaltation. All except Vingo.

Vingo sat there stunned, looking at the oak tree. It was covered with yellow handkerchiefs, twenty of them, thirty of them, maybe hundreds, a tree that stood like a banner of welcome blowing and billowing in the wind, turned into a gorgeous yellow blur by the passing bus. As the young people shouted, the old con slowly rose from his seat, holding himself tightly, and made his way to the front of the bus to go home.

Questions and ideas for discussion:

1. The thesis of the essay is implied rather than stated directly. See if you can state the thesis in your own words.

2. In paragraph 11, it writes, "Vingo seemed very shy." Find at least two pieces of evidence in the passage to support the idea.

3. It is implied that despite his crime, Vingo was a honorable man. Find evidence that support this point.

4. What transition words or coherence devices the writer used to keep the flow of his narration?

Writing assignment:

1. Write an essay narrating an experience in which a certain emotion was dominant. The emotion might be happiness, disappointment, frustration, any of the following, or some other:

Love   Shock   Loss   Loneliness   Silliness
Nostalgia   Hate   Anger   Terror   Fear

2. Tell the story of some unusual events in the lives of people whom you know well. Use the first person narration, characterize them at least briefly in the beginning in addition to locating the reader in time and place. Be sure to make your narrative meaningful.

3. Write a narrative essay recounting an event you witnessed on your trip or a journey back home.

1.4　Exposition

Exposition means expounding or explaining. It is probably the most common type of writing—in reports, term papers, prose, critical essays, etc. Although exposition often contains description and narration, its role is not merely to paint a word picture or to tell a story. Instead, its main objective is to expose—to set forth and explain—information and ideas about a particular subject.

Seldom is any piece of writing pure exposition. Just as the lecture tells a story or uses maps, charts to interest his audience and clinch his point, so the expository writer may turn for aid to narration or description. The writing of exposition begins, therefore, in an understanding of the broad purpose to be achieved. It begins, like all composition, in the writer's head. What specific point do I intend to make? For whom am I writing? How can I best convey my point to my readers? Deciding upon readers and purpose is easily half the task of writing. Once the writer has determined what point he intends to make, the writer has saved himself time by eliminating several false starts, and he has already resisted temptation to lose himself and his readers in the thickets and bypaths of his subject. With his readers in mind he has already solved many of his problems of diction and tone as well. In a word, the first requirement of all writing—a definite point for definite readers.

The particulars of exposition are patterns of logic and evidence, patterns that may shape individual paragraphs, a group of several paragraphs, or the composition in its entirety. The expository writer, therefore, uses the common methods of logic and thinking: he develops his material by offering examples as evidence, by comparing or contrasting, by giving reasons, by classifying and dividing his subject, by showing cause and effect, by defining, by arguing from premise to conclusion. The following give examples of each of the common types of expository.

(1) Illustration

In the illustration essay, the writer uses a number of carefully chosen examples to illustrate or support his thesis. The essay usually begins with an introduction that includes the thesis statement, which is supported by examples in the body of the essay. Each body paragraph may develop a separate example, present a point illustrated by several brief examples. The conclusion then provides a brief summary of what the examples illustrate and reinforces the controlling idea of the essay. At times, however, variation of this basic pattern are advisable and even necessary. For instance, begin a paper with a striking example to stimulate the reader's interest and curiosity or end the writing with one to vividly reinforce the thesis. Well-used examples make writing more effective and persuasive.

Sample essay:

The American Character
by Bradford Smith

The temptation is strong to lump all Americans together. Yet those who look a little deeper are puzzled by the seeming contradictions in American life. It is true that

Americans as a whole work hard. But they also play hard. They spend more time and money in traveling, camping, hunting, watching sports, drinking, smoking, reading. Yet they also spend more money on churches, social services, hospitals and all kinds of charities. They are always in a hurry, yet they spend more time relaxing. They are at the same time sensitive to the rights of the individual and habitual conformists. They worship bigness yet idealize the little man, whether he be the small business man as opposed to the big one or the plain citizen as opposed to the big wheel.

Americans love work. It is meat and drink to them. If it's skiing, they throw themselves at it with an effort that would kill a horse. They like to be handy at all things. College professors go in for making furniture or remodelling an old house in the country. Bankers don aprons and become expert barbecue chefs. Nearly everyone knows how to use tools, make simple repairs to plumbing or electrical fixtures, refinish furniture or paint a wall. Far from being thought a disgrace if he performs these "menial" task, a man is thought ridiculous if he does not know how to perform them.

Americans carry with them an appearance which is more a result of attitude than of clothing. This attitude combines a lack of class consciousness, a somewhat jaunty optimism and an inquisitiveness which in combination look to the European like naivete. Also a liking for facts and figures, an alertness more muscular and ocular than intellectual, and above all a desire to be friendly.

To boil it down to the briefest summary, American characteristics are the product of response to an unusually competitive situation combined with unusual opportunity.

Americans are a peculiar people. They work like mad, then give away much of what they earn. They play until they are exhausted, and call this a vocation. They love to think of themselves as tough-minded business men, yet they are pushovers for any hard luck story. When meeting, they are always telling each other, "Take it easy," then they rush off like crazy in opposite directions. They play games as if they were fighting a war, and fight wars as if playing a game. They marry more, go broke more often and make more money than any other people. They crowd their highways with cars while complaining about the traffic, flock to movies and television while griping about the quality and the commercials, go to church but don't care much for sermons, and drink too much in the hope of relaxing—only to find themselves stimulated to even bigger dreams.

There is, of course, no typical American. But if you added them all together and then divided by 226000000 they would look something like what this chapter has tried to portray.

Questions and ideas for discussion:

1. What're the author's views on the American character? What examples does he use to support his points?

2. Does the author believe in a single pattern of national behaviour and attitude? In what sense does he use the term "the American Character" then? Do you think him justified?

Writing assignment:

1. Write an illustrative essay on one of the following topics:
- The advantages of temporary jobs for college student
- Problems with my apartment
- Benefits of television

2. Apart from your family, who has influenced you most? Give specific examples to show how you have been influenced.

3. Write an essay in which you discuss some of the positive or negative characteristics of people in a city. You can use your family and friends as examples.

(2) Process analysis

A process analysis essay explains how to do something or how something occurs. It presents a sequence of steps and show how those steps lead to an expected or planned result. There are two types of process analysis essays: those that instruct or direct and those that explain or analyze. Directional essays tell how to do something, and process analysis essays that explain or analyze tell how something works, how something happened, how something is or was done.

Usually the introduction of the process essay is a brief paragraph indicating the process to be described and the purpose for describing it. The arrangement of the body will depend on the process and the steps involved. The sequence of the steps is important and each step must be covered with enough details so that the reader will have no question. The conclusion is a nature place to emphasize the value of the explanation and make the reader feel like he has learned something worthwhile.

Sample 1:

Cheesemaking

Hundreds of different names for cheese are used throughout the world, but the general principles of making cheese from milk have changed little for nearly 3,000 years. The aroma, texture, and taste of cheese depend on slight variations of the process used to produce it, but all methods consist of two to four basic steps. The first step consists of the coagulation of the protein "casein" by adding acid or enzyme to the milk, usually cow's milk, but sometimes the milk of the sheep, goat, mare, ass, reindeer, llama, yak, camel, or buffalo. Next, the liquid, called whey, is drained, leaving a semi-solid cheese, called curds, which may be eaten in this form or processed further. All soft or cream cheese are of this type. Hard cheese undergoes two additional steps in the process. The semi-solid cheese is matured until it reaches the required level of acidity, at which time it is salted and pressed into forms or moulds to gibe it the distinctive shape and size of a particular cheese. The final step is the aging process during which the world's most famous cheese acquire their unique flavours from the place and length of storage. Changes in the manufacture and storage produce different kinds of cheeses, but cheese is one of the universal foods from the regions of the world where mild-producing mammals live and varies only slightly in the basic manufacturing process.

Sample 2:

How to Prepare for Earthquakes

Ideally, people would like to know when an earthquake is going to happen and how bad it will be. In both Japan and China, people have long believed that earthquakes can be forecast. In Japan, scientists have wired the Earth and sea to detect movements. The Chinese have traditionally watched animal and plants for warning signs of earthquakes. For example, the Chinese have noted that before an earthquake, hens refuse to enter their cages at night, and dogs bark a lot. Perhaps most interesting, and most easily measured, is a chemical change in ground water before a quake. Experimental data seem to indicate that the amount of radon in the water under the surface of the Earth waxes before an earthquake.

People would also like to be able to prevent the great destruction of property caused by earthquakes. After all, most of the people who die in earthquakes are killed by falling buildings. Therefore, building structures that can withstand the power of earthquakes is a major concern. Steel seems to be the best material, but not if it is welded to form a rigid structure. Many new structures are built with a new type of steel joint, an I-joint, which appears to be the most durable type of joint.

Besides working to improve build structures, people in areas where earthquakes are common need to prepare for the possibility of a great earthquake. They should regularly check and reinforce their homes, place heavy objects in low positions, attach cupboards and cabinets to walls, and fasten doors so that they will not open accidentally during an earthquake.

In addition to preparing their houses, people in these regions need to prepare themselves. They should have supplies of water and food at home and at work. It is best to store several gallons of water per person, store one week's food for each person. Earthquake survival supplies include a radio receiver, a torch, extra batteries, first aid supplies, a spade, a tent, some rope, and warm clothing. Experts also suggest the following:

Keep a fire extinguisher handy. You should have one at home, at work, and in your car. The fire extinguisher should be able to put out any type of fire. Have the proper tools to turn off gas and water lines if necessary.

Every family needs to have earthquake emergency plans. How will family members leave the area during the chaos following an earthquake? Everyone should agree on a meeting point outside of the area—perhaps in a town several miles away. Also important is an arrangement for family members to communicate if there is an earthquake. If an earthquake happens in a large city, many of the telephone lines within the city are likely to be down. The few remaining working lines will be busy with the calls that naturally occur after a disaster and it will be difficult to call from one part of the city to another. It might, however, be possible to call outside the city. A sensible arrangement is to have all of the members of the family call to check in with a friend or relative who lives more than a hundred miles away.

Although scientists still cannot predict earthquakes, they are learning a great deal about how the large plates in the Earth's crust move, the stresses between plates, how earthquake work, and the general probability that a given place will have an earthquake. Someday soon it may actually become possible to predict earthquakes with accuracy. And education concerning how to survive an earthquake should be a major emphasis for all government programs and earthquake-related research projects.

Writing assignment:
Any one of the topics below can be written as a process paper:
- How to break a bad habit
- How to do well in a job interview
- How to add romance to your life
- How to care for an aging relative

(3) Cause and effect analysis

The main purpose of a cause-and-effect essay is to explain to your audience: the causes of a particular event or situation; the effects of an event or a situation; or more rarely, a combination of both.

The type of cause-and-effect essay will depend on the topic you choose and the main point you wish to communicate. If, for example, your purpose is to tell readers about the impact a special teacher had on your life, your essay would focus mainly on the *effect* of that person. However, if your purpose is to explain why you hate to live in the apartment on campus, your essay would focus on the *cause* of your direction.

Here are some useful transitions and expressions in cause-and-effect essay:

a. Transitions in phrase: *because of*, *as a result of*, *to result from*, *to be due to*, *to lead to*, *to contribute to*, *to result in*, *in consequence of*;

b. Transitional expressions between sentences: *thus*, *therefore*, *consequently*, *for this reason*, *as a result*, *then*, *accordingly*;

c. Coordinating conjunctions as transitions: *so* (indicating a result), *for* (indicating a cause);

d. Adverbial clauses of cause or result: Both *because* and *since* can be added to sentences to make adverbial clauses of cause. Adverbial clauses of result are made by connecting sentences with *so/such...that*.

Sample 1:

Iron deficiency is very common among women in general, affecting one in four female teenagers and one in five women aged 18 to 45, respectively. But the ratio is even greater among active women, affecting up to 80 percent of female endurance athletes. This means, Lyle says, that "too many women ignore the amount of iron they take in". Women of childbearing age at great risk, since their monthly bleeding is a major source of iron loss. Plus, many health-conscious women increase their risk by rejecting red meat, which contains the most easily absorbed form of iron. And because women often restrict their diet in an effort to control weight, they may not consume enough iron-rich food, and are liable to experience a deficiency.

Sample 2:

Does Exercise Have Unexpected Benefits?

Just as exercise strengthens the heart and lungs, bones and muscles, it may also power up the brain. A succession of scientific studies of animal implies that physical activity has a positive effect on mental functioning.

"It's clear that the brain benefits from exercise." says brain scientist William Greenough of the University of Illinois at Urbana-Champaign. His studies with rats have demonstrate two primary effects of activity: Vigorous physical exercise provides the brain with more fuel, and skill-based exercise increases the formation of connections in the brain, which according to the proposals of some scientists, may make the brain better able to process information.

In one experiment, laboratory rats were separated into three groups. One group took exercise by running inside an automatic wheel, a second group improved their skills in a complicated obstacle course, and a third group was inactive.

"The animals that learned to go through the obstacle course exhibited a great number of brain connections than the animals in the exercised or inactive groups," Greenough said, "In contrast, the animals that exercised inside the automatic wheel possessed a greater density of blood vessels in the brain than either of the other two groups of animals did. " Though animals aren't people, he says it is logical to make the inference that an effect found in rats may also apply to humans.

Human studies have focused primarily on old adults and suggest that regular exercise can improve the speed with which the brain processes information. Measurements made by Arthur Krammer at the University of Illinois demonstrated that inactive adults, aged 63 to 82, could hit buttons faster in response to a tone after they went through a 10-week water exercise course. A corresponding control group that didn't exercise showed no improvement.

This boost in reaction time after exercise training may occur because declines associated with getting old could actually stem from declines in physical condition. Some scientists speculate the reduction in mental function often attributed to getting old may really be a penalty of neglecting to stay physically active, in addition to related factors such as medicines and poor diet.

Numerous studies show that children who engage in regular physical activity do better in school than their inactive classmates. But until recently the academic edge gained by participants in sports was thought to come from the increase of self-confidence, the better mood, and the ability to concentrate that comes from burning off steam in exercise. Now, however, some scientists have revised their ways of thinking, and point to possible physical connections.

Pierce J. Howard, another expert, says new research indicates that physical exercise increase the amount of certain brain chemicals that stimulate the growth of nerve cells. Consequently, the brains of people who exercise may be better equipped to tackle mental challenges.

Inactivity may also have negative effects on mind and body alike. "Scientists recognize that mind is body, and body is mind," comments Howard. The most beneficial forms of exercise, he says, engage both.

(4) Comparison and contrast

Both comparison and contrast are ways of understanding one subject by putting it next to another. In the narrowest sense, comparison shows how two or more things are similar, and contrast shows how they are different.

There are two patterns the writer may follow to organize the body of the essay. The first is the **block** method. In this method, the writer describes the characteristics of one subject and then the other. This method works best if the essay is short and there are only few characteristics.

Take this thesis for example: The Teaching Styles Are Different Between English Oral and Writing Class

Subject (Block) 1 the oral class
　　Point 1: students activities
　　Point 2: teacher's guides
　　Point 3: the class atmosphere
Subject (Block) 2 the writing class
　　Point 1: students activities
　　Point 2: teacher's guides
　　Point 3: the class atmosphere

The second pattern of comparing and contrasting is called the **point-by-point** method. In this method, the writer compares or contrasts the two subjects feature by feature. Each time something is said about one subject, the same characteristics is addressed regarding the other subject, for example:

Thesis statement: Cultural Differences in Western and Japanese Decision-Making

Point 1: the communication style
　　A: in Japan
　　B: in Western countries
Point 2 the management behaviour
　　A: in Japan
　　B: in Western countries

Transition words are very important for compare/contrast essays. They help remind the readers of what is happening in the composition.

Transition words for comparing, like: just as...so; like...; likewise; similarly; in the same way; as well as; much the same as; in addition to...

Transition words for contrast, like: although; in contrast; while; however; conversely; different from; despite; instead; on the contrary; on the one hand... on the other hand; still; yet; whereas

Sample essay:

The English and the American
by Edward T. Hall

It has been said that the English and the Americans are two great people separated by one language. The differences for which language gets blamed may not be due so much to words as to communications on other levels beginning with English intonation and continuing to ego-linked ways of handling time, space, and materials. If there were two cultures in which differences of the proxemic details are marked, it is in the educated (public school) English and the middle-class Americans. One of the basic reasons for this wide disparity is that in the United States we use space as a way of classifying people and activities, whereas in England it is the social system that determines who you are. In the United States, your address is an important cue to status (this applies not only to one's home but to the business address as well). The Joneses from Brooklyn and Miami are not as "in" as the Joneses from Newport and Palm Beach. Greechwich and Cape God are worlds apart from Newark and Miami. Business located on Madison and Park avenue have more tone than those on Seventhe and Eighth avenue. A corner office is more prestigious than one next to the elevator or at the end of a long hall. The Englishman, however, is born and brought up in a social system. He is still Lord—no matter where you find him, even if it is behind the counter in a fishmonger's stall. In addition to class distinctions, there are differences between the English and ourselves in how space is allotted.

The middle-class American growing up in the United States feels he has a right to have his own room, or at least part of a room. American women who want to be alone can go to the bedroom and close the door. The closed door is the sign meaning "Do not disturb" or "I'm angry." An American is available if his door is open at home or at his office. He is expected not to shut himself off but to maintain himself in a state of constant readiness to answer the demands of others. Closed doors are for conferences, private conversations, and business, study, resting, sleeping, work that requires concentration, etc.

The middle and upper-class Englishman, on the other hand, is brought up in a nursery shared with brothers and sisters. The oldest occupies a room by himself which he vacates when he leaves for boarding school, possibly even at the age of nine or ten. The difference between a room of one's own and early conditioning to shared space, while seeming inconsequential, has an important effect on the Englishman's attitude toward his own space. He may nerve have a permanent "room of his own" and seldom expects one or feels he is entitled to one. Even Members of Parliament have no offices and often conduct their business on the terrace overlooking the Thames. As a consequence, the English are puzzled by the American need for a secure place in which to work, an office. Americans working in England may become annoyed if they are not provided with what they consider appropriate enclosed work space. In regard to the need for walls as a screen for the ego, this places the Americans somewhere between the Germans and the English.

The contrasting English and American patterns have some remarkable implications, particularly if we assume that man, like other animals, has a build-in need to shut himself off from others from time to time. An English student in one of my seminars typified what happens when hidden patterns clash. He was quite obviously experiencing stain in his relationships with Americans. Nothing seemed to go right and it was quite clear from his remarks that we did not know how to behave. An analysis of his complaints showed that a major source of irritation was that no American seemed to be able to pick up the subtle clues that there were times when he didn't want his thoughts intruded on. As he stated it, "I'm walking around the apartment and it seems that whenever I want to be alone my roommate starts talking to me. Pretty soon he's asking, 'What's the matter?' and wants to know if I'm angry. By then I am angry and say something."

It took some time but finally we were able to identify most of the contrasting features of the American and British problems that were in conflict in this case. When the American wants to be alone he goes into a room and shut the door—he depends on architectural features for screening. For an American to refuse to talk to someone else present in the same room, to give them the "silent treatment" is the ultimate form of rejection and a sure sign of great displeasure. The English, on the other hand, lacking rooms of their own since childhood, never developed the practice of using space as a refuge from others. They have in effect internalized a set of barriers, which they erect and which others are supposed to recognized. Therefore, the more the Englishman shuts himself off when he is with an American the more likely the American is to break in to assure himself that all is well. Tension lasts until the two get to know each other. The important point is that the spatial and architectural needs of each are not the same at all.

Questions and ideas for discussion:
1. What is the thesis statement in this essay?
2. What kind of compare and contrast patterns are used in the essay?
3. Besides comparison and contrast, what other exposition devices are used in the essay?

(5) Definition

Definition is the process of explaining a word, term, object, or idea in such a way that the reader knows as precisely as possible what we mean. In a particular writing situation, a definition may be essential because a term has more than one meaning, because we are using it in an unusual way, or because we believe the term is specialized or unfamiliar to readers. For example, definition can explain abstractions like *romantism* or controversial terms like *right to life* or slang terms.

Definition can be objective or subjective. An objective definition explains what a term exactly means by placing it in a class to which it fits and by supplying the characteristics that distinguish that term from all other items in that class. A sentence or formal definition usually strives for objectivity. For example, *Sociology* may be defined as *the branch of science which studies the development and principles of social organization. It is concerned with group behaviour as distinct from the behaviour of individuals in the group.*

An extended definition, a longer, more complex definition that requires a paragraph, an essay, or even a whole book tends to be subjective. That is, it may define a term in a way that reflects your attitude toward the subject or your reason for defining it. For example, a more personal, artistic and spiritual definition on *love*:

What is love? For some it is like a resting place, a shelter from the storm. It exists to give you comfort, it is there to keep you warm. Perhaps love is like a window, perhaps an open door, it invites you to come closer, it wants to show you more.

Sample essay:

Plot
by E. M. Forster

Let us define a plot. We have defined a story as a narrative of events arranged in their time-sequence. A plot is also a narrative of events, the emphasis falling on causality. "The king died and then the queen died," is a story. "The king died, and then the queen died of grief," is a plot. The time-sequence is preserved, but the sense of causality overshadows it. Or again: "The queen died, no one knew why, until it was discovered that it was through grief at the death of the king." This is a plot with a mystery in it, a form capable of high development. It suspends the time-sequence, it moves as far away from the story as its limitations will allow. Consider the death of the queen. If it is in a story we say "and then?" If it is in a plot we ask, "why?" That is the fundamental difference between these two aspects of the novel. A plot cannot be told to a gaping audience of cave men or to a tyrannical sultan or to their modern descendant the movie-public. They can only be kept awake by "and then—and then." They can only supply curiosity. But a plot demands intelligence and memory also.

Curiosity is one of the lowest of the human faculties. You will have noticed in daily life that when people are inquisitive they nearly always have bad memories and are usually stupid at bottom. The man who begins by asking you how many brothers and sisters you have, is never a sympathetic character, and if you meet him in a year's time he will probably ask you how many brothers and sisters you have, his mouth again sagging open, his eyes still bulging from his head. It is difficult to be friends with such a man, and for two inquisitive people to be friends must be impossible. Curiosity by itself takes us a very little way, nor does it take us far into the novel—only as far as the story. If we would grasp the plot we must add intelligence and memory.

Intelligence first. The intelligent novel-reader, unlike the inquisitive one who just runs his eye over a new fact, mentally picks it up. He sees it from two points of view: isolated, and related to the other facts that he has read on previous pages. Probably he does not understand it, but he does not expect to do so yet awhile. The facts in a highly organized novel (like *The Egoist*) are often of the nature of cross-correspondences and the ideal spectator cannot expect to view them properly until he is sitting up on a hill at the end. This element of surprise or mystery—the detective element as it is sometimes rather emptily called—is of great importance in plot. It occurs through a suspension of the time-sequence, a mystery is a pocket in time, and it occurs crudely, as in "why did the queen die?", and more subtly in half-explained gestures and words, the true meaning of which only dawns pages ahead. Mystery is essential to a plot, and cannot be appreciated without intelligence. To the curious it is just another "and then—" To appreciate mystery, part of the mind must be left behind, brooding, while the other part goes marching on.

That brings us to our second qualification: memory. Memory and intelligence are closely connected, for unless we remember we cannot understand. If by the time the queen dies we have forgotten the existence of the king we shall never make out what killed her. The plot-maker expects us to remember, we expect him to leave no loose ends. Every action or word ought to count; it ought to be economical and spare; even when complicated it should be organic and free from dead matter. It may be difficult or easy, it may and should contain mysteries, but it ought not to mislead. And over it, as it unfolds, will hover the memory of the reader (that dull glow of the mind of which intelligence is the bright advancing edge) and will constantly rearrange and reconsider, seeing new clues, new chains of cause and effect, and the final sense(if the plot has been a fine one) will not be of clues or chains, but something aesthetically compact, something which might have been shown by the novelist straight away, only if he had shown it straight away it would never have become beautiful. We come up against beauty here—for the first time in our inquiry: beauty at which a novelist should never aim, though he fails if he does not achieve it. I will conduct beauty to her proper place later on. Meanwhile please accept her as part of a completed plot. She looks a little surprised at being there, but beauty ought to look a little surprised: it is the emotion that best suits her face, as Botticelli knew when he painted her risen from the waves, between the winds and the flowers. The beauty who does not look surprised, who accepts her position as her due—she reminds us too much of a prima donna.

(From *Aspects of the Novel*)

Questions for discussion:

1. What is the genus of plot?
2. Does Mr. Forster differentiate plot explicitly or implicitly?

Writing assignment:

1. Write a definition of *healthy lifestyle*, using examples wherever appropriate. Your definition might focus on both mental and physical health and might include some living habits.

Alternatively, you might decide to take a playful point of view and write an essay defining an *unhealthy lifestyle*.

2. Write an essay of definition in which you define a human quality, such as "tactlessness", "arrogance", "cautiousness".

(6) Division and classification

Division and classification means dividing or classifying a subject according to a single principle. Once you decide to use a division/classification pattern, you need to identify your yardstick of classification. Every group of people, things, or ideas can be categorized in many ways. When you organize things in an essay, the yardstick according to which things are divided and classified is determined by your writing situation—your purpose, your audience, and your special knowledge and interests. The important thing is to remain consistent and use only one yardstick for division and classification in an essay.

Some words and expressions are commonly used in division and classification essay, like: fall into, divide... into, classify... into, be divided into, be classified into, etc.

Sample Essay:

Study Habits

In college in any class, you will find widely different types of people, not only in personality but also in scholastic attitude. This same range from one extreme to the other can also be observed in their study habits. In fact, students can be divided into distinct groups based on their study habits. There are basically three categories: the perpetual learner, the average learner, and the crammer.

The perpetual learner is a rare breed indeed. But they exist and they aren't very hard to spot. They usually sit in the front of the class and write about three pages of notes a day regardless of how much material the instructor covers. They don't talk to anyone except to answer questions, and that only at the end of class when the lecture is over. When a perpetual learner goes home, before he does anything else, he takes out all his books and begins studying for the classes that he has the next day. When he is informed that he has a test, he will begin preparing for it at least five days in advance unless, of course, he is told less than five days previous to the test, in which case he will study until he has covered all the notes he has at least ten times or until he knows the material backwards and forwards. Although the perpetual learner does well in school, he usually misses out on social life. There are a select few who maintain something of a social life, but this is rare. Most of them never meet new people except in situations where they are forced to, such as meeting their roommates at the start of school. However, they will graduate with a 4.0 grade point average and be successful in life—as long as they don't choose careers that require many social skills.

The majority of students fall into a category that I refer to as the average learner. This person studies sufficiently but doesn't work more than necessary. He may put in anywhere from two to six hours a day studying during the week leaving Friday and Saturday for his social life and then spend from four to eight hours studying on Sunday. The average learner takes his education seriously and will study with friends much more often than the perpetual learner will. He will have a good time getting an education. For him the line between education and having a good time is a lot thinner than with the perpetual learner. The average learner will leave college with at least a solid education and will be much more socially adept than the perpetual learner.

The third type of learner is the crammer. This type of person studies only when the threat of taking that class over is very great. When he studies for a test, he doesn't begin until the night before or the morning of the test. He spends most of his time doing anything that doesn't have to do with school. Their homework is last on their list of things to do. Cleaning the room even takes precedence over homework—not to mention sleep. But at the very last minute—before the axe falls, so to speak—they will hit the books.

The crammers are easily recognized in any classroom. They sit in the place farthest from the teacher, and they usually group together. They seem to have the attitude that they are in class to do nothing but have a good time and attract attention. They may enjoy interrupting class. Although some of the crammers won't last for four years, most of them will graduate. They will leave college, though, with little education and few social skills.

It can be argued, of course, that there should be a forth category—the never learner, one who quite literally never studies not even at the very last minute. But then, this person doesn't remain classified as a student for very long.

Writing assignment:

1. Write an essay in which you classify different reactions to a particular story, song, or television program.

2. Classify the different types of roommates in your school. Label each type of roommate like "the messy type", "the neatnik", or "the loud-music-lover", etc., and explain what it would be like to live with them.

1.5 Argumentation

1.5.1 An Overview

While exposition explains and judgment unfolds a question and measures out an answer, argument persuades. More exactly, it persuades by appealing to reason. The essence of argument, then, is reason. The ability to put forth sound and compelling arguments is an important skill in everyday life.

1.5.2　Strategies for Argumentation

(1) The use of tactful, courteous language

In an argumentation essay, you are attempting to persuade readers to accept your viewpoint. It is important, therefore, not to anger them by referring to them or their opinions in rude or belittling terms. Stay away from sweeping statements like "everybody knows that..." or "people with any intelligence agree that..." Also, keep the focus on the issue you are discussing, not on the people involved in the debate.

(2) The use of sufficient evidence

Any thesis statement containing opinions and ideas is based on facts. Evidence that can be used to develop an argument can be of many kinds. The major kinds of evidence you will need to support your thesis include the following:

- Examples

Examples can be very persuasive in support of arguments. They help create atmosphere and make complex theories plainer. Remember to choose concrete, illustrative and representative examples.

- Facts

Some facts are readily accepted because they are a part of general knowledge—we know they are true and they can be verified.

- Statistics

Reports with figures are always helpful for their vividness and accuracy. Remember to select statistics carefully and avoid presenting a long list of figures. Keep in mind the purpose for which you select statistics and put them together.

- Authorities

Most readers regard government publications, standard reference works, books, and periodicals published by established firms as recognized and reliable sources. In addition, opinions from experts, who are knowledgeable and experienced in certain fields, are likely to be accepted by the reader.

(3) The use of emotional appeal

The emotional appeal to readers can be used to assist argumentation. Emotion appeals to the reader's self interest or their need for survival, safety, love or esteem. Probably the most common use of emotion to persuade is in advertising, like the star effect used in TV commercials to lead consuming. Appeal to feelings can be very powerful.

(4) The use of logic appeal

A good piece of argumentative writing requires clear logic in reasoning, and reason may work in two ways: by induction and by deduction.

- Inductive reasoning

The process of inductive reasoning leads the reader to move from various items of specific evidence to some related generalization. That is, you first present facts and then arrive at a particular conclusion. In this process, you establish the cause or causes of something. This pattern wins its popularity for it is easy to be used.

The technique of inductive reasoning is good for establishing probability or arriving at generalization. Nevertheless, you should avoid basing a generalization on too little evidence; otherwise, that generalization will seem hasty and unfounded.

- Deductive reasoning

This writing argues from particular facts to broad conclusion. The reasoning is based on a three-part formula: a major premier, a minor premise, and a conclusion. Here is an example:

Major premise: Big cities can be dangerous.

Minor premise: New York is one of the big cities.

Conclusion: New York can be dangerous.

If both premises are right, then readers have no choice but to accept your conclusion. To reach a valid conclusion, be sure to state an accepted major premise and a factual minor premise of that generalization. Meanwhile, avoid faulty syllogism like this:

Major premise: People can't be trusted.

Minor premise: Jerry is a person.

Conclusion: Jerry can't be trusted.

Here the illogical reasoning results from a faulty major premise (or generalization), which is not generally accepted.

Sample Essay 1:

Cocksure Women and Hensure Men

by D. H. Lawrence

It seems to me there are two aspects to women. There is the demure and the dauntless. Men have loved to dwell, in fiction at least, on the demure maiden whose inevitable reply is: "Oh, yes, if you please, kind sir!" The demure maiden, the demure spouse, the demure mother—this is still the ideal. A few maidens, mistresses and mothers are demure. A few pretend to be. But the vast majority are not. And they don't pretend to be. We don't expect a girl skilfully driving her car to be demure, we expect her to be dauntless. What good would demure and maidenly Members of Parliament be, inevitably responding: Oh, yes, if you please, kind sir! — Though of course there are masculine members of that kidney. —And a demure telephone girl? Or even a demure stenographer? Demureness, to be sure, is outwardly becoming, it is an outward mark of femininity, like bobbed hair. But it goes with inward dauntlessness. The girl who has got to make her way in life has got to be dauntless, and if she has a pretty, demure manner with it, then lucky girl. She kills two birds with two stones.

With the two kinds of femininity go two kinds of confidence: there are the women who are cocksure, and the women who are hensure. A really up-to-date woman is a cocksure woman. She doesn't have a doubt nor a qualm. She is the modern type. Whereas the old-fashioned demure woman was sure as a hen is sure, that is, without knowing anything about it. She went quietly and busily clucking around, laying the eggs and mothering the chickens in a kind of anxious dream that still was full of sureness. But not mental sureness. Her sureness was a physical condition, very soothing, but a condition out of which she could easily be startled or frightened.

It is quite amusing to see the two kinds of sureness in chickens. The cockerel is, naturally, cocksure. He crows because he is certain it is day. Then the hen peeps out from under her wing. He marches to the door of the henhouse and pokes out his head assertively: Ah ha! Daylight, of course, just as I said! —and he majestically steps down the chicken ladder towards terra firma, knowing that the hens will step cautiously after him, drawn by his confidence. So after him, cautiously, step the hens. He crows again: Ha-ha! Here we are! —It is indisputable, and the hens accept it entirely. He marches towards the house. From the house a person ought to appear, scattering corn. Why does the person not appear? The cock will see to it. He is cocksure. He gives a loud crow in the doorway, and the person appears. The hens suitably impressed but immediately devote all their henny consciousness to the scattered corn, pecking absorbedly, while the cock runs and fusses, cocksure that he is responsible for it all.

So the day goes on. The cock finds a tit-bit, and loudly calls the hens. They scuffle up in henny surety, and gobble the tit-bit. But when they find a juicy morsel for themselves, they devour it in silence, hensure. Unless, of course, there are little chicks, when they most anxiously call the brood. But in her own dim surety, the hen is really much surer than the cock, in a different way. She marches off to lay her eggs, she secures obstinately the nest she wants, she lays her eggs at last, then steps forth again with prancing confidence, and gives that most assured of all sounds, the hensure cackle of bird who has laid her egg. The cock, who is never so sure about anything as the hen is about the egg she has laid, immediately starts to cackle like the female of his species. He is pinning to be hensure, for hensure is so much surer than cocksure. Nevertheless, cocksure is boss. When the chicken-hawk appears in the sky, loud are the cockerel's calls of alarm. Then the hens scuffle under the verandah, the cock ruffles his feathers on guard. The hens are numb with fear, they say: "Alas, there is no health in us! How wonderful to be a cock so bold!"—And they huddle, numbed. But their very numbness is hensurety.

Just as the cock can cackle, however, as if he had laid the eggs, so can the hen bird crow. She can more or less assume his cocksureness. And she is never so easy, cocksure, as she used to be when she was hensure. Cocksure, she is cocksure, but uneasy. Hensure, she trembles, but is easy.

It seems to me just the same in the vast human farmyard. Only nowadays all the cocks are cackling and pretending to lay eggs, and all the hens are crowing and pretending to call the sun out of bed. If women today are cocksure, men are hensure. Men are timid, tremulous, rather soft and submissive, easy in their very henlike tremulousness. They only want to be spoken to gently. So the women step forth with a good loud *Cock-a-doole-do*!

The tragedy about cocksure women is that they are more cocky, in their assurance, than the cock himself. They never realize that when the cock gives his loud crow in the morning, he listens acutely afterwards, to hear if some other wretch of a cock dare crow defiance, challenge, danger and death on the clear air; or the possibility thereof.

But, when the hen crows, she listens for no defiance or challenge. When she says *Cock-a-doodle-do*! Then it is unanswerable. The cock listens for an answer, alert. But the hens knows she is unanswerable. *Cock-a-doodle-do*! and there it is, take it or leave it!

And it is this that makes the cocksureness of women so dangerous, so devastating. It is really out of scheme, it is not in relation to the rest of things. So we have the tragedy of cocksure women. They find, so often, that instead of having laid an egg, they have laid a vote, or an empty ink-bottle, or some other absolutely unhatchable object, which means nothing to them.

It is the tragedy of the modern woman. She becomes cocksure, she puts all her passion and energy and years of her life into some effort or assertion, without ever listening for the denial which she ought to take into count. She is cocksure, but she is a hen all the time. Frightened of her own henny self, she rushes to mad lengths about votes, or welfare, or sports, or business: she is marvellous, out-manning the man. But alas, it is all fundamentally disconnected. It is all an attitude, and one day the attitude will become a weird cramp, a pain, and then it will collapse. And when it has collapsed, and she looks at the eggs she has laid, votes, or miles of typewriting, years of business efficiency—suddenly, because she is a hen and not a cock, all she has done will turn into pure nothingness to her. Suddenly it all falls out of relation to her basic henny self, and she realize she has lost her life. The lovely henny surety, the hensureness which is the real bliss of every female, has been denied her: she had never had it. Having lived her life with such utmost strenuousness and cocksureness, she has missed her life altogether. Nothingness!

Questions and ideas for discussion:

1. Where does the author present his thesis statement? Identify the author's basis for his views.

2. In reasoning, the author draws an analogy between human life and the life of cock and hen. Do you agree with some of his views?

3. The language is quite lively in this essay. The author even creates some words, like "hensure" to polish his expression. List some words you consider used most vividly and give your reasons.

Sample Essay 2:

Should the Press Be Human?

by Katharine Whitehorn

If you were asked who shot Lee Harvey Oswald you would probably say Jack Buby. But there's another possible answer to the question: the photographer who shot those staggering pictures of Ruby gunning him down. And what has teased my mind ever since is wondering whether, if he had dropped his camera and grabbed the gunman, we might, with Oswald alive, know more than we will now ever be able to find out about why Kennedy died.

Journalists and TV people, we know, are supposed to record what goes on; but in trying to get the best record they can, they may sometimes seem amazingly cold-blooded. In the massacre that followed the British quitting India, there was a photographer who made sorrowing India family bury and rebury its dead several times till he got a perfect shot. A BBC sound man held up a Nigerian execution for half an hour while he adjust his sound equipment; yet you could say it didn't make any difference to the final outcome, but it doesn't make you feel especially warm towards the man concerned.

Should these journalists and photographers join in, or just stand back and watch while people kill one another? It's a tricky ethical question, not just a matter of how brave anyone is feeling at the time; because without authentic pictures, how will the world know, how should the world believe what atrocities are committed? One dead photographer does not do much for the cause he cares about, even if he did feel compelled to weigh in and take sides.

Our professional ethic enjoins us to stay uncommitted and report the facts; and, if we have to have guidelines, that's probably as good a one as any. Certainly some of the seediest of journalists, whether we're talking about the Middle East or Northern Ireland, are those who pile on one set of adjectives—squalid, butchering, oppressive—for terrorism of whose aims they disapprove, and quit another set—committed, dedicated, idealistic—for the same thing done by those they like.

But it leaves out a lot. "My complaint against journalists," a friend of mine once said, "is not that they behave badly in the course of duty, but their inability to recoil into a human being when it's over." I have not forgotten an occasion over 20 years ago, when a birdman was going to jump from a Press-filled Rapide. He got his equipment tangled with the aeroplane in some way, and plunged to his death. As most of them watched in shocked horror, one newsman ran down the plane with words: "My God, what a story!"

To stay out of the fight, to write down what's going on, to treat equally with both sides, as a doctor will stitch up soldiers in either uniform or a lawyer argue for either side—that is supposed to be our code; and when it comes to the crunch, we probably do better trying to stick to that, than rushing off on individual impulse.

But is there not a point in any profession where you are forded back against the wall as a human being, where a doctor should hand Jack the Ripper over to the police and a lawyer refuse to suppress the bloodstained evidence that proves his client a torturer? I think there is,... During the Algerian confusion, some Tunisian soldiers were preparing to shoot their prisoners ("What a story"). One journalists, an Italian, walked over and just calmly stood in front of the wretched men, implying that if the soldiers shot them, they would have to shoot him too. Finally some officers arrived and defused the explosive situation, and just a handful of the lives that went up in that particular bonfire were saved.

A newshound may start out just to get a good story, but it is not impossible, all the same, for him to end as a man.

Questions and ideas for discussion:

1. Find out the thesis of this essay. Is it a debatable point?

2. Is there adequate evidence to convince the reader? What kinds of evidence does the essay provide?

3. Is the writer's reasoning logical and effective?

Writing assignment:

Write an essay on one of the following topics. In the essay you should give your argument on the subject and support it with evidence. Your reasoning should be logical.

- Internet may cause depression
- My view on artistic education of children
- Boarding school or day school
- Silence is not always good

Chapter 2　Rhetorical Devices in English

2.1　理论简介

2.1.1　西方修辞学传统

西方修辞学传统起源于公元前4世纪柏拉图时期到奥古斯丁时期。从这一时期到古罗马时期的西方修辞学被称为"古典修辞学"。当时的修辞学称为"演讲术"或"论辩术"更为合适，因为那时的修辞学研究仅限于演讲训练和公开演说或辩论的艺术，是口头的、劝说性的。而 rhetoric 一词也正是源于希腊语中的 rhetor（演说者）一词。亚里士多德是西方古典修辞学领域中最为著名的一位修辞学家，他认为修辞学相当于辩证法：辩证法是逻辑论辩的艺术；修辞学是演讲的艺术，修辞是"在任何给定情况下运用已有劝说手段的能力"（the faculty of observing, in any given case, the available means of persuasion）（从莱庭、徐鲁亚，2007）。也就是说，修辞学的目的就是劝说他人接受你的观点和立场，这也正是修辞的本质。这种以口头表达为主的修辞源于古希腊的民主制度，也因此服务于政治目的。古希腊时期和古罗马时期都涌现了许多修辞学家，如科拉克斯（Corax）、蒂西雅斯（Tisias）、伊索格拉底（Isocrates）、柏拉图、亚里士多德、西塞罗（Cicero）、昆体利安（Quitilian）等。

中世纪的修辞学主要用于传教和书信写作。文艺复兴时期，古希腊时期的修辞学著作重新被发现并得到重视。从古希腊时期起直到文艺复兴时期，修辞学在西方的教育体系中始终处于中心地位，与语法、逻辑学并称为三大学科。修辞学家们更是创造出了两百多种不同的修辞格，并被广泛应用在演说、文学和写作领域。

17—19世纪是西方修辞学的现代修辞学时期。在这一时期，一些修辞学家试图从哲学、逻辑学、心理学和美学角度阐释修辞的属性，将修辞学应用从演说、写作扩大到了文艺批评。20世纪初，西方修辞学不但复兴了古希腊的修辞学传统，而且向哲学、心理学、社会学、文艺批评等学科延伸。现代修辞学家将研究重点转移到解释上，由关注说和写转为关注听和读。修辞学已经不仅仅局限于应用语言的范围，而是发展成为包括实践修辞学、论辩修辞学、小说修辞学、语体学、风格学、辞格理论等分支的一门庞大的学科。

2.1.2 修辞与写作

无论是口头表达还是书面表达,我们都希望自己的语言得体,通过自己的语言表达可以感动、说服或影响他人。这就需要根据表达目的、受众的要求,合理安排语言材料,选取适当的语言手段,对语言进行加工和润色。我们为了达到这一目的而运用的语言手段就是修辞。所以,每个人在言语实践中都在有意无意地使用修辞手段。修辞的使用可以使我们的语言准确生动,形象易懂,富有感染力,加深听众或读者的印象,使他人产生共鸣;同时有助于我们更清楚地了解他人想要表达的意思,更深入地欣赏和分析文学作品。例如,英语中那些语言优美、慷慨激昂、广为传颂的演讲词,都是使用修辞的典范,只有当我们感受到那些修辞手段的效果,才能够更好地领略其魅力。

修辞与写作更是有着密切的关系。每一次用词的选择与词语的使用和组合都是修辞手段的使用。因此,每一位写作者都不可避免地在使用修辞。一篇优秀的作品不仅仅是一些优美辞藻和句子的组合。面对与你有着不同的思维方式和认知的读者,要想让他们理解你的观点或思想,引起他们的关注,甚至促使他们思考,你的作品必须有趣、清晰、具有说服力、令人难忘,只有这样,读者才能注意到你的文字传达的信息,然后理解、相信并记住这些信息。要做到这一点,除了要有明确的主题和充分的论据之外,文章结构的安排、语言和风格的运用对于能否有效地传递信息,达到最佳表达效果至关重要,而这些都需要对修辞的恰当使用。因此,要写出好的作文,就要学会如何运用各种修辞手段。

2.1.3 修辞格

西方修辞学有广义和狭义之分,广义上包括修辞格和写作,而狭义上仅仅指修辞格,分别对应 Rhetoric 和 Figure of Speech。Rhetoric 通常指广义上的修辞,即人们在运用语言传递信息、表情达意的过程中借助于一些手段和技巧追求最佳表达效果的言语实践,如词的选择,句子结构的运用,表达的得体性和生动性,语篇的连贯等等。而 Figure of Speech 则是修辞格,一种有意识且巧妙地偏离常规的语言表达方式,是人们在追求语言最佳表达效果的过程中长期形成的并为社会所公认的对语言进行组织、调整和修饰的模式,具有特定结构、特定方法、特定功能。古典修辞学研究说、写者,现代修辞学更加注重对听、读者的研究,也就是说,写者如何通过语言手段引起听、读者的兴趣、关注和情感。而在所有这些手段中,最常用的就是修辞格。所以,修辞格是修辞学研究的核心之一。

我国的修辞学家陈望道先生将修辞分为消极修辞(Passive Rhetoric)和积极修辞(Active Rhetoric)。前者指锻词炼句和谋篇布局,以通顺、准确和生动为目的;后者则指各种修辞格的积极运用,力求表达鲜明、生动和形象。写作中这两种修辞手段缺一不可。本章着重介绍一些英语写作中常用的修辞格,使读者了解并通过实践掌握各种修辞格的用法,然后巧妙地应用在写作中。

2.1.4 修辞格的使用

英语修辞格主要分为三大类:音韵修辞格、语义修辞格和句法修辞格。每一大类中都包括更详细的区分。要正确而巧妙地运用这些修辞格,首先需要对各种修辞格进行了解和掌握。但这并不意味着一篇文章中修辞格使用得越多就越好。修辞格的使用,需要考虑以下几个因素:

1)文章的语体

不同的语体有不同的特点和目的,因而对文字的风格有不同的要求,自然对修辞格的选取和使用也有不同的要求。因此,修辞格的使用要与一定的语体相适应。书面语体包括事务语体、科技语体、政论语体和文艺语体。政论语体以说理为主,其目的是宣传观点或鼓动民众,需要极强的感染力和说服力,因此通常大量使用排比、反问、反复、对比、比喻等修辞格;以描绘和抒情为主的艺术语体几乎可以使用任何一种修辞格;而事务语体以客观简洁为主要特征,科技语体要求准确、严密,所以这两种语体很少使用修辞格。但是,交叉语体如艺术政论语体、通俗科技语体等,可以视需要和表达目的使用一些修辞格。

2)特定的语境

语言表达是否得体与语境息息相关,适合语境,语言就是得体优美的,否则就不得体。修辞格必须用在合适的语境中才能起到画龙点睛的作用。同一种修辞格,在一种语境下使用加强了表达效果,但在另一种语境中可能就会起到反作用。比如,反语可以用来表示讽刺,也可以产生幽默效果;反复可以增强语气,也可能让人觉得啰嗦;双关的使用和理解更是与语境关系密切,不同的语境下,不同的受众会产生不同的解读。

3)文章的整体风格

所有的文章都有一个统一的格调,体现作者的情感和立场。使用修辞格时,要和整个格调相一致,或严肃准确,或诙谐幽默,或褒或贬,或赞扬或批评,只有选取与文章整体风格协调的修辞格,才能服务于文章的主题,获得好的表达效果。

掌握修辞格的用法需要大量的练习和尝试。但是,修辞手段的使用是用来帮助写作的,而不是写作的目的,所以不要将修辞格的使用当做任务。过多、过于频繁地使用修辞格或是其他修辞手段都可能会适得其反。

掌握了修辞格的使用技巧,你就可以自由地使用各种修辞格,使文章更加优美,重点更加突出,表达更加有效。

2.2 Rhetorical Devices in English

A rhetorical device, also known as a figure of speech, refers to the technique of using language to achieve a special effect or heighten the wanted effect in expression. In general, rhetorical devices are classified into three categories: phonological rhetorical devices that make use of the phonological features of words including onomatopoeia, alliteration and assonance; semantic rhetorical devices that rely on the semantic associations and linguistic alterations including simile, metaphor, allusion, metonymy, transferred epithet, personification, hyperbole, irony, euphemism, pun, oxymoron, zeugma, contrast, etc.; syntactical rhetorical devices recurring to the balance of sentence structures or the highlighting of key information like repetition, parallelism and rhetorical question.

The proper employment of rhetorical devices can give clarity, emphasis, accuracy, vividness to an expression or create humorous effect or suggestive imagery. "They are the special tools of our language, and as such, should be handled with care; if used skillfully they add strength and beauty, but if awkwardly used they make the user appear affected and makes him a subject of ridicule." (Charles Morris, 1992) Therefore, a careful and systematic study of figure of speech is of great use and importance.

2.3 Phonological Rhetorical Devices

A phonological rhetorical device is a figure of speech that makes use of the phonological features of words. The use of such a device can create some sound effect in a piece of writing.

2.3.1 Onomatopoeia

2.3.1.1 Definition of Onomatopoeia

Onomatopoeia is defined by *Merriam-Webster* (*Unabridged*) as the formation of words in imitation of natural sounds; the name of a thing or action by a more or less exact reproduction of the sound associated with it. The onomatopoeic words are mostly used in descriptive literature to make the description more lively and real so that "we read not only with our eyes but also with our ears" (James Kilpatrick, 2007). They are widely used in poetry and nursery rhymes or other literature for children producing strong images that can both delight and amuse kids when the stories, poets or rhymes are read to them. "The smallest child, learning to read by reading about bees, needs no translation for buzz" (James Kilpatrick, 2007). Onomatopoeic words also provide the writers with more options in wording to meet the need of the context and effectively avoid repetition on the part of the writers. They can be used as nouns, verbs, adjectives and adverbs.

Here is a good example of children's poem making use of onomatopoeia entitled "I Speak, I Say, I Talk" from *Mice Squeak, We Speak* by Tomie de Paola.

Cats purr. 猫咪喵喵
Lions roar. 狮子咆哮
Owls hoot. 夜枭鸣叫
Bears snore. 大熊呼噜
Crickets creak. 蟋蟀嘎嘎
Mice squeak. 老鼠叽吱
Sheep baa. 绵羊咩咩
But I SPEAK. 但我说话

Monkeys chatter. 猴子唧唧
Cows moo. 母牛哞哞
Ducks quack. 鸭子嘎嘎
Doves coo. 鸽子咕咕
Pigs squeal. 猪仔尖叫
Horses neigh. 马儿嘶鸣
Chickens cluck. 小鸡咯咯
But I SAY. 但我能说

Flies hum. 苍蝇嗡嗡
Dogs growl. 狗儿狂吠
Bats screech. 蝙蝠尖鸣
Coyotes howl. 郊狼号叫
Frogs croak. 青蛙呱呱
Parrots squawk. 鹦鹉嘎嘎
Bees buzz. 蜜蜂嗡嗡
But I TALK. 但我能聊

All together 21 kinds of animal sounds are listed here making the poem a good piece of material for young children to learn to differentiate animal sounds.

2.3.1.2 Classification of Onomatopoeia

Since onomatopoeic words are imitation of sounds, based on the producer of the sound, onomatopoeic words can be roughly divided into four types.

1) Imitation of human sounds

e.g. chuckle(抿着嘴轻声地笑), gurgle(咯咯笑), ouch(哎呀), hush(嘘), murmur(咕哝), mutter(轻声低语), giggle(咯咯笑声), hum(哼), whoop(喘气声), babble(胡言乱语,含糊不清地说)

Johnnie had seen him too and ran to the gate. Then <u>clatter</u>, <u>clatter</u> up the stairs, Johnnie knocked at the door.

The word "clatter" portrays the sound of the footsteps when Johnnie went upstairs. Readers feel as if they were in the room upstairs listening to the coming of Johnnie.

2) Imitation of animal sounds

e.g. cock—crow, hen—cackle, chicken—cheep, duck—quack, goose—cackle, dove—coo, magpie—chatter, parrot—squawk, pig—grunt, sheep—baa, horse—neigh, lion—roar, cow—moo, dog—bark, fox—yelp, monkey—jabber, tiger—growl, cat—mew, elephant—trumpet, wolf—bowl, bee—buzz, mosquito—hum, cicada—chirp, snake—hiss, cricket—chirp, frog—croak

The moment the <u>hawker</u> rushed in, the white geese set up an excited <u>quacking</u>, to be joined by hens <u>chucking</u>, dog <u>barking</u>. (周立波《暴风骤雨》)

Four onomatopoeic words "hawker", "quacking", "chucking" and "barking" greatly enhance the effect of the description.

Among all the onomatopoeic words, those imitating animal sounds are the largest in number and therefore are the most important in writing. The following is a list of onomatopoeic words imitating animal sounds.

Ape: gibber
Ass: bray, heehaw
Bear: growl
Bee: buzz, hum, murmur, drone
Beetle: drone
Bird: chatter, chirp, flap, sing, squawk, twitter
Bull: bellow, bow
Camel: grunt
Cat: miaow, meow, purr
Cattle: low
Chicken: cheep, peep

Cock: crow, cock-a-doodle-do
Cow: boo, low, moo
Cricket: chirp
Crow: caw, croak
Deer: beat
Dog: bark, bay, bow-wow, grow, how, whine, yap, yelp
Donkey: bray, hee-haw
Dove/pigeon: coo
Duck: quack, screech
Eagle: scream
Elephant: trumpet

Fly: buzz, hum, drone
Fox: yelp, bark
Frog: croak
Goose: cackle, gabble, gaggle, hiss
Goat/sheep: bleat, baa
Hawk: scream
Hen: cackle, chuckle
Horse: whiney, neigh, snort
Hound: bay
Insect: chirp
Lark: sing, warble
Lion: roar
Magpie: chatter
Mouse: peep, squeak
Monkey: chatter, japer, screech
Owl: hoot, screech, scream
Ox: bo, how, moo
Parrot: talk, quack
Pig: oink, grunt
Snake: hiss
Sparrow: chatter, chirp, twitter
Swallow: twitter
Swan: cry
Tiger: roar, growl
Turkey: gobble
Whale: blow
Wild goose: honk
Wolf: howl, growl

In fact, because of the great number of animals as well as the countless sounds produced by animals, it is impossible to cover all the animal sounds in a list. What's more, the creation of an onomatopoeic word is sometimes a personal experience. So in some cases, writers may coin onomatopoeic words that can most vividly reflect the animal sounds and that can best fit into the context.

Spring
(by Thomas Nashe)
Spring, the sweet Spring, is the year's pleasant king;
Then blooms each thing, then maids dance in a ring;
Cold doth not sting, the pretty birds do sing:
Cuckoo, jug jug, pu we, to witta woo!

This poem describes the beautiful scene in spring. It ends with four onomatopoeic words imitating the singing of four different birds: cuckoo, nightingale, lapwing and owl. But "pu we" and "to witta woo" are the writer's own creation. These words bring readers into a beautiful spring day with all kinds of birds singing beside you.

3) Imitation of sounds by machines or metals

e. g. click 咔嚓(剪刀, 门, 按钮), clack 铿锵(刀叉, 碗碟, 机器), clink 叮叮(金属, 玻璃), clank 叮当(铁链, 刀枪), clang 发出铿锵(或叮当)声, rumble 轰隆声(雷, 风, 炮, 车), toot 嘟嘟(火车, 汽车, 轮船), ticktack 滴答(钟表), bang 砰声(枪等), boom 轰隆声(大炮等), pop 砰声(枪等), rattle 嘎嘎声(窗等).

As you approach it, a <u>tinkling</u> and <u>banging</u> and <u>clashing</u> begins to impinge on your ear.

The three onomatopoeic words give a vivid depiction of the copper-smith's job.

4) Imitation of sounds in nature

There are many different sounds in nature such as the sounds of water(babble, murmur), the sounds of wave(swish), the sounds of wind (whisper, whirl, roar), the sounds of rain(spatter), the sounds of thunder(crack, rumble) and so on. The use of onomatopoeic words could immensely beautify a piece of writing.

The ice was here, the ice was there,
The ice was all around:
It <u>cracked</u> and <u>growled</u>, and <u>roared</u> and <u>howled</u>,
Like noises in a swound!

(Samuel T. Coleridge: The Rime of the Ancient Mariner)

"Cracked", "growled", "roared" and "howled" are the sounds made by the breaking of ice. They present a true to life scene of the collapse of iceberg on the sea.

Note: When translating onomatopoeic words between English and Chinese, the translator has to consider the different habits in using onomatopoeic words in the two languages.

Tasks:

1. Please put the following English sentences containing onomatopoeic words into Chinese.

a. Nothing was heard but the voice of the master and the scratching of pens on paper.

b. On the way through the mountains to school, we can see the babbling water in the brook, hear the frogs croaking, cuckoo cuckooing, birds singing, sparrows chirping in the forest.

c. When Miss Martha was reaching for bread there was a great tooting, a clanging, and a fire engine came rumbling past.

d. The angry husband shut the door with a bang.

e. The drunken driver drove bang into the store window.

f. Presently Ben Rogers came in sight. He was eating an apple, giving a long melodious whoop at intervals, followed by a deep-toned ding-dong-dong, ding-dong-dong, for he was personating a steamboat. (Mark Twain: *The Adventures of Tom Sawyer*)

g. The ticking of the clock was the only sound that greeted him, for not a soul remained. (Hardy: *The Return of the Native*)

h. The metal tool clanged when it hit the wall.

  i. During his fever he babbled without stopping.

  j. He babbled the secret out to his friends.

  k. He burbled on (*talked*) for hours.

  l. I heard many birds twittering in the woods.

  m. His stomach rumbled/growled (*when hungry*).

  n. He saw nothing and heard nothing but he could feel his heart pounding and then he heard the clack on stone and the leaping, dropping clicks of a small rock falling. (*Ernest Hemingway*: *For Whom the Bell Tolls*)

  o. She brought me into touch with everything that could be reached or felt—sunlight, the rustling of silk, the noises of insects, the creaking of a door, the voice of a loved one.

  p. Ancient girders creak and groan, with the squeaking and rumbling of the grinding wheels, and the occasional grunts, and sight of the camels.

  q. The night shift had already begun and the air was vibrating with the hum and clatter of machinery.

  2. Please put the following Chinese sentences into English. Pay attention to the use of onomatopoeic words.

  a. 火车"哐唧哐唧"驶出车站。

  b. 午餐时女孩们"叽里呱啦"地谈个不停。

  c. 盘子、碗碰得"叮叮当当"响。

  d. 远处雷声隆隆。

  f. 站在身后的人们一直"唧唧喳喳"个没完。

  g. 钟声"滴滴答答",火声"噼噼啪啪"。

  h. 大约在这个时候,有人从窗户外面抛了一块砖进来,"噼里啪啦"砸得很响。

  i. 钟声"滴答滴答"地把时间打发走了。

  j. 她把匣子"砰"的一下摔在桌子上。

  k. 那人"砰"的一声把门关上了。

  l. 风在松林中飒飒作响。

  m. 那些老屋梁神秘地发出裂开的响声。

  n. 万籁俱寂,她唯一听到的是常青藤轻扣玻璃的声音。

  o. 他猛然坐到一把椅子上,椅子被压得"吱吱"作响。

  p. 小伙子冲进来,"呼哧呼哧"上气不接下气。

  q. 他把手儿一扬,千万人的眼睛跟着它滴溜溜地转。

3. Appreciate the use of onomatopoeic words.

a. *My souls, how the wind did scream along! And every second or two there'd come a glare that lit up the white-caps for a half a mile around, and you'd see the islands looking dusty through the rain, and the trees thrashing around in the wind, then comes a h-wack! -bum! bum! bumble-umble-um-bum-bum bum and the thunder would go rumbling and grumbling away, and quit—and then rip comes another flash and another sockdolager.* (*Mark Twain: The Adventures of Huckleberry Finn*)

b. *"What be ye looking at?" asked a man who had not observed the incident.*

"Ho-ho-ho!" laughed dark Car.

"Hee-hee-hee!" laughed the tippling bride, as she steadied herself on the arm of her fond husband.

"Heu-heu-heu!" laughed dark Car's mother, stroking her moustache as she explained laconically. "Out of the frying-pan into the fire."

(*Thomas Hardy: Tess of the D'urbervilles*)

c. *I chatter over stony ways,*

In little sharps and trebles,

I bubble into eddying bays,

I babble on the pebbles.

(*Alfred Tennyson: The Brook*)

2.3.2 Alliteration, Consonance and Assonance

In addition to onomatopoeia, alliteration, consonance and assonance are also ways of enhancing the sound effect in writing.

2.3.2.1 Alliteration

Alliteration is the repetition of an initial consonant sound or consonant cluster in two or more neighboring words.

e. g.

a **p**eck of **p**ickled **p**epper

safe and **s**ound

through **th**ick and **th**in

All **r**ivers **r**un into sea.

No **s**weet without **s**weat.

Used not only in poetry and prose, but also in advertising, journalism and speech, alliteration is good for sound rhyme and emphasis. It conveys and emphasizes vivid images hence lending force and memorability to the materials. Here are some examples of advertisement using alliteration.

Health, **H**umor and **H**appiness.   (*Tourism*)
Cut **c**osts without **c**utting **c**orners.   (*Car*)
Form **F**ollows **F**un.   (*BMW*)

The repetition of consonants "h", "k" and "f" in the three pieces of ads leaves a deep impression on the audiences, and as a result, effectively draws the audiences' attention to the advertised products or service.

2.3.2.2 Consonance

Consonance, according to *Merriam-Webster's Collegiate Dictionary*, refers to "recurrence or repetition of consonant sounds especially at the end of stressed syllables without the similar correspondence of vowels". Like alliteration, it is also often used in poetry, advertisement or speech to create a musical and impressive image.

(1) *They left half a loaf in the sa**fe**.*
(2) *The downtown area is a scene of hu**stle** and bu**stle**.*
(3) *Thinking is one of the most wonder**ful** and power**ful** tools we have.*

2.3.2.3 Assonance

Assonance is the repetition of the same or similar vowel sounds in the stressed syllables of a sequence of words, preceded and followed by different consonants.

(1) *The sergeant asked him to b**o**mb the l**aw**n with h**o**tp**o**ts.*
(2) *Thanks to the hurric**a**ne, the pl**a**ne was m**a**de l**a**te to reach Wuhan.*
(3) *The gl**a**ss h**a**rdly fell off the table when J**a**ck gr**a**sped it.*

Usually, alliteration, consonance and assonance are employed together to form a good rhyme as in "*please put plenty of paper in Peter's pocket and throw all the waste paper into the waste-paper basket*" and "*much more man came home that day than we ever expected*". The use of the three devices at the same time can make the speech or writing more rhythmic and appealing.

Tasks:

1. Tongue twisters are examples of alliteration, consonance and assonance. Read the tongue twisters below. Can you say this fives times fast?

    a. *Peter Piper picked a peck of pickled peppers.*
       Did Peter Piper pick a peck of pickled peppers?
       If Peter Piper picked a peck of pickled peppers,
       where's the peck of pickled peppers Peter Piper picked?
    b. *She sells sea-shells by the sea-shore,*
       And the shells she sells are sea-shells, I'm sure.

So if she sells shells by the sea-shore,
The shells she sells are sea-shells, for sure.

(*Phyllis Flowerdew: Susan Sells Sea Shells*)

2. Study the following idioms or sayings and point out the phonological rhetorical devices used in them.

thick and thin

black and blue

now or never

then and there

cut and carve

bed and board

sink or swim

A fall into the pit, a gain in your wit.

mend or end

first and last

Spare the rod, and spoil the child.

by hook or crook

Fit most, and survive at last.

No pains, no gains.

Man proposes, God disposes.

A lazy youth, a lousy age.

Three cobblers combined, makes a genius mind.

3. Read and appreciate the excerption from Thomas Gray's poem ***Elegy Written in a Country Churchyard.***

The curfew tolls the knell of parting day,
The lowing herd winds slowly o'er the lea,
The ploughman homeward plods his weary way,
And leaves the world to darkness and to me.

Now fades the glimmering landscape on the sight,
And all the air a solemn stillness holds,
Save where the beetle wheels his droning flight,
And drowsy tinklings lull the distant folds;

Save that from yonder ivy-mantled tower
The moping owl does to the moon complain

Of such as, wandering near her secret bower,
Molest her ancient solitary reign.

Beneath those rugged elms, that yew-tree's shade,
Where heaves the turf in many a mouldering heap,
Each in his narrow cell for ever laid,
The rude Forefathers of the hamlet sleep.

The breezy call of incense-breathing morn,
The swallow twittering from the straw-built shed,
The cock's shrill clarion, or the echoing horn,
No more shall rouse them from their lowly bed.

2.4　Semantic Rhetorical Devices

In using semantic rhetorical devices, a word or phrase diverges from its normal meaning or literal meaning (from Wikipedia), in which case the word or phrase is said to be used figuratively and convey meanings in a more vivid and impressive manner.

2.4.1　Simile

2.4.1.1　Definition of Simile

Simile is a figure of speech that makes a comparison between two dissimilar things having certain qualities or characteristics in common. It consists of three parts: tenor(本体), vehicle(喻体), and indicator of resemblance(比喻词).

The moon is like a silver coin.

In this sentence, "the moon" is the tenor; "a silver coin" is the vehicle; "like" is the indicator of resemblance.

2.4.1.2　Indicators of Resemblance Used in Simile

In simile, to form the comparison, different indicators of resemblance are employed.

1) Prepositions

(1) As

Beauty is as summer fruits, which are easy to corrupt and cannot last…

(Bacon: Of Studies)

Beauty is compared to fruits in summer, which tells the audiences how transient and fragile beauty is.

Out of the sleeves came strong bony wrists and hands gnarled knotted and hard <u>as</u> peach branches. (John Steinbeck)

His young daughter looks <u>as</u> red <u>as</u> a rose.

(2) Like

Paris is a morgue without you; before I knew you, it was Paris, and I thought it heavens; but now it is a vast desert of desolation and loneliness. It is <u>like</u> the face of a clock, bereft of its hands. (Sarah Bernhardt to Victorian Sardou)

Living without an aim is <u>like</u> sailing without a compass. (John Ruskin)

(3) Of

He has the heart <u>of</u> a lion, but he does everything in a down-to-earth way.

He has a heart <u>of</u> stone and will <u>of</u> iron.

2) Conjunctions

A crowd of people were around him, touching his body, feeling his legs, and bidding for him <u>as if</u> he had been a horse.

They stood upon a bleak and desert moor, whose monstrous masses of stone were cast about <u>as though</u> it were the burial place of giants.

The best work is done <u>the way</u> ants do things—by tiny, tireless and regular additions.

3) Verbs

Her face <u>resembled</u> a silver moon.

He <u>treats</u> his child <u>as</u> the apple in the eye.

Shakespeare <u>compared</u> the world <u>to</u> a stage. (Wood)

You can <u>liken</u> your eye <u>to</u> a camera. (Neal)

His nose was particularly white and his large nostrils, correspondingly dark, <u>reminded</u> me <u>of</u> an oboe when they dilated.

His strength is <u>similar to</u> a horse.

4) Phrases

Our village is <u>no less</u> beautiful <u>than</u> this picture.

A student can <u>no more</u> obtain knowledge without studying <u>than</u> a farmer can get harvest without plowing.

He never listens—you <u>might as well</u> talk to a brick (as talk to him).

A home without love is <u>no more than</u> a body without a soul.

He is, <u>as it were</u>, a walking dictionary.

The traffic manager has in the hollow of his hand, <u>so to speak</u>, the traffic of the whole system.

2.4.1.3　The Use of Simile in Writing

Simile is one of the simplest and most frequently used rhetorical devices, which makes the expression succinct, vivid and lively. So writers use it to make what they want to express more descriptive and entertaining, in particular in poems or songs.

O my love's like a red, red rose,
That's newly sprung in June;
O my love is like the melodie,
That's sweetly played in tune.　　　　　　　　　　　　　　　*(Robert Burns)*

These are the lines taken from the famous poem *A Red Red Rose* by Robert Burns who in this poem portrays the beauty of his love. As the first stanza of the poem, it contains two similes which present the audience with a most pleasing picture—a pretty young girl is as beautiful as flower, and as sweet as melody.

My heart is <u>like</u> a singing bird
Whose nest is on a watered shoot;
My heart is <u>like</u> an apple-tree
Whose boughs are bent with thick-set fruit;
My heart is <u>like</u> a rainbow shell
That paddles in a halcyon sea;
My heart is gladder than all these
Because my love is come to me.　　　　　　　　　　　　　　　*(Rossetti)*

In this poem, "my heart" is compared to "singing bird", "apple tree" and "rainbow shell". These comparisons of abstract feeling to concrete objects vividly express "my" pleasure.

Simile can tell audience a lot more than mere description, but sometimes it is not as easy as thought, it also takes a wide range of knowledge and good understanding to tell what it really means.

Once, the <u>Boy Scout law</u> read like the chivalrous <u>code of King Arthur and his knights</u>. But if Timothy Curran and Elliott Welsh prevail, the law could soon sound more like the credo of <u>the American Civil Liberties Union</u>. (*David Whitman*: *Beyond Thrifty and Loyalty*)

The sentences are the opening remarks of an article about the identity crisis of the Boy Scouts(男童子军). To make out what they mean, you have to know about the background information of the three items involved in the comparison. Firstly, what is Boy Scout law? It refers to a set of rules a boy scout must abide by which requires a scout to be trustworthy, loyal, helpful, friendly, courteous, kind, obedient, cheerful, thrifty, brave, clean, and reverent. Secondly, what is the code of King Arthur and his knights? This originates from the legend of King Arthur and his knights of the round table who live by a code of chivalry: *To never do outrage nor murder. Always to flee treason. To by no means be cruel but to give mercy unto him who asks for mercy. To always do ladies, gentlewomen and widows succor. To never force ladies, gentlewomen or widows. Not to take up battles in wrongful quarrels.* Today, King Arthur and his Knights are symbols of bravery, loyalty and trustworthiness. Lastly, what is the credo of the American Civil Liberties Union? The ACLU is an organization dedicated to the protection of individual rights and freedom including the freedom of speech and press, freedom of religion and privacy. After learning all the background information, readers would sense the subtle similarity between the Boy Scout and the chivalrous knights and what would happen to Boy Scout once "Timothy Curran and Elliott Welsh prevail". Without too many words, the author puts what he wants to say quite clearly.

Many idioms and old sayings contain similes which have become clichés, such as "as clear as crystal", "as white as snow", "as busy as bee", "as firm as a rock", "as cool as a cucumber", etc. They have been used so many times that the application of these expressions may, instead of adding vividness and interest to your writing, leaves a negative impression on the readers. Similarly, the overuse or misuse of simile is always destructive. Only an original simile that fits well in the context can produce the wanted effect.

Tasks:

1. The following sentences are taken from Winston S. Churchill's Speech on Hitler's invasion of the USSR. In the underlined sentence, Churchill compares German soldiers to locusts. Why does he make such a comparison? What effect can it achieve?

I see... in hideous onslaught the Nazi war machine with its clanking, heel-clicking, dandified Prussian officers, its crafty expert agents fresh from the cowing and tying down of a dozen countries. <u>I see also the dull, drilled, docile, brutish masses of the Hun soldiery plodding on like a swarm of crawling locusts.</u>

2. Mr. Zhu Ziqing is a literary master who is good at using simile in his works. The following sentences are taken from his works, all of which use similes. Put the sentences into English and pay attention to the use of similes.

1. 叶子出水很高,像亭亭的舞女的裙。
2. 层层的叶子中间,零星地点缀着些白花,有袅娜地开着的,有羞涩地打着朵的;正如一粒粒的明珠,又如碧空里的星星,又如刚出浴的美人。

3. 微风过处,送来缕缕清香,仿佛远处高楼上渺茫的歌声似的。
4. 这时候叶子与花也有一丝的颤动,像闪电般,霎时传过荷塘的那边去了。
5. 叶子本是肩并肩密密地挨着,这便宛然有了一道凝碧的波痕。
6. 月光如流水一般,静静地泻在这一片叶子和花上。
7. 叶子和花仿佛在牛乳中洗过一样;又像笼着轻纱的梦。
8. 丛生的灌木,落下参差的斑驳的黑影,峭楞楞如鬼一般。
9. 光与影有着和谐的旋律,如梵婀玲上奏着的名曲。
10. 树色一例是阴阴的,乍看像一团烟雾。

3. Translate the following sentences into English using the given indicators of resemblance.

1. 鲸不是鱼,正如马也不是鱼一样。(not any more... than)
2. 每一次读到一本好书,对我来说我好像交了一位新朋友。(as if)
3. 你不能动摇我的决心,正如你不能使河水倒流一样。(not any more than)
4. 有时候他似乎脾气不好,但他的心眼可好了。(of)
5. 他们挥金如土。(like)
6. 我像一朵浮云独自漫游。(as)
7. 我可以像猫嗅老鼠那样闻出它的气味来。(the way)
8. 她的笑容像玫瑰花一样漂亮。(resemble)
9. 我觉得人生就像一条河。(compare)
10. 我感到好像大地在脚下滑动。(as though)

2.4.2 Metaphor

2.4.2.1 Definition of Metaphor

Like simile, metaphor also makes a comparison between two unlike elements, but different from simile, this comparison is implied rather than stated without the use of indicator of resemblance. As Lakoff G. & Johnson puts it in *Metaphors We Live By*, metaphor is pervasive in our daily life; it happens not only in human's language but also in human's thinking and behavior (束定芳,1998). The use and the understanding of metaphors are trickier than that of similes, but metaphor is more concise and interesting.

For example,

Similes	Metaphors
1. <u>Life is like an isthmus</u> between two eternities.	1. <u>Life is an isthmus</u> between two eternities.
2. <u>Happiness is like sunshine</u>; it is made up of very little beams.	2. <u>The sunshine of life is made up of</u> very little beams.
3. <u>Habit may be likened to a cable</u>; every day we weave a thread, and soon we cannot break it.	3. <u>Habit is a cable</u>; every day we weave a thread, and soon we cannot break it.

2.4.2.2　Classification of Metaphor Based on the Basic Components

In Metaphor, there are three basic components: tenor, vehicle, and ground(喻底), which means the similarities between the tenor and the vehicle. According to the three basic components in metaphor, metaphor is classified into four types.

1) Metaphors in which both the tenor and the vehicle emerge

e.g. *The streets were a furnace, the sun an executioner.*

(*Cynthia Ozick*: *Rosa*)

This sentence contains two metaphors, "the streets" and "the sun" are tenors; while "a furnace" and "an executioner" are vehicles. The ground of the metaphor is easy to understand—the sun is burning hot as if it can kill people with its heat; the streets, under the sunshine, is also so hot that people walking on the street feel as if they were in a huge furnace.

What is the tenor, vehicle and ground in the sentence below?

If the fatherland is sound, my personal troubles are only a flea bite.

2) Metaphor in which the tenor is implied

e.g. *Laws catch flies but let wasps go free.*

In this sentence, "law" is compared to "cobwebs". Both "flies" and "wasps" are vehicles but tenors do not emerge. In fact, "flies" refer to those petty criminals, and "wasps" mean those who really commit serious crimes or do great harm to society. So this sentence means only those petty criminals are punished by law; those who commit serious crimes always run away with their bad deeds. Through the use of the metaphor, the meaning of the sentence is not directly stated and therefore is more forceful and striking. With just eight words, a picture depicting the cruel reality is presented to the readers.

3) Metaphors in which the vehicle is implied

e.g. *Some books are to be tasted, others swallowed, and some few to be chewed and digested.*

In this sentence, "books" are tenors but vehicles are absent. All the verbs used here "taste", "swallow", "chew", and "digest" are related to food. So it is clear that "books" are compared to "food". If the word "food" appears in this sentence, the effect would be greatly diminished and the sentence would be one of the platitudes.

What is the tenor, vehicle and ground in the sentence below?

She wished she could stop time and freeze this day so that it would never end.

4) Metaphors in which the tenor, the vehicle and the ground all emerge

In this case, the meaning of the sentence is easy to understand. Many metaphors belong to this type.

e. g. *My life is one long curve, full of turning points.*

It is obvious that in the sentence "my life" is the tenor, "long curve" is the vehicle, and the ground is "full of turning points", which is the common points between "my life" and "long curve".

2.4.2.3　Classification of Metaphor Based on the Form

1) Noun metaphors

As the name indicates, noun metaphors involve the use of nouns. The typical pattern is "A is B" or "B of A". This kind of metaphor is easy to use and to understand. It can be changed into a simile "A is like B".

All the world's a stage, and all the men and women merely players.

(*William Shakespeare*)

Money is a bottomless sea, in which honor, conscience, and truth may be drowned.　　　　　　　　　　　　　　　　　　　　　　　　　(*Kozlay*)

Marriage is a book of which the first chapter is written in poetry and remaining chapters in prose.　　　　　　　　　　　　　　　　(*Beverley Nichols*)

She was an angel of a wife.

2) Verb metaphors

The case snowballed into one of the most famous trials in U. S. history.

"Snowball into" means "gradually develop into like a snowball", describing how the insignificant case became more and more serious.

All day long, whilst the women were praying ten miles away, the lines of the dauntless English infantry were receiving and repelling the furious charges of the French horsemen. Guns which were heard at Brussels were ploughing up their ranks, and comrades falling, and the resolute survivors closing in.

(*W. H. Thackeray*: *Vanity Fair*)

"Plough" is usually followed by "field" or "land". The use of this word implies how hard the soldiers fought the battle just like farmers toil and sweat in the fields.

3) Adjective metaphors

It is a thorny problem.

A "thorn" is difficult to handle and always hurts people. Similarly, a "problem" may be hard to solve and bring danger to you.

His speech touched off a stormy protest.

"A stormy protest" means "a protest as strong as a storm".

4) Adverbial metaphors

Time passed at a snail's pace.

As "snail" crawls slowly, the sentence means "time passed as slowly as a snail."

5) Proverbs serving as metaphors

There are many proverbs in English that are often used to illustrate an abstract idea or a similar situation. When used in this way, it is also a kind of metaphor. The following proverbs are frequently used as metaphors.

Too many cooks spoil the broth. 人多坏事。
Do not put the cart before the horse. 勿将本末倒置。
Do not wash your dirty linen in public. 家丑不可外扬。
Give him an inch and he will make a mile. 得寸进尺。
Look before you leap. 三思而后行。
Strike the iron while it is hot. 趁热打铁。
You can not make an omelet without breaking eggs. 做事不可畏首畏尾。
Tomorrow is another (a new) day. 重整旗鼓,东山再起。
A little pot is soon hot. 小人易怒,小锅易沸。
Fish sticks at the head. 上梁不正下梁歪。
A new broom sweeps clean. 新官上任三把火。
A bird in the hand is worth two in the bush/wood. 双鸟在林,不如一鸟在手。
Every dog has its/his day. 人人皆有得意时。
Still waters run deep. 水静流深,人静心深。

2.4.2.4　The Use of Metaphors in Writing

In President Obama's inauguration speech, metaphors are used frequently lending strength and appeal to the speech.

Forty-four Americans have now taken the presidential oath. The words have been spoken during rising tides of prosperity and the still waters of peace. Yet, every so often the oath is taken amidst gathering clouds and raging storms. At these moments, America has carried on not simply because of the skill or vision of those in high office, but be-

cause *We the People have remained faithful to the ideals of our forbearers*, *and true to our founding documents.*

Both "tide" and "water" are used metaphorically here. "Tide" means "trend" and "rising tide of prosperity" means "the rising trend to get prosperous". "Still waters of peace" refers to "the stable and peaceful situation". "Gathering clouds and raging storms" refers to the difficulties, problems and potential crisis that are facing the U. S. Instead of using plain expressions, President Obama skillfully makes use of the metaphors to imply that under his administration, the U. S. will go out of all the troubles and crisis into a period of peace and stabilization, setting people thinking about the past and present state of the U. S. , and looking forward to the bright future with him as their leader.

Metaphor is useful and important in the use of language, as Max Black puts it, "It would be more illuminating to say that the metaphor creates the similarity than to say that it formulates some similarity antecedently existing." (Max Black, 1962) However, it's not an easy task to acquire the skill of using metaphors. Aristotle once said, "... the greatest thing by far is to be a master of metaphor." The words point out the difficulty in as well as the significance of using metaphors skillfully. An effective metaphor should have freshness and originality so as to give readers a forceful impact. When two or more metaphors are used to illuminate the same tenor, the metaphors should be consistent with each other or supporting each other. Only when a metaphor is used aptly, can it enhance the effect, and this takes a wide vocabulary and a sound knowledge of the connotations of words.

Note: In addition to simile and metaphor, there is another rhetorical device that is used to make comparisons: analogy. However, while simile and metaphor make comparison on the point of resemblance, analogy aims at what is common between two things of different classes and draws a parallel between them. Usually one thing is unfamiliar, difficult or abstract hence the need for clarifying, and the other is familiar and easy which is utilized to help explain the unfamiliar thing. Through the comparison, the reader can better understand an idea not so simple to define. The typical pattern is "A is to B what C is to D".

e. g. *Judicious praise is to children what the sun is to flowers.*

In this sentence, it is "the importance of praise to children" that is compared to "the importance of sun to flowers". With sunshine, flowers grow faster and bloom more beautifully. With judicious praise, children can grow and develop better.

But this sentence's pattern is not the only way to make an analogy. In *Hit the*

Nail on the Head by Alan Warner, the opening remark is impressive:

Have you ever watched a clumsy man hammering a nail into a box? He hits it first to one side, then to another, perhaps knocking it over completely, so that in the end he only gets half of it into the wood. <u>A skillful carpenter, on the other hand, will drive home the nail with a few firm, deft blows, hitting it each time squarely on the head. So with language; the good craftsman will choose words that drive home his point firmly and exactly.</u> A word that is more or less right, a loose phrase, an ambiguous expression, a vague adjective, will not satisfy a writer who aims at clean English. He will try always to get the word that is completely right for his purpose.

This analogy is not designed to equate a skillful carpenter with a language master. It shows that "the way a skillful carpenter hits a nail" is similar to "the way how a language master uses words". A good language user should learn to choose exact words to best express his own ideas, just as a good carpenter knows where to hit to most effectively drive a nail home.

What should be noted is that in making an analogy, make sure that the analogy is meaningful and only those details that can best serve the purpose are included.

Tasks:

1. Find out which types of metaphor are used in the following sentences according to the three basic components in metaphor.

a. Love is an alchemist that can transmute poison into food—and a spaniel that prefers even punishment from one hand to caresses from another.

b. The rain came down in long knitting needles.

c. Her son had been damaged in a crash.

d. I am no better than the old lightening-struck chestnut tree in the orchard.

e. He is deep in love.

f. Investments in restructuring companies involve substantial risks, and deciphering the details of a company's finances and plans for re-emergence is akin to penetrating a legal jungle.

g. Men's words are bullets, that their enemies take up and make use of against them.

h. While most of us are too ready to apply to others the cold wind of criticism, we are somehow reluctant to give our fellows the warm sunshine of praise.

2. Find out which types of metaphor are used in the following sentences based on the form and translate the sentences into Chinese.

a. Education is not the <u>filling of a pail</u>, but the <u>lighting of a fire</u>.

(William B. Yeats)

b. The boy is <u>shooting up</u> fast.

c. Don't <u>monkey</u> with the new radio.

d. Beauty, strength, youth, are <u>flowers</u> but fading seen; duty, faith, love are <u>roots</u>, and ever green.　　　　　　　　　　　　　　　　(George Peele)

e. The human <u>tide</u> was rolling westward.　　　　　　　　(Dickens)

f. We regard it as a <u>burning</u> shame to have lagged behind.

g. I've got the <u>devil</u> of a toothache.

h. They escaped <u>by a hair's breath</u>.

i. Misfortune <u>dogged</u> him at every turn.

j. He is a walking <u>dictionary</u>.

k. The boy <u>wolfed down</u> the food the moment he grabbed it.

l. He <u>needled</u> his way through the crowd.

m. She has a <u>photographic</u> memory for detail.

n. By this hour the <u>volcanic</u> fires of his nature had burnt down, and having drunk no great quantity as yet he was inclined to acquiesce.　　(Thomas Hardy)

o. Waves <u>thundered</u> against the rocks.

p. They lived <u>from hand to mouth</u>.

q. She was born <u>with a silver spoon in her mouth</u>.

3. The following paragraphs are excerption from President Obama's inauguration speech. Pick out the metaphors used in the paragraphs and figure out their meaning. Analyze the effect these metaphors have achieved.

This is the journey we continue today. We remain the most prosperous, powerful nation on Earth. Our workers are no less productive than when this crisis began. Our minds are no less inventive, our goods and services no less needed than they were last week or last month or last year. Our capacity remains undiminished. But our time of standing pat, of protecting narrow interests and putting off unpleasant decisions—that time has surely passed. Starting today, we must pick ourselves up, dust ourselves off, and begin again the work of remaking America.

For everywhere we look, there is work to be done. The state of the economy calls for action, bold and swift, and we will act—not only to create new jobs, but to lay a new foundation for growth. We will build the roads and bridges, the electric grids and digital lines that feed our commerce and bind us together. We will restore science to its rightful place, and wield technology's wonders to raise health care's quality and lower its cost. We will harness the sun and the winds and the soil to fuel our cars and run our factories. And we will transform our schools and colleges and universities to meet the demands of a new age. All this we can do. And all this we will do.

4. Read the poem and appreciate the use of metaphors in this poem.

Poetry

(*by Eleanor Farjeon*)

What is poetry? Who knows?
Not a rose, but the scent of the rose;
Not the sky, but the light in the sky;
Not the fly, but the gleam of the fly;
Not the sea, but the sound of the sea;
Not myself, but what makes me
See, hear, and feel something that prose
Cannot: and what it is, who knows?

2.4.3 Personification

2.4.3.1 Definition of Personification

Personification is a figure of speech that gives inanimate object human form or feelings, qualities or abilities. In other words, with personification, a thing or abstraction is represented as a person. For example, "the sun shone brightly down on me as if she were shining for me alone". Personification is considered by many scholars a type of metaphor in that personification also consists of tenor, vehicle and ground, often without using indicator of resemblance. This device is preferably used in poems, fables or descriptive writings. Many proverbs are also good examples of personification.

Justice has long arms.

Walls have long ears.

Love is blind.

Necessity is the mother of invention.

Time is the best physician/healer.

Procrastination is the thief of time.

Lies have short legs.

2.4.3.2 Formation of Personification

Personification can be formed through words of different classes. Verbs, adjectives, nouns or pronouns that are usually applied to a person can all be used to describe the inanimate object.

1) Personification through the use of pronouns and nouns in relation to human beings

Death *will come when **he** is least expected.*

"Death" is personified through the use of the pronoun "he" instead of "it", creating a masculine image as if death is a muscular and strong man with immense power which no one can defy.

*When **winter** comes, **she** always finds the earth cold and bare.*

In this sentence, "winter" is implied as a lady striking readers as loving and gentle.

So it can be concluded that "he" is often related to "power", "violence", and "cruelty"; whereas "she" reminds people of "gentleness", "gracefulness", and "peace". That's why native country is sometimes referred to as "motherland", while on some other occasions as "fatherland".

In some personifications, some nouns are used in relation to human beings lending the lifeless objects human traits. But quite often, the nouns are used together with adjectives or verbs to get the expected effect.

e. g.

Oreo: Milk's favorite cookie.   (*slogan on a package of Oreo cookies*)

Only a human with the ability to taste, to eat, to think, to choose and to judge can decide what his favorite cookie is. Hence, in this sentence, milk is animated.

I have always wished that I can fly freely like the clouds; the clouds must be enjoying their freedom very much.

The clouds flow randomly in the sky, which in human beings' eyes, is freedom. As freedom is what many people are looking forward to, it is something that should be enjoyed.

2) Personification through the use of verbs applied to a person

The autumn wind is sighing.

With the word "sigh" instead of "blow", a sense of coldness and desolation strikes readers.

The noise killed the music.

The word "kill" gives both "the noise" and "the music" life making readers feel pitiful for the beautiful music while detesting the abominable noise.

Since bird flu first appeared in 1997, it has taken more than 100 lives.

Through the use of the word "take", it implies that it is easy for people to die of bird flu, hence the seriousness of the situation.

3) Personification through the use of adjectives modifying a person

The hungry flame tore up the buildings faster than anything I had seen.

The word "hungry" presents readers with a striking picture in which the fire destroys all the buildings in a second as if a person who has been starved for a long time finally takes hold of something to eat and therefore is eating greedily.

But the houses were cold, closed, and <u>unfriendly.</u>

In fact, it is not the house that is unfriendly, but the people living in the house. Yet standing in front of a closed door, all one can feel is indifferent, cold and unfriendly.

To describe the blowing of the wind, different verbs are used to imply different meanings.

The wind is sighing/whistling/shouting/roaring.

The four verbs put readers under different impressions which vividly tell us how the wind is blowing.

"Fear <u>knocked</u> on the door. Faith <u>answered</u>. There was no one there."

(Proverb quoted by Christopher Moltisanti, The Sopranos)

In most cases, personification is formed through the employment of nouns, pronouns, verbs and adjectives together. In this way, the effect is highly enhanced.

Dawn Stepping Down

(by J. R. Rowland)

Dawn <u>stepping down</u> into the garden

Stepping down

Lightly about the roofs, <u>sets</u> in bare trees

Heavy lumps of birds, wood pigeons; places

Ladder against wall, <u>uncovers</u>

The houses' <u>naked sleeping faces</u>

And <u>closed eyes</u>.

In this poem, verbs applied to a person are used including "step", "set" and "uncover", all of which are to describe the coming of dawn as if the dawn is a person who gets up early and wakes everything up. Adjectives modifying a person are "naked", "sleeping" and "closed". Together with "faces" and "eyes", they impart a sense of sleepiness to readers.

2.4.3.3 Classification of Personification Based on the Types of Tenor

According to the type of the tenor, personification can be classified into four types:

1) Personification of natural phenomenon or objects

The current <u>lingers</u> along gently. It comes flowing softly through the midmost privacy and deepest heart of a wood which <u>whispers</u> it to be quiet; while the stream <u>whispers</u> back again from its sedgy borders, as if the river and wood were hushing one another to <u>sleep</u>. Yes, the river <u>sleeps</u> along its course and <u>dreams of</u> the sky and of the clustering foliage, amid which fall showers of broken sunlight, imparting specks of vivid cheerfulness.

 Both the river and the wood are given life as if they can think and feel like human beings. The audiences cannot but imagine that in such a fairyland, they can communicate with everything around them.

The rain to the wind <u>said</u>
"You <u>push</u> and I'll <u>pelt</u>,"
They so smote the garden bed
That the flowers actually <u>knelt</u>
And lay <u>lodged</u>—though not <u>dead</u>
I know how the flowers <u>felt</u>.

(Robert Frost)

 In this poem, wind and rain become people who are cold and cruel. They destroy flowers without mercy, arousing the readers' sympathy for flowers which are the symbol of beauty.

 2) Personification of machines

With a wild rattle and clatter, and an inhuman <u>abandonment of consideration</u> not easily <u>understood</u> in these days, the carriage dashed through streets and swept round corners, with women screaming before it, and men clutching each other and clutching children out of its way. At last, swooping at a street corner by a fountain, one of its wheels came to a <u>sickening little jolt</u>, and there was a loud cry from a number of voices.

(Charles Dickens)

 The carriage is described as a person who cannot think and behave normally. A frightening scene is thus created.

 3) Personification of animals and plants

The next morning when the little tree was <u>awake</u>, it had its needle once more. It was so glad to have them again that it <u>laughed</u>, and all the trees of the forest <u>laughed</u> with it. And always after that the little tree was <u>contented</u>.

(Story of the Little Pine Tree)

 The little tree is like a lovely child. Readers would smile together with the trees.

 It is useless for the sheep <u>to pass resolutions in favour of vegetarianism</u> while the wolf <u>remains of a different opinion</u>.   (W. R. Inge)

The animals are depicted as human beings in order to achieve an ironical effect. It is a reflection of human society.

4) Personification of abstract ideas or objects

Bitterness *fed on* the man who had made the world laugh.

Time is like *a fashionable host*, that slightly *shakes his passing guest* by th' hand; and *with his arms stretched*, as he would fly, *grasps in the comer*. The welcomes ever *smile*, and farewell *goes out sighing*.　　　　　　　　　(William Shakespeare)

Tasks:

1. Read the following sentences containing personification and figure out the meanings of the sentences.

 a. *She watched the moonlight dancing on the lake.*

 b. *The glow of the setting sun is kissing the hills.*

 c. *Monday morning found Jack miserable.*

 d. *Those years witnessed great changes in the country.*

 e. *A beautiful view greeted her eyes.*

 f. *She was seized by fear.*

 g. *Justice is blind.*

 h. *Necessity is the mother of invention.*

 i. *My computer hates me.*

 j. *The sun kissed the flowers.*

 k. *The ancient tower spoke to her of the disaster, and the sea waves sobbed with sorrows.*

 l. *The gentle breeze caressed my cheeks and soothed my anger.*

 m. *My rocking chair was making noises all night; it's getting very old.*

 n. *The flower was very pretty, it smiled at me and its perfume had such a nice smell.*

 o. *My computer is protesting about how I'm using it too much.*

 p. *In the winter when I am standing outside, my teeth keep on protesting how it's so cold.*

 q. *The apple was too sour, my teeth didn't like it.*

 r. *The journey was very long, my feet got very tired.*

 s. *One day I was packing for my trip, but I couldn't fit everything into my suitcase; I bet my suitcase would start crying if I stuff it anymore.*

 t. *When I was little I always talked to the maple tree beside my home every time when I felt sad; the tree always nodded its leaves in understanding.*

 u. *When guns speak it is too late to argue.*

v. Mosquitoes were using my ankles for filling stations.

2. Point out the parts using personification in the following passages and poems.

a. "Only the champion daisy trees were serene. After all, they were part of a rain forest already two thousand years old and scheduled for eternity, so they ignored the men and continued to rock the diamondbacks that slept in their arms. It took the river to persuade them that indeed the world was altered."   (Toni Morrison: Tar Baby)

b. The wind stood up and gave a shout.
   He whistled on his fingers and
   Kicked the withered leaves about
   And thumped the branches with his hand
   And said he'd kill and kill and kill,
   And so he will and so he will.   (James Stephens: The Wind)

c. "Do villainy, do, since you protest to do't,
   Like workmen. I'll example you with thievery.
   The sun's a thief, and with his great attraction
   Robs the vast sea; the moon's an arrant thief,
   And her pale fire she snatches from the sun;
   The sea's a thief, whose liquid surge resolves
   The moon into salt tears; the earth's a thief,
   That feeds and breeds by a composture stolen
   From general excrement: each thing's a thief."
       (William Shakespeare: Timon in Timon of Athens)

d. The Eagle
   He clasps the crag with crooked hands,
   Close to the sun in lonely lands,
   Ringed with the azure world, he stands.
   The wrinkled sea beneath him crawls;
   He watches from his mountain walls,
   And like a thunderbolt he falls.
                           (Alfred: Lord Tennyson)

3. Appreciate the following passages, poems or sentences in which personification is used.

a. Slowly, silently, now the moon
   Walks the night <u>in her silver shoon</u>;

　　　　This way, and that, <u>she peers</u>, and <u>sees</u>
　　　　Silver fruit upon silver trees...

　　　　　　　　　　　　　　　　　　　　　(Walter de la Mare: Silver)

　　b. *A tree whose <u>hungry mouth</u> is prest*
　　　　Against the earth's <u>sweet flowing breast</u>;
　　　　A tree that <u>looks at</u> God all day,
　　　　And <u>lifts her leafy arms to pray</u>;

　　　　　　　　　　　　　　　　　　　　　(Joyce Kilmer: Trees)

　　c. It may be well for these <u>timid</u>, lowland trees to <u>tremble</u> with all their leaves, or <u>turn their paleness</u> to the sky, if a rush of rain passes by them; or to let fall their leaves at last, <u>sick and sere</u>. But we pines must <u>live</u> amidst the wrath of clouds. We only <u>wave</u> our branches to and fro when the storm pleads with us, as men toss their arms in a dream.

　　d. Money <u>talks</u>; money <u>prints</u>; money <u>broadcasts</u>; money <u>reigns</u>; and kings and labor leaders alike have to register its decrees, and even, by a staggering paradox, to finance its enterprises and guarantee its profits.

　　　　　　　　　　　　　　　　　(G. Bernard Shaw: The Apple Cart, Preface)

　　e. The clock on the wall ticked <u>loudly and lazily</u>, as if it had time to <u>spare</u>. Outside the rattling windows there was a <u>restless</u>, <u>whispering</u> wind. The room grew light and dark, and wondrous light again, as the moon <u>played hide-and-seek</u> through the clouds.

　　　　　　　　　　　　　　　　　　　　(Henry van Dyke: The Blue Flower)

2.4.4　Metonymy

2.4.4.1　Definition of Metonymy

　　Metonymy is a figure of speech in which the name of one object or concept is used to substitute that of another object or concept. In metonymy, unlike metaphor, the two objects or concepts do not have similarities or common points, but are intimately associated with each other. It is easy to confuse metonymy and metaphor. As metaphors are meant to emphasize the similarities between two referents, there is always a transfer of qualities from one referent to another in metaphor, which is absent in metonymy. For instance, "the pen (words) is mightier than the sword (forces)". Similarly, "crown" can be used to mean "king", and "throne" refers to "kingship".

2.4.4.2　The Formation of Metonymy

　　Generally speaking, metonymy is formed in the following ways.

1) The replacement of people or objects by their features

When someone or something has a special feature, it can be used to refer to the man or the thing, thus making the language more interesting and impressive.

(1) *She said coldly, "I asked how much."*
The piggy eyes blinked. "Ten thousand dollars."

"The piggy eyes" refers to the man with pig-like eyes.

(2) *Have I in conquest stretch'd my arms so far*
To be afraid to tell graybeards the truth? (*William Shakespeare: Julius Caesar*)

"Graybeards" refers to those old men wearing grey beard. The use of this feature for the "old men" emphasizes the fact that those men are so old that it is impossible for "me" to fear them and not to tell them the truth.

(3) *Soapy stood still with his hands in his pockets and smiled at the sight of brass buttons.*   (*O. Henry: The Cop and the Anthem*)

As policemen in the U. S. wears uniform with brass button, "brass button" means policeman.

2) The substitution of objects for the user or the owner of the objects

(1) *His pen sways over half of the civilized world.*

"Pen" refers to works. The sentence means "his works influenced over half of the civilized world".

(2) *But in spite of himself, he became deeply interested in this Polish girl with the intense gray eyes and delicate features, who was as keen on test tubes as himself.*

This sentence describes how Curry fell in love with Ms. Curry. "Test tube" refers to chemical experiment.

3) The substitution of names of writers or artists for their literary or artistic works

(1) *I am reading Thoreau.*

Thoreau refers to Thoreau's works.

(2) *She is interested in Picasso.*

Picasso refers to Picasso's paintings.

4) The substitution of certain animals for a nation, people or a place

For example, "dragon" can substitute for China, "John Bull" for England or typical Englishman, and "bear" for Russia

5) The use of names of places or building to replace organizations or governmental departments

For instance, "the Capital Hill", the physical location of the Congress of the United States refers to the legislative branch of the federal government; "the White

House", which is the official presidential residence in Washington, D. C. refers to the US President, his staff and close advisors; "the Wall Street" represents American financial and banking center and industry, while "Hollywood" stands for American film and television industry.

(1) *Business lobbyists on <u>Capital Hill</u> are keeping close tabs on what is known as the Family and Medical Leave Act.* (*Paul Hoffmon*)

(2) *A Beli or a Bailly may gain greater glory than the Brahmins, but he'll never equal their entrée into <u>White House</u>.* (*Paul Hoffmon*)

6) The substitution of the container for its contents

(1) *The <u>kettle</u> boils.*

In fact, it is the water in the kettle that boils. As kettle is the container of water, it can be used to refer to water.

(2) *He has undoubtedly the best <u>stable</u> in the country.*

"Stable" refers to the horses in the stable.

(3) *He set <u>the room</u> roaring with laughter.*

"The room" means the people in the room.

(4) *The coat would be beyond his miserable <u>pocket</u>.*

"Pocket" refers to the money in the pocket. So the sentence means "he doesn't have enough money to buy the coat". "His" miserable condition is well presented through this expression.

7) The substitution of a human organ for its function

(1) *<u>Brain</u> is mightier than <u>muscle</u>.*

"Brain" means intelligence or knowledge as brain is the organ for thinking; "muscle" refers to brute force since muscle reminds people of physical strength. "Brain" is also used to mean "talented people" or "idea", so the leaving of talents is called "brain drain".

(2) *Mark Twain honed and experimented with his new writing <u>muscles</u>.* (*Noel Grove*)

In this sentence, "muscle" doesn't mean physical strength, but means ability.

(3) *She has a ready <u>tongue</u>.*

When people talk, they use tongue. So "tongue" means the ability to talk. This sentence means "she is very articulate".

(4) *She was, to be sure, a girl who excited the emotions, but I was not one to let my <u>heart</u> rule my <u>head</u>.* (*Max Shulman*)

"Heart" is always related to emotions (e. g. break one's heart), while "head" (e. g. lose one's head) refers to thinking or sensibility. So the sentence means "I would not lose my sensibility because of strong emotions".

8) The substitution of a concrete object for an abstract idea

(1) In the book of *Genesis 3:19*, after the Lord God found Adam and Eve had eaten the forbidden fruit, he said to Adam:

"... The ground is cursed because of you. You will eat from it by means of painful labor all the days of your life. It will produce thorns and thistles for you, and you will eat the plants of the field. You will eat bread by the sweat of your brow until you return to the ground, since you were taken from it. For you are dust, and you will return to dust."

"Sweat" refers to the hard labor that Adam will have to endure to produce the food that will sustain his life. "The sweat of your brow" vividly presents a picture of how hard he has to work.

(2) *The rather arresting spectacle of little old Japan adrift amid beige concrete skyscrapers is the very symbol of the incessant struggle between the kimono and the miniskirt.*   (Jacques Danvoir)

"Kimono" stands for the traditional Japanese culture while "miniskirt" represents the modern Western culture. These two words form a sharp contrast hence lending force to the expression.

(3) *Play the man*!

"Man" refers to the qualities a man should have. "Play the man" means "behave as a man should do".

(4) *He lives by the pen.*

In this sentence, "pen" no longer means "works", but "writing".

9) The substitution of an abstract idea for a concrete object

(1) *It was not only writers, you know, it was a thoroughly representative gathering—science, politics, business, art, the world.*

"Science", "politics", "business" and "art" refer to people in these lines. "The world" means people from all walks of life.

(2) *It is a pity that there is more ignorance than knowledge in the country.*

"Ignorance" refers to people who are ignorant or ill-educated and "knowledge" refers to those well-educated ones.

(3) *The proposals were expected to be unacceptable to capital.*

"Capital" means the investor, the one who provides the capital.

2.4.4.3　The Use of Metonymy in Writing

In metonymy, the association between the two objects or concepts is usually established on the close connections between them.

(1) The Peaceful Shepherd
(by Robert Frost)

If heaven were to do again,
And on the pasture bars,
I leaned to line the figures in
Between the dotted stars.
I should be tempted to forget,
I fear, the <u>Crown</u> of Rule,
The <u>Scales</u> of Trade, the <u>Cross</u> of Faith,
As hardly worth renewal.
For these have governed in our lives,
And see how men have warred.
The <u>Cross</u>, the <u>Crown</u>, the <u>Scales</u> may all
As well have been the Sword.

In the poem, "cross" is used by Christians and stands for church here; "crown" which is worn by king or queen stands for imperial power; "scales" used by business people stands for trade and business. The three words are used metonymically to represent what are closely related to them.

(2) In the book of *Genesis 27:28*, Isaac smelled his son Jacob's clothes and blessed him:

Ah, the smell of my son is like the smell of a field that the Lord has blessed. May God give to you—from the dew of the sky and from the richness of the land—an abundance of <u>grain and new wine</u>.

"Grain and wine" here means money and material possessions. "An abundance of grain and wine" means Jacob will attain a lot of wealth.

Examples of metonymy can be found in many literary works or poetry. The use of metonymy establishes strong word association hence adding variation and adornment to literary works and changing the thought pattern of readers. An understanding of metonymy aids a reader to better interpret a piece of writing.

(3) In the poem *Out, Out* by Robert Frost, the injured boy holds up his hand "as if to keep the life from spilling". Literally, this line means to keep the blood from spilling; metonymically, it means the boy's life is in mortal danger. Here is this poem:

Out, Out
(*by Robert Frost*)

The buzz-saw snarled and rattled in the yard
And made dust and dropped stove-length sticks of wood,
Sweet-scented stuff when the breeze drew across it.
And from there those that lifted eyes could count
Five mountain ranges one behind the other
Under the sunset far into Vermont.
And the saw snarled and rattled, snarled and rattled,
As it ran light, or had to bear a load.
And nothing happened: day was all but done.
Call it a day, I wish they might have said
To please the boy by giving him the half hour
That a boy counts so much when saved from work.
His sister stood beside them in her apron
To tell them "Supper." At the word, the saw,
As if to prove saws knew what supper meant,
Leaped out at the boy's hand, or seemed to leap—
He must have given the hand. However it was,
Neither refused the meeting. But the hand!
The boy's first outcry was a rueful laugh,
As he swung toward them holding up the hand
Half in appeal, but half <u>as if to keep</u>
<u>The life from spilling.</u> Then the boy saw all—
Since he was old enough to know, big boy
Doing a man's work, though a child at heart—
He saw all spoiled. "Don't let him cut my hand off—
The doctor, when he comes. Don't let him, sister!"
So. But the hand was gone already.
The doctor put him in the dark of ether.
He lay and puffed his lips out with his breath.
And then—the watcher at his pulse took fright.
No one believed. They listened at his heart.
Little—less—nothing! —and that ended it.
No more to build on there. And they, since they
Were not the one dead, turned to their affairs.

Tasks:

1. In the following list, the original meanings of the words are given. Choose the meanings of these words in metonymic use from the list.

word	original meaning	meaning in metonymic use
1. damages	Destructive effects	_____
2. Detroit	The largest city in Michigan	_____
3. Downing street	A street in the city of Westminster, on which is located the official residence of the UK Prime Minister	_____
4. Foggy Bottom	A neighborhood in Washington, D. C.	_____
5. the press	Printing press	_____
6. Fleet street	A street in London	_____
7. tongue	Oral muscle	_____
8. word	A unit of language	_____
9. Broadway	An avenue running the length of Manhattan Island in New York City	_____
10. Langley	An unincorporated community in Virginia	_____
11. sweat	The perspiration	_____
12. Madison Avenue	An avenue in the borough of Manhattan in New York City	_____
13. The Kremlin	A fortified construction in historic cities of Russia and the Soviet Union	_____
14. The Palace	Buckingham Palace	_____
15. The Pentagon	A large government office building in Arlington, Virginia	_____
16. Westminster	A city in Greater London	_____
17. Whitewall	A street in the city of Westminster	_____
18. Houston	The largest city in Texas	_____
19. Vatican	The Vatican City State	_____

Meaning in metonymic use:

a. Money paid in compensation

b. A promise; a conversation

c. Hard work

d. A language or dialect

e. The news media

f. NASA mission control

g. The American automobile industry

h. The government of Russia

i. The Central Intelligence Agency of the United States
j. The United States Department of State
k. The American advertising industry
l. The live theater district of New York
m. The United States Department of Defense
n. The British Prime Minister's office
o. The UK monarch's office
p. The UK Government
q. The British Civil service or a Government Department
r. The British press, particularly newspapers
s. The Pope and Magisterium of the Roman Catholic Church

2. Point out the metonymies used in the following sentences and figure out their meanings.

a. He writes a fine hand.
b. The house was called to order.
c. We have always remained loyal to the crown.
d. He is a man of the cloth.
e. He is fond of the bottle.
f. Grey hairs should be respected.
g. Life is not just a journey from diaper to shroud.
h. He is booked out for the whole season.
i. She is the first violin in the band.
j. There is much of the schoolboy in him.
k. The blue eyes walked into the office.
l. To solve the dispute, labor put forward three proposals.
m. He has done me kindnesses.
n. He has five mouths to feed.
o. Many hands make light work.
p. There's bread and work for all.
q. He is her admiration.
r. The practiced ear can recognize a classic favor.
s. She has the eye for the fair and the beautiful.
t. A thousand mustaches can live together, but not four breasts.   (A proverb)
u. The wolf and the pig mingled together in his face.
v. The whole village rejoiced at news.

w. He is in his cups again.

x. He keeps a good table and one gets plenty to eat and drink in his house.

2.4.5 Hyperbole

2.4.5.1 Definition of Hyperbole

Hyperbole, also called overstatement, is a rhetorical device in which statements are deliberately exaggerated to evoke strong emotional response or to leave a deep impression, or to create emphasis. To put it simply, hyperbole is a way of describing something in order to make it sound bigger, smaller, better, worse, etc. than it really is. It is frequently used for humor, and not meant to be taken literally.

For instance:

(1) *He almost died laughing.*

The sentence vividly depicts a picture in which a person who keeps laughing and cannot stop so that he can neither straighten up nor speak—he cannot even breathe normally. Reading this sentence, the readers can't help smiling.

(2) *I tried a thousand times.*

Of course, "I" couldn't have tried as many as a thousand times. But with exaggeration, the anxiety of the speaker is well reflected and conveyed.

(3) *I will love you until the sky falls and the sea runs dry.*

It is impossible that the sky falls or the sea runs dry, so it means "I will love you forever". The use of the exaggerated statements shows the speaker's deep love for his/her beloved.

Hyperbole is sometimes confused with a simile or a metaphor because it often involves a comparison of two objects. But a hyperbole always contains an exaggeration which is not found in both simile and metaphor.

For example:

(4) *His feet are as big as a barge.*

The sentence looks like a simile in terms of its form as it compares foot size to the size of a barge. But it is obvious that no one's feet can be that big (a barge is approximately 700 feet long).

(5) *The waves are mountain high.*

Seemingly, the sentence contains a metaphor as it can be changed into a simile "as high as mountains". But in fact waves cannot reach the height of mountains. The use of exaggeration describes the hugeness of waves in a dramatic way.

Hyperbole is not only an important device in literary works, but also common in casual speech. The media and the advertising industry often use hyperbole when speaking of an accident, to increase the impact of the story causing sensation among the audiences or appealing to a wider audience.

The effect of hyperbole is well described in the following words:

"Hyperbole is the polished mirror into which the black imagination gazes with every other rhyme, laughing as it sees itself refracted and distorted in a phantasmagorical kaleidoscope. The language of hyperbole amplifies reality by carrying us beyond the boundaries of rational thought... Hyperbole makes extraordinary demands on the imagination." (Onwuchekwa Jemie)

2.4.5.2 Classification of Hyperbole

1) Extended hyperbole and reduced hyperbole

Hyperbole can be classified as **extended hyperbole** that amplifies the image or function of an object or that maximizes the amount or degree of the object, and **reduced hyperbole** that minimizes the features of an object.

For example:

His eloquence would split rocks! (extended hyperbole)

It is the last straw that breaks the camel's back. (reduced hyperbole)

2) Classification of hyperbole based on form

Based on the forms of hyperbole, it is classed into five types:

(1) Hyperbole through the use of numerals

e. g.

This made him roar like a thousand bulls.

(*George Eliot: The Mill on the Floss*)

It can be imagined how loud it is if a thousand bulls roar together. Then it is not hard for readers to visualize the scene.

I loved Ophelia: forty thousand brothers could not, with all their quantity of love make up my sum.   (*William Shakespeare: Hamlet*)

It is impossible to measure one's love. But through the use of the concrete number, the audiences may have a clear idea of how deep and strong Hamlet's love for Ophelia is.

(2) Hyperbole through the use of verbs, nouns, adjectives and adverbs

a. Hyperbole through the use of verbs

e. g.

He nearly exploded with indignation.

A man cannot explode because of anger. But the sentence vividly describes "his" irrepressible rage.

The sound of drums and gongs reached the stars.

The sentence means the sound of drums and gongs is deafening loud and carries a long way so that it can be heard from the distance.

b. Hyperbole through the use of nouns

e. g.

She left in a storm of tears.

How can one shed so many tears that it is like a storm? But this expression is more vivid than simply saying "She left crying." We can almost see a girl with tears all over her face.

It's a crime to stay inside on such a good day.

When it is a fine day, people should go out to enjoy themselves. When staying inside has become a "crime", it can be known how beautiful the weather is.

c. Hyperbole through the use of adjectives

e. g.

Divorce has become a lucrative process, simple to arrange and easy to forget, and ambitious females can repeat it as often as they please and parlay their winnings to astronomical figures. (Roald Dahl: Mrs Bixby and the Colonel's Coat)

"Astronomical" tells the readers how appalling the figure is and corresponds to the word "lucrative".

Most Americans remember Mark Twain as the father of Huck Finn's idyllic cruise through eternal boyhood and Tom Sawyer's endless summer of freedom and adventure.
(Noel Grove: Mark Twain—Mirror of America)

The use of the words "eternal" and "endless" reflects the long-lasting influence of the work on the audiences.

d. Hyperbole through the use of adverbs

e. g.

The hills are heavenly beautiful.

The sentence can be changed into "The hills are as beautiful as heaven". No one has ever seen what heaven is like; the only thing that is known about heaven is that it is extremely beautiful. So instead of reading the long description of the beautiful scenery, readers could give full play to their imagination.

Madame Loisel now knew the horrible life of the need. But she took her part heroically. (Guy de Maupassant: The Necklace)

"Heroically" portrays Madame Loisel's feelings about the hard life—she was scared, but had to confront it. This lady has to face the harsh reality with great courage like a hero.

(3) Hyperbole using the comparative and superlative degree of adjectives

a. Hyperbole using comparative degree of adjectives

e. g.

She has <u>more</u> goodness in her little finger <u>than</u> he has in his whole body.

(*Jonathan Swift*)

The sentence is to compare the two persons. Without many words depicting how good and moral "she" is while how evil and sinful "he" is, the sharp contrast between the morality of the two persons is self-evident.

b. Hyperbole using superlative degree of adjectives

e. g.

The <u>most effective</u> water power in the world—women's tears. (*Wilson Mizner*)

Is that all the affection and pride you can muster, for the nation that bore you— for the <u>noblest, most civilized</u> nation on the face of this planet?

(*Peter Stone and Sherman Edwards*)

Sometimes, "as (so)... as" is used to form hyperbole. For instance:

He is <u>as proud as proud can be</u>.

None is <u>so blind as</u> those that won't see.

Both sentences have a superlative degree of adjectives hidden in them.

(4) Hyperbole through the use of subjunctive mood

As subjunctive mood can be used for supposition or assumption, it is often used to form a hyperbole.

e. g.

A knife <u>could have cut</u> the tension during the seemingly endless trip back to the plantation. (*Alex Haley: Roots*)

The atmosphere is so tense as if the air has been caked and a knife can curt through it.

Some movie stars wear their sunglasses even in churches; they're afraid God <u>might recognize</u> them and <u>ask for autograph</u>. (*Fred Allen*)

The expression is both hyperbolic and ironical.

(5) Hyperbole formed together with other rhetorical devices

In some cases, hyperbole is formed in the form of other rhetorical devices.

e. g.

<u>A drop of ink</u> may make <u>a million think</u>.   (*George G. Byron*)

The sentence contains metonymy, contrast, hyperbole and consonance. "Ink" stands for the enlightening words or articles (metonymy). "A drop" forms a contrast with "a million" for emphasis. "Ink" and "think" use the same consonant. Both "a drop" and "a million" are hyperbolic.

Miss Bolo went straight home in <u>a flood of tears</u> and sedan chair.

(*Charles Dickens*)

"A flood of tears" is a metaphor in form with a hyperbolic function at the same time.

How many rhetorical devices are used in the following sentence?

A lie can <u>travel half way around the world</u> while the truth is <u>putting on his shoes</u>.

(*Mark Twain*)

Hyperbole may be used for serious, comic, or ironic effect. If properly used, it can reveal the nature of an object or event, intensify the effect and provoke associations or inspirations. So hyperbole must be based on reality yet clearly distinguishing from the truth and it should be original and used in the right context.

Tasks:

1. Analyze how the following hyperboles are formed.

a. My feet are killing me.

b. Life is happiness, each minute might have been an age of happiness.

(*Fyodor Dostoevsky to His Brother Mihail*)

c. There's no one within miles of him as a cricketer.

d. He is blind drunk.

e. The Pacific is the deep of deeps.

f. The young porkers who are sitting in front of me, every one of you will scream your lives out at the block within a year.   (*George Orwell: Animal Farm*)

g. She is as poor as poor can be.

h. I wondered what mortal controlled it, in what must be one of the loneliest, most forbidding spots on earth.   (*V. Sackville-West: No Signposts in the Sea*)

i. He is diabolically clever.   (*John Steinbeck*)

j. We had held this conversation in a low voice, well knowing my guardian's ears to be the sharpest of the sharp.   (*Charles Dickens*)

k. He smoked like a chimney.

l. They ran like greased lightning.

m. When you come to think of it, there is nothing in the world more potent and more impotent than words.

n. The church is calm enough, I am sure; but it might be a steam-power loom in full action, for any sedative effect it has on me.

o. Guns, thunder, earthquakes would not have awakened the men just then.

p. They are sitting on a volcano, which might erupt at any moment.

q. My left leg weighs three tons.　　　(*Thomas Baily Aldrich*: *Marjorie Daw*)

r. After twenty minutes my legs had turned to water again.

s. Ornamental columns supported a ceiling that displayed whole universe of electric bulbs.

t. There I saw him, lying on his back, with his legs extending to I don't know where, gurgling taking place in his throat, stoppages in his nose, and his mouth open like a post office.　　　(*Charles Dickens*)

u. Your mama's hair is so short she could stand on her head and her hair wouldn't touch the ground.

v. My toaster has never once worked properly in four years. I follow the instructions and push two slices of bread down in the slots, and seconds later they rifle upwards. Once they broke the nose of a woman I loved dearly.

　　　(*Woody Allen*: *My Speech to the Graduates*)

2. Translate the following sentences into English using hyperbole.
1. 坦克轰隆轰隆地沿着路开过来。
2. 他们捧腹大笑。
3. 他们像连珠炮似的向我提了几个问题。
4. 食品价格飞涨。
5. 她高兴得心里飘飘然。
6. 她疲倦得要命。
7. 这两个城市千差万别。
8. 我试过很多次了。
9. 办公室里有很多的职员。
10. 他通晓中国历史。
11. 天冷得要命。
12. 这个人庸俗不堪。
13. 使你感到不便,我真抱歉。
14. 他们是极有才能的人。

15. 她的发音极好。
16. 这是荒谬绝伦的事。
17. 她的父母一贫如洗。
18. 他的口才可以把石头都说得动起来。
19. 没有比他更负责的教师了。
20. 他很大年纪了。
21. 他非常勤劳。
22. 这项工作进展缓慢。
23. 消息传来,犹如晴天霹雳。
24. 我绝对不会去跳舞。
25. 我告诉过你很多次不要撒谎。
26. 我排队等了半天。
27. 我手头有一大堆事情要做。
28. 她哭了很久。
29. 所有的人都盯着我看。
30. 我们应当寸土必争。

2.4.6 Understatement

2.4.6.1 Definition of Understatement

Understatement is the opposite of hyperbole. It is a restrained statement in ironic contrast to what might be said, a studied avoidance of explicit emphasis or exaggeration. It is "a form of irony: the ironical contrast inheres in the discrepancy between what one would be expected to say and his actual refusal to say it" (Cleanth Brooks, 1950). It achieves its purpose of emphasizing a fact by deliberately making it seem less important or serious, impressing the listener or the reader by what is implied or left unsaid.

For instance:

It is no laughing matter.

What the speaker really wants to say is "it is a very serious matter".

We are none of us getting any younger.

The sentence implies "we are both of us getting much old".

2.4.6.2 Classification of Understatement by Devices

Understatement can be achieved through lexical and grammatical devices.

1) Understatement using lexical devices

Words or expressions with less force are often used to describe a serious situation.

Those of us who are quitting are the impatient ones who <u>lack the imagination</u> to believe that the bright dream will glow again.

(*Caskie Stinnett*: *Farewell*, *My Unlovely*)

By "lack the imagination", the writer means "do not believe". The use of the word "imagination" is full of irony and the effect is much stronger than direct statement.

I have to have this operation. It <u>isn't very serious</u>. I have this <u>tiny little</u> tumor on the brain. (*J. D. Salinger*: *Holden Caulfield in The Catcher in the Rye*)

2) Understatement using grammatical devices

No one was <u>more</u> willing to do a favor for friend and neighbor <u>than</u> he.

The sentence, through a comparison, tells the readers that "he" is the most helpful person.

I know he is honest, and <u>I wish I could</u> add he were capable.

Subjunctive mood is employed to mean "he is not capable enough".

"Don't you figure out that I might have had something to do with it?" said Soapy, <u>not without sarcasm</u>, but friendly, as one greets good fortune.

(*O. Henry*: *The Cop and the Anthem*)

Double negation is used to emphasis when Soapy made the remark, he was saying with sarcasm.

2.4.6.3 Classification of Understatement by Ways of Expression

In terms of its way of expression, understatement consists of litotes and meiosis.

1) Litotes （反叙）

Litotes is a type of understatement "in which an affirmative is expressed by the negative of the contrary". In other words, the negative word is used for the opposite effect.

e. g.

(1) *Who <u>can not</u> rely on such an honest man?*

It means "everybody can rely on such an honest man". The negative form is used for the affirmative purpose. The effect is much stronger and impressive.

(2) *He has <u>no small</u> chance of success.*

It means "he has great chance of success".

(3) *You <u>cannot</u> begin the practice <u>too</u> early.*

The sentence means "the earlier you begin the practice, the better".

(4) *A final agreement to set up trade offices with consular functions came after*

high-profile maneuvering by Seoul at last month's Asian Games in Beijing. A generous Korean contribution to the cash-short event <u>didn't hurt</u>. Now analysts expect last year's $3.1 billion in indirect two-way trade to leap quickly to a $5-billion-a-year clip.

(*Gerson Yalowitz*)

Considering the fact that it is a generous contribution and that the sports event is "cash-short", the contribution should be highly appreciated. However, for political and diplomatic reasons, the appreciation cannot be overly expressed. Therefore, litotes is used to give an objective account of the event without too much embellishment.

Here are more examples:

(5) *If you can tell the fair one's mind, it will be <u>no small proof</u> of your art, for I dare say it is more than she herself can do.* (*Alexander Pope*)

(6) *He who examines his own self will <u>not long remain ignorant</u> of his failings.*

(7) *Overall the flavors of the mushrooms, herbs, and spices combine to make the dish <u>not at all disagreeable</u> to the palate.*

2) Meiosis(弱陈)

Meiosis is a figure of speech by which the impression is intentionally conveyed that a thing is less in size, importance, etc., than it really is. While litotes uses negative expressions to strengthen the opposite effect, meiosis uses affirmative form to downplay the effect. Downtoners like rather, quite, almost, a bit, a little, some (thing), sort/kind of, scarcely, hardly, pretty, almost are employed instead of very (much). It is used when a reserved assessment is made.

(1) *Mr. Li is <u>something</u> of a philosopher.*

It is likely that Mr. Li is not a philosopher by profession, but a person who talks or behaves in a way a philosopher does. So it is improper to say Mr. Li is a philosopher, and "something of" can well meet the need. Suppose Mr. Li is indeed a philosopher, this statement is ironical.

(2) *I'm <u>sort/kind of</u> angry at your rudeness.*

Usually when this remark is made, it doesn't really mean the speaker is only a little angry, but more likely he is very angry. But for politeness and for the consideration of the listener's feeling, anger is downplayed.

(3) *During last year's Central Park Bicycle Race, five of the racers were attacked and had their bikes stolen while the race was in progress. This is <u>something of</u> a handicap in a bicycle race.* (*Caskle Stinnett*)

This is a journalistic report of the attack on the racers and the theft of their bikes. The wording are carefully studied and chosen and the tone is not radical. In this way, the journalist avoids offending the organizers of the race and avoids causing others to think he is gloating over the misfortune.

2.4.6.4   The Use of Understatement in Writing

Understatement is used usually for humorous or ironic emphasis. It is sometimes used to employ the reader's own powers of description.

For example:

(1) *Henry and Catherine were married, the bells rang, and everybody smiled.... To begin perfect happiness at the respective ages of twenty-six and eighteen is to do pretty well....*   (*Jane Austen*)

(2) *Last week I saw a woman flayed, and you will hardly believe how much it altered her person for the worse.*   (*Jonathan Swift*)

(3) *You know I would be a little disappointed if you were to be hit by a drunk driver at two a.m., so I hope you will be home early.*

In these cases the writers leave enough space for the readers to use their own knowledge of the facts and fill out a more vivid and personal description than the writer might have.

More noticeably, understatement is also used as a tool for modesty and tactfulness. Whenever you represent your own accomplishments, and often when you just describe your own position, an understatement of the facts will help you to avoid the charge of egotism on the one hand and of self-interested puffery on the other. A person proud of his own achievements or qualities is always unpopular, leaving a bad impression on others. Conversely, a person modest of his own talents wins our admiration easily—this is where understatement is needed. Understatement is especially useful in showing your disagreement, because most people don't like objections, and view disagreement as a sign of contempt for their intellect or ability. Understatement, even if carrying the same point, sounds much less offensive.

Compare the following two sentences and point out which statement is more acceptable:

A. *This plan will not work.*

B. *This is a good plan, but there may be some difficulties carrying it out.*

It is clear that the first statement might well offend the proposer and the result may not be what you wanted. Since the goal of a speech or a piece of writing is to persuade others to accept your idea, you should avoid offending others. The use of understatement allows you to show some respect for the audiences' feelings and understanding, eliminating the possible hostility, and sets the stage for further communication and elucidation until finally you reach your goal.

Tasks:

1. Read the following sentences, and find out how understatement is used.

a. "I am just going outside and may be some time."

(Captain Lawrence Oates, Antarctic explorer, before walking out into a blizzard to face certain death, 1912)

b. "Well, that's cast rather a gloom over the evening, hasn't it?"

(Dinner guest, after a visit from the Grim Reaper, in Monty Python's "The Meaning of Life")

c. There is also poverty, convincingly etched in the statistics, and etched too, in the lives of people like Hortensia Cabrera, mother of 14, widow.

"Money," she says with quiet understatement, "is kind of tight. But I manage."

(Griffin Smith Jr.)

d. I see myself, with Agnes at my side journeying along the road of life. I see our children and our friends around us; and I hear the roar of many voices, not indifferent to me as I travel on. (Charles Dickens: David Copperfield)

e. ... there was a loud cry from a number of voices, and the horses reared and plunged.

But for the latter inconvenience, the carriage probably would not have stopped; carriages were often known to drive on, and leave their wounded behind, and why not?

(Charles Dickens: A Tale of Two Cities)

f. It was no small feat to harness the energies of an entire nation for a united show of hospitality and good will for visitors from around the world.

(Kyuk-Ho Shin)

g. "It's just a flesh wound".

(Black Knight, after having both arms cut off, in Monty Python and the Holy Grail)

h. A soiled baby, with a neglected nose, cannot be conscientiously regarded as a thing of beauty. (Mark Twain)

i. The face wasn't a bad one; it had what they called charm.

(John Galsworthy)

j. He was, he said, rather a precocious boy that he was permitted an amount of initiative that most children scarcely attain by seven or eight. (Wells)

k. You may have something of a Roosevelt, something of a Newton in yourself, you may have something very much greater than either of these men manifested waiting your help to give it expression.

l. I have never committed one act that was not in the interests of my people.

(W. Epton)

m. Bassanio, in his grief, replied that there was nothing he could not sacrifice.

(Ch. Lamb)

n. The British are feeling the pinch in relation to recent terrorist bombings and threats to destroy nightclubs and airports, and therefore have raised their security level from "Miffed" to "Peeved." Soon, though, security levels may be raised yet again to "Irritated" or even "A Bit Cross." Brits have not been "A Bit Cross" since the Blitz in 1940 when tea supplies all but ran out.

2. Rewrite the following sentences using understatement.

a. He is wise.

b. Every week, he finds fault with me.

c. It is agreeable to be rich.

d. He knows the use of all weapons.

e. Similar mistakes are common.

f. All rules have exception.

g. Only with high political consciousness, can we serve the people well.

h. He was a very good orator.

i. This problem is easy for us.

j. I am quite early, I see.

k. I'm very happy.

l. Only fools have ever believed it.

m. He was always satisfied with my work.

n. She is very happy in her present post.

o. We are much concerned about our political study.

p. Everyone has some fault.

q. Be sure to come to us.

r. Our efforts were fruitful.

3. Read the following sentences to see how understatement is used.

a. He did not go to Oxford for nothing.

b. He is no stranger to computers.

c. They didn't start a moment too soon.

d. A teacher cannot be too patient with his students.

e. Good manners cannot be too much valued.

f. I can't thank you enough for your kind help.
g. We can't do enough for our socialist educational cause.
h. Her pronunciation is rather good.
j. He has written quite a number of books.
k. The place is some distance off.
l. There was a slight disturbance in the city yesterday. All the shops were shut.

2.4.7 Euphemism

2.4.7.1 Definition of Euphemism

Euphemism is the substitution of an agreeable or mild expression for an unpleasant or offensive one, usually obscene, vulgar, ominous and profane words. By using euphemism, unpleasantness, embarrassment, impoliteness, etc. can be avoided.

For instance:

You've lost your license.

In different situation, the sentence has different interpretations as "license" may be understood literally, but may have other implied meanings. In addition to the literal meaning, this sentence can also mean "your fly is open" or "your suit is untimely". In both cases, the use of this euphemistical expression is a good way to avoid embarrassment.

2.4.7.2 Traditional Euphemism and Stylistic Euphemism

There are a huge number of euphemisms in English. Some are traditional euphemism while others are stylistic euphemism.

1) Traditional euphemism

Traditional euphemisms are reflections of social taboos including expressions related to illness, disability, aging, death, human body and human needs. Here are some traditionally used euphemisms.

(1) Euphemisms for illness

e.g.

soft in the head—mad; the big c/long illness—cancer; Hansen's disease—leprosy; irregularity—constipation; problem skin—acne; mental hospital—madhouse; look off color—be ill; social disease—AIDS

(2) Euphemisms for death

e.g.

join the silent majority; pass away; go to heaven; fall asleep; pass beyond; fade; be called to God; safe in the arms of Jesus; be gone to a better land; pop off (the hooks); get off the hooks; go to his long home; kick the bucket; go to sleep forever; be no more; go west; be at rest; go the way of all flesh; join one's ancestors; return to dust; breathe one's last; run one's race; be no longer with us

(3) Euphemisms for defecate and urinate

go to stool; pass water; go to the bathroom; answer nature's call; make water; empty one's bladder; go to public lavatory; go to men's(women's); go to washroom; pay a call; go to the bank; spend a penny; wash one's hands; see Johnny; consult Mr. Jones; powder one's nose; want to make one self comfortable

(4) Euphemisms for sex

e. g.

go all the way; have relations with; go to bed with; make love; do it; live together

(5) Euphemisms for pregnancy

"She is pregnant." is euphemistically put in the following ways:

She has cancelled all her social engagement;

She is in an interesting condition;

She is in a delicate condition;

She is knitting bootees;

She is in the family way;

She is expecting;

She is eating for two;

She swallows a watermelon seed;

She learns all about diaper folding;

She is rehearsing lullabies;

She wears the apron high.

2) Stylistic euphemism

Stylistic euphemisms refer to those euphemisms used to show politeness, to avoid disrespect or for some other communication purposes.

(1) Euphemisms for occupations

e. g.

tree-trimmer→tree surgeon; hair dresser (barber)→beautician; floor-sweeper →custodian engineer; bootblack→foot-wear maintenance engineer; cobbler→shoe rebuilder; dustman (garbage collector)→street orderly/sanitary engineer; hired girl →domestic help; maid→day help; housekeeper→live-in help; head-waiter→captain; butcher→meat technologist; funeral undertaker→grief therapist

(2) Euphemisms for social problems

e. g.

murder→take care of/dispose of/remove/rub out/put away/touch off;

prostitution→the oldest profession in the world;

prostitute→a lady of the town/call girl/streetwalker;

prison→the big house/correctional center;

steal→take things without permission;

burglary→surreptitious entry;

violence→action;

cocaine→Lady Snow

(3) Euphemisms for disability

e. g.

disabled students → special students; the crippled → the handicapped; blind students→visually retarded students; deaf→hard of hearing; stupid students→slow learners/under-achievers; he is dull (foolish)→he is a bit slow for his age

(4) Euphemisms for aging

e. g.

getting on years; advanced in age; elderly; senior; past one's prime; feeling one's age; golden age; sunset years

(5) Political, economic, military and diplomatic euphemisms

e. g.

economic crisis→recession/depression;

attack→active defense;

aggression→involvement;

pullout→retreat/light and scattered action/break off contact with enemy;

death penalty→capital punishment;

strike→industrial action/industrial dispute;

racial extinction→final solution;

nuclear accidents→core rearrangement;

electric chair→hot seat;

solitary confinement cells→adjustment centers/quiet cells;

dismiss→lay off/ease out/give sb. the walking ticket

In addition to using the euphemisms that have been generally acknowledged, writers sometimes create some euphemistic expressions to fit into the context and to achieve a better effect.

And, it being low water, he <u>went out with the tide</u>.

(*Charles Dickens*: *David Copperfield*)

Instead of saying "he was drowned to death", the writer chooses an indirect but touching expression.

He was both <u>out of pocket</u> and out of spirits by that catastrophe, failed in his health and prophesied the speedy ruin of the empire.

(*John M. Thackeray*: *Vanity Fair*)

"Out of pocket" is used to describe a man "poor" or "bankrupt" and forms correspondence with "out of spirits".

We have come to dedicate a portion of that field as <u>a final resting place</u> for those who here <u>gave their lives</u> that nation might live.

(*Abraham Lincoln*: *Gettysburg Address*)

The tomb is replaced by "a final resting place", and "gave their lives" substitutes "died" to show respect to the soldiers who sacrificed their lives for the nation.

2.4.8 Zeugma

2.4.8.1 Definition of Zeugma

Zeugma is a figure of speech in which a single word (usually a verb or a noun) is used to modify or to govern two or more words in a sentence that are not semantically related. The modifying or governing word either makes sense to only one word or properly applies to all the words it governs in different senses.

For example:

The sun shall not burn you by day, nor the moon by night.

Obviously, the moon is not hot enough to burn. So the verb "burn" only makes sense to the word "sun".

She opened the door and her heart to the homeless boy.

"Open" modifies both "door" and "heart", but in totally different meanings.

This rhetorical device can greatly increase the liveliness and humor of the language, and show the relationships between ideas and actions more clearly. A zeugma always employs ellipsis (the omission of words which are easily understood) and parallelism (the balance of several words or phrases).

2.4.8.2 Classification of Zeugma

In terms of the structure of zeugma, namely, the position of the governing word and the governed words, zeugma can be divided into several types.

1) Prozeugma

Prozeugma is a zeugma in which a verb employed in the first part of a series of clauses is elided in the latter clauses as it also governs the latter clauses.

(1) Pride <u>oppresses</u> humility; hatred love; cruelty compassion.

(Henry Peacham)

The verb "oppress" is omitted in the latter two clauses.

(2) Poverty <u>hath gotten conquest of</u> thy riches, shame of thy pride, danger of thy safety, folly of thy wisdom, weakness of thy strength, and time of thy imagined immortality.

(Henry Peacham)

Likewise, "has got conquest of" appears only in the first clause and is elided in the following ones to avoid repetition.

When using prozeugma, the subjects are not necessarily different. It can be used in a sentence where the subject of the several clauses or phrases is the same one.

(3) He (Mr. Finching) <u>proposed</u> seven times once in a hackney-coach once in a boat once in a pew once on a donkey at Tunbridge Wells and the rest on his knees.

(Charles Dickens: Little Dorrit)

2) Mesozeugma

Mesozeugma is a zeugma where a verb is placed in the middle of the sentence to govern several parallel clauses on either side.

What a shame is this, that neither hope of reward, nor fear of reproach could any thing <u>move</u> him, neither the persuasion of his friends, nor the love of his country.

(Henry Peacham)

3) Hypozeugma

Hypozeugma is a zeugma in which a verb falls at the end of a series of clauses, words or phrases and governs the preceding parallel clauses, words or phrases. In other words, hypozeugma forms a sentence in which several subjects are followed by one predicate. Hypozeugma can cause a sense of suspense in listeners and readers until they reach the end of the sentence.

(1) Neither rain nor fog nor dragons will <u>slow this knight on his quest</u>.

Hypozeugma is a good way to arouse the audiences' curiosity and draw their attention. While the audiences are making a guess at what is to be said in the end, the writer or speaker may make some unexpected observations causing shock or other dramatic effect on the audiences' part.

(2) Does not the nightly watch of the Palatine, does not guard of the city, does

not the fear of the people, does not the union of all good men, does not the holding of the senate in this most defensible place, do not the looks and faces of these people move you? (*Cicero*)

Cicero intends to take the listeners off guard by suspending the verb until the end. Before he utters the final words, the listeners are unable to determine what action the atrocities will cause.

4) Diazeugma

Diazeugma is a zeugma where one subject governs several verbs or verbal constructions which are usually arranged in parallel expressing a similar idea or some related ideas. It is further classified as diazeugma disjunction and diazeugma conjunction according to the placement of the subject and verbs.

Diazeugma disjunction is the structure in which the subject appears in the initial place of the sentence followed by verbs or verbal constructions.

(1) *The book reveals the extent of counterintelligence operations, discusses the options for improving security, and argues for an increase in human intelligence.*

(2) *Physical beauty: with disease it fades; with age it dies.*

Diazeugma conjunction is the structure in which the subject appears in the middle of a sentence.

(3) *Stands accused, threatens our homes, revels in his crime, this man guilty of burglary asks our forgiveness.*

The subject "this man" is placed in the middle of the sentence, governing the verbs preceding and following it.

2.4.8.3 Zeugma and Syllepsis

There is another figure of speech—syllepsis which is considered by many a special type of zeugma. However, some scholars try to differentiate the two as distinct devices. Syllepsis is a figure of speech in which one verb or verbal phrase is used to govern two or more words, phrases or clauses, the meaning changing with each expression. One expression is to be understood literally, while the other may be used figuratively. It can be used for comic effect due to the unusual connections and ambiguity involved.

For example:

(1) *While he was fighting, and losing limb and mind, and dying, others stayed behind to pursue education and career.*

"Losing one's limbs" is used literally, but "losing one's mind" is figurative which means to go mad.

(2) I *left my heart and my wallet* in San Francisco.

"Left my wallet" is literal, what does "left my heart" mean?

It can be concluded that in both form and meaning, there is not much difference between syllepsis and zeugma. Therefore syllepsis can be regarded as a special type of zeugma which makes use of polysemy and idiomatic usage of words. In comparison, zeugma does not necessarily use the same word in different meanings.

a. He *grabbed* his hat from the rack in the closet, his gloves from the table near the door, and his car keys from the punchbowl.

Prozeugma is used in this sentence as the verb "grab" appears only in the first part and elided in the latter part of the sentence. The meaning of "grab" remains the same in the three expressions.

b. He *grabbed* his hat from the rack by the stairs and a kiss from the lips of his wife.

In form, this sentence is similar to sentence *a*, but this sentence employs syllepsis as in "grabbed his hat" and "grabbed a kiss", the verb "grab" is interpreted differently—the former is literal while the latter is metaphorical.

Whereas zeugma enables a concise or even poetic statement of a situation (especially if the verb is at the end), syllepsis emphasizes incongruity between meanings of a verb or different fields of meaning of nouns. The use of the zeugmatic devices is economical and thought provoking as they avoid the repetition of words and create ingenious ideas through the connection of words either grammatically or rhetorically. Zeugma enables us to express ideas concisely and powerfully, yet the proper use of the device requires good understanding of language as well as creative thinking.

Tasks:

1. Point out which types of zeugma are used in the following sentences.

a. *Despairing in the heat and in the sun, we marched, cursing in the rain and in the cold.*

b. *The Romans destroyed Numantia, razed Carthage, obliterated Corinth, overthrew Fregellae.* (Ad Herennium)

c. *Her voice pierces my ears; her words, my heart.* (Cicero)

d. *The freshman excelled in calculus; the sophomore, in music; the senior, in drama.*

e. *When at Nightmare Abbey, he would condole with Mr. Glowry, drink Madeira with Scythrop, crack jokes with Mr. Hilary, hand Mrs. Hilary to the piano, take charge of her fan and gloves, and turn over her music with surprising dexterity, quote*

Revelations with Mr. Toobad, and lament the good old times of feudal darkness with the Transcendental Mr. Flosky. (*Thomas Love Peacock*)

    f. I speak sense, you nonsense.

    g. Hours, days, weeks, months, and years do pass away. (*Sherry*)

    h. With one mighty swing he knocked the ball through the window and two spectators off their chairs.

    i. Both determination and virtue will prevail; both dedication and honor, diligence and commitment.

    j. He smashed the clock into bits and his fist through the wall.

    k. To generate that much electricity and to achieve that kind of durability would require a completely new generator design.

    l. The little baby from his crib, the screaming lady off the roof, and the man from the flooded basement were all rescued.

    m. Friends, Romans, Countrymen, lend me your ears.

(*William Shakespeare*: *Julius Caesar*)

    n. Family, religion, friendship. These are the three demons you must slay if you wish to succeed in business. (*Mr. Burns*: *The Simpsons*)

    o. Neither his father nor his mother could persuade him; neither his friends nor his kinsmen.

    2. The following sentences employ syllepsis. Find out the meanings of the two expressions formed with the same word in each sentence.

    a. She went home in a huff and a taxi.

        In a huff:

        In a taxi:

    b. Don't forget to put out the cat and the lights before going to bed.

        Put out the cat:

        Put out the light:

    c. He had to eat his words and his lunch.

        Eat his words:

        Eat his lunch:

    d. He took his coat and his leave.

        Took his coat:

        Took his leave:

    e. His boat and his dreams sank.

        His boat sank:

His dream sank:

f. Fix the problem and not the blame.

Fix the problem:

Fix the blame:

g. You held your breath and the door for me.

(Alanis Morissette: Head over Feet)

Held the breath:

Held the door:

h. He lost his coat and his temper.

Lost his coat:

Lost his temper:

i. I live in shame and the suburbs.

Live in shame:

Live in suburbs:

j. When I address Fred I never have to raise either my voice or my hopes.

(E. B. White: Dog Training)

Raise my voice:

Raise my hopes:

k. I finally told Ross, late in the summer, that I was losing weight, my grip, and possibly my mind. (James Thurber: The Years with Ross)

Lose weight:

Lose my grip:

Lose my mind:

l. You took my hand and breath away. (Tyler Hilton: You, My Love)

Took my hand:

Took my breath away:

m. It's a small apartment. I've barely enough room to lay my hat and a few friends. (Dorothy Parker)

Lay my hat:

Lay a few friends:

n. The secret to becoming a writer is to persist—to keep on writing regardless of whether you're paid any heed or money.

Pay you heed:

Pay you money:

o. He picked up his hat and his courage.

Picked up his hat;
Picked up his courage;
p. He got up early and caught the train and a cold.
Caught the train;
Caught a cold;

2.4.9 Other Semantic Rhetorical Devices

There are so many semantic rhetorical devices that it is impossible to cover all of them in a chapter. In addition, some of the devices are not so frequently used. So they are only briefly introduced in this part.

2.4.9.1 Paradox

Paradox is a figure of speech consisting of a statement which seems self-contradictory, absurd or contrary to established fact or practice, but which proves to be true and meaningful. Many proverbs or sayings are examples of paradox and they take a second thought to find out the truth.

For instance:

More haste, less speed.
Too many hands spoil the broth.
The child is the father to the man.

2.4.9.2 Oxymoron

Oxymoron is a figure of speech which conjoins two contrasting or contradictory terms for emphasis, wit or special effect.

Oxymoron is usually formed in the following five ways.

1) An adjective-noun relationship

For instance: *living death, eloquent silence, sweet sorrow, open secret, proud humility, conspicuous absence, glorious defeat*

2) An adjective-adjective relationship

For example: *sour-sweet memories, bitter-sweet feelings, poor-rich man*

3) An adverb-adjective relationship

For example: *inertly strong, deliciously tired, falsely true*

4) A verb-adverb relationship

For example: *shine darkly, smile bitterly*

5) A noun-noun relationship

For example: *the sound of silence, a love-hate relationship*

Among the five ways of forming oxymoron, the adjective-noun relationship is the most commonly used one.

Oxymoron is used not only in phrases, but also in sentences.

e. g.

The coach had to be *cruel* to be *kind* to his trainees.

During his *useful* life he often felt he was *useless*.

In most cases, oxymoron, like paradox, is to show the complexity of a situation or idea when two opposite or contradictory objects are both true like "wise fool", "tender cruelty", or "studied carelessness", etc. It can be used for irony when things are contrary to expectation, or assertion, or when you disagree with the other.

Senator Rosebud calls this a useless plan; if so, it is *the most helpful useless plan we have ever enacted*.

The cost-saving program became *an expensive economy*.

An oxymoron is usually not a widely accepted or established expression; instead, it should be unique and fit well into the context. So a good writer should avoid using others' and create his own oxymoronic expression.

2.4.9.3 Pun

Pun is a play on words, either on different senses of the same word, or on the similar sense or sound of different words. In this way, the same expression contains two different meanings, resulting in humor and fun.

For instance:

A cannon-ball took off his legs, so he laid down his *arms*.

"Arms" can mean a person's body or weapons.

—I'd like a book, please.

—Something *light*?

"Light" has two meanings, either not heavy or relaxing.

Seven days without water make one weak (week).

2.4.9.4 Irony

Irony is a figure of speech that achieves emphasis by saying the opposite of what is meant. If it is strong and is meant to hurt others, it is sarcasm.

For example:

This morning, I was late for work; at noon, I had my bike stolen; on the way home this afternoon, I slipped down in the street. So today, *I am certainly enjoying myself*.

Thanks to his help, we are now in real troubles.

You believe what he said? *You are really smart*!

2.4.9.5 Transferred Epithet

Transferred epithet is a figure of speech in which an epithet (an adjective or a descriptive phrase) which usually applies to one object is transferred to another object to which it does not really apply or belong.

For instance: *a sleepless night, a toothless smile, a busy life, a thoughtful/an amazed silence, isolated ignorance, a hungry market*

The old man put a <u>reassuring hand</u> on my shoulder.

This is the <u>cheapest market</u> in this country.

In an age of <u>pressurized happiness</u>, *we sometimes grow insensitive to subtle joys.*

As the transferred epithet is unusual and striking, it can instantly catch readers' attention and therefore effectively emphasize an idea.

2.5 Syntactical Rhetorical Devices

2.5.1 Parallelism

2.5.1.1 Definition of Parallelism

According to *Concise English Dictionary*, parallelism is a balanced construction of a verse or sentence, where one part repeats the form or meaning of the other. In parallelism, several sentences or parts of a sentence are repeated or expressed in a similar way in terms of structure or function to show ideas in the sentences or the parts of the sentence are equally important or closely related. As one of the common rhetorical devices in English, parallelism is widely used in poetry, prose, novels, plays and speeches. Parallelism can establish a balanced and rhythmic structure, add clarity to the expression, and hence make the writing more effective and impressive. Parallelism can happen at any linguistic levels, be it word and phrase or clause and sentence. At the word and phrase level, coordinating conjunctions like "and" or "or" are often used to join the parallel structure.

2.5.1.2 Classification of Parallelism

1) Parallelism at the word level

Almost any sentence elements and words of any class can be paralleled.

(1) Nouns:

Subject:

<u>Lumber</u>, <u>corn</u>, <u>tobacco</u>, <u>wheat</u>, and <u>furs</u> moved downtown to the delta country.

(*Noel Grove: Mark Twain—Mirror of America*)

Object:

We hate what we fear and so where hate is, fear is lurking. Thus we hate what threatens our <u>person</u>, our <u>liberty</u>, our <u>privacy</u>, our <u>income</u>, our <u>popularity</u>, our <u>vanity</u> and our <u>dreams</u> and <u>plans</u> for ourselves. (*Cyril Connolly*: *The Unquiet Crave*)

Object of preposition:

Civilized men arrived in the Pacific, armed with <u>alcohol</u>, <u>syphilis</u>, <u>trousers</u> and <u>the Bible</u>. (*H. Ellis*)

Predicative:

Those who huddled pitifully together on the left were <u>the old</u>, <u>the infirm</u>, <u>the ill</u>, <u>the very young</u>.

Parallel modifiers can be attached to the nouns.

I like <u>rich deserts</u>, <u>fast card games</u> and <u>difficult riddles</u>.

<u>Ferocious dragons</u> breathing fire and <u>wicked sorcerers</u> casting their spells do their harm by night in the forest of Darkness.

(2) Adjectives:

The letter, <u>short</u>, <u>cold</u>, <u>sharp-tongued</u>, was unexpected.

Her fiancé is <u>tall</u>, <u>bland</u> and <u>handsome</u>.

(3) Verbs:

I have always <u>sought</u> but seldom <u>obtained</u> a parking space near the door.

(4) Adverbs:

Bob does his work <u>quickly</u>, <u>carefully</u>, and <u>efficiently</u>.

(5) Prepositions:

They are laughing <u>at</u> me, not <u>with</u> me. (*Bart Simpson*: *The Simpsons*)

2) Parallelism at the phrase level

(1) Prepositional phrases:

Studies serve <u>for delight</u>, <u>for ornament</u>, and <u>for ability</u>.

(*Francis Bacon*: *Of Studies*)

He found it difficult to vote <u>for an ideal truth</u> but <u>against his own self interest</u>.

(2) Infinitive phrases:

Read not <u>to contradict and confuse</u>; nor <u>to believe and take for granted</u>; nor <u>to find talk and discourse</u>; but <u>to weigh and consider</u>. (*Francis Bacon*: *Of Studies*)

Note: In a parallel structure formed by infinitive phrases, "to" can be used before all the verbs or only before the first one.

(3) Gerunds:

Peter enjoys <u>going to movies</u>, <u>listening to music</u>, and <u>playing cards</u>.

(4) Verbal phrases:

A money lender <u>serves you in the present tense</u>, <u>lends you money in the conditional mood</u>, <u>keeps you in the subjunctive</u> and <u>ruins you in the future.</u>　　(Joseph Addison)

(5) Participial:

He left the engine on, <u>idling erratically</u> and <u>heating rapidly.</u>

3) Parallelism at the clause level

(1) Noun clause:

Most students are eager to obtain knowledge, but they lack the sense of <u>what is good</u>, or <u>what is necessary</u> and <u>how such a deficiency in the concept of viewing the situation as a whole would mislead them.</u>

(2) Adverbial clause of time:

<u>When a person wants to discover and change his "losing streak"</u>, <u>when he wants to become more like the winner he was born to be</u>, he can use gestalt-type experiments and transactional analysis to make change happen.　　(Howard Kendler)

(3) Adverbial clause of place:

They vanish from a world <u>where they were of no consequences</u>; <u>where they achieved nothing</u>; <u>where they were a mistake and failure and a foolishness</u>; <u>where they left no sign that they had existed.</u>　　(Noel Grove: Mark Twain—Mirror of America)

(4) Attributive clause:

These critics—<u>who point out the beauties of style and ideas</u>, <u>who discover the faults of false constructions</u>, and <u>who discuss the application of the rules</u>—usually help a lot in engendering an understanding of the writer's essay.

(5) Object clause:

The coach told the players <u>that they should get a lot of sleep</u>, <u>that they should not eat too much</u>, and <u>that they should do some warm up exercise before the game.</u>

4) Parallelism at the sentence level

At the sentence level, parallelism is often used together with repetition, that is, part of the sentences is repeated, so that the effect is greatly enhanced.

The world listens. The world watches. The world waits to see what we will do.

We are caught in war, wanting peace. We are torn by division, wanting unity.

2.5.1.3　Features of Parallelism

From the above examples, it can be found out that parallel structures have two features.

1) At any linguistic levels, when parallelism is employed, the parallel structure is usually formed by three linguistic elements, as this can give clarity to the expres-

sion and naturally lead the expression to the climax.

e. g.

I came; I saw; I conquer.

The famous remark is made by Julius Caesar, the ruler of the ancient Rome. The use of the three parallel words gives full expression to the confidence and bravery of this ancient warrior.

In fact, on account of the forceful tone parallel of three linguistic elements creates, it is widely used not only in literary works, but also in speeches as it can effectively exert influence on the audiences. Almost every American president, in his inauguration speech, makes use of parallel structure of three linguistic elements at various linguistic levels. Take President Obama's inauguration speech for instance, in his speech, parallelism is used several times.

I stand here today <u>humbled by the task before us</u>, <u>grateful for the trust you have bestowed</u>, <u>mindful of the sacrifices borne by our ancestors</u>. I thank President Bush for his service to our nation, as well as the generosity and cooperation he has shown throughout this transition.

As the opening remark of the speech, the words show President Obama's complicated feeling through the use of the three parallel phrases. The audiences soon get to understand the president better and will appreciate his sincerity and modesty.

In reaffirming the greatness of our nation, we understand that greatness is never a given. It must be earned. Our journey has never been one of shortcuts or settling for less. It has not been the path for the faint-hearted—for those who prefer leisure over work, or seek only the pleasures of riches and fame. Rather, it has been the <u>risk-takers</u>, the <u>doers</u>, the <u>makers of things</u>—some celebrated but more often men and women obscure in their labor, who have carried us up the long, rugged path towards prosperity and freedom.

Three nouns are used in parallel structure to reassert that the greatness of the nation is hard-earned. Only through struggle, hard work in spite of all the difficulties can the American people attain freedom and prosperity.

But our time <u>of standing pat</u>, <u>of protecting narrow interests</u> and <u>putting off unpleasant decisions</u>—that time has surely passed. Starting today, we must <u>pick ourselves up</u>, <u>dust ourselves off</u>, and <u>begin again the work of remaking America</u>.

Both sentences contain parallel structures formed by three phrases making a comparison between the period that Americans have just gone through and the future work they need to do. The first sentence presents a vivid picture of the previous situation in America—avoiding any reforms, being afraid of losing vested interest and being contented with the present situation. The second sentence shows President Obama's strong determination to change the present situation which sounds fairly encouraging.

Homes have been lost; jobs shed; businesses shuttered.

The sentence consists of three clauses in parallel structure. As the three clauses have the same structure, the last two clauses leave out "have been". This sentence is a description of the difficulties American people are facing as a result of the financial crisis. Short as it is, it truly reflects the people's living conditions so that President Obama would surely be identified with by the people.

For us, they packed up their few worldly possessions and traveled across oceans in search of a new life.

For us, they toiled in sweatshops and settled the West; endured the lash of the whip and plowed the hard earth.

For us, they fought and died, in places like Concord and Gettysburg; Normandy and Khe Sanh.

"They" refers to the forefathers who made sacrifice for and contribution to America. Three sentences are paralleled, each standing as an independent paragraph. Within the sentences, parallelism is again used. The entire part reviews the labor and sacrifices of the ancestors. The use of parallelism makes this part touching and impressive.

Not only President Obama is a master of parallelism in his speech, so are other presidents of America.

This great Nation will endure as it has endured, will revive and will prosper.

(*Franklin D. Roosevelt*)

President Roosevelt uses three parallel verbs describing the future of their nation—the three stages the nation will experience. With the use of the three different words, people's confidence will also be strengthened bit by bit.

Let us take as our goal: where peace is unknown, make it welcome; where peace is fragile, make it strong; where peace is temporary, make it permanent.

(*Richard Milhous Nixon*)

President Nixon employs three parallel sentences expressing his wish for a peaceful and beautiful world.

2) The second feature of parallelism is that the parallel elements in a sentence or the parallel sentences should have the same or similar functions and grammatical

forms. For example, a parallel structure that begins with clauses must keep on with clauses. Changing to another pattern or even changing the voice of the verb will break the parallelism. Similarly, an infinitive phrase should be paralleled with another infinitive phrase instead of a gerund, though the meaning of the sentence remains the same. When this occurs, the structure is a faulty parallel.

Faulty Parallel:
I like reading, singing, and <u>to listen to music</u>.
Correct Parallel:
I like reading, singing, and listening to music.
Faulty Parallel:
They can learn cooking, canoeing, swimming, or <u>how to make ropes</u>.
Correct Parallel:
They can learn cooking, canoeing, swimming, or rope-making.
Faulty Parallel:
The production manager was asked to write his report quickly, accurately, and <u>in a detailed manner</u>.
Correct Parallel:
The production manager was asked to write his report quickly, accurately, and <u>thoroughly</u>.
Faulty Parallel:
The hurricane <u>not only destroyed</u> the fishing fleet but also the homes of the fishermen.
Correct Parallel:
The hurricane destroyed not only the fishing fleet but also the homes of the fishermen.
Faulty Parallel:
The coach told the players that they should get a lot of sleep, that they should not eat too much, and <u>to do some warm-up exercises before the game</u>.
Correct Parallel:
The coach told the players that they should get a lot of sleep, that they should not eat too much, and that they should do some warm-up exercises before the game.
Faulty Parallel:
The salesman expected that he would present his product at the meeting, that there would be time for him to show his slide presentation, and <u>that questions would be asked by prospective buyers</u>.

Correct Parallel:

The salesman expected that he would present his product at the meeting, that there would be time for him to show his slide presentation, and that prospective buyers would ask him questions.

The use of parallel structure in a piece of writing can make the writing more concise, help the writer present the ideas in a clearly and orderly way, and help the readers follow the writer's thoughts more easily. As Claire K. Cook observes, "The value of parallel structure goes beyond aesthetics.... It points up the structure of the sentence, showing readers what goes with what and keeping them on the right track." (Claire K. Cook, 1985) In a word, if well used, parallelism definitely imparts grace and power to a piece of writing.

Tasks:

1. Complete the following sentences using parallel structure.

a. Having no job or _____, the student had to drop out of school.

b. Because I used a computer to do my research paper, I could easily correct spelling errors, move paragraphs around to achieve better organization, and _____.

c. While I was in college, I worked as a waitress, as a typist, and _____.

d. He is a man known for his integrity and _____.

e. Because he was ill and _____, the auto worker left his job.

f. The professor walked through the door, looked at the students, and _____.

g. A farmer spends his life tilling the soil, sowing the seeds, and _____.

h. I was surprised to discover that in person the rock star was warm, friendly, unassuming and _____.

i. Quickly and _____ he walked around the corner to buy the book.

j. As one of modern college students, I get online everyday to acquire the information I need, _____, and _____.

k. We can gain knowledge by reading, by reflection, _____ or _____.

2. Decide whether the examples below are faulty parallel (F) or correct parallel (C) and revise the faulty ones.

_____ a. A Bachelor of Business degree in Marketing, work experience in sales and with people, and my farming background qualify me to contribute to the sales staff at JCPenney.

_____ b. The fabric must be washed in cold water, line-dried, and pressed with a cool iron.

_____ c. Whether it be closing a sale in Chinese, bidding a price to Chile in Spanish, hedging a sale at the Board of Trade or completing the international accounting work, I have the educational background to fill this position and contribute to Columbia's success.

_____ d. Come to the seminar prepared to take notes and with some questions to ask.

_____ e. The schedule is as follows:
Week 1. Research of pamphlets and interviews with balloonists.
Week 2. Read books and magazines and begin to compile information into a report.
Week 3. Final report prepared and sent to printer.

_____ f. We have finished work on the report on schedule. The first week we reviewed our files and researched turf literature to review methods of turf grass establishment. The second week an on-site analysis of your property was conducted to check for micro-climates which may influence turf grass establishment.

_____ g. The pilot walked down the aisle, through the door, and into the cockpit, singing "Up, Up, and Away."

_____ h. I was involved in making research technique decisions, in measuring the market for particular products, helped develop ideas for new products, and worked with R&D to produce models of new products.

_____ i. Joe wants you to get groceries, wash the car, pay the electric bill, and return his CD player.

_____ j. He left the engine on, idling erratically and heating rapidly.

_____ k. To think accurately and writing with precision are interrelated goals.

_____ l. He ran up to the bookshelves, grabbed a chair standing nearby, stepped painfully on his tiptoes, and pulled the fifty-pound volume on top of him, crushing his ribs and impressing him with the power of knowledge.

_____ m. Slowly and full of confidence, he walked to the witness stand.

_____ n. The teacher said that he was a poor student because he waited until the last minute to study for the exam, completed his lab problems in a careless manner, and his motivation was low.

_____ o. He was well-known, well-respected, and well-loved.

_____ p. The dictionary can be used for these purposes: to find word mean-

ings, pronunciations, correct spellings, and looking up irregular verbs.

_____ *q. Machiavelli advocates relying on one's own strength, leaving as little to chance as possible, and the need to get rid of sentimental attachments.*

3. The following sentences are good examples of parallelism, appreciate and study them.

a. An Englishman thinks seated; a Frenchman, standing; an American, pacing; an Irishman, afterward. (*O' Malley*)

b. The past, with its crimes, its follies, and its tragedies, flashes away.
(*Churchill*)

c. The nodules vary in almost every respect you can think of: in size, from one to 15 centimeters; in color, from redbrown to jetblack; in shape, from spherical to what is known in nodule jargon as "hamburger-shaped"; and in structure, from those that are very hard to those that crumble in your hand. (*Stuart Harris*)

d. It is rather for us to be here dedicated to the great task remaining before us, that from these honored dead we take increased devotion to that cause for which they here gave the last full measure of devotion; that we here highly resolve that these dead shall not have died in vain; that this nation, under God, shall have a new birth of freedom, and that government of the people, by the people, for the people, shall not perish from the earth. (*Abraham Lincoln: Gettysburg Address*)

e. Any man or state who fights on against Nazidom will have our aid. Any man or state who marches with Hitler is our foe. (*W. S. Churchill*)

f. No one can be perfectly free till all are free; no one can be perfectly moral till all are moral; no one can be perfectly happy till all are happy.
(*Herbert Spencer: Social Statistics*)

g. We can never be satisfied as long as the Negro is the victim of the unspeakable horrors of police brutality. We can never be satisfied as long as our bodies, heavy with the fatigue of travel, cannot gain lodging in the motels of the highways and the hotels of the cities. We can never be satisfied as long as our children are stripped of their selfhood and robbed of their dignity by signs stating "For Whites Only." We cannot be satisfied as long as the Negro's basic mobility is from a smaller ghetto to a larger one... (*Martin Luther King: I Have a Dream*)

h. To that work I now turn, with all the authority of my office. I ask the Congress to join with me. But no president, no Congress, no government, can undertake this mission alone. (*Bill Clinton*)

i. Steadfast in our faith in the Almighty, we will advance toward a world where man's freedom is secure. To that end we will devote our strength, our resources, and our firmness of resolve. With God's help, the future of mankind will be assured in a world of justice, harmony, and peace.　　　　　　　　　　(Harry S. Truman)

j. We are creating a nation once again vibrant, robust and alive. But there are many mountains yet to climb.　　　　　　　　　　　　　　(Ronald Reagan)

k. We were in the midst of shock—but we acted. We acted quickly, boldly, decisively.　　　　　　　　　　　　　　　　　　　　(Franklin D. Roosevelt)

l. America is ready to encourage, eager to initiate, anxious to participate in any seemly program likely to lessen the probability of war, and promote that brotherhood of mankind which must be God's highest conception of human.　(Warren G. Harding)

m. With this, we can build a great cathedral of the spirit—each of us raising it one stone at a time, as he reaches out to his neighbor, helping, caring, doing.
　　　　　　　　　　　　　　　　　　　　　　(Richard Milhous Nixon)

n. Conceived in justice, written in liberty, bound in union, it (covenant) was meant one day to inspire the hopes of all mankind; and it binds us still.
　　　　　　　　　　　　　　　　　　　　　　(Lyndon Baines Johnson)

o. We renew our pledge of support—to prevent it (the United Nations) from becoming merely a forum for invective—to strength its shield of the new and the weak— and to enlarge the area in which its writ may run.　　　　(John F. Kennedy)

p. We must act on what we know. I take as my guide the hope of a saint: in crucial things—unity; in important things—diversity; in all things, generosity.
　　　　　　　　　　　　　　　　　　　　　　　　(George Bush)

q. Let history say of us: These were golden years—when the American Revolution was reborn, when freedom gained new life, when America reached for her best.
　　　　　　　　　　　　　　　　　　　　　　　　(Ronald Reagan)

r. Our transportation crisis will be solved by a bigger plane or a wider road, mental illness with a pill, poverty with a law, slums with a bulldozer, urban conflict with a gas, racism with a goodwill gesture.　(Philip Slater: The Pursuit of Loneliness)

s. With this faith, we will be able to work together, to pray together, to struggle together, to go to jail together, to stand up for freedom together, knowing that we will be free one day.　　　　　　　　　　(Martin Luther King: I Have a Dream)

2.5.2　Antithesis

2.5.2.1　Definition of Antithesis

Antithesis is a figure of speech which deliberately arranges two contrasting or opposite objects, ideas, qualities or conditions in a parallel structure (phrases, clauses or sentences) to achieve emphasis. Though antithesis is presented in the parallel form, it is different from parallelism in that. In parallelism, the objects are related and equally important, while antithesis focuses on the contrasting relationship between the two objects.

For instance:

Speech is silver; silence is golden.

The two short sentences clearly show the qualities of two opposite behaviors, emphasizing the value of remaining silent.

Money is a good servant but a bad master. (Holy Bible)

"A good servant" and "a bad master" vividly reflect the role of money in people's life. If people use money wisely, it can serve people well. Yet if people become its slave, possessed by it, it can ruin people.

2.5.2.2 The Functions of Antithesis

Antithesis creates a definite and systematic relationship between ideas, reveals the truth through some seemingly simple witty remarks, and has good rhythmic effect, therefore it is widely used in proverbs, speeches, newspaper reports and other literary works. It can be used in various styles, whether it is descriptive or argumentative, narrative or sentimental. In most cases, it is used to show contrast.

e. g.

To err is human; to forgive, divine. (Pope)

That short and easy trip made a lasting and profound change in Harold's outlook.

That's one small step for a man, one giant leap for mankind. (Neil Armstrong)

Antithesis can convey certain sense of complexity in a person, a situation or an idea by admitting opposite or contrasting truths.

e. g.

If we try, we might succeed; if we do not try, we cannot succeed.

Success makes men proud; failure makes them wise.

Antithesis can also be used to make fine distinctions.

e. g.

In order that all men may be taught to speak truth, it is necessary that all likewise should learn to hear it. (Samuel Johnson)

I agree that it is legal; but my question was, is it moral?

2.5.2.3 The Use of Antithesis in Writing

An antithesis is formed either to contrast two objects or the two aspects of one object.

1) Antithesis of contrasting two objects

Any man or state who fights on against Nazidom will have our aid. Any man or state who marches with Hitler is our foe. (*Churchill*)

Antithesis is formed through the contrast of two sentences. Churchill's attitude and his strong determination to fight against Hitler and Nazidom are fully expressed.

<u>Sink</u> or <u>swim</u>, <u>live</u> or <u>die</u>, <u>survive</u> or <u>perish</u>, I give my hand and my heart to this vote. (*Daniel Webster*)

John Adams made the remark when he was calling for people to support the independence of South America. Three pairs of antithesis in the sentence greatly enhance the tone, emphasizing the fact that it is a critical moment for the people of South America and clearly showing Adam's strong determination.

It was the <u>best of times</u>, it was the <u>worst of times</u>; it was the <u>age of wisdom</u>, it was the <u>age of foolishness</u>; it was the <u>epoch of belief</u>, it was the <u>epoch of incredulity</u>; it was the <u>season of Light</u>, it was the <u>season of Darkness</u>; it was the <u>spring of hope</u>, it was the <u>winter of despair</u>; we had <u>everything before us</u>, we had <u>nothing before us</u>; we were all going direct to <u>Heaven</u>, we were all going direct to <u>the other way</u>.

(*Charles Dickens*: *A Tale of Two Cities*)

This is the opening words of Dickens' *A Tale of Two Cities* and also a good example of antithesis. A series of antithesis is used to present to the audiences the social background of the story—a turbulent period which is on the whole moving forward yet is full of troubles and wars; while there is hope for a better society, no one is sure about the final result; everything is changing and everything is uncertain. The language is full of strength and expressiveness.

2) Antithesis of contrasting two aspects of one object

Antithesis contrasting the two aspects of one object can reveal the nature of an object, telling people a truth and is therefore provoking and meaningful.

America is <u>the paradise</u> for the rich and <u>the hell</u> for the poor.

This is a vivid depiction of the diametrically different situations of the rich and the poor in America. The sharp words pinpoint the reality that while the rich are enjoying a happy and comfortable life, the poor are suffering.

As Caesar <u>loved</u> me, I <u>weep</u> for him; as he was <u>fortunate</u>, I <u>rejoice</u> at it; as he was <u>valiant</u>, I <u>honor</u> him; but as he was <u>ambitious</u>, I <u>slew</u> him. There is <u>tears for his love</u>; <u>joy for his fortune</u>; <u>honor for his valor</u>; and <u>death for his ambition</u>.

(*W. Shakespeare*: *Julius Caesar*)

Antithesis is not necessarily formed between two phrases or clauses. In this sentence, antithesis is used twice. Both of the structures include four sentences or phrases, the last one of which is contrasting with the first three ones.

Tasks:

1. Translate the following English sentences into Chinese and pay attention to the use of antithesis.

a. From them all Mark Twain gained a keen perception of the human race, of the difference between what people claim to be and what they really are. (Noel Grove)

b. They are wonderful when they are good, he thought. There is no people like them when they are good and when they go bad, there is no people that is worse.
(E. Hemingway: *For Whom the Bell Tolls*)

c. A bank is a place where they lend you an umbrella in fair weather and ask for back again when it begins to rain. (Robert Frost)

d. Crafty men condemn studies, simple men admire them.

e. A world will lament them a day and forget them forever.

f. United we stand; divided we fall.

g. Penny wise and pound foolish.

h. Think like a man of action, act like a man of thought.

i. We must learn to live together as brothers or perish together as fools.
(Martin Luther King)

j. Love is an ideal thing, marriage a real thing. (Goethe)

k. Hatred stirs up strife, but love covers all sins.

2. Translate the following Chinese sentences into English.

a. 希望是一顿美好的早餐,但是一顿糟糕的晚餐。

b. 基督教徒认为人类来自于天上,而进化论者则认为人类必定来自于地下。

c. 你们不要问你们的国家能够为你们做什么,而要问你们为自己的国家做些什么。

d. 他干得越多,得到的就越少。

e. 统治易,管理难。

f. 谋事在人,成事在天。

g. 她物质丰富,精神贫乏。

h. 有些人贪婪自私,而另一些人善良慷慨。

i. 更多的危险来自于伪装的朋友,而不是公开的敌人。

2.5.3 Other Syntactical Rhetorical Devices

2.5.3.1 Chiasmus

Chiasmus is a figure of speech in which the second half of an expression is balanced against the first half in reversed order. It is also called "reverse parallelism" as the two parts of the sentence parallel with each other, only in reversed order.

For example:

(1) *He led bravely, and we bravely followed.*

In the first clause, the verb is followed by the adverb. In the second, the verb follows the adverb.

Chiasmus may be useful for those sentences in which you want balance, but which cannot be paralleled effectively, either because they are too short, or because the emphasis is placed on the wrong words. Through the inversion of word order, readers' attention is drawn to the ends of sentences and therefore the emphatic effect is achieved. In addition, it may serve the purpose of being serious, witty or humorous and may add to the variety of sentence structures, making the wiring more interesting and beautiful.

Any grammatical part in the sentence can be reversed in the sentence.

(2) *Tell me not of your many perfections; of your great modesty tell me not either.*

In the second part of the sentence, the prepositional phrase is moved from the end to the initial place for emphatic purpose.

(3) *If you come to them, they are not asleep; if you ask and inquire of them, they do not withdraw themselves; they do not chide if you make mistakes; they do not laugh at you if you are ignorant.* (Richard de Bury)

In the third and fourth sentence, the order of the subordinate clause and main clause is changed.

Other sentence elements can also be moved around to form chiastic structures. The effect is rather emphatic.

(4) *The melody was old, old also were the words.*

(5) *He labors without complaining and without bragging rests.*

(6) *It is boring to eat, to sleep is fulfilling.*

(7) *He was an angel on the surface, but at heart a knave.*

Note: A special type of chiasmus is called antimetabole which involves the repetition of the same word or idea in inverse order. (However, in many cases it is not necessary to make such a subtle distinction.) Here are some examples:

1) Repetition of the words in reverse order

(1) Live simply, so that others may simply live.
(2) Truth is beauty, and beauty is truth.
(3) Forty is the old age of youth; fifty is the youth of old age. (Victor Hugo)
(4) Let us never negotiate out of fear, but let us never fear to negotiate.
(5) One loves that for which one labors, and one labors for that which one loves.
(6) Know something of everything and everything of something.
(7) An optimist sees an opportunity in every calamity, a pessimist sees a calamity in every opportunity. (Reginald B. Mansell)

2) Repetition of the syntactic elements in reverse order

(1) He went to the theatre, but home went she.
(2) Lack of confidence is not the result of difficulty, the difficulty comes from lack of confidence.
(3) A man may not always be what he appears to be. But what he appears to be is always a significant part of what he is. (Willard Gaylin)

Task:

Compare the versions of these sentences, written first in chiastic and then in strictly parallel form. Which one do you think is better in each case?

a.
(1) On the way to school, my car ran out of gas; then it had a flat on the way home.
(2) On the way to school, my car ran out of gas; then on the way home it had a flat.

b.
(1) We swam in silence and in silence we dressed in our wet clothes.
(2) We swam in silence and we dressed in our wet clothes in silence.

c.
(1) Sitting together at lunch, the kids talked incessantly; but they said nothing at all sitting in the dentist's office.
(2) Sitting together at lunch, the kids talked incessantly; but sitting in the dentist's office, they said nothing at all.

d.
(1) The computer is now on sale; available also at a discount is the latest software.
(2) The computer is now on sale; the latest software is also available at a discount.

e.
(1) Just as the term "menial" does not apply to any honest labor, so no dishonest work can be called "prestigious."
(2) Just as the term "menial" does not apply to any honest labor, so "prestigious" does not apply to any dishonest work.

2.5.3.2 Climax and Anticlimax

1) Climax

Climax is a figure of speech in which a series of words or expressions rise step by step, beginning with the least important and ending with the most important. It is derived from the Greek word for "ladder" (that is *klimax*) and implies the progress of ideas in accordance with the rising of significance or intensity, just like climbing a ladder, each idea outweighing the preceding one until reaching a summit.

For example:

(1) *I came, I saw, I conquered.*

(2) *Reading makes a full man; conference a ready man; and writing an exact man.*

(3) *We strive for the good, aim for the better, and seize the best.*

(4) *Lincoln recognized worth in the common people; he loved the common people; he fought for the common people; and he died for the common people.*

Climax is often used to stir up feelings and emotions of audiences or to emphasize a point. Such a structure must ascend at least three steps and is always used together with repetition and parallelism.

(5) *What light is to the eyes, what air is to the lungs, what love is to the heart, liberty is to the soul of man.* (R. G. Ingersoll)

(6) *The world watches. The world listens. The world waits to see what we will do.* (Richard Nixon)

2) Anticlimax

Opposite to climax, anticlimax involves stating a series of ideas in a descending order of significance or intensity, from strong to weak, form significant to unimportant, from weighty to light. It is used to achieve emphasis, to ridicule or satirize, for being comic or humorous. Unlike climax, it needs only two steps of descending to gain emphasis. Still in most cases, three or more steps are used.

For instance:

(1) *He pawned his life, his watch and his word.*

(2) *Where shall we find hope, happiness, friends, and cigarettes?*

(3) *Religion, credit and the eye are not to be touched.*

(4) *If once a man indulges himself in murder, very soon he comes to think little of robbing; and from robbing he comes next to drinking and Sabbath-breaking, and from that to incivility and procrastination.*

The successful construction of climax and anticlimax requires good command of vocabulary and originality of thought. The use of these two devices can leave a deep impression on the audiences, contributing to the persuasiveness of the writing or speech.

2.5.3.3 Rhetorical Question

Rhetorical question is a question to which the answer is obvious or immediately provided by the questioner and therefore not expected. It is used by writers or speakers to assert or deny something. As it forces the audiences to think about the answers, it can intensify the wanted effect.

For example:

(1) *How was it possible to walk for an hour through the woods and see nothing worthy of note?*

(2) *Shall we allow those untruths to go unanswered?*

(3) *Marriage is a wonderful institution, but who would want to live in an institution?*

(*H. L. Mencken*)

(4) *If practice makes perfect, and no one's perfect, then why practice?*

(*Billy Corgan*)

2.5.3.4 Repetition

Repetition is a figure of speech in which words or phrases are repeated to emphasize certain facts or ideas. It is a major rhetorical strategy for producing emphasis, clarity, amplification, or emotional effect. It always appears together with several rhetorical devices, such as parallelism, antithesis, and chiasmus. Words or phrases, clauses or ideas in any places of the sentence or a piece of writing, can be repeated to produce a rhythmic beauty in language, to emphasize a point, and to produce a certain atmosphere. According to the repeated parts and the places of the repeated parts, repetition can be further classified into many types. But it is not going to be discussed in detail here.

(1) *She stroked her kitty cat very softly, very slowly, very smoothly.*

(2) *I am exactly the man to be placed in a superior position, in such a case as that; I am above the rest of mankind, in such a case as that; I can act with philosophy, in such a case as that.*

(3) *I want her to live. I want her to breathe. I want her to aerobicize.*

(4) *My conscience hath a thousand several tongues,*
  And every tongue brings in a several tale,
  And every tale condemns me for a villain.

(*William Shakespeare: Richard III*)

2.5.4 Sample Speeches Employing Rhetorical Devices

The following are famous speeches which are also good examples of employing rhetorical devices. Read the speeches and find out what rhetorical devices are used in each speech and how they are used.

Sample 1:

Winston S. Churchill's Speech on Hitler's Invasion of the USSR

The Nazi regime is indistinguishable from the worst features of Communism. It is devoid of all theme and principle except appetite and racial domination. It excels in all forms of human wickedness, in the efficiency of its cruelty and ferocious aggression. No one has been a more consistent opponent of Communism than I have for the last twenty-five years. I will unsay no words that I've spoken about it. But all this fades away before the spectacle which is now unfolding.

The past, with its crimes, its follies and its tragedies, flashes away. I see the Russian soldiers standing on the threshold of their native land, guarding the fields which their fathers have tilled from time immemorial. I see them guarding their homes; their mothers and wives pray, ah yes, for there are times when all pray for the safety of their loved ones, for the return of the breadwinner, of the champion, of their protectors.

I see the 10,000 villages of Russia, where the means of existence was wrung so hardly from the soil, but where there are still primordial human joys, where maidens laugh and children play. I see advancing upon all this, in hideous onslaught, the Nazi war machine, with its clanking, heel-clicking, dandified Prussian officers, its crafty expert agents, fresh from the cowing and tying down of a dozen countries. I see also the dull, drilled, docile brutish masses of the Hun soldiery, plodding on like a swarm of crawling locusts. I see the German bombers and fighters in the sky, still smarting from many a British whipping, so delighted to find what they believe is an easier and a safer prey. And behind all this glare, behind all this storm, I see that small group of villainous men who planned, organized and launched this cataract of horrors upon mankind.

And then my mind goes back across the years to the days when the Russian armies were our Allies against the same deadly foe when they fought with so much valor and constancy and helped to gain a victory, from all share in which, alas, they were, through no fault of ours, utterly cut off.

I have lived through all this and you will pardon me if I express my feelings and the stir of old memories. But now I have to declare the decision of His Majesty's Government, and I feel sure it is a decision in which the great Dominions will, in due course, concur. And that we must speak of now, at once, without a day's delay. I have to make the declaration, but can you doubt what our policy will be?

We have but one aim and one single irrevocable purpose. We are resolved to destroy Hitler and every vestige of the Nazi regime. From this nothing will turn us. Nothing. We will never parley; we will never negotiate with Hitler or any of his gang. We shall fight him by land; we shall fight him by sea; we shall fight him in the air, until, with God's help, we have rid the earth of his shadow and liberated its people from his yoke.

Any man or State who fights against Nazism will have our aid. Any man or State who marches with Hitler is our foe. This applies not only to organized States but to all representatives of that vile race of Quislings who make themselves the tools and agents of the Nazi regime against their fellow-countrymen and against the lands of their births. These Quislings, like the Nazi leaders themselves, if not disposed of by their fellow-countrymen, which would save trouble, will be delivered by us on the morrow of victory to the justice of the Allied tribunals. That is our policy and that is our declaration.

It follows, therefore, that we shall give whatever help we can to Russia and to the Russian people. We shall appeal to all our friends and Allies in every part of the world to take the same course and pursue it as we shall, faithfully and steadfastly to the end.

We have offered to the Government of Soviet Russia any technical or economic assistance which is in our power and which is likely to be of service to them. We shall bomb Germany by day as well as by night in ever-increasing measure, casting upon them month by month a heavier discharge of bombs and making the German people taste and gulp each month a sharper dose of the miseries they have showered upon mankind.

It is noteworthy that only yesterday the Royal Air Force, striking inland over France, cut down with very small loss to themselves twenty-eight of the Hun fighting machines in the air above the French soil they have invaded, defiled and profess to hold.

But this is only a beginning. From now henceforward the main expansion of our air force proceeds with gathering speed. In another six months the weight of the help we are receiving from the United States in war materials of all kinds, especially in heavy bombers, will begin to tell. This is no class war. It is a war in which the whole British Empire and Commonwealth of Nations is engaged without distinction of race, creed or party.

It is not for me to speak of the action of the United States, but this I will say: If Hitler imagines that his attack on Soviet Russia will cause the slightest division of aims or slackening of effort in the great democracies, who are resolved upon his doom, he is woefully mistaken. On the contrary, we shall be fortified and encouraged in our efforts to rescue mankind from his tyranny. We shall be strengthened and not weakened in our determination and in our resources.

This is no time to moralize upon the follies of countries and governments which have allowed themselves to be struck down one by one when by united action they could so easily have saved themselves and saved the world from this catastrophe.

But, when I spoke a few minutes ago of Hitler's bloodlust and the hateful appetites which have impelled or lured him on his Russian adventure, I said there was one deeper motive behind his outrage. He wishes to destroy the Russian power because he hopes that if he succeeds in this he will be able to bring back the main strength of his army and air force from the East and hurl it upon this island, which he knows he must conquer or suffer the penalty of his crimes.

His invasion of Russia is no more than a prelude to an attempted invasion of the British Isles. He hopes, no doubt, that all this may be accomplished before the Winter comes and that he can overwhelm Great Britain before the fleets and air power of the United States will intervene. He hopes that he may once again repeat upon a greater scale than ever before that process of destroying his enemies one by one, by which he has so long thrived and prospered, and that then the scene will be clear for the final act, without which all his conquests would be in vain, namely, the subjugation of the Western Hemisphere to his will and to his system.

The Russian danger is therefore our danger and the danger of the United States just as the cause of any Russian fighting for his hearth and home is the cause of free men and free peoples in every quarter of the globe.

Let us learn the lessons already taught by such cruel experience. Let us redouble our exertions and strike with united strength while life and power remain.

Sample 2:

President Barack Obama's Inauguration Speech

My fellow citizens:

I stand here today humbled by the task before us, grateful for the trust you have bestowed, mindful of the sacrifices borne by our ancestors. I thank President Bush for his service to our nation, as well as the generosity and cooperation he has shown throughout this transition.

Forty-four Americans have now taken the presidential oath. The words have been spoken during rising tides of prosperity and the still waters of peace. Yet, every so often the oath is taken amidst gathering clouds and raging storms. At these moments, America has carried on not simply because of the skill or vision of those in high office, but because We the People have remained faithful to the ideals of our forbearers, and true to our founding documents.

So it has been. So it must be with this generation of Americans.

That we are in the midst of crisis is now well understood. Our nation is at war, against a far-reaching network of violence and hatred. Our economy is badly weakened, a consequence of greed and irresponsibility on the part of some, but also our collective failure to make hard choices and prepare the nation for a new age. Homes have been lost; jobs shed; businesses shuttered. Our health care is too costly; our schools fail too many; and each day brings further evidence that the ways we use energy strengthen our adversaries and threaten our planet.

These are the indicators of crisis, subject to data and statistics. Less measurable but no less profound is a sapping of confidence across our land—a nagging fear that America's decline is inevitable, and that the next generation must lower its sights.

Today I say to you that the challenges we face are real. They are serious and they are many. They will not be met easily or in a short span of time. But know this, America—they will be met.

On this day, we gather because we have chosen hope over fear, unity of purpose over conflict and discord.

On this day, we come to proclaim an end to the petty grievances and false promises, the recriminations and worn out dogmas, that for far too long have strangled our politics.

We remain a young nation, but in the words of Scripture, the time has come to set aside childish things. The time has come to reaffirm our enduring spirit; to choose our better history; to carry forward that precious gift, that noble idea, passed on from generation to generation: the God-given promise that all are equal, all are free, and all deserve a chance to pursue their full measure of happiness.

In reaffirming the greatness of our nation, we understand that greatness is never a given. It must be earned. Our journey has never been one of short-cuts or settling for less. It has not been the path for the faint-hearted—for those who prefer leisure over work, or seek only the pleasures of riches and fame. Rather, it has been the risk-takers, the doers, the makers of things—some celebrated but more often men and women obscure in their labor, who have carried us up the long, rugged path toward prosperity and freedom.

For us, they packed up their few worldly possessions and traveled across oceans in search of a new life.

For us, they toiled in sweatshops and settled the West; endured the lash of the whip and plowed the hard earth.

For us, they fought and died, in places like Concord and Gettysburg; Normandy and Khe Sahn.

Time and again these men and women struggled and sacrificed and worked till their hands were raw so that we might live a better life. They saw America as bigger than the sum of our individual ambitions; greater than all the differences of birth or wealth or faction.

This is the journey we continue today. We remain the most prosperous, powerful nation on Earth. Our workers are no less productive than when this crisis began. Our minds are no less inventive, our goods and services no less needed than they were last week or last month or last year. Our capacity remains undiminished. But our time of standing pat, of protecting narrow interests and putting off unpleasant decisions—that time has surely passed. Starting today, we must pick ourselves up, dust ourselves off, and begin again the work of remaking America.

For everywhere we look, there is work to be done. The state of the economy calls for action, bold and swift, and we will act—not only to create new jobs, but to lay a new foundation for growth. We will build the roads and bridges, the electric grids and digital lines that feed our commerce and bind us together. We will restore science to its rightful place, and wield technology's wonders to raise health care's quality and lower its cost. We will harness the sun and the winds and the soil to fuel our cars and run our factories. And we will transform our schools and colleges and universities to meet the demands of a new age. All this we can do. And all this we will do.

Now, there are some who question the scale of our ambitions—who suggest that our system cannot tolerate too many big plans.

Their memories are short. For they have forgotten what this country has already done; what free men and women can achieve when imagination is joined to common purpose, and necessity to courage.

What the cynics fail to understand is that the ground has shifted beneath them—that the stale political arguments that have consumed us for so long no longer apply. The question we ask today is not whether our government is too big or too small, but whether it works—whether it helps families find jobs at a decent wage, care they can afford, a retirement that is dignified. Where the answer is yes, we intend to move forward. Where the answer is no, programs will end. And those of us who manage the public's dollars will be held to account—to spend wisely, reform bad habits, and do our business in the light of day—because only then can we restore the vital trust between a people and their government.

Nor is the question before us whether the market is a force for good or ill. Its power to generate wealth and expand freedom is unmatched, but this crisis has reminded us that without a watchful eye, the market can spin out of control—and that a nation cannot prosper long when it favors only the prosperous. The success of our economy has always depended not just on the size of our Gross Domestic Product, but on the reach of our prosperity; on our ability to extend opportunity to every willing heart—not out of charity, but because it is the surest route to our common good.

As for our common defense, we reject as false the choice between our safety and our ideals. Our Founding Fathers, faced with perils we can scarcely imagine, drafted a charter to assure the rule of law and the rights of man, a charter expanded by the blood of generations. Those ideals still light the world, and we will not give them up for expedience's sake. And so to all other peoples and governments who are watching today, from the grandest capitals to the small village where my father was born: know that America is a friend of each nation and every man, woman, and child who seeks a future of peace and dignity, and that we are ready to lead once more.

Recall that earlier generations faced down fascism and communism not just with missiles and tanks, but with sturdy alliances and enduring convictions. They understood that our power alone cannot protect us, nor does it entitle us to do as we please. Instead, they knew that our power grows through its prudent use; our security emanates from the justness of our cause, the force of our example, the tempering qualities of humility and restraint.

We are the keepers of this legacy. Guided by these principles once more, we can meet those new threats that demand even greater effort—even greater cooperation and understanding between nations. We will begin to responsibly leave Iraq to its people, and forge a hard-earned peace in Afghanistan. With old friends and former foes, we will work tirelessly to lessen the nuclear threat, and roll back the specter of a warming planet. We will not apologize for our way of life, nor will we waver in its defense, and for those who seek to advance their aims by inducing terror and slaughtering innocents, we say to you now that our spirit is stronger and cannot be broken; you cannot outlast us, and we will defeat you.

For we know that our patchwork heritage is a strength, not a weakness. We are a nation of Christians and Muslims, Jews and Hindus—and non-believers. We are shaped by every language and culture, drawn from every end of this Earth; and because we have tasted the bitter swill of civil war and segregation, and emerged from that dark chapter stronger and more united, we cannot help but believe that the old hatreds shall someday pass; that the lines of tribe shall soon dissolve; that as the world grows smaller, our common humanity shall reveal itself; and that America must play its role in ushering in a new era of peace.

To the Muslim world, we seek a new way forward, based on mutual interest and mutual respect. To those leaders around the globe who seek to sow conflict, or blame their society's ills on the West—know that your people will judge you on what you can build, not what you destroy. To those who cling to power through corruption and deceit and the silencing of dissent, know that you are on the wrong side of history; but that we will extend a hand if you are willing to unclench your fist.

To the people of poor nations, we pledge to work alongside you to make your farms flourish and let clean waters flow; to nourish starved bodies and feed hungry minds. And to those nations like ours that enjoy relative plenty, we say we can no longer afford indifference to suffering outside our borders; nor can we consume the world's resources without regard to effect. For the world has changed, and we must change with it.

As we consider the road that unfolds before us, we remember with humble gratitude those brave Americans who, at this very hour, patrol far-off deserts and distant mountains. They have something to tell us today, just as the fallen heroes who lie in Arlington whisper through the ages. We honor them not only because they are guardians of our liberty, but because they embody the spirit of service; a willingness to find meaning in something greater than themselves. And yet, at this moment—a moment that will define a generation—it is precisely this spirit that must inhabit us all.

For as much as government can do and must do, it is ultimately the faith and determination of the American people upon which this nation relies. It is the kindness to take in a stranger when the levees break, the selflessness of workers who would rather cut their hours than see a friend lose their job which sees us through our darkest hours. It is the firefighter's courage to storm a stairway filled with smoke, but also a parent's willingness to nurture a child, that finally decides our fate.

Our challenges may be new. The instruments with which we meet them may be new. But those values upon which our success depends—hard work and honesty, courage and fair play, tolerance and curiosity, loyalty and patriotism—these things are old. These things are true. They have been the quiet force of progress throughout our history. What is demanded then is a return to these truths. What is required of us now is a new era of responsibility—a recognition, on the part of every American, that we have duties to ourselves, our nation, and the world, duties that we do not grudgingly accept but rather seize gladly, firm in the knowledge that there is nothing so satisfying to the spirit, so defining of our character, than giving our all to a difficult task.

This is the price and the promise of citizenship.

This is the source of our confidence—the knowledge that God calls on us to shape an uncertain destiny.

This is the meaning of our liberty and our creed—why men and women and children of every race and every faith can join in celebration across this magnificent mall, and why a man whose father less than sixty years ago might not have been served at a local restaurant can now stand before you to take a most sacred oath.

So let us mark this day with remembrance, of who we are and how far we have traveled. In the year of America's birth, in the coldest of months, a small band of patriots huddled by dying campfires on the shores of an icy river. The capital was abandoned. The enemy was advancing. The snow was stained with blood. At a moment when the outcome of our revolution was most in doubt, the father of our nation ordered these words be read to the people:

"Let it be told to the future world... that in the depth of winter, when nothing but hope and virtue could survive... that the city and the country, alarmed at one common danger, came forth to meet."

America. In the face of our common dangers, in this winter of our hardship, let us remember these timeless words. With hope and virtue, let us brave once more the icy currents, and endure what storms may come. Let it be said by our children's children that when we were tested we refused to let this journey end, that we did not turn back nor did we falter; and with eyes fixed on the horizon and God's grace upon us, we carried forth that great gift of freedom and delivered it safely to future generations.

Sample 3:

Obama's 2008 Presidential Acceptance Speech

Hello, Chicago.

If there is anyone out there who still doubts that America is a place where all things are possible; who still wonders if the dream of our founders is alive in our time; who still questions the power of our democracy, tonight is your answer.

It's the answer told by lines that stretched around schools and churches in numbers this nation has never seen; by people who waited three hours and four hours, many for the very first time in their lives, because they believed that this time must be different; that their voice could be that difference.

It's the answer spoken by young and old, rich and poor, Democrat and Republican, black, white, Latino, Asian, Native American, gay, straight, disabled and not disabled—Americans who sent a message to the world that we have never been a collection of Red States and Blue States: we are, and always will be, the United States of America.

It's the answer that led those who have been told for so long by so many to be cynical, and fearful, and doubtful of what we can achieve to put their hands on the arc of history and bend it once more toward the hope of a better day.

It's been a long time coming, but tonight, because of what we did on this day, in this election, at this defining moment, change has come to America.

I just received a very gracious call from Senator McCain. He fought long and hard in this campaign, and he's fought even longer and harder for the country he loves. He has endured sacrifices for America that most of us cannot begin to imagine, and we are better off for the service rendered by this brave and selfless leader. I congratulate him and Governor Palin for all they have achieved, and I look forward to working with them to renew this nation's promise in the months ahead.

I want to thank my partner in this journey, a man who campaigned from his heart and spoke for the men and women he grew up with on the streets of Scranton and rode with on that train home to Delaware, the Vice President-elect of the United States, Joe Biden.

I would not be standing here tonight without the unyielding support of my best friend for the last sixteen years, the rock of our family and the love of my life, our nation's next First Lady, Michelle Obama. Sasha and Malia, I love you both so much, and you have earned the new puppy that's coming with us to the White House. And while she's no longer with us, I know my grandmother is watching, along with the family that made me who I am. I miss them tonight, and know that my debt to them is beyond measure.

To my campaign manager David Plouffe, my chief strategist David Axelrod, and the best campaign team ever assembled in the history of politics—you made this happen, and I am forever grateful for what you've sacrificed to get it done.

But above all, I will never forget who this victory truly belongs to—it belongs to you.

I was never the likeliest candidate for this office. We didn't start with much money or many endorsements. Our campaign was not hatched in the halls of Washington—it began in the backyards of Des Moines and the living rooms of Concord and the front porches of Charleston.

It was built by working men and women who dug into what little savings they had to give five dollars and ten dollars and twenty dollars to this cause. It grew strength from the young people who rejected the myth of their generation's apathy; who left their homes and their families for jobs that offered little pay and less sleep; from the not-so-young people who braved the bitter cold and scorching heat to knock on the doors of perfect strangers; from the millions of Americans who volunteered, and organized, and proved that more than two centuries later, a government of the people, by the people and for the people has not perished from this Earth. This is your victory.

I know you didn't do this just to win an election and I know you didn't do it for me. You did it because you understand the enormity of the task that lies ahead. For even as we celebrate tonight, we know the challenges that tomorrow will bring are the greatest of our lifetime—two wars, a planet in peril, the worst financial crisis in a century. Even as we stand here tonight, we know there are brave Americans waking up in the deserts of Iraq and the mountains of Afghanistan to risk their lives for us. There are mothers and fathers who will lie awake after their children fall asleep and wonder how they'll make the mortgage, or pay their doctor's bills, or save enough for college. There is new energy to harness and new jobs to be created; new schools to build and threats to meet and alliances to repair.

The road ahead will be long. Our climb will be steep. We may not get there in one year or even one term, but America—I have never been more hopeful than I am tonight that we will get there. I promise you—we as a people will get there.

There will be setbacks and false starts. There are many who won't agree with every decision or policy I make as President, and we know that government can't solve every problem. But I will always be honest with you about the challenges we face. I will listen to you, especially when we disagree. And above all, I will ask you join in the work of remaking this nation the only way it's been done in America for two-hundred and twenty-one years—block by block, brick by brick, calloused hand by calloused hand.

What began twenty-one months ago in the depths of winter must not end on this autumn night. This victory alone is not the change we seek—it is only the chance for us to make that change. And that cannot happen if we go back to the way things were. It cannot happen without you.

So let us summon a new spirit of patriotism; of service and responsibility where each of us resolves to pitch in and work harder and look after not only ourselves, but each other. Let us remember that if this financial crisis taught us anything, it's that we cannot have a thriving Wall Street while Main Street suffers—in this country, we rise or fall as one nation; as one people.

Let us resist the temptation to fall back on the same partisanship and pettiness and immaturity that has poisoned our politics for so long. Let us remember that it was a man from this state who first carried the banner of the Republican Party to the White House—a party founded on the values of self-reliance, individual liberty, and national unity. Those are values we all share, and while the Democratic Party has won a great victory tonight, we do so with a measure of humility and determination to heal the divides that have held back our progress. As Lincoln said to a nation far more divided than ours, "We are not enemies, but friends... though passion may have strained it must not break our bonds of affection." And to those Americans whose support I have yet to earn—I may not have won your vote, but I hear your voices, I need your help, and I will be your President too.

And to all those watching tonight from beyond our shores, from parliaments and palaces to those who are huddled around radios in the forgotten corners of our world—our stories are singular, but our destiny is shared, and a new dawn of American leadership is at hand. To those who would tear this world down—we will defeat you. To those who seek peace and security—we support you. And to all those who have wondered if America's beacon still burns as bright—tonight we proved once more that the true strength of our nation comes not from the might of our arms or the scale of our wealth, but from the enduring power of our ideals: democracy, liberty, opportunity, and unyielding hope.

For that is the true genius of America—that America can change. Our union can be perfected. And what we have already achieved gives us hope for what we can and must achieve tomorrow.

This election had many firsts and many stories that will be told for generations. But one that's on my mind tonight is about a woman who cast her ballot in Atlanta. She's a lot like the millions of others who stood in line to make their voice heard in this election except for one thing—Ann Nixon Cooper is 106 years old.

She was born just a generation past slavery; a time when there were no cars on the road or planes in the sky; when someone like her couldn't vote for two reasons—because she was a woman and because of the color of her skin.

And tonight, I think about all that she's seen throughout her century in America—the heartache and the hope; the struggle and the progress; the times we were told that we can't, and the people who pressed on with that American creed: Yes we can.

At a time when women's voices were silenced and their hopes dismissed, she lived to see them stand up and speak out and reach for the ballot. Yes we can.

When there was despair in the dust bowl and depression across the land, she saw a nation conquer fear itself with a New Deal, new jobs and a new sense of common purpose. Yes we can.

When the bombs fell on our harbor and tyranny threatened the world, she was there to witness a generation rise to greatness and a democracy was saved. Yes we can.

She was there for the buses in Montgomery, the hoses in Birmingham, a bridge in Selma, and a preacher from Atlanta who told a people that "We Shall Overcome." Yes we can.

A man touched down on the moon, a wall came down in Berlin, a world was connected by our own science and imagination. And this year, in this election, she touched her finger to a screen, and cast her vote, because after 106 years in America, through the best of times and the darkest of hours, she knows how America can change. Yes we can.

America, we have come so far. We have seen so much. But there is so much more to do. So tonight, let us ask ourselves—if our children should live to see the next century; if my daughters should be so lucky to live as long as Ann Nixon Cooper, what change will they see? What progress will we have made?

This is our chance to answer that call. This is our moment. This is our time—to put our people back to work and open doors of opportunity for our kids; to restore prosperity and promote the cause of peace; to reclaim the American Dream and reaffirm that fundamental truth—that out of many, we are one; that while we breathe, we hope, and where we are met with cynicism, and doubt, and those who tell us that we can't, we will respond with that timeless creed that sums up the spirit of a people:

Yes We Can.

Thank you, God bless you, and may God Bless the United States of America.

Sample 4:

The Audacity of Hope

Keynote Address at the 2004 Democratic National Convention

On behalf of the great state of Illinois, crossroads of a nation, land of Lincoln, let me express my deep gratitude for the privilege of addressing this convention. Tonight is a particular honor for me because, let's face it, my presence on this stage is pretty unlikely. My father was a foreign student, born and raised in a small village in Kenya. He grew up herding goats, went to school in a tin-roof shack. His father, my grandfather, was a cook, a domestic servant.

But my grandfather had larger dreams for his son. Through hard work and perseverance my father got a scholarship to study in a magical place: America, which stood as a beacon of freedom and opportunity to so many who had come before. While studying here, my father met my mother. She was born in a town on the other side of the world, in Kansas. Her father worked on oil rigs and farms through most of the Depression. The day after Pearl Harbor he signed up for duty, joined Patton's army and marched across Europe. Back home, my grandmother raised their baby and went to work on a bomber assembly line. After the war, they studied on the GI Bill, bought a house through FHA, and moved west in search of opportunity.

And they, too, had big dreams for their daughter, a common dream, born of two continents. My parents shared not only an improbable love; they shared an abiding faith in the possibilities of this nation. They would give me an African name, Barack, or "blessed," believing that in a tolerant America your name is no barrier to success. They imagined me going to the best schools in the land, even though they weren't rich, because in a generous America you don't have to be rich to achieve your potential. They are both passed away now. Yet, I know that, on this night, they look down on me with pride.

I stand here today, grateful for the diversity of my heritage, aware that my parents' dreams live on in my precious daughters. I stand here knowing that my story is part of the larger American story, that I owe a debt to all of those who came before me, and that, in no other country on earth, is my story even possible. Tonight, we gather to affirm the greatness of our nation, not because of the height of our skyscrapers, or the power of our military, or the size of our economy. Our pride is based on a very simple premise, summed up in a declaration made over two hundred years ago, "We hold these truths to he self-evident, that all men are created equal. That they are endowed by their Creator with certain inalienable rights. That among these are life, liberty and the pursuit of happiness."

That is the true genius of America, a faith in the simple dreams of its people, the insistence on small miracles. That we can tuck in our children at night and know they are fed and clothed and safe from harm. That we can say what we think, write what we think, without hearing a sudden knock on the door. That we can have an idea and start our own business without paying a bribe or hiring somebody's son. That we can participate in the political process without fear of retribution, and that our votes will he counted—or at least, most of the time.

This year, in this election, we are called to reaffirm our values and commitments, to hold them against a hard reality and see how we are measuring up, to the legacy of our forbearers, and the promise of future generations. And fellow Americans—Democrats, Republicans, Independents—I say to you tonight: we have more work to do. More to do for the workers I met in Galesburg, Illinois, who are losing their union jobs at the Maytag plant that's moving to Mexico, and now are having to compete with their own children for jobs that pay seven bucks an hour. More to do for the father I met who was losing his job and choking back tears, wondering how he would pay $4,500 a month for the drugs his son needs without the health benefits he counted on. More to do for the young woman in East St. Louis, and thousands more like her, who has the grades, has the drive, has the will, but doesn't have the money to go to college.

Don't get me wrong. The people I meet in small towns and big cities, in diners and office parks, they don't expect government to solve all their problems. They know they have to work hard to get ahead and they want to. Go into the collar counties around Chicago, and people will tell you they don't want their tax money wasted by a welfare agency or the Pentagon. Go into any inner city neighborhood, and folks will tell you that government alone can't teach kids to learn. They know that parents have to parent, that children can't achieve unless we raise their expectations and turn off the television sets and eradicate the slander that says a black youth with a book is acting white. No, people don't expect government to solve all their problems. But they sense, deep in their bones, that with just a change in priorities, we can make sure that every child in America has a decent shot at life, and that the doors of opportunity remain open to all. They know we can do better. And they want that choice.

In this election, we offer that choice. Our party has chosen a man to lead us who embodies the best this country has to offer. That man is John Kerry. John Kerry understands the ideals of community, faith, and sacrifice, because they've defined his life. From his heroic service in Vietnam to his years as prosecutor and lieutenant governor, through two decades in the United States Senate, he has devoted himself to this country. Again and again, we've seen him make tough choices when easier ones were available. His values and his record affirm what is best in us.

John Kerry believes in an America where hard work is rewarded. So instead of offering tax breaks to companies shipping jobs overseas, he'll offer them to companies creating jobs here at home. John Kerry believes in an America where all Americans can afford the same health coverage our politicians in Washington have for themselves. John Kerry believes in energy independence, so we aren't held hostage to the profits of oil companies or the sabotage of foreign oil fields. John Kerry believes in the constitutional freedoms that have made our country the envy of the world, and he will never sacrifice our basic liberties nor use faith as a wedge to divide us. And John Kerry believes that in a dangerous world, war must be an option, but it should never he the first option.

A while back, I met a young man named Shamus at the VFW Hall in East Moline, Illinois. He was a good-looking kid, six-two or six-three, clear-eyed, with an easy smile. He told me he'd joined the Marines and was heading to Iraq the following week. As I listened to him explain why he'd enlisted, his absolute faith in our country and its leaders, his devotion to duty and service, I thought this young man was all any of us might hope for in a child. But then I asked myself: Are we serving Shamus as well as he was serving us? I thought of more than 900 service men and women, sons and daughters, husbands and wives, friends and neighbors, who will not be returning to their hometowns. I thought of families I had met who were struggling to get by without a loved one's full income, or whose loved ones had returned with a limb missing or with nerves shattered, but who still lacked long-term health benefits because they were reservists. When we send our young men and women into harm's way, we have a solemn obligation not to fudge the numbers or shade the truth about why they're going, to care for their families while they're gone, to tend to the soldiers upon their return, and to never ever go to war without enough troops to win the war, secure the peace, and earn the respect of the world.

Now let me be clear. We have real enemies in the world. These enemies must be found. They must be pursued and they must be defeated. John Kerry knows this. And just as Lieutenant Kerry did not hesitate to risk his life to protect the men who served with him in Vietnam, President Kerry will not hesitate one moment to use our military might to keep America safe and secure. John Kerry believes in America. And he knows it's not enough for just some of us to prosper. For alongside our famous individualism, there's another ingredient in the American saga.

A belief that we are connected as one people. If there's a child on the south side of Chicago who can't read, that matters to me, even if it's not my child. If there's a senior citizen somewhere who can't pay for her prescription and has to choose between medicine and the rent, that makes my life poorer, even if it's not my grandmother. If there's an Arab American family being rounded up without benefit of an attorney or due process, that threatens my civil liberties. It's that fundamental belief—I am my brother's keeper, I am my sister's keeper—that makes this country work. It's what allows us to pursue our individual dreams, yet still come together as a single American family. "E pluribus unum." Out of many, one.

Yet even as we speak, there are those who are preparing to divide us, the spin masters and negative ad peddlers who embrace the politics of anything goes. Well, I say to them tonight, there's not a liberal America and a conservative America—there's the United States of America. There's not a black America and white America and Latino America and Asian America; there's the United States of America. The pundits like to slice-and-dice our country into Red States and Blue States; Red States for Republicans, Blue States for Democrats. But I've got news for them, too. We worship an awesome God in the Blue States, and we don't like federal agents poking around our libraries in the Red States. We coach Little League in the Blue States and have gay friends in the Red States. There are patriots who opposed the war in Iraq and patriots who supported it. We are one people, all of us pledging allegiance to the stars and stripes, all of us defending the United States of America.

In the end, that's what this election is about. Do we participate in a politics of cynicism or a politics of hope? John Kerry calls on us to hope. John Edwards calls on us to hope. I'm not talking about blind optimism here—the almost willful ignorance that thinks unemployment will go away if we just don't talk about it, or the health care crisis will solve itself if we just ignore it. No, I'm talking about something more substantial. It's the hope of slaves sitting around a fire singing freedom songs; the hope of immigrants setting out for distant shores; the hope of a young naval lieutenant bravely patrolling the Mekong Delta; the hope of a millworker's son who dares to defy the odds; the hope of a skinny kid with a funny name who believes that America has a place for him, too. The audacity of hope!

In the end, that is God's greatest gift to us, the bedrock of this nation; the belief in things not seen; the belief that there are better days ahead. I believe we can give our middle class relief and provide working families with a road to opportunity. I believe we can provide jobs to the jobless, homes to the homeless, and reclaim young people in cities across America from violence and despair. I believe that as we stand on the crossroads of history, we can make the right choices, and meet the challenges that face us. America!

Tonight, if you feel the same energy I do, the same urgency I do, the same passion I do, the same hopefulness I do—if we do what we must do, then I have no doubt that all across the country, from Florida to Oregon, from Washington to Maine, the people will rise up in November, and John Kerry will be sworn in as president, and John Edwards will be sworn in as vice president, and this country will reclaim its promise, and out of this long political darkness a brighter day will come. Thank you and God bless you.

Chapter 3　Introduction of Stylistics

3.1　理 论 简 介

　　根据秦秀白(2000:12)的论述,文体学是运用现代语言学理论和方法研究文体的学科。文体有广义和狭义之分。狭义的文体涉及作家的写作风格;广义的文体较宽泛,涉及一种语言的各类文体(王佐良、丁往道,1987:i)。目前,文体学的研究呈现一派繁荣的景象,原因在于研究角度和方法不一,于是产生了普通文体学、文学文体学、形式文体学、功能文体学、话语文体学等分支。

　　文本分析可以在词汇、句法、篇章等各个层面上进行。秦秀白提出了在文本分析方面应该注意的两点:首先,文本分析不同于语法分析,"语法分析有规则可循,受规则制约(rule-governed);文本分析无规则可循,受原则制约(principle-governed)"(2000:12),相同的语言结构在不同的语境中会产生不同的语体效果;很可能,不同的语言结构也会产生相同的语体效果。其次,文本分析过程中,不能分离语言描写和阐释活动,原因是"脱离阐释活动的语言描写往往忽视文本的思想内容和作者意图,容易盲目地把文本当做验证某种语言学模式的'实验基地',故曾招致诸多方面的批评,例如美国文论家 Stanley E. Fish 曾把文体分析称做'一种过于容易玩的游戏'"(秦秀白,2000:15—16)。

　　根据丁祥珍的研究,语体学研究对象是语言体裁,指的是运用同一语言的人在不同场合所运用的语言品种的变体。语体不具有自己独特的语音、词汇和语言特征,仅仅在某些同义成分的选择频率上显现自己的特征,语言使用者可以依据不同的语境在不同程度上改变语体。语体和语言品种不同,语言品种有自己独特的语音、词汇和语法特征。语体是相沿成习的,相同的语言社团一般运用同一语体成分。语体和个人语言特点也不相同,它展现的是同一语言社团的语言共性。比如,"现代英语按语体品种可以分成十六个语体:英国英语语体、美国英语语体、会话语体、新闻语体、广播电视语体、广告语体、科技语体、宗教语体、经济贸易语体、书信语体、法律语体、军事语体、电脑语体、黑人英语语体、体育语体以及其他讲英语国家语体。这十六种语体既有共性,又具有各自的特点,共同构成了世界英语"(丁祥珍,2002:110)。

　　就新闻语体而言,潘麦玲指出该语体的语言风格具有大众性、趣味性、节俭性。其词汇特点体现在如下四个方面:运用有新闻色彩的词汇;运用小词;广泛运用缩略词;临时拼凑词汇以满足表达需要。该语体的句法特点有:时态多用现在时;多运用带有修饰成分的简单句;标题较多运用省略句;使用高度浓缩的前置修饰语。汪燕华谈到了意识流小说的语言特点:语言片段支离破碎;句法很不完整,"语义上仅保留了'核心信息',摒除了一切日常交际话语中为了表达清晰而采用的'剩余信息'"(2003:92)。

3.2 The Noun Phrase

The noun phrase is composed of a noun plus its modifiers which can be classified as pre-modifiers and post-modifiers. In the text, the author will resort to modification to create some stylistic effect. Common sense is that the role of the modifiers can not be ignored. The modifiers can assist the author in communicating his ideas vividly, simultaneously they can also allow the reader to bring his imagination into full play, consequently, a thorough understanding of the essay is possible. In many cases, some modifiers can function as an attributive or adverbial clause does. In addition, some anonymous researchers on the Internet hold the point that the modifiers are necessary for the author to express complex ideas, which is also very clear manifestation of the economic principle, according to which people will communicate more information using fewer linguistic units.

Discuss the stylistic effect the modifiers create in the following paragraphs.

As far as eye could see, the pool with its winding margin was covered with trim leaves, which rose high out of the water like the flared skirts of dancing girls. And starring these tiers of leaves were white lotus flowers, alluringly open or bashfully in bud, like glimmering pearls, stars in an azure sky, or beauties fresh from the bath. The breeze carried past gusts of fragrance, like the strains of a song faintly heard from a far-off tower. And leaves and blossoms trembled slightly, while in a flash the scent was carried away. As the closely serried leaves bent, a tide of opaque emerald could be glimpsed. That was the softly running water beneath, hidden from sight, its color invisible, though the leaves looked more graceful than ever.

Moonlight cascaded like water over the lotus leaves and flowers, and a light blue mist floating up from the pool made them seem washed in milk or caught in a gauzy dream. Though the moon was full, a film of pale clouds in the sky would not allow its rays to shine through brightly; but I felt this was all to the good—though refreshing sleep is indispensable, short naps have a charm all their own. As the moon shone from behind them, the dense trees on the hills threw checkered shadows, dark forms loomed like devils, and the sparse, graceful shadows of willows seemed painted on the lotus leaves. The moonlight on the pool was not uniform, but light and shadow made up a harmonious rhythm like a beautiful tune played on a violin.

3.3　The Verb Phrase

The verb serves as the important part of a sentence, being very expressive and adding color to the text. The verb plays a main role in manifesting the author's ideas. There is no exaggeration that the verb acts as the soul of the sentence. The vividness of the essay and full expression of the author's idea can be embodied in the verb. Actually, not only can well-chosen verbs present one's thoughts vividly and precisely but also communicate more than literal meaning. For example, in the following sentence, "She banged saucepans around irritably." The word "banged" reveals the lady's bad mood. Even without the word "irritably", we can still sense her awful state of mind. In view of that, in the process of the appreciation of the literary works, analysis of the use of the verb constitutes a very important part, hence, carefully choosing the verb receives much attention from the author.

Discuss the effect the verbs create in the following paragraphs and translate them into English.

1. 我付了茶钱,还了胡琴,辞别三家村的青年们,坐上车子。

(丰子恺 《山中避雨》)

2. 当地报纸编辑昂首阔步,高声喊叫,趾高气扬,欣喜若狂,他终于诚心诚意地体谅我,邀我到药房去,在亲切的气氛中,干一杯"法涅斯托克驱虫剂",以便洗刷掉一切怨恨。　　(马克·吐温 《我的第一次文学尝试》)

3. 他向着大方凳,坐在小凳上;便很惊惶地站了起来,失了色瑟缩着……我即刻伸手折断了胡蝶的一支翅骨,又将风轮掷在地下,踏扁了。

(鲁迅 《风筝》)

4. 虽然因为作者要凑成三十六天罡七十二地煞勉勉强强地写满了一百零八人的数目,我觉得也比没有人物个性的《荡寇志》强多了。

(冰心 《忆读书》)

5. 我们的心曾经铺满落叶
　　时光也曾在某个冬天
　　剪走我们多余的枯枝
　　但现在三月的小耳朵上

一串串鸟声的项链
摇醒了我们的嘴唇

让我吻吧,在你的嘴唇上摘一片柳叶
初春的江水高过我们的心跳
两株远离岸边的芦苇
在风中晃动内心的温柔

石头的内心绿起来
我们要让目光紧紧拥抱
直到我们的忧伤
也绿起来 直到阳光
拧出春天多余的雨水

(竹林一闲 《绿》)

6. 闪在青石旁。那只大虫又饥又渴,把两只前爪在地上按了一按,望上一扑,从半空窜下来,武松吃那一惊,酒都变作冷汗出了。说时迟,那时快,武松见大虫扑来,一闪,闪在大虫背后。大虫背后看人最难,就把前爪搭在地上,把腰胯一掀。武松一闪,又闪在一边。大虫见掀他不着,吼一声,就像半天里起了个霹雳,震得那山岗也动了。接着把铁棒似的虎尾倒竖起来一剪。武松一闪,又闪在一边。

(施耐庵、罗贯中 《水浒传》)

3.4 The Function of the Pronoun

The consecutive use of the pronoun can produce much stylistic effect. As suggested by some anonymous researchers on the Internet, the author can impress the reader and change the reader's attitude by taking advantage of the pronoun.

For example, in many essays, when the author conveys his or her own view, it is not necessary that the author has to choose "I". The author can also resort to "we" to convey his ideas. "We" not only embodies the author's view but also sounds more polite because "we" implies whatever is related to the reader.

In addition, as claimed by Saitz & Baumwoll (1975), when the author reports the first-hand experience, the first person pronoun is still a top priority.

As far as the second person pronoun "you", it does not refer to the single form alone. Common wisdom is that "you" can bear the generic reference. The generic reference performs the function of capturing the readers' attention directly. The generic reference can allow the author to easily develop the empathy between the readers and the author, as a consequence, the readers are more likely to accept the author's ideas.

Still, as suggested by Saitz & Baumwoll, to convey a personal view of a particular person's style, the author will turn to the personalized discourse.

Task 1. Please translate the following paragraphs into English, and then analyze the effect the pronouns create in the paragraphs.

1. 在一篇《要能容忍根除刑讯逼供的副作用》的评论中,编辑这样写道:

"……或者假如警方将赵作海起诉到了法院,法院以警方对赵作海刑讯逼供为由将赵作海无罪释放,你能接受吗?"

2. 2008 年 6 月 1 日,《南方都市报》社论《孩子,节日给你,哀伤给我》这样写道:

"孩子,今天是你的节日。地震灾区的孩子,今天是你的节日。无论你在家与否,也无论你是否还在病床上,今天的阳光都为你存在……"

3. 2010 年 4 月 11 日,《北京青年报》社评《你应该为富士康"跳楼门"感到羞愧》:

"一个工人不是机器,也不仅仅是可以奉献出利润的劳动者,他还是某人的儿子、某人的父亲或兄长。每一起坠楼事件的发生,所了断的并不仅仅是当事人的生命,还有一个家庭的幸福和欢乐。它伤害的不仅仅是亲人和朋友,也严重打击了人们对一个物质极大丰富的时代的美好想象,它在整个社会的文化肌体上留下了创伤。如果我们明知还会有人从富士康的楼上跳下去,却不作任何努力去阻止和挽救,难道我们不该感到羞愧吗?"

Task 2. Discuss the usage of the first person pronoun "we".

Task 3. Discuss the usage of the second person pronoun "you".

Task 4. Identify the usage of the second person pronoun "you" in the following paragraph.

Although some of the most charming toys in the world are made in China, there are almost no toys whatever among the poor in the country districts. But the children are good at making games for themselves out of whatever comes handy. They play a kind of hopscotch game, marking the squares and circles in the dirt with their fingers. Or perhaps they manage to make the end of an old barrel into a hoop which they roll. Some play a game with a pair of sticks laid across an open hole. The top stick is placed in such a way that if you hit the upper end, it will go quite a distance. The object is to see how far you can make the stick go. The children who have had schooling may own chalk and little smooth wooden slabs used like slates, but they are unlikely to own any books.

3.5 The Function of the Tense

The tense is closely related to the type of the text. Generally speaking, when we related something in the past, the past tense is commonly chosen, the present things the present tense. However, on many occasions, the above rule will be violated so that some effect will be created. As is well known, the function of the present tense connotes what is happening at the present time. Hence, the author can apply the present tense to creating a sense of what is happening now and being close to the readers, therefore, the urgency and importance of the matter can be sensed by the readers. Therefore, even when the author expresses things in the past, sometimes the author will resort to the present tense to create the immediacy. In the fictional stories, even when the author relates what will be in the future, for instance, what the earth will evolve into in the future within millions of years, the present tense is still preferred to the future tense. As stated in the grammar books, the present tense can implement the function of the future tense. The very reason is that the present tense can assist the author in trying to make all more likely to come true.

Task 1. Discuss the functions of all types of tense in English.

Task 2. Discuss and compare the functions of tense in both Chinese and English.

3.6 Ellipsis

Ellipsis does not mean that something is omitted. For example, it can communicate the author's hesitation about providing more information about the relevant topic. The relevant reasons are various. Anyway, this act is intentional, in other words, the author intends to hide something from the readers for some purpose. On many occasions, ellipsis bears more expressive force. Cited from anonymous researchers' findings on the Internet, ellipsis sometimes implies such meanings as discontinuity, hesitation, interruption, silence, etc. What is more, one more function is worthy of note. That is, ellipsis can be a very good manifestation of the on-going thinking process.

Background: the teacher points to a beautiful picture
Teacher: What does the picture say?
Student: It is very beautiful,...

In the above sentence, ellipsis reveals that the student failed to find the proper words to depict the picture, possibly still meditating on the picture.

Task 1. Discuss and classify the functions of ellipses in both English and Chinese.

Task 2. Discuss the effect ellipses can create in various discourses.

3.7 The Discourse Markers

What is a discourse marker? Common knowledge is that a discourse marker is a linguistic item which bears only the procedural meaning devoid of propositional content. Here is a list of the widely used discourse markers:

I mean, right, actually, just, so, after all, like, sort of, almost, then, and, moreover, therefore, now, anyway, basically, because, but, oh, ok, or, really, well, yes, you know, you see, etc.

The importance of the discourse markers is self-evident. It is recognized that the function of a language is to communicate information. So to speak, the discourse markers make up the important components in the effective communication. So far as the discourse marker "like" is concerned, as suggested by many researchers and the author's own research, some functions of "like" as a discourse marker are put in this way: First, the discourse marker "like" implies being approximate. Here is one example, "that was like one hundred dollars". Second, the discourse marker "like" can introduce examples, for instance, "have you ever been to any places of interest in China, like, the Great Wall".

In view of the above, the mastery of the functions of the discourse markers is necessary for language learners to learn a language well. Hence, researches into the factors are necessary and of much significance in affecting how the language learners apply the discourse markers. The author once made a survey of the functions of the widely used discourse markers. One of the findings is that the Chinese learners of English turn to their Chinese counterparts in applying the corresponding English discourse markers. Except for the influence from the mother tongue, many other factors are worthy of further research. One factor is the learning environment, which wins many researchers' agreement. As is known, in the foreign language learning environment, the language learners failed to receive a systematic study of the functions of the discourse markers. Based on the author's survey, the learners learn the functions of the discourse markers from such sources as TV and film programs, native speakers or

English speakers, listening materials, etc. So far, no systematic teaching of the functions of the discourse markers is adopted. Viewing that the discourse markers count much in promoting effective communication, a systematic pedagogic program of the teaching of the discourse markers is necessary.

Task 1. List the functions of the discourse markers you are familiar with and create some dialogues using them.

Task 2. List the functions of the discourse markers "I mean", "now", "like", "well" and "you know".

Task 3. List the Chinese discourse markers you are familiar with and relate their functions.

# 参 考 答 案

2.3 Phonological Rhetorical Devices
2.3.1 Onomatopoeia
Tasks：

1. Please put the following English sentences containing onomatopoeic words into Chinese.

　　a. 除了老师的声音和笔在纸上的"沙沙"声，什么也听不到。

　　b. 在去学校的山路上，上学路上，我们能看见溪中的潺潺流水，能听见青蛙鸣、杜鹃啼、麻雀叫。

　　c. 正当玛莎小姐拿面包时，门外突然想起警笛，一阵"铿锵"声，随后一辆消防车"轰隆轰隆"地开过。

　　d. 愤怒的丈夫"砰"的一声把门关上。

　　e. 醉醺醺的司机开车"砰"地撞进商店的橱窗。

　　f. 忽然，本·罗杰斯从远处走来。他一边啃着大苹果，一边不时地发出阵阵悦耳的"嘟嘟"声，接着他模仿着轮船低沉的笛声，"叮当当,叮当当"走了过来。

　　g. 迎接他的只有"滴答滴答"的钟声，因为再也没有一个人留下了。

　　h. 这金属工具击墙时发出"铿锵"声。

　　i. 他在高烧中不停地说胡话。

　　j. 他向朋友们胡乱说话，泄漏了秘密。

　　k. 他滔滔不绝地说了几个小时。

　　l. 我听到许多鸟儿在林里"唧唧喳喳"。

　　m. 他的肚子"咕噜咕噜"地叫了起来。

　　n. 他什么也看不见，什么也听不到，但是他能够感觉到自己"怦怦"的心跳，接着他听到有东西撞击在石头上的声音和落下的小块岩石碰撞时发出的"咔嗒"声。

　　o. 她让我触摸所有能摸到或感觉到的东西——阳光、丝绸摩擦的"沙沙"声、昆虫的叫声、门的"吱呀"声，还有爱人的声音。

　　p. 古木大梁压得"嘎吱"作响，缆索开始绷紧，接着便见一滴滴的油沿着一条石槽流入一只废旧汽油桶里。

q. 夜班已经上工,空中荡漾着机器开动的嘈杂响声。

2. Please put the following Chinese sentences into English. Pay attention to the use of onomatopoeic words.

a. The train clattered out of the station.

b. The girls clattered away at their luncheon.

c. The dishes and bowls slid together with a clatter.

d. The thunder rolled in the distance.

f. Those standing behind whispered and chattered all the time.

g. The clock ticked, the fire cracked.

h. About this time a brick came through the window with a splintering crash.

i. The clock ticked away the minutes.

j. She slammed the box on the table.

k. The man shut the door with a bang.

l. The wind whispered in the pines.

m. Old beams began to crack mysteriously.

n. A profound silence prevailed over all and the only thing she could hear was the tap of ivy on the pane.

o. He crashed down on a protesting chair.

p. The lad rushed in, gasping for breath.

q. When he raised his hand, ten thousand eyes followed it.

2.2 Alliteration, Consonance and Assonance

Tasks:

2. Study the following idioms or sayings and point out the phonological rhetorical devices used in them.

thick and thin	Alliteration
black and blue	Alliteration
now or never	Alliteration
then and there	Alliteration
cut and carve	Alliteration
bed and board	Alliteration Consonance
sink or swim	Alliteration
A fall into the pit, a gain in your wit.	Assonance Consonance
mend or end	Assonance Consonance
first and last	Consonance

*S*pare the ro*d*, and *s*poil the chil*d*.　　　Alliteration Consonance
by h*ook* or cr*ook*　　　Assonance Consonance
Fit m*ost*, and survive at la*st*.　　　Consonance
No p*ains*, no g*ains*.　　　Assonance Consonance
Man prop*oses*, God disp*oses*.　　　Assonance Consonance
A *l*a*zy* youth, a *l*ousy age.　　　Alliteration Consonance
Three cobblers comb*ined*, makes a genius m*ind*.　　Assonance Consonance

2.4 Semantic Rhetorical Devices
2.4.1 Simile
Tasks:

2. Mr. Zhu Ziqing is a literary master who is good at using simile in his works. The following sentences are taken from his works, all of which use similes. Put the sentences into English and pay attention to the use of similes.

a. The leaves rose high out of the water, like the flared skirts of dancing girls.

b. Starring these tiers of leaves were white lotus flowers, alluringly open or bashfully in bud, like glimmering pearls, stars in an azure sky, or beauties fresh from the bath.

c. The breeze carried past gusts of fragrance, like the strains of a song faintly heard from a far-off tower.

d. At this moment, a tiny thrill shoots through the leaves and flowers, like a streak of lightening, straight across the forest of lotuses.

e. As the closely serried leaves bent, a tide of opaque emerald could be glimpsed.

f. Moonlight cascaded like water over the flowers and leaves.

g. The flowers and leaves looked as if they had been bathed in milk, or like a dream wrapped in hazy hood.

h. The dense trees threw checkered shadows, and dark forms looked like devils.

i. The light and shadow made up a harmonious rhythm like a beautiful melody played on a violin.

j. All the trees were sober as dense smoke.

3. Translate the following sentences into English using the given indicators of resemblance.

a. A whale is not a fish any more than a horse is.

b. Every time I read an excellent book, it is to me just as if I had gained a new friend.

 c. You cannot hope to move me any more than expect a river to flow backward.

 d. He is sometimes bad-tempered but really he's got a heart of gold.

 e. They spent money like water.

 f. I wandered lonely as a cloud.

 g. I can smell it the way a cat smells a mouse.

 h. Her smile resembles a beautiful rose flower.

 i. I'd like to compare life to a river.

 j. I felt as though the ground was slipping under my feet.

2.4.2 Metaphor

Tasks：

1. Find out which types of metaphor are used in the following sentences according to the three basic components in metaphor.

 a. Metaphor in which both the tenor and the vehicle emerge.

 b. Metaphor in which the tenor is implied.

 c. Metaphor in which the vehicle is implied.

 d. Metaphor in which the vehicle is implied.

 e. Metaphor in which the vehicle is implied.

 f. Metaphor in which the tenor is implied.

 g. Metaphor in which the tenor, the vehicle and the ground all emerge.

 h. Metaphor in which both the tenor and the vehicle emerge.

2. Find out which types of metaphor are used in the following sentences based on the form and translate the sentences into Chinese.

 a. Noun metaphor 教育不是注满一桶水，而是点燃一把火。

 b. Verb metaphor 这个小孩长得特快。

 c. Verb metaphor 不要乱动新收音机。

 d. Noun metaphor 美貌、体力、青春，就像花朵，终将衰尽；义务、信念、爱情，就像树根，万古长青。

 e. Noun metaphor 人流向西涌去。

 f. Adjective metaphor 我们把落后看成是奇耻大辱。

 g. Noun metaphor 我牙痛不堪。

 h. Adverbial metaphor 他们死里逃生。

 i. Verb metaphor 灾难老是折磨着他。

 j. Noun metaphor 他是一本活词典。

 k. Verb metaphor 那男孩儿一抓到食物便狼吞虎咽般地吃了下去。

l. Verb metaphor 他穿过人群。

m. Adjective metaphor 她对细节有照相机般的记忆力。

n. Adjective metaphor 到这时候,他天性中那种暴烈的火焰已经燃烧殆尽,酒还喝得不多,他就打算加以默认了。

o. Verb metaphor 水浪猛烈地拍打着岩岸。

p. Adverbial metaphor 他们收入仅够糊口。

q. Adverbial metaphor 她生于富贵人家。

3.3 Personification

Tasks:

1. Read the following sentences containing personification and figure out the meaning of the sentences.

a. 她看着月光洒在湖面上。

b. 夕阳的余晖照在山上。

c. 周一的早上,杰克很惨。

d. 那些年,这个国家发生了巨大的变化。

e. 美丽的景色跃入她的眼帘。

f. 她感到一阵恐惧。

g. 法律是不讲情面的。

h. 需要是发明之母。

i. 我的电脑总是出问题。

j. 阳光照耀着花朵。

k. 古老的塔楼诉说着那场灾难,海浪悲伤地呜咽着。

l. 微风轻拂我的面颊,消去了我的怒气。

m. 我的摇椅整晚都"吱吱呀呀"的,它已经用了太久了。

n. 花儿很美丽,它仿佛在向我微笑,散发出怡人的芬芳。

o. 我的电脑出问题了,大概是我用得太多了。

p. 冬天站在外面,我冻得上下牙直打架。

q. 苹果太酸了,我的牙受不了。

r. 路途遥远,我已经走不动了。

s. 一天,我在收拾行李,但是行李箱连一件东西也塞不进去了。我敢说要是我再往里塞东西的话,行李箱就要开始哭了。

t. 小的时候,每次我难过的时候,我都会对着我家旁边的一颗枫树说话。树叶晃动,好像那棵树听懂了我的话在点头。

u. 待到炮声响,辩论已莫及。

v. 蚊子们把我的<u>脚脖子</u>当做加油站。

2. Point out the parts using personification in the following passages and poems.

a. "Only the champion daisy trees <u>were serene</u>. After all, they were part of a rain forest already two thousand years old and <u>scheduled</u> for eternity, so they <u>ignored</u> the men and continued to <u>rock</u> the diamondbacks that <u>slept</u> in their <u>arms</u>. It took the river to <u>persuade</u> them that indeed the world was altered." (Toni Morrison: Tar Baby)

b. The wind <u>stood up</u> and <u>gave a shout</u>.
He <u>whistled on his fingers</u> and
<u>Kicked</u> the withered leaves about
And <u>thumped</u> the branches with <u>his hand</u>
And said he'd kill and kill and kill,
And so <u>he</u> will and so <u>he</u> will.

(James Stephens: The Wind)

c. "Do villainy, do, since you protest to do't,
Like workmen. I'll example you with thievery.
The sun's a <u>thief</u>, and with <u>his</u> great attraction
<u>Robs</u> the vast sea; the moon's <u>an arrant thief</u>,
And <u>her</u> pale fire <u>she snatches</u> from the sun;
The sea's a <u>thief</u>, whose liquid surge resolves
The moon into salt <u>tears</u>; the earth's a <u>thief</u>,
That <u>feeds</u> and <u>breeds</u> by a composture <u>stolen</u>
From general excrement: each thing's a <u>thief</u>."

(William Shakespeare: Timon in Timon of Athens)

d. The Eagle
He <u>clasps</u> the crag with crooked <u>hands</u>,
Close to the sun in lonely lands,
Ringed with the azure world, <u>he stands</u>.
The <u>wrinkled</u> sea beneath <u>him crawls</u>;
He <u>watches</u> from <u>his</u> mountain walls,
And like a thunderbolt <u>he</u> falls.

(Alfred: Lord Tennyson)

2.4.4 Metonymy

Tasks:

1. In the following table, the original meanings of the words are given. Choose the meaning of these words in metonymic use from the list.

1. a 2. g 3. n 4. j 5. e 6. r 7. d 8. b 9. l 10. i 11. c 12. k 13. h 14. o 15. m 16. p 17. q 18. f 19. s

2. Point out the metonymy used in the following sentences and figure out their meanings.

a. He writes a <u>fine hand</u>.
"Fine hand" means good handwriting.

b. <u>The house</u> was called to order.
"The house" means people in the house.

c. We have always remained loyal to <u>the crown</u>.
"The crown" means the monarch.

d. He is <u>a man of the cloth</u>.
"A man of the cloth" means a clergyman.

e. He is fond of <u>the bottle</u>.
"The bottle" means alcohol.

f. <u>Grey hairs</u> should be respected.
"Grey hairs" means old people.

g. Life is not just a journey from <u>diaper</u> to <u>shroud</u>.
"Diaper" means birth or infantry; "shroud" means death.

h. <u>He</u> is booked out for the whole season.
"He" means his performance.

i. She is the first <u>violin</u> in the band.
"Violin" means violin player.

j. There is much of <u>the schoolboy</u> in him.
"Schoolboy" means the characteristics of a schoolboy.

k. <u>The blue eyes</u> walked into the office.
"The blue eyes" means the man with blue eyes.

l. To solve the dispute, <u>labor</u> put forward three proposals.
"Labor" means workers.

m. He has done me <u>kindnesses</u>.
"Kindness" means kind things, good deeds.

n. He has five <u>mouths</u> to feed.

"Mouth" means person.

o. Many <u>hands</u> make light work.

"Hands" means people.

p. There's <u>bread</u> and work for all.

"Bread" means food.

q. He is her <u>admiration</u>.

"Admiration" means person admired.

r. The <u>practiced ear</u> can recognize a classic favor.

"Practiced ear" means the person who has practiced ears.

s. She has the <u>eye</u> for the fair and the beautiful.

"Eye" means taste or judgment.

t. A thousand <u>mustaches</u> can live together, but not four <u>breasts</u>. (A proverb)

"Mustache" means man; "breast" means woman.

u. The <u>wolf</u> and the <u>pig</u> mingled together in his face.

"Wolf" and "pig" mean the characteristics of wolf and pig, namely ferocity and greediness.

v. <u>The whole village</u> rejoiced at news.

"The whole village" means all the villagers.

w. He is in his <u>cups</u> again.

"In his cups" means drinking.

x. He keeps <u>a good table</u> and one gets plenty to eat and drink in his house.

"A good table" means good dishes.

2.4.5 Hyperbole

Tasks:

2. Translate the following sentences into Chinese using hyperbole.

1. Tanks <u>thunders</u> down the road.
2. They <u>split/burst</u> their sides with laughing.
3. They <u>bombarded</u> me with a number of questions.
4. The price of food is <u>soaring</u>.
5. She was <u>walking on air</u>.
6. She was tired to the <u>world</u>.
7. There is a <u>world</u> of difference between these two cities.
8. I have tried <u>heaps</u> of times.
9. There are <u>clouds</u> of clerks in the office.
10. He has an <u>encyclopedia</u> knowledge of Chinese history.

11. It's so plaguy cold.
12. The man is beastly vulgar.
13. I'm frightfully sorry I inconvenienced you.
14. They are fearfully talented people.
15. She has the best pronunciation in the world.
16. It is the most absurd thing on earth.
17. Her parents were the poorest of the poor.
18. His eloquence would have moved a stone to action.
19. A more responsible teacher than him could never have been found.
20. He is a hundred years old.
21. No one could be more industrious.
22. The work progressed like a snail.
23. The news came like a bolt form the blue.
24. I would rather die than dance.
25. I've told a thousand times not to lie.
26. I've waited in the line for the whole year.
27. I've a sea of work to do.
28. She has cried for an eternity.
29. The whole world is staring at me.
30. We must fight for every inch of land.

2.4.6 Understatement

Tasks:

2. Rewrite the following sentences using understatement.

a. He is no fool.
b. There is never a week without his finding faults with me.
c. It is not a disagreeable thing to be rich.
d. There isn't a weapon he doesn't know the use of.
e. Similar mistakes are not uncommon.
f. There is no rule without exception.
g. We can't serve the people well without high political consciousness.
h. He was no mean orator.
i. This problem is not above us.
j. I am not quite too late, I see.
k. I couldn't be more happier.
l. None but fools have ever believed it.

m. He was never dissatisfied with my work.
n. She is not unhappy in her present post.
o. We are not careless of our political study.
p. No one is free from faults.
q. Never fail to come to us.
r. Our efforts were not in vain.

2.4.8 Zeugma

Tasks:

1. Point out which types of zeugma are used in the following sentences.

a. Prozeugma

b. Diazeugma

c. Prozeugma

d. Prozeugma

e. Diazeugma

f. Prozeugma

g. Hypozeugma

h. Prozeugma Diazeugma

i. Prozeugma

j. Prozeugma Diazeugma

k. Prozeugma

l. Prozeugma

m. Prozeugma

n. Prozeugma

o. Mesozeugma

2. The following sentences employ syllepsis. Find out the meanings of the same word in each sentence.

a. She went home in a huff and a taxi.
   In a huff: 怒气冲冲地
   In a taxi: 坐计程车

b. Don't forget to put out the cat and the lights before going to bed.
   Put out the cat: 把猫放到外面
   Put out the light: 关灯

c. He had to eat his words and his lunch.
   Eat his words: 食言
   Eat his lunch: 吃午饭

d. He took his coat and his leave.

    Took his coat：拿外套

    Took his leave：离开

e. His boat and his dreams sank.

    His boat sank：他的船沉了

    His dream sank：他的希望破灭了

f. Fix the problem and not the blame.

    Fix the problem：解决问题

    Fix the blame：归罪（于他人）

g. You held your breath and the door for me.

                                         （Alanis Morissette：Head over Feet）

    Held the breath：屏住呼吸

    Held the door：（帮某人）拉着门

h. He lost his coat and his temper.

    Lost his coat：丢外套

    Lost his temper：发脾气

i. I live in shame and the suburbs.

    Live in shame：活在屈辱中

    Live in suburbs：住在郊区

j. When I address Fred I never have to raise either my voice or my hopes.

                                         （E. B. White：Dog Training）

    Raise my voice：提高声音

    Raise my hopes：燃起希望

k. I finally told Ross, late in the summer, that I was losing weight, my grip, and possibly my mind. （James Thurber：The Years with Ross）

    Lose weight：减肥

    Lose my grip：（情绪）失去控制

    Lose my mind：发疯

l. You took my hand and breath away. （Tyler Hilton：You, My Love）

    Took my hand：抓住我的手

    Took my breath away：让我窒息

m. It's a small apartment. I've barely enough room to lay my hat and a few friends. （Dorothy Parker）

    Lay my hat：放我的帽子

    Lay a few friends：安顿几个朋友

n. The secret to becoming a writer is to persist—to keep on writing regardless of whether you're paid any heed or money.

Pay you heed：对你注意

Pay you money：付给你钱

o. He picked up his hat and his courage.

Picked up his hat：捡起帽子

Picked up his courage：鼓起勇气

p. He got up early and caught the train and a cold.

Caught the train：赶上火车

Caught a cold：感冒

2.5 Syntactical Rhetorical Devices

2.5.1 Parallelism

2. Decide whether the examples below are faulty parallel (F) or correct parallel (C) and revise the faulty ones.

a. C b. F c. C d. F e. F f. F g. F h. C i. C j. F k. F l. C m. F n. F o. C p. F

2.5.2 Antithesis

Tasks：

1. Translate the following English sentences into Chinese and pay attention to the use of antithesis.

a. 从他们身上,马克·吐温对人类有了敏锐的深刻认识,看清了他们口头说的和实际做的的区别。

b. 他想,他们好的时候真了不起。他们好的时候,谁也比不上他们;他们坏的时候,可谁都不如他们恶毒。

c. 银行,是在天晴之时借伞给你,到了下雨之时就催你还回去的地方。

d. 艺术家谴责学问,普通的人崇拜学问。

e. 世界为他们会痛苦一时,但最终会永远忘记他们。

f. 团结则存,分裂则亡。

g. 大事糊涂,小事聪明。

h. 思考要像实干家,行动要像思想家。

i. 我们要么像手足一样一起生活,要么像傻瓜一样一起毁灭。

j. 爱情是理想的事情,婚姻是现实的事情。

k. 恨挑起争端,爱宽容过错。

2. Translate the following Chinese sentences into English.

a. Hope is a good breakfast, but a bad supper.

b. The Christian believes that man came from above. The evolutionist believes that he must have come from below.

c. Ask not what your country can do for you; ask what you can do for your country.

d. The more he did, the less he got.

e. To rule is easy, to govern difficult.

f. Man proposes, God disposes.

g. She is rich in goods but poor in spirit.

h. Some people are greedy and selfish, while some others are kind and generous.

i. There is more danger from a pretended friend than from an open enemy.

参考文献

1. Skeat, Walter W., *Concise Dictionary of English*, Wordsworth Editions Ltd, 2007.
2. Black, Max, *Models and Metaphors: Studies in Language and Philosophy*, Cornell University Press, 1962.
3. Brooks, Cleanth, *Fundamentals of Good Writing: A Handbook of Modern Rhetoric*, Harcourt, 1950.
4. Cook, Claire K., *Line by Line*, Houghton Mifflin, 1985.
5. Burentt, Frances Hodgson, *A little Princess*, Wordsworth Editions Ltd, 1994.
6. Jemie, Onwuchekwa, *Yo Mama!: New Raps, Toasts, Dozens, Jokes, and Children's Rhymes from Urban Black America*, Temple University Press, 2003.
7. Kilpatrick, James, "Listening to What We Write", *The Columbus Dispatch*, Aug. 1, 2007.
8. Langan, John, *College Writing Skills with Readings (6th Edition)*, Foreign Language Teaching and Research Press, 2007.
9. Alcott, Louisa May, *Little Women*, Aladdin Paperbacks Simon & Schuster, 2000.
10. Mish, Frederick C. *et al.*, *Merriam-Webster's Collegiate Dictionary (11th edition)*, Harper Collins Publisher Inc., 2003.
11. Morris, Charles, *The Home Cyclopedia of Business and Commerce*, W. E. Scull, 1992.
12. Simpson, J. & Weimer, E., *The Oxford English Dictionary (2nd edition)*, Oxford University Press, 1989.
13. Virginia Woolf, *To the Light House*, The Penguin Group, 1996.
14. Bunce, Peter, *Figures of Speech*, http://www.earnestspeakers.com/figuresofspeech.html, visited at 2011-04-04.
15. Hit the Nail on the Head, http://course.cug.edu.cn/cugThird/ad_english/kcnr/analysis/anly1-1.htm, visited at 2011-02-17.
16. *Look Up: Understatement*, http://www.encyclo.co.uk/define/understatement, visited at 2011-04-04.
17. *Examples of Simile*, http://www.greatsongwriting.com/examples-of-simile.html, visited at 2011-05-04.
18. Wikipedia, *Figure of Speech*, http://en.wikipedia.org/wiki/Figure_of_speech, visited at 2011-05-04.
19. Onomatopoeia, http://hi.baidu.com/herminawsm/blog/item/0d14868e1ffc4ee8f11f361f.html, visited at 2011-03-23.
20. Long, Bill, *Zeugma and Syllepsis*, http://www.drbilllong.com/EvenMoreWords/Zeugma.html, visited at 2011-03-23.
21. 〔美〕桑德拉·希斯内罗丝:《芒果街上的小屋》,苏伶童译,译林出版社2006年版。

22. 〔美〕Nancy Herzfeld-Pipkin 编著:《高级实用英语写作》,中国人民大学出版社 2007 年版。
23. 〔英〕M. D. M. 麦肯齐、L. J. 韦斯特伍德:《英国背景》,周宛湘、曾绍红注释,世界图书出版公司 1995 年版。
24. 陈望道:《修辞学发凡》,复旦大学出版社 2008 年版。
25. 从莱庭、徐鲁亚编著:《西方修辞学》,上海外语教育出版社 2007 年版。
26. 丁往道等编著:《英语写作手册》,外语教学与研究出版社 1994 年版。
27. 汪福祥编著:《英语写作技巧新编》(中文版),外文出版社 2004 年版。
28. 〔英〕Laura Wright、Jonathan Hope:《实用文体学教程》,秦秀白导读,外语教学与研究出版社 2000 年版。
29. 张强、陈莉编译:《经典小品文选粹》,武汉测绘科技大学出版社 1997 年版。
30. 张汉熙主编:《高级英语》,外语教学与研究出版社 1995 年版。
31. 麻保金等编:《大学英语写作教程》,河南大学出版社 1992 年版。
32. 黄任编著:《英语修辞与写作》,上海外语教育出版社 1996 年版。
33. 冀成会主编:《高级英语写作教程》,外语教学与研究出版社 2009 年版。
34. 丁祥珍:《用英语语体学理论指导大学英语泛读课教学》,载《安徽农业大学学报》2002 年第 6 期。
35. 潘麦玲:《从新闻英语的语体特点看新闻英语的翻译》,载《新闻知识》2009 年第 11 期。
36. 束定芳:《论隐喻的本质及语义特征》,载《外国语》1998 年第 6 期。
37. 汪燕华:《意识流小说的语体特点和翻译策略》,载《咸宁学院学报》2003 年第 5 期。
38. 郑树棠主编:《新视野大学英语读写》(3),外语教学与研究出版社 2003 年版。
39. 马少华:《评论中人称代词的特殊效果》,载《新闻与写作》2010 年第 7 期。
40. 《省略号除了内容省略还有什么作用?》,http://zhidao.baidu.com/question/50382736.html,2011 年 2 月 18 日访问。
41. 《妙用动词,文章增色》,http://wenku.baidu.com/view/ccae683231126edb6f1a10a3.html,2010 年 10 月 22 日访问。
42. 楚神奇:《最基本而有效的技巧——添加修饰语》,http://www.zuowenweb.com/mimi/2010/08/459.html,2011 年 2 月 23 日访问。
43. 沈彩初:《就竹林一闲〈绿〉浅谈新诗动词的妙用效果》,http://bbs.shigebao.com/viewthread.php?tid=272895,2010 年 12 月 28 日访问。
44. 吴长青:《动词连用的表达效果》,http://xxzb.tl100.com/200907/49756.shtml,2010 年 12 月 28 日访问。